Theory-Building and Data Analysis in the Social Sciences

Theory-Building and Data Analysis in the Social Sciences

Herbert B. Asher, Herbert F. Weisberg,
John H. Kessel, and W. Phillips Shively

Published by the University of Tennessee Press
in cooperation with the Midwest Political Science Association

Library of Congress Cataloging in Publication Data

Main entry under title:

Theory-building and data analysis in the social sciences.

Contains articles from the American journal of political
science.
Bibliography: p.
Includes index.
1. Social sciences—Methodology—Addresses, essays,
lectures. I. Asher, Herbert B. II. Midwest Political
Science Association (U.S.) III. American journal of
political science.
H61.T467　1983　　　300'.72　　　83-3458
ISBN 0-87049-398-1
ISBN 0-87049-399-X (pbk.)

Preface

In recognition of the changing nature of the political science discipline and the increased demands placed upon social scientists in the area of research methodology, the *American Journal of Political Science* under the editorship of John Kessel instituted in its February 1974 issue a special Workshop section devoted to articles describing research procedures in terms understandable to the broader social science profession. This section remains a distinctive feature of *AJPS*. About forty articles have now been published in the Workshop section under the editorships of John Kessel, Phil Shively, ourselves, and now Bob Erikson, articles spanning the research process, from its philosophy of science underpinnings and the role of formal theory to a variety of methods of data analysis.

This first volume of Workshop articles consists of ten pieces originally published during Kessel's editorship. They were chosen for reprinting here because together they cover central concerns of social science research. Part I of the book includes articles on theory building, with sections on philosophy of science and on formal political theory. Part II of the book emphasizes data analysis, with sections on measures of association, regression analysis, and scaling techniques. Additionally, we have written four new essays to present background material which supplements the Workshop articles. These essays also include some updated references relevant to the Workshop articles. It is naturally impossible to cover all appropriate topics and new analysis procedures in one volume; the interested reader is invited to check through the continuing series of Workshop articles in the *American Journal of Political Science* for presentations on other topics.

We appreciate the efforts of the many people who have helped make this project possible. Foremost among them is John Kessel, who initiated the Workshop section and published the articles that appear in the volume. Kessel was succeeded as editor by Phil Shively, who continued the Workshop enterprise and built upon the high standards established by Kessel. It was the efforts of Kessel and Shively that have made the Workshop section the valuable resource that it is today for the social science community. A major debt of gratitude is also owed to the authors of the Workshop articles who admirably fulfilled their task of writing about complex methodological topics in an informative and accessible fashion. We thank the officers of the Midwest Political Science Association and the people at the Journals Department of the University of Texas Press for working through the complex process underlying publication of this volume; a special debt of gratitude goes to Mac Jewell for handling some of the negotiations. Marilyn Dantico has provided us with helpful comments on our chapters. The staff of the Department of Political Science of the Ohio State University and our editorial assistants on the journal, Sandy Davis and Rich Pacelle, have provided valuable help throughout our work on this volume. Finally, we would like to thank Mavis Bryant of the University of Tennessee Press for her encouragement, suggestions, and patience throughout the many lives of this project.

                                        Herb Asher   Herb Weisberg
January 1983
Columbus, Ohio

Contents

Part I

Theory-Building

HERBERT B. ASHER

The Research Process

Although the research process is often described as an orderly, sequential activity, the actual conduct of research is much more unpredictable. Nevertheless, it is possible to lay out a series of steps which are common to almost all research endeavors. Thus the chapter first discusses problem formulation and theorizing followed by a discussion of the operationalization of concepts central to one's research. With respect to operationalization, major attention is given to the use of multiple indicators and to the properties of reliability and validity. The chapter concludes with a discussion of data generation and data collection procedures with particular emphasis on experiments and surveys.

It is tempting to describe the conduct of research as an orderly, sequential process in which we routinely follow a carefully laid out series of steps which ultimately leads to important substantive findings. Yet, as any practitioner will readily admit, the research process is not so neat and tidy. Even when following a carefully constructed plan of research, the investigator must inevitably be prepared to adapt his or her research efforts to the unforeseen occurrence, the unanticipated problem, and the serendipitous discovery.

Nevertheless, it is possible to lay out certain stages and tasks, the completion of which is critical to most research endeavors. In the ensuing discussion, we will consider the various stages of the research process. Before we do so, two admonitions about research must be considered. The first is simply that decisions made early in the research process will be very consequential for the subsequent stages of the process. This is such an obvious assertion that its utility might be questioned. Yet all too often research founders at the later stages, particularly in data analysis, because of the inadequacy of decisions made at the initial stages. For example, it is extremely frustrating at the data analysis stage to observe a relationship between two variables yet be unable to test whether that relationship is spurious, because the potential confounding variable has not been identified at the theorizing and design phase and hence has not been measured. Likewise, it is frustrating for the investigator who wishes to employ a certain data analysis technique to learn that certain additional variables needed to have been measured in order to use the technique properly. Even more importantly, the analyst who realizes too late that his or her measurement strategies are not faithful to the "true" meaning of the concepts of interest may be unable to perform any meaningful analysis of data whatsoever.

These examples can be multiplied endlessly; they should suffice to support our second admonition, namely that the researcher should take a prospective, anticipatory view of the research process. To the extent that we look ahead, the requirements of later stages might be anticipated and the necessary decisions and choices made early. The techniques for data analysis discussed in the second part of this book are reasonably straightforward. If the research process has generated "good" data ("good" will be defined shortly), then if we make a mistake in performing the statistical analysis, we can simply redo the analysis. However, if the research process has not resulted in "good" data, it most likely will be impossible because of resource constraints to reformulate measurement definitions and repeat the data collection. Hence, it cannot be emphasized too strongly that even as the investigator conducts research in a step-by-step fashion, at some point a major commitment to an anticipatory posture is warranted.

Problem Formulation and Theorizing

Research problems emerge from many sources. The values and concerns of the broader society in which the social scientist is working may determine the research program. For example, the major emphasis given to voting studies in political science is in part a reflection of the heavy emphasis in American political thought given to free and open electoral competition as a core characteristic of a democratic polity.

The nature of the discipline in which we have been trained may affect our research agenda. In some disciplines there may be widespread agreement about the core questions to be asked and about the methods and approaches by which those questions will be addressed. Such disciplines are said to be characterized by a dominant research paradigm.

Of course, there are many disciplines in which there is little consensus on the key questions, let alone on the appropriate methods by which the researcher pursues truth. In such cases research problems may emerge from a broader research program defined by the analyst, or research problems may reflect more narrowly defined puzzles that have intrigued observers. Many is the research project that began when the investigator observed anomalous behavior in some setting and had his or her curiousity piqued. Research topics can thus arise from many sources. The key point is that once a problem has been identified it is necessary to formulate a program of research to address that problem. And most often the research begins with a careful theoretical elaboration of the problem.

The Ball article in this volume, by analyzing the work of Thomas Kuhn and Imre Lakatos, examines how science progresses. Ball first criticizes the Kuhnian view that one research paradigm is suddenly replaced by another; Ball argues that paradigms are more likely to erode gradually, a point conceded by Kuhn in his later work. Ball describes the scientific enterprise as dynamic but not cumulative in a simplistic sense, since "facts, hypotheses and theories are not building blocks which can be stacked one on top of the other. Disciplines do not grow and develop by simple accretion."

According to Ball, one of Kuhn's major contributions was to refute the notion of naive falsification—the idea that theories could be simply falsified by facts. Ball introduces here the work of Imre Lakatos, who details three types of falsification. For Lakatos (and Ball) the appropriate perspective is one of sophisticated methodological falsification. In the view of Lakatos, scientific progress is to be assessed by examining the success or failure of a series of theories, "each sharing common core assumptions." This is called a "research program" and consists of a "hard core" of not directly challengable assumptions. In this view, theories are falsified in a relative and not an absolute sense. Ball argues that we have treated our research programs too harshly, that because of a narrow falsification approach we have rejected potentially interesting theories too quickly. Hence, Ball issues a plea for tolerance in theoretical matters, a posture that holds promise for richer development and testing of our theories and research programs.

Ball's article focuses on how we view our theories; it does not actually detail the processes involved in theorizing. For our purposes we can view the theorizing process as the generation of explanations of phenomena of interest. There are many ways in which theories and explanations are developed, the most logically elegant of which is by means of an axiomatic or formal-deductive approach. The Fiorina article in this volume considers the role of formal models in the social sciences. According to Fiorina, all formal models have three elements in common: a set of primitives or undefined terms, additional concepts defined with respect to the primitives and other previously defined terms, and assumptions of various types (e.g., behavioral, institutional or about the language in which the model is cast).

Fiorina argues that the formal modeling approach has a number of advantages: it forces precision in our arguments, it makes assumptions explicit, it makes it easier to check for logical consistency in an argument, and it facilitates the fuller development of the logical implications of the model. By a process of logical deduction, we can work through a formal model and generate a set of theoretical statements.

Models are by their nature unrealistic; at the minimum, they represent a vast oversimplification of reality. In many cases, the assumptions built into models seem patently absurd in light of our real world insights and experiences. Nevertheless, formal models are of great help to us. By constructing a model consisting of a small set of concepts and relationships to represent complex phenomena and by working through the implications of that model, we can gain understanding and insight into real world processes. Even though some modelers are unconcerned with real world correspondences and adopt the Friedman view that models should be judged on the accuracy of their predictions and not on the plausibility of their assumptions, increasingly we are seeing a concern for relaxing restrictive, unrealistic assumptions in the model. Moreover, we are witnessing greater efforts at testing the logical implications of formal models against real world data, a welcome development.

Formal models have been used to address many important problems, such as the effect of institutional mechanisms on voting in legislatures, voters' decisions whether to vote and for which party to vote, and the linkages between constituents and their representatives. The Plott article in this volume considers some central questions of democratic theory from a formal perspective. In particular, Plott considers at length the work of Kenneth Arrow, who demonstrated that a number of conditions that most observers agree should characterize a just and fair political system are in fact logically inconsistent. Plott's article shows that the dichotomy between normative political concerns and formal political analysis is indeed a false one. Although the part of the Plott article reprinted here gives essentially "negative" results, the last part of this article (omitted here because of space limitations) gives new results that are more "positive" in character—such as providing axiomatic characterizations of several existing social choice processes (e.g., simple majority rule), examining the procedural features of some social choice processes (e.g., the secret ballot), and suggesting how we might identify institutional structures by using axiomatic models of process behavior ("the theory of revealed institutions"). This last part of his article shows that there are exciting directions forthcoming in the social choice arena, with models more directly relevant to empirical political and social settings.

The mode of theorizing outlined in the Fiorina chapter has little recourse to real world observations at the outset of the theorizing process. There are many instances, however, in which the researcher might proceed in an inductive fashion, moving from observations of certain events and behaviors to generalizations about those dependent phenomena based upon the observations. Although ideally data would be generated from guidelines provided by some prior theory, the inductive approach is a legitimate one which can result in the development of a more general, testable theory.

Yet another style of theorizing and explanation-generation is retroduction (Selltiz et al., pp. 32–35). Here we reason from conclusions to reasons for conclusions. In many ways retroduction is a more accurate description of how the theorizing and analysis processes actually work than is deduction or induction. That is, there is often a major interplay between theory and data analysis in research. We may observe a certain relationship, propose a certain explanation for it, reason that if that explanation is valid some other relationship should be observed, and test whether the latter relationship is indeed observed. This kind of interplay can go through multiple stages of analysis and argument.

Our theoretical statements will most often be expressed in terms of relationships among concepts, abstractions or symbols representing our key theoretical terms. The question arises as to the source of our concepts. In his article in this volume, Jones discusses the paradox of conceptualization. He argues that we need a good theory to arrive at the proper concepts, yet proper concepts are needed to generate a good theory—hence the paradox. He suggests that the paradox is not a serious problem for political science (and other social sciences), not because political science is a well-developed discipline with a paradigm that identifies theory and concepts, but for just the opposite reason. It is the undeveloped state of political science (and other social sciences) that enables and even forces us to be bold and imaginative in the process of conceptualization. Hence, for Jones, "doing before knowing" means identifying concepts before paradigms; it does *not* mean data collection before concepts.

The articles in the first part of this book focus on the theorizing and problem formulation stages of research just discussed, while the articles in the second part consider specific data analysis strategies and techniques. Between the theorizing and data analysis stages are many other crucial steps of the research process, particularly operationalization—the translation of concepts into a set of measurement operations—and data generation and collection. Although no articles on these topics have been included in this volume, it is still important to discuss them at some length in order to present a more nearly complete picture of the research process.

Operationalization

The translation of concepts into measurement operations is a critical step in the research process and one at which much research goes astray. Often in our theories we use such grand concepts as economic development, political culture, and democracy, which present serious if not intractable measurement problems. Even with some of our more mundane concepts, operationalization entails some difficult measurement choices. For example, in analyzing the assertion, "The more competitive the legislative district from which a representative is elected, the more likely the representative is to follow the district's wishes on policy matters before the legislature," let us consider how the first concept—district competitiveness—might be measured. Immediately we have a basic choice to make: should we rely on a subjective measure such as the representative's perception of the district's competitiveness or on an objective measure such as the representative's margin of victory? If we opt for an objective measure (perhaps on the practical grounds that resources are inadequate to allow personal interviewing of legislators), there are still many choices facing us. Is a competitive district one that was won by less than 55% of the vote or by less than 60%? Or is a competitive district one that has changed party hands some number of times over the past set of elections? Or is a competitive district one in which the representative's margin of victory has dropped from some previously higher level? Or perhaps competitiveness is a combination of all of these. If so, what kind of combination? Should each indicator be weighted equally or should certain components count more? Are multiple indicators of competition preferable to a single indicator?

Multiple Indicators

It is often suggested that investigators adopt a multiple indicators strategy in measuring concepts. One rationale for this advice comes from psychometric theory, in which it is argued that any single indicator of a concept is likely to contain different kinds of error, one type of which is random measurement error. The use of a single indicator which contains random measurement error decreases reliability and yields attenuated results. Therefore it is argued that combining multiple indicators (each of which contains error) into an index will lead to more reliable measures and stronger relationships because the random measurement error components will tend to be cancelled.

Guilford (1954) shows how the addition of homogeneous indicators to a test or measuring instrument will increase the reliability of that instrument. ("Reliability" and "validity" will be formally defined shortly.) The word "homogeneous" is critical here; the additional indicator should "not only resemble the old ones in form and kind of content but also (be) of equal difficulty and have equal correlation with one another and with the old items" (Guilford, p. 352). This is the situation that Leege and Francis (1974) describe as multiple indicators of the same kind or what others call multiple indicators obtained by the same method. The main point is that the psychometric justification for combining multiple indicators rests on the gain in reliability that we obtain. For example, in survey research which is characterized by substantial random error, we often observe that an index correlates more highly with some other variable than do the separate items comprising the index.

Multiple indicators need not be homogeneous and may instead be based on different measurement strategies. The rationale for multiple indicators based upon different measurement operations has been presented by Hyman (1955, p. 183), who argued that the use of such measures "precludes the possibility that the finding is an accident of some peculiarity in the procedure underlying the particular relationship." Cook and Selltiz develop further the rationale for (non-homogeneous) multiple indicators. They observe that inconsistencies inevitably arise between different measures of the same trait and urge that we "work with a number of different measures, in each of which an effort is made to eliminate or control in some systematic way some identifiable influence on response other than the attitude in question" (Cook and Selltiz, p. 24). They then discuss the advantages and disadvantages of five different ways of measuring attitudes.

Campbell and Fiske (1969) relate the use of multiple indicators more systematically to a strategy of validation. Their multitrait-multimethod matrix method requires the measurement of multiple traits (variables) by a variety of methods, yielding multiple indicators obtained by different methods which suggest the relative importance of trait vs. method variance. An examination of the trait-method correlation matrix gives us evidence about convergent and discriminant validation; if these are achieved, then we might move to other validity questions. We will say more about the Campbell and Fiske approach shortly.

The abovementioned reasons for using homogeneous multiple indicators and multiple indicators obtained by different measurement operations might be termed methodological in that they were concerned with the consequences of measurement error, method effects, and the like. There is a more substantive justification for multiple indicators which argues that, since many of the concepts we work with are multifaceted, no single indicator of the concept can capture its complexity. Certainly, if a multidimensional concept is measured by a single indicator, important information will be lost. For example, it is fortunate that political efficacy was traditionally measured by four indicators even though it was conceptualized as unidimensional and the four indicators initially scaled in a Guttman sense (see chapter 12). The availability of the four indicators made it possible for Balch (1974) and Converse (1972) to identify two aspects of efficacy, a discovery that would have been impossible had only a single indicator been used. Originally the four efficacy items were viewed as homogeneous indicators of the same unidimensional concept; the advantage of the four items over any one of them was that the four could be combined into an index or scale that would lessen the effect of random measurement error. Although subsequent research has not consistently confirmed the existence of two components of efficacy, nevertheless, it is still useful to view the four efficacy items as consisting of two homogeneous multiple indicators each for each of the two components of efficacy. This approach, in contrast to the lumping together of all four efficacy indicators, holds greater promise for uncovering the antecedents and consequences of efficacy.

In general, if we have a multidimensional concept, we should construct multiple indicators for each aspect of the concept. We may then decide to combine the indicators for each aspect to reduce error, or we may treat them separately to yield more tests of hypotheses. Leege and Francis (1974, p. 140) assert that "sound measurement is more likely to occur when multiple indicators, some of the same kind but others based on different operations, are used." When our multiple indicators are not of the same kind, we would not want to combine them; rather, we might use them to check for convergence of results as in the multitrait-multimethod matrix method.

Even though the general injunction to use multiple indicators is an appropriate one, there may be times when the single item indicator is to be preferred, most likely on theoretical and substantive grounds. For example, in our earlier discussion of district competitiveness, we might decide on *a priori*, theoretical grounds that it is the perception of electoral safety and marginality that is most likely to affect the representative's behavior, and hence we would opt for the subjective measure of competition over the objective ones.

There may be times when multiple indicators appear to be available, but closer inspection reveals that each indicator is tapping fundamentally different things. For example, we can measure change (e.g., change in the amount of money spent for a program) in terms of absolute change, percentage change, or residualized change scores (Van Meter). These indicators are not interchangeable, nor should they be combined into an index. Each has its own unique meaning and interpretation, and the choice of which measure to use should be determined by the substantive thrust of the research.

Finally, the injunction to use multiple indicators may create major validity problems when the unsophisticated researcher devotes too much time to collecting multiple measures relevant to his or her concepts and does not give sufficient prior thought to theorizing and operationalization. This occurs for a variety of reasons. One reason is that certain concepts may be very difficult to work with, because of either their complexity or their conceptual fuzziness. This may lead the investigator to collect hordes of indicators on such variables without first trying to sort out the complexity or remedy the fuzziness. Often, resources are available for such massive data gathering exercises and the data themselves may be readily accessible. Thus the researcher compensates for theoretical shortcomings and intellectual untidiness by a strategy of indicator overkill. In the ideal world, operationalization and data collection would proceed from some theoretical perspective within which measurement decisions would naturally emerge. But this procedure is often bypassed, perhaps because the theoretical problems are intractable, while the data collection is relatively easy.

Some investigators behave as if validation concerns can be left to a post–data collection stage, and to a limited extent they are probably correct. That is, some researchers collect many indicators of each variable so that they can use such techniques as the multitrait-multimethod matrix method and factor analysis (see chapter 12) to arrive at a measure of validity. Such procedures can tell us which indicators hang together and what the complexity and dimensionality of our measures looks like. However, results, whether confirming our initial expectations or not, are more interpretable when embedded in some theoretically derived relationships. And, when results contradict our expectations, we are in much better shape for sorting out the various sources of the discrepancies when there is some theoretical underpinning for our initial selection of indicators.

For example, one problem in relying upon the results of factor analysis to guide our decisions about indicator validity is that results contrary to our expectations can be attributed to a variety of sources. Our expectations (implicit theory) may have been in error. Or perhaps our expectations were correct, but the translation from concept to indicator was flawed. Or perhaps the operational definitions were satisfactory, but the data collection shoddy. The greater the confidence we have in the theory underlying the choice and measurement of indicators, the less likely unexpected results will leave us befuddled.

Of course, there are many situations in which we cannot proceed so neatly from theory and concepts to operational definitions and data. Theory may be sparse, concepts undeveloped, and optimal data unavailable. In such situations, an interplay between theory and data seems entirely legitimate; we may define some variables, collect some data, perhaps factor analyze the data, examine the results, and then reconceptualize the variables. There is nothing inherently unscientific about this procedure. But there may come the point where such a process becomes mindless data snooping.

Reliability and Validity

Whether we use single or multiple indicators, the key criteria for assessing the quality of the measurement strategies are reliability and validity. In simple terms, reliability refers to the consistency of the performance of the measuring instrument, while validity refers to whether the measuring instrument actually taps the underlying concept it is supposed to.

There are two general classes of reliability measures—measures of stability and measures of equivalence. The stability of a measuring instrument is determined by applying that instrument to the same cases on two different occasions and correlating the two sets of responses. For example, in the context of survey research, the instrument would be a questionnaire and the cases people (respondents). The respondents' answers to the same item administered the two different times would be correlated to yield an estimate of the test-retest reliability of that item. The higher the correlation, the greater the test-retest reliability.

There are some obvious problems with test-retest reliability estimates. The estimate obtained will in part be a function of the time interval between the measurements. In general, the longer the time period, the lower the reliability estimate. But if there is a lengthy interval between measurements, then there is a greater probability (in the survey context) that genuine attitude change would have occurred, which of course reduces the stability coefficient but does not actually indicate low reliability. If the time interval between the administration of the two tests is too short, then the reliability estimate may be artificially inflated if respondents recall their earlier answers and attempt to remain consistent over time. This problem of memory effects is sometimes handled by employing a second form of the instrument that is parallel in content to the first instrument, although the particular items in each are not identical. At t_1 the first form is used, at t_2 the second form, and the reliability estimate is obtained by correlating the two sets of responses. A final problem with test-retest measures is the reactivity effect: the t_1 measurement may sensitize and activate respondents with respect to the questionnaire, thereby inducing attitude change, which in turn may give the incorrect impression of low reliability estimates.

The problems inherent in the test-retest measures have led analysts to consider measures of equivalence to assess reliability. Equivalence measures deal with two general situations: the extent to which different investigators using the same measurement instrument on the same cases at the same time obtain consistent results and the extent to which different measures applied to the same cases at the same time yield similar results. Underlying equivalence measures is the idea that whenever we construct a testing instrument we are selecting only a sample of the potentially infinite set of items that might comprise the instrument. The question becomes how the selection of one set of items vs. another affects our results. It is this concern that motivates the use of such approaches as alternate forms.

With alternate forms, we construct two equivalent versions of the instrument and administer it to the same subjects. The correlation between the observations generated by each of the equivalent (though not identical) forms indicates the consistency of the forms in measuring the variable of interest; the higher the correlation, the better the reliability. The split-half method can be viewed as a special case of alternate forms; here we construct a large number of items designed to tap the same trait and then randomly assign them to the groups, thereby creating two indices which supposedly measure that trait. The higher the correlation between the results obtained using the two indices, the better the reliability.

Validity is a more difficult property to ascertain than reliability. A simple definition of validity is that an instrument is valid if it taps the concept it is supposed to measure. An example of a potentially invalid survey item is the following question on school desegregation asked in election surveys of the Center for Political Studies: "Do you think the government in Washington should see to it that white and black children go to the same schools or stay out of this area as it is not its business?" If this question is used to measure desegregation attitudes, it may be invalid because it contains two stimuli— desegregation and the government in Washington. It is possible that a person might support desegregation but not feel it is the responsibility of the government in Washington.

A very simple kind of validity is face validity, which in actuality is little more than the assertion that the instrument appears to be tapping what it is supposed to measure. A more demanding type of validity is pragmatic or criterion-related validity. Here we are concerned with how well the instrument serves as an indicator or predictor of some other property of the case. For example, if we measured a concept such as sense of citizen or civic duty, we might try to validate the measurement by linking it to some related behavior, such as turnout in elections. Presumably, persons with higher levels of citizen duty should have a higher electoral turnout; if this turns out not to be the case, it would call into question how validly civic duty was measured in the first place. Likewise, if we have measured religious orthodoxy, we might check whether the more or-thodox attend church more regularly.

Often there is no single criterion such as election turnout or church attendance to help validate the measure, and thus other validation strategies have to be considered, the most prominent of which is construct validation. Hofstetter (1971) provides a useful statement of the process of construct validation:

Construct validation requires that the analyst place a concept in the context of a nomological network of other concepts, preferably a series of logically interrelated propositions forming a theory. Relationships between the concept to be validated and other concepts in the network are then derived on the basis of theory (or, less preferably, discrete research findings). Measures for all variables that are theoretically related to the concept to be validated are generated, and inter-correlations are calculated. Confidence in the validity of the measure to be validated is then directly proportional to the extent to which the theoretically generated predictions are confirmed in the correlational analysis.

Construct validation is a demanding task. We must measure not only the concept to be validated but also the other concepts to which it has been related theoretically; this of course implies that there is some theory underlying the enterprise. Moreover, the subsequent correlational analysis may not yield a definitive judgment as to validity; the expected patterns may hold, but only weakly, or there may be inconsistencies which might be due to the measurement of the concept to be validated or to the measurement of the other concepts or to inadequacies in the underlying theory.

Campbell and Fiske have argued that we should pay more attention to the measure of the concept before examining its linkages with other variables. They state that two kinds of information are needed about a measure prior to analyzing its relationships to other measures. The first is convergent validation, the notion that different measures of the same construct yield similar results. The second is discriminant validation, the idea that the construct as measured can be differentiated from other constructs. Their multitrait, multimethod matrix approach requires that multiple traits each be measured by multiple methods; such an approach enables us to assess the relative importance of trait vs. method effects in measurement. For example, if presumably different traits measured by the same method have very high similarity, this would suggest that method effects are pronounced or that the traits are not so distinctive as initially thought. Likewise, if the same trait measured by different methods yields similar results, this would argue that the trait is well measured and method effects are not dominant.

Most of our examples have discussed reliability and validity in the context of survey research and attitude measurement, in part because much of the core work on reliability and validity originated in psychometrics. However, reliability and validity concerns are central to all measurement strategies and types of data, even though they may take on forms particular to those strategies. For example, in experimental design, validity is considered under the rubrics of internal and external validity, topics discussed later. Hermann has analyzed validity problems in games and simulations. When we are utilizing data from the public record, a major validity concern is source bias. For example, one kind of data used widely in international politics research is events data, which represent the foreign policy behaviors of nations relative to each other. The events data are generated from such sources as the New York Times and Deadline Data. Analysts have warned that we should not rely too heavily on any single source for events data. For example, regional sources may overemphasize events of that region at the expense of the larger set of international events. Likewise, certain sources may be more likely to report certain types of events than others. Such problems can be minimized by using multiple sources.

Reliability concerns also take on a distinctive hue in certain research strategies. For example, in doing content analysis, we often begin with a raw data base consisting of words (not numbers), most often coming from the written, public record—newspapers, official government records and documents, and the like. These words are then categorized and coded to yield information about the phenomenon under study. For example, if we were interested in understanding the outbreak of war in a region, we might monitor regional news sources to determine whether the charges and threats issued by nations of the region reached some critical or threshold point prior to the onset of war. We would then generate a coding scheme that would classify different charges and threats in terms of the degree of conflict and hostility that they represented.

Hence coding is a central task of content analysis, and coding involves various kinds of reliability. One kind is intercoder reliability, the extent to which different coders using the same coding rules (the measuring instrument) on the same set of materials agree in their judgments and classification. Obviously, low intercoder reliability would be a cause for concern, for it would indicate that classifications were coder specific, which in turn would seriously undermine the obtained results.

Intercoder reliability is a function of how well trained and prepared the coders are. It is also a function of another kind of reliability—category reliability—the extent to which the investigator can construct categories and coding rules that are distinct and meaningful to trained judges. A large number of categories with very minor distinctions between them may result in substantial intercoder disagreements. But a smaller number of more broadly defined categories may be too inclusive for the purposes of the research even though it results in high intercoder reliability.

The above discussion should serve to demonstrate how crucial the properties of reliability and validity are. If concepts are not well measured, then the subsequent data analysis, although technically correct, may generate nonsense results. It cannot be emphasized too strongly that the soundness of the operational definitions given our concepts is central to the quality of the research output.

Data Generation and Collection

There are myriad ways to generate and collect data, and clearly the choice among these is primarily a function of the needs and requirements of the research conditioned by the practical resource constraints that most research projects confront. We can generate data through extensive reliance on the public record, using such approaches as content analysis. Or we might employ observational techniques in which the investigator directly observes the behavior or phenomenon of interest (McCall and Simmons). For many research topics, less obtrusive, more indirect modes of data collection are required (Phillips). Probably the two most prominent data collection designs in the social sciences are surveys and experiments, and it is these two that will be the focus of attention in the remainder of this section.

Survey designs are undoubtedly the most familiar to the social science audience and to citizens in general. Almost everyone has heard of the Gallup and Harris polls, which predict election outcomes, assess presidential popularity, and tap public opinion on issues. Survey research and popular polling have become so widespread that there is a mistaken impression that survey research is easily done and applicable to almost any research question.

Because many fine texts on survey research are available (Babbie; Backstrom and Hursh-César; Weisberg and Bowen), we will simply touch upon some of the central points. Most survey research involves selecting a sample of respondents from some population, interviewing these respondents in some fashion, and generating statements about the population based upon information provided by the sample. Because only a sample has been selected from the population, the population parameters can be estimated only approximately; the difference between the sample results and the true population values is called sampling error.

There are a number of types of sample survey designs. The simplest and most common is the cross-section, which is merely a representative sample interviewed at one point in time. This design is particularly useful for assessing the general characteristics of the population and the relationships among variables at one time. An extension of this design is successive cross-sections, the selection of different samples from the same population at different times. This design is particularly useful in talking about trends and attitude change, although only the net amount of attitude change can be assessed with this design.

A more difficult yet more informative design is the panel study, in which successive surveys with the *same* sample are conducted at multiple points in time. A panel enables us to measure the net and the gross amount of attitude change that has occurred in the interval between interviews. Panel studies have a number of unique problems. One is mortality—respondents may move or vanish or even die after the first interview, and tracking them down for a re-interview can be a very expensive proposition. Panels also have the problem of contamination: the first interview may sensitize the person to the topic at hand and induce attitude change. Or the respondent may recall his/her earlier responses and strive to be consistent.

In conducting a survey, two basic questions must be addressed: What kind of sampling scheme will be used, and how will the questionnaire be administered? Will we use a random sample, a systematic sample, or a more complex multi-stage area sample? Will we rely on personal interviews or telephone interviews or self-administered mail questionnaires? These choices and the factors that affect them are discussed extensively in many texts on the research process; certainly the substantive nature of the research and the availability of resources to conduct the research will affect these decisions.

The steps involved in survey research are straightforward once the research problem has been well formulated—select a good sample, construct a reliable and valid questionnaire, administer that instrument appropriately, and analyze the data correctly. These steps are covered thoroughly in many texts. There is one aspect of survey research that does not receive sufficient attention—the problem of measuring non-attitudes (Converse, 1970). Too often we assume in survey research that questions which are meaningful to the investigator are also meaningful to the survey respondent. One danger in survey research is that people give answers to questions even when they have no real opinion on that matter. The very process of asking questions generates responses even when we try to screen out non-attitudes by making it easy for the respondent to say that he or she has never thought about the issue at hand. The analysis of non-attitudes is the analysis of noise, not genuine information; as such, the substantive significance of such data is at best dubious.

Surveys usually have the desirable property of being representative, which means that we can generalize from the sample results to the broader population from which that sample was drawn. Unfortunately, survey designs are generally low in control over outside factors that may be affecting the survey results. This lower control is partially a function of the survey being conducted in the natural setting—the real world—and of the fact that in a (cross-sectional) survey there is a little meaningful temporal ordering in the measurement of variables.

A design that contrasts sharply to a survey with respect to the properties of representativeness and control is an experiment which tends to be high on control and low on representativeness. The basic outline of an experiment is simple. One is attempting to ascertain the impact of some experimental or causal variable or treatment on some dependent variable of interest. There is often an experimental group which is exposed to the treatment and a control group which is not, with pre- and postmeasurements on both groups. The two groups may then be compared to determine the impact of the treatment on the dependent variable. This is the simplest outline of an experiment; in the real world, experimental designs get much more complex with multiple control groups, differential patterns of pre- and posttreatment measurements, and elaborate efforts to insure that the control and experimental groups are equivalent at the outset.

Campbell and Stanley discuss two types of validity relevant to an experiment. Internal validity refers to whether the effects observed in the experiment can actually be attributed to the experimental variable or treatment. External validity refers to the extent we can accurately generalize from the results of the experiment to other populations or other treatments. Campbell and Stanley systematically analyze a number of factors that can upset internal validity (e.g., history, maturation, pretest effects, statistical regression, etc.) and external validity (e.g., pretest-treatment interaction) and outline different experimental designs which handle these factors.

The advantage of an experiment, as noted earlier, is that it is high in control; the experimenter can structure the research setting so as to be able to isolate the effects of the treatment. But how representative the results of experiments in social science are and how far they may be generalized may often be in doubt. The subjects studied are disproportionately college students; the laboratory setting itself is likely to be a very artificial one. Nevertheless, a well-constructed experiment is one of the best ways for making causal statements about the impact of one variable on another.

In this section, we have considered a number of designs, focusing primarily on surveys and experiments. As stated earlier, the choice of which design to use should follow from the nature of the research question to be addressed. Designs are not interchangeable; the choice of one design over another can actually affect the substantive results obtained. For example, researchers have long been interested in the impact of political communications and propaganda on attitudes and attitude change. Both survey and experimental designs have been employed to study this topic, with the survey results generally indicating that communications are not effective in inducing attitude change and experimental studies indicating the opposite.

It is likely that these different results are due in part to features of the respective designs themselves (Converse, 1970; Hovland). For example, in an experiment the subjects in the experimental group are fully exposed to the communication, while in the natural setting of the survey there may be many other things competing for the respondent's attention. Moreover, in an experiment, the effect of the communication is often measured shortly after exposure to it, while in the survey study the time interval between exposure and measurement of effect is likely to be much longer. In an experiment, the communication may appear to have the implicit sponsorship of a credible source such as the investigator conducting the research; the authoritative source may be less common in the real world.

Other differences between surveys and experiments could be cited; the point is that the design chosen to pursue the research goals may affect the results obtained. Hence it is imperative that the researcher give serious thought to the choice of design and to the consequences of that choice. Often resource constraints prevent us from employing the optimum design; compromise on design is a fact of research life. However, the investigator should try to anticipate what the consequences of this compromise might be.

Conclusion

Throughout this chapter we have discussed the stages of the research process with an emphasis on the factors that might upset inferences based upon our data. Once reliable and valid data have been collected, the next step is to analyze them to answer the substantive questions of the research. Data analysis is the focus of the second half of this book. A good strategy of data analysis is to begin with simpler procedures, such as an examination of the univariate properties of the data followed by an analysis of the bivariate relationships linking the variables. This procedure is worthwhile because it gives the investigator insight into the basic properties of the data, thereby helping determine which of the more complex, multivariate statistical techniques are appropriate to apply to the data. The second part of the book reflects this data analysis strategy; it begins with simple measures of association appropriate for the analysis of bivariate relationships and moves on to more complex, multivariate techniques such as regression analysis, multidimensional scaling, and factor analysis.

REFERENCES

Babbie, Earl R. 1973. *Survey Research Methods*. Belmont, California: Wadsworth.

Backstrom, Charles H., and Hursh-César, Gerald. 1981. *Survey Research*, 2nd ed. New York: John Wiley.

Campbell, Donald T., and Fiske, Donald W. 1959. "Convergent and Discriminant Validation by the Multitrait-Multimethod Matrix," *Psychological Bulletin*, March 1959, pp. 81–104.

Campbell, Donald T., and Stanley, Julian C. 1963. *Experimental and Quasi-Experimental Designs for Research*. Chicago: Rand McNally.

Converse, Philip E. 1970. "Attitudes and Non-Attitudes: Continuation of a Dialogue," in Edward R. Tufte, ed., *The Quantitative Analysis of Social Problems*. Reading, Mass.: Addison-Wesley.

Converse, Philip E. 1972. "Change in the American Electorate," in Angus Campbell and Philip E. Converse, eds., *The Human Meaning of Social Change*. New York: Russell Sage Foundation.

Cook, Stuart W., and Selltiz, Claire. 1964. "A Multiple Indicator Approach to Attitude Measurement," *Psychological Bulletin*, July 1964, pp. 36–55.

Guilford, J. P. 1954. *Psychometric Methods*. New York: McGraw-Hill.

Hermann, Charles. 1967. "Validation Problems in Games and Simulations with Special Reference to Models of International Politics," *Behavioral Science*, May 1967, pp. 216–231.

Hofstetter, C. Richard. 1971. "The Amateur Politician: A Problem in Construct Validation," *Midwest Journal of Political Science*, February 1971, pp. 31–56.

Hovland, Carl I. 1959. "Reconciling Conflicting Results Derived from Experimental and Survey Studies of Attitude Change," *American Psychologist*, January 1959, pp. 8–17.

Hyman, Herbert. 1955. *Survey Design and Analysis*. New York: The Free Press.

Leege, David C., and Francis, Wayne L. 1974. *Political Research*. New York: Basic Books.

McCall, George J., and Simmons, J. L., eds. 1969. *Issues in Participant Observation*. Reading, Massachusetts: Addison-Wesley.

Phillips, Derek L. 1971. *Knowledge from What?* Chicago: Rand McNally.

Selltiz, Claire, et al. 1976. *Research Methods in Social Relations*, 3rd ed. New York: Holt, Rinehart and Winston.

Van Meter, Donald S. 1974. "Alternative Methods of Measuring Change: What Difference Does It Make?" *Political Methodology*, Fall 1974, pp. 125–140.

Weisberg, Herbert F., and Bowen, Bruce D. 1977. *An Introduction to Survey Research and Data Analysis*. San Francisco: W. H. Freeman.

Philosophy of Science

TERENCE BALL

From Paradigms to Research Programs: Toward a Post-Kuhnian Political Science*

This paper traces the reception of T.S. Kuhn's *Structure of Scientific Revolutions* by political scientists through three stages—the first two of uncritical acceptance, the third of rejection. I argue that a critical reading of Kuhn supports none of these positions in toto. I then go on to catalogue the main strengths and weaknesses of Kuhn's theory of scientific choice and change. This examination leads to a consideration of Imre Lakatos' more satisfactory theory of scientific progress. I then go on to suggest what bearing Lakatos' theory has upon the actual practice of political science.

The clash between . . . Kuhn [and his critics] is not about a mere technical point in epistemology. It concerns our central intellectual values, and has implications not only for theoretical physics but also for the underdeveloped social sciences and even for moral and political philosophy.

Imre Lakatos (1970, p. 93)

A decade has passed since political scientists first "discovered" Thomas Kuhn's *Structure of Scientific Revolutions.* The influence of that book upon the thinking of political scientists has been both profound and curious: profound, because political scientists have not only read Kuhn's book but have, as they believe, taken its message to heart; and curious, because few can say with certainty what that message is and what its implications might be for political-scientific inquiry. My aim here is not to provide yet another paean to Kuhn's "relevance" for political science. I want instead to trace the reception of his work by political scientists through three stages—the first two of uncritical acceptance, the third of outright rejection; to suggest that a critical

*Many of the themes and arguments in this essay grew out of conversations with Donald Moon, Stephen Toulmin, and the late Imre Lakatos. It is a pleasure to record my debt to them. I should also like to thank Moon and an anonymous referee for the *American Journal of Political Science* for criticizing an earlier version of this paper.

Reprinted from AMERICAN JOURNAL OF POLITICAL SCIENCE, Vol. XX, No. 1, February 1976, pp. 151-177, Terence Ball, "From Paradigms to Research Programs: Toward a Post-Kuhnian Political Science," by permission of the University of Texas Press.

reading of Kuhn supports none of these positions; to note several respects in which Kuhn's account of scientific change is unsatisfactory; to explicate the more satisfactory alternative to be found in Lakatos' notion of "research programs"; and finally to suggest what bearing Lakatos' perspective has upon the way we practice political science. By these means I hope to outline for political scientists a new methodology (broadly understood) which has lately gained widespread currency among philosophers of science. This methodology purports to meet two criteria. First of all, it supplies a *rational* standard or "demarcation criterion" for distinguishing science from nonscience; and in so doing it denies the Kuhnian contention that our demarcation criteria are nonrational and historically mutable. And secondly, this methodology purports to accord with the history of science—and in particular with the way in which scientific theories have been criticized, amended, and even, eventually, rejected. In being historical (*not* historicist), this new methodology has much more commonsense appeal than does the formalistic and ahistorical methodology associated with traditional "positivist" philosophy of science. It thus enables us to steer a middle course between the Scylla of Kuhnian relativism and the Charybdis of positivist formalism.

A Plethora of Paradigms

Kuhn's reception by political scientists has in the past decade gone through three more or less distinct phases. At first Kuhn's work was hailed by proponents of "scientific" or "behavioral" political science as providing (among other things) an explanation for the persistent tendency of political scientists to talk past each other: they have been operating within different "paradigms" of political inquiry; and so long as no authoritative single paradigm emerges, they will continue to do so, and political science will remain in its present "backward" ("underdeveloped," "immature," or "revolutionary") condition. But then, as Kuhn has shown, the natural sciences themselves have at times been similarly unsettled. And this was taken by some political scientists as a sign of hope. Political science had, they believed, undergone its own "revolutionary" phase (lasting two decades, three centuries, or 2,500 years, depending upon how one measures it), but was now about to become a "normal" or "mature" science in Kuhn's sense. This, at least, was the hope expressed in two A.P.S.A. presidential perorations (Truman, 1965; Almond, 1966). One, indeed, went to far as to suggest that "a new more surely scientific [*sic*] paradigm" was emerging in political science (Almond, 1966, p. 869). Others expressed similar hopes. The only trouble was that no one agreed as to whether the emerging paradigm was to be interest-group analysis, structural functionalism, mathematical game theory, or even "behavioralism" as a whole.[1] Kuhn's own warning to the contrary notwithstanding (1962, p. 15) political scientists—along with other social scientists[2]—joined in searching for "paradigms" in their respective fields.

If this was the season of hope, it proved to be remarkably short-lived. For the opponents of a "scientific" political science soon found in "their" Kuhn an able ally. And in a kind of pincer movement they pressed a renewed attack upon political "science." These critics focused first upon Kuhn's account of "normal" science and the sociology of settled scientific communities. Following Kuhn, they emphasized the narrowing of focus and the "dogmatism" characteristic of "normal science." If that is what a normal or mature science looks like, then political scientists should want no part of it. Paradigms do not (on their reading of Kuhn) merely dominate, they tyrannize; and so political scientists committed to free inquiry should resist all blandishments to make theirs a "normal" science (Euben, 1969; Wolin, 1968, 1969; Ryan, 1972; Beardsley, 1974). Political science should rather strive, as one commentator put it, to "attain a multiparadigmatic condition" (Beardsley, 1974, p. 60). Or, to put it in Kuhn's terms: political science should remain in its present "immature" state.

The second part of this pincer movement proceeded by drawing out the nonrational and relativistic implications of Kuhn's account of scientific change. In *The Structure of Scientific Revolutions* Kuhn averred that the decision to abandon one paradigm in favor of another is not a rational affair at all, but is rather more closely akin to a conversion experience (1962, pp. 150, 157). This claim, and its implications, did not go unheeded by opponents of "behavioral" political science. For Kuhn had (as they believed) shown the natural sciences to be quite as "subjective" and "normative" as the behavioralists' caricature of "traditional political theory" held that enterprise to be. And so, these new relativists maintained, the acceptance of one paradigm and the rejection of another is not a rational process but a matter of personal "values" and even "existential" choice (Gunnell, 1968, 1969; Miller, 1972). A further and rather more ominous implication (to which I will return in the next section) is that meaningful communication, and indeed truth itself, is necessarily *intra*paradigmatic, i.e. between adherents of different

[1] For a sophisticated analysis of would-be paradigms in political science, see Holt and Richardson (1970). On the role of paradigms in the history of political theory, see Wolin (1968).

[2] Here I include sociology (Friedrichs, 1971; Smolicz, 1970; Lebowitz, 1971), psychology (Palermo, 1971; Welmes, 1973; Boneau, 1974), and economics (Coats, 1969; Stanfield, 1974).

paradigms no rational communication would be possible; and so a permanent failure to communicate would be the inevitable accompaniment of a "multi-paradigmatic" political science.

The third—and present—phase of Kuhn's reception by political scientists can best be characterized as outright repudiation (Landau, 1972a, ch. 2, 1972b; Stephens, 1973). Frightened by the specter of epistemological relativism, political scientists are nowadays tempted to resort to pre-Kuhnian clichés about objectivity, testability and falsification, and the like. This temptation, although understandable, should be resisted, inasmuch as it represents a retreat to the comfortable—albeit questionable—pre-Kuhnian verities. Fortunately, we need not choose between retreat and surrender. We have another option. For we can—to extend the military metaphor—advance to new and more defensible ground. Lakatos has suggested one way of getting there. In a later section I will explicate his strategy. But first I should outline several persuasive reasons for attempting to move beyond Kuhn to a genuinely *post*-Kuhnian position.

Normal Science or Permanent Revolution?

Although Kuhn's views are too well known to warrant a detailed recounting here, several points should be noted. In *The Structure of Scientific Revolutions* Kuhn disputed the "cumulative" or "text book" conception of scientific change, viz.: that the growth of scientific knowledge is piecemeal, cumulative, and pacific; that such growth results from applying the neutral instrument of "scientific method" to independently existing reality; that this method requires, among other things, that theories be tested against reality and, should they fail, be discarded as "falsified"; and that scientific advance consists in the gradual accumulation of ever-truer hypotheses and theories. This vision of scientific development is plausible, Kuhn argues, only if one ignores the actual (as distinguished from the "textbook") history of science. Close and careful study of the history of science reveals significant conceptual and methodological *discontinuities,* sometimes of "revolutionary" proportions. Revolutions are, however, relatively infrequent. The greater part of the history of science is the story of "normal science," i.e., the enterprise of resolving the "puzzles" which arise, as a matter of course, in attempting to force recalcitrant nature into the conceptual pigeonholes of an exemplary theory or "paradigm." More often than not, natural phenomena can be conceptualized, interpreted—and, if need be, reinterpreted—so as to square with the expectations generated by the dominant paradigm. Sometimes, however, would-be puzzles turn into "anomalies"—that is, phenomena for which the master theory affords no plausible explanation. The presence, and indeed the proliferation, of anomalies does not, of itself, suffice to falsify the theory. Instead, the members of the scientific community devote their energies and attention to solving the soluble. During such periods, scientific advance conforms to the textbook picture: it is steady, continuous, and cumulative. This idyll may nevertheless be interrupted by the appearance of a rival paradigm which, Athena-like, springs fully formed from the head of a master theoretician and purports to account for the anomalies of the old even as it indicates new directions for research. The appearance of a rival paradigm signals the onset of a "crisis" and even, quite possibly, a thoroughgoing revolution. A revolution, in science as in politics, succeeds when scientists' loyalties and allegiances are transferred from the old to the new paradigm. And this victory, in its turn, inaugurates a new era of normalcy.

My purpose in briefly recounting the original (1962) Kuhnian conception of scientific change is to suggest that—contrary to a widely held misconception—it is *not* the role assigned to "paradigms" that distinguishes Kuhn's account. Indeed, the concept of theoretical "paradigms" is, in the history of philosophy, rather old hat.[3] It is, rather, Kuhn's distinction between "normal" and "revolutionary" science that distinguishes, and must carry the weight of, his account of scientific change. That being so, two questions ought now be asked. The first is formal: Is the distinction between normal and revolutionary science a coherent one? I maintain that when the distinction is drawn in one way, Kuhn's account of scientific change is incoherent, i.e., *internally inconsistent;* but, when drawn in another way, it is not. In *The Structure of Scientific Revolutions* Kuhn sometimes appears to draw the distinction in the first way; in subsequent "clarifications" of his position he has drawn it in the second way. Because political scientists are more likely to

---

[3] Although Kuhn has popularized the term "paradigm," he did not coin it. Our word "paradigm" derives from the Greek *paradeigma,* meaning model, pattern, or exemplar. In the *Republic,* for example, Plato speaks of his ideal polity as a "paradigm ($\pi\alpha\rho\dot{\alpha}\delta\epsilon\iota\gamma\mu\alpha$) laid up in heaven" (592 b). The first to speak of paradigms in the natural sciences was the eighteenth-century philosopher Georg Christoph Lichtenberg, for whom a paradigm was an accepted standard model or pattern into which we attempt to fit unfamiliar phenomena; and when we have done so we say we have "explained" or "understood" them. It is in this sense also that Wittgenstein (1968) spoke of paradigms and Austin (1970, p. 202) of "thought-models." This earlier use of the term is rather more precise and restricted than Kuhn's original (1962) use of "paradigm" as a portmanteau concept enclosing exemplary scientific achievements, theories, successful experiments, *Gestalten,* and world-views, among other notions (Masterman, 1970). Wanting to control such terminological inflation, Kuhn now (1970a, 1974) prefers to speak instead of exemplary theories, or "exemplars" for short.

know Kuhn's book than his later work, I will direct most of my criticisms against the claims advanced there. Having done that, I will move on to a second, empirical question: Does the history of science support the distinction between normal and revolutionary science?

Whether Kuhn's theory of scientific change is internally consistent or inconsistent depends upon which of two theses he subscribes to. The first I shall call the *thesis of perfect (or strict) incommensurability*; it holds that the phenomena of scientific investigation count as (relevant) facts solely by virtue of their being statable in a theoretical language. All meaningful observation reports are, on this view, "theory-laden." And furthermore, there being no neutral observation language common to any two theories, the observation reports of the one are not translatable into (or recognizable as meaningful) observation reports in the other. The second thesis—the *thesis of imperfect (or partial) commensurability*—holds that scientific theories are, in a way roughly analogous to natural languages, to some degree mutually intertranslatable.[4] That is, at least some phenomena-reporting sentences of a theory T will have roughly corresponding meaning-equivalents in another theory T'. Communication between theories in a given domain (e.g., microphysics), however partial and unsatisfactory, is at least possible.

In his book, especially, Kuhn appears to subscribe to the thesis of strict incommensurability (1962, pp. 4, 91, 102, 111, 147); in other essays he denies it explicitly (1970a, 1970b). In any event I shall argue that *if* in fact Kuhn *were* to subscribe to the strict thesis, his theory of scientific change would be internally inconsistent. For consider: According to Kuhn any master theory or "paradigm" permits one not only to explain certain phenomena but also to recognize other phenomena as (presently) inexplicable or anomalous. The solving of "puzzles" and the unearthing of "anomalies" are part of normal science. Now just as any number of compatible facts do not suffice to confirm a theory, neither can any number of recalcitrant phenomena—anomalies—serve to disconfirm it. Even so, as Kuhn acknowledges, recalcitrant facts do accumulate and may eventually undermine the scientists' confidence in the paradigm, thus paving the way for the appearance of a rival paradigm which, in a successful revolution, replaces the older anomaly-ridden master theory.

The question immediately arises, however, as to how—given the thesis of strict incommensurability—the second theory (T') could possibly be adjudged *better* than the first (T). Surely it is not "better" in that it "fits the facts"

---

[4] The analogy between paradigms and natural languages is drawn by Popper (1970) and accepted, with amendments, by Kuhn (1970a, pp. 200–204; 1970b, pp. 267–271).

more closely, since (1) the facts that T' explains cannot be (the same as) those that T explains and, further, (2) the phenomena that T *fails* to explain cannot be the (same) ones that T' does explain (Shapere, 1964, 1966). In other words: if "facts" are recognized as such only in the light of a theory, and if theories are strictly incommensurable, then T and T' necessarily explain quite *different* phenomena. Therefore Kuhn cannot without contradiction subscribe to the strict incommensurability thesis *and* maintain that one theory T' explains phenomena that are anomalous with respect to another theory T. Wholly incommensurable theories cannot—*logically* cannot—even recognize, much less explain, the "same" phenomena. From this it follows that one theory or paradigm cannot, strictly speaking, "rival" another.

In recent "clarifications" of his position Kuhn denies that he ever subscribed to the thesis of strict incommensurability (1970a, 1970b, 1974). He now insists that he accepts the thesis of partial commensurability, and so his theory of scientific change is at least internally consistent.

Internal coherence, however, is not everything. We may still ask whether the history of science supports the distinction between normal and revolutionary science. Is the distinction an accurate and useful one? In his book Kuhn maintained that the history of science is, for the most part, the story of "normal" science, interrupted infrequently by scientific "revolutions." He characterized these revolutions as thoroughgoing "changes of world view" or "gestalt switches" (1962, ch. 10). But, as Kuhn's critics hastened to note, the history of science does not conform to this schema. For example, changes of theory—"paradigm shifts"—are not the sudden all-or-nothing changes that Kuhn pictures them to be, but are more likely to take many years. Scientific change is also rather more piecemeal and continuous than Kuhn suggests. A paradigm does not fall in a great cataclysmic crash; it is more likely to erode over time (Toulmin, 1970). For example, the Newtonian paradigm was not a monolith until Einstein demolished it utterly; it was, rather, a ravaged shell of a theory, cracked in many places, and no longer able to support the ever-increasing weight of the evidence against it. Kuhn's "big bang," or revolutionary, account of scientific change does not fit the facts, even here.

Kuhn now concedes as much. Small-scale minirevolutions, he now maintains (1970b, pp. 249–50), occur frequently in the history of science. The upshot of Kuhn's concession to his critics was, however, to undercut—and render incoherent—his original distinction between "normal" and "revolutionary" science, which after all had been the linchpin of his theory of scientific change. For now all "normal" science is (to some unspecified degree) "revolutionary." Kuhn's account of scientific change is thus transformed into a theory of permanent revolution (as Trotsky might have said) or a "revolution in perpetuity" (as Toulmin [1972, p. 114] did in fact say). But then Kuhn, having rendered otiose the distinction between normal and revolutionary science, has emptied it of much of its supposed heuristic and explanatory value. Ironically, Kuhn's attempted "revolutionizing" of normal science lends support not to a revolutionary theory of scientific change but to an *evolutionary* one.[5] The boldest and most original aspects of Kuhn's account of scientific change—the ideas of self-contained paradigms, normal and revolutionary science, and the rest—have now been either watered down considerably or abandoned entirely.

In the face of these, and other, apparently decisive objections to Kuhn's account, political scientists are inclined to wring their hands in despair, lamenting that "We are back where we started before the Kuhnian paradigm [*sic*] was adopted by political science" (Stephens, 1973, p. 488). I disagree. Far from going back to Square One, we have made some progress—progress too easily overlooked if we focus only on the errors and omissions of Kuhn's original account. To suggest that we are "back where we started" is to go much farther than Kuhn's critics would have us go.

Even Kuhn's most ardent critics readily acknowledge the value and importance of his contribution to the history and philosophy of science. We must count among Kuhn's achievements the undermining (if not outright destruction) of the "textbook" conception of scientific progress as a steady growth-by-accumulation of ever-truer hypotheses and theories. For all its rhetorical exaggeration, Kuhn's conception of scientific change-through-revolution has had the signal merit of reminding us that the scientific enterprise is above all a dynamic and not wholly "cumulative" one. No one, with the possible exception of Sir Karl Popper, has done more than Kuhn to call this feature to our attention. As a result no political scientist would nowadays maintain that "A science of politics which deserves its name must build from the bottom up . . . . An empirical discipline is built by the slow, modest, and piecemeal accumulation of relevant theories and data" (Eulau, 1964, p. 9). Whatever their view of scientific development, Kuhn and his critics are agreed in repudiating this vision of growth-through-accumulation; facts, hypotheses and theories are not building blocks which can be stacked one on top of the other. Disciplines do not grow and develop by simple accretion.

---

[5] Kuhn *now* says that his "view of scientific development is fundamentally evolutionary" (1970b, p. 264); if so, his view has changed dramatically. For two rather different "evolutionary" theories of scientific change, see Popper (1972, ch. 7) and Toulmin (1967, 1972).

Another of Kuhn's important contributions is his recognition of the inseparability of "history" and "philosophy" of science: neither can proceed successfully without the other. Here, too, most of his critics agree with Kuhn. Where they disagree with Kuhn is over his further implication that an historical approach commits one to an *historicist* position in epistemology (Rudner, 1972, p. 827).

Another, even more important, contribution is Kuhn's undermining of naive falsificationism, i.e., the doctrine that *facts* can falsify or confute *theories.* Just as Popper showed that the "test of experience" cannot "prove" or verify the truth of a theory, so Kuhn has shown that the test of experience never suffices, of itself, to refute a theory. Theories are never falsified *simpliciter,* not even by rank anomalies. Therefore falsifiability cannot serve as the "demarcation criterion" for distinguishing science from nonscience (or pseudoscience). On this point Kuhn and his critics are agreed. They disagree, however, with Kuhn's contention that there can be no methodological demarcation criterion, but only, as it were, a *sociological* one; that is, that only the Powers That Be in a given scientific community can decide what is science and what is not, and that their standards of judgment are extrascientific and historically variable—a matter of taste and fashion only, and therefore beyond rational criticism (1962, ch's. 3, 10–12). Kuhn's contention has spurred others—Lakatos foremost among them—to formulate defensible demarcation criteria; that is, criteria more liberal—and therefore more acceptable, from an historical perspective—than the criterion of falsifiability, but which also make the demarcation between science and pseudoscience rationally defensible. With the aid of such a methodological demarcation criterion, we can view the choice between theories or paradigms as a *rational* one made for methodologically sound reasons, rather than—as with Kuhn—an arbitrary and rationally inexplicable "shift" of "allegiance" or "loyalties."

Lakatos' Alternative to Kuhn

Lakatos and Kuhn are agreed on this much: the history of science does not support the view that an elegant theory can be killed (or "falsified") by an ugly fact. Theories are made of sterner stuff, and facts are not so hard and unyielding as classical empiricists had supposed. But if science purports to say anything about the world, then scientists—and philosophers of science—must retain and take seriously the idea of an empirical basis. The mistake of the older empiricists was to assume that facts and theories are wholly separable in all cases, and that the truth content of the latter can be ascertained by reference to the former. I want now to outline Lakatos' reasons for believing this view to be mistaken.

Lakatos begins by distinguishing three species of falsificationism, which he terms "dogmatic," "methodological," and "sophisticated methodological falsificationism," respectively. *Dogmatic falsificationism* holds that while "facts" never suffice to *prove* theories, they do suffice to *disprove* them. "Falsifiability" thus serves as the demarcation criterion between science and nonscience. For in order to qualify as "scientific" a proposition or a theory must be potentially falsifiable: criteria of refutation must be specified and one or more "crucial experiments" conducted; if the theory or proposition fails in its direct encounters or "confrontations" with Nature, it must be given up (Lakatos, 1970, pp. 95–97).

Dogmatic falsificationism rests, however, upon two mistaken assumptions. The first is that there is some clear-cut dividing line between "observational" and "theoretical" propositions.[6] The second assumption upon which dogmatic falsificationism rests is that if a proposition qualifies as a "basic" or "observational" one, then it is either incorrigibly true or incorrigibly false; that is, "one may say that it was *proved* [or disproved] from facts." Lakatos (1970, pp. 97–98) calls this "the doctrine of observational (or experimental) proof."

Both these assumptions are, however, mistaken—the first mistaken in fact, the second in logic. The first is mistaken inasmuch as there is in fact no clear-cut borderline between observational and theoretical propositions. "For there are and can be no sensations unimpregnated by expectations and therefore there is no natural (i.e., psychological) demarcation between observational and theoretical propositions" (Lakatos, 1970, p. 98). By way of example, Lakatos cites the case of Galileo's supposed "refutation" of the Aristotelian theory of flawless celestial spheres:

Galileo claimed that he could "observe" mountains on the moon and spots on the sun and that these "observations" refuted the time-honoured theory that celestial bodies are faultless crystal balls. But his "observations" were not "observational" in the sense of being observed by the—unaided—senses: their reliability depended on the reliability of his telescope—and of the optical theory of the telescope—which was violently questioned by his contemporaries. It was not Galileo's—pure, untheoretical—*observations* that con-

[6] Popper terms this "the naturalistic doctrine of observation"; Nietzsche called it—rather more colorfully—"the dogma of immaculate perception."

[7] On this much, at least, Kuhn and Lakatos are agreed. For extended discussions of the "theory-laden" character of observation, see Hanson (1958), Spector (1966), Feyerabend (1970), and Machamer (1971, 1973).

fronted Aristotelian *theory* but rather Galileo's "observations" in the light of his optical theory that confronted the Aristotelians' "observations" in the light of their theory of the heavens. This leaves us with two inconsistent theories, *prima facie* on a par.

Even our most "direct" observations are impregnated with expectations; thus there is no natural dividing line between "basic" or "observational" propositions and "theoretical" ones.[7]

The second assumption upon which dogmatic falsificationism rests—its doctrine of experimental (dis)proof—is also mistaken, but for a different reason. It is mistaken, Lakatos says, because of "a basic point in elementary logic," viz.: "Propositions can only be derived from [and be consistent or inconsistent with] other propositions." Therefore "no factual proposition can ever be proved [or disproved] from an experiment" (1970, p. 99). Dogmatic falsificationism mistakenly posits a world of hard facts that is both independent of and comparable with our systems of propositions, i.e., theories. But it is not independent, inasmuch as no natural line of demarcation separates observation from theory; and it is not comparable, inasmuch as propositions can be compared only with other propositions. Dogmatic falsificationism is therefore untenable.

But dogmatic falsificationism is not the only kind. There is a second and less objectionable kind, which Lakatos calls *methodological* falsificationism. As against dogmatic falsificationism, it holds that the dividing line between observational and theoretical propositions is not natural but conventional; i.e., *where* to draw it is a methodological decision. For example, the sorts of basic or "observational" propositions against which we test the predictions of a theory T' are not pure and unsullied "protocol sentences" but are, rather, propositions drawn from another, "touchstone" theory. To return to the Galileo example cited above: What Galileo did in "testing" the Aristotelian theory of celestial bodies was to admit as "basic" or "observational" propositions the *theoretical* propositions of another theory—in this case his (still unrefined) optical theory. For purposes of testing—and falsifying—one theory, we use another. "The methodological falsificationist," says Lakatos, "uses our most successful theories as extensions of our senses . . ." (1970, p. 107). In other words, a proposition which is a "theoretical" one in T may be accorded "observational" status in T'.[8]

[8] Lest one think that such "observational" propositions are somehow suspect, if not indeed inferior to direct "eyeball observation," Lakatos reminds us that "calling the reports of our human eye 'observational' only indicates that we 'rely' on some vague physiological theory of human vision" (1970, p. 107).

Methodological falsificationism adopts a demarcation criterion which is, to say the least, more liberal than that proposed by dogmatic falsificationism: it admits as "scientific" any theory which has "potential falsifiers," even if they derive from some other, as yet unfalsified, theory. Consequently, many more theories may now be regarded as scientific ones. Both kinds of falsificationism hold, however, that a theory enjoys "scientific" status by continually "sticking its neck out." The scientist puts his theory's head on the block by "specifying, in advance, an experiment such that if the result contradicts the theory, the theory has to be given up" (Lakatos, 1970, pp. 96, 112). The difference between the dogmatic and methodological falsificationist is that the latter's conception of "observation" and "testing"—and hence "falsification"—is more liberal than the former's.

Even so, Lakatos argues that methodological falsificationism is not liberal enough. Its standards of falsification are too strict. It does not square with, or do justice to, the history of science. For if we apply its standards, many of the most respected theories of yesteryear would be accounted unscientific (or pseudoscientific). Theorists are almost never inclined to bet their theories on a crucial experiment (in which the theory is not "confirmed" once and for all, but merely not-falsified *this* time). Such an all-or-nothing go-for-broke attitude is, Lakatos says, "reckless" and "daredevil" (1970, p. 112). In fact, however, scientists tend to be bold in their conjectures but cautious in their refutations; good theories being hard to come by, they hold fast to what they have already.[9] And yet: theories *do* get falsified; one theory is rejected in favor of another; the scope and explanatory power of successive theories increases. But how is this sort of progress possible? If we are to answer that question we must first ask: How—by what standards, on what grounds— is one theory to be rejected as inferior to another? Any satisfactory answer to that question, Lakatos avers, cannot be given in isolation from, or in ignorance of, the actual history of science. But then, he says (1970, p. 114), "If we look at the history of science, if we try to see how some of the most celebrated falsifications happened, we have to come to the conclusion that either some of them are plainly irrational, *or* that they rest on rationality principles different from those [espoused by dogmatic and/or methodological falsificationists]." Faced with this choice, Kuhn opts for the former: choosing between rival theories or paradigms is not a wholly rational matter. Lakatos, by contrast, opts for the latter: there *are* principles of scientific rationality, criticism, and falsifiability—only they are *not* the ones advanced

[9]Up to this point Lakatos agrees with Kuhn. But Kuhn differs from Lakatos in viewing this as a social-psychological fact about the behavior of scientists, rather than as a methodological maxim or principle implicit in scientific practice.

by dogmatic and/or methodological falsificationists. To formulate and defend these principles is the task that Lakatos set himself.

Against Kuhn and earlier falsificationists alike, Lakatos advanced his own "methodology of scientific research programs." The linchpin of his theory of criticism and scientific change is to be found in his doctrine of "sophisticated methodological falsificationism" (or "sophisticated falsificationism" for short). On this account a theory is to be adjudged "scientific" by virtue of its being "falsifiable" in a new, and methodologically more sophisticated, sense:

The sophisticated falsificationist regards a scientific theory T as falsified if and only if another theory T' has been proposed with the following characteristics: (1) T' has excess empirical content over T: that is, it predicts *novel* facts, that is, facts improbable in the light of, or even forbidden by, T; (2) T' explains the previous success of T, that is, all the unrefuted content of T is contained (within the limits of observational error) in the content of T'; and (3) some of the excess content of T' is corroborated (Lakatos, 1970, p. 116).

Sophisticated falsificationism has two signal merits. First, it squares with the history of science;[10] and secondly, it avoids the sort of irrationalism implied by Kuhn's earlier (1962) account of scientific choice and change.[11]

For the sophisticated falsificationist the problem is no longer how to distinguish between science and pseudoscience *simpliciter,* but rather, "how to demarcate between scientific and pseudoscientific *adjustments,* between rational and irrational changes of theory" (Lakatos, 1970, p. 117). What Lakatos proposes, then, is to provide not merely a descriptive account of scientific change, but a *theory of scientific progress*—and progress, moreover, of an eminently critical and rational sort.

Scientific progress, according to Lakatos, can only be gauged by looking at the successes and failures not of single theories but of successive *series of theories,* each sharing common core assumptions. Such a series he calls a "research program." A research program consists of a "hard core" of not-directly-criticizable assumptions.[12] The hardness of this hard core is a

---

[10] Squares, that is, with a "rational reconstruction" of the history of science: see Lakatos (1971).

[11] Lakatos does not supply us with a wholly rational method for *choosing* a research program, but rather with a means of "keeping score" in the contest between rival research programs (1971, p. 101).

[12] The idea that such assumptions subtend all scientific inquiry is not a new one. Burtt (1954) speaks of "metaphysical foundations," Collingwood (1940) of "absolute presuppositions," Popper (1962, ch. 4) of "myths," and Toulmin (1961, ch's. 3–4) of "ideals of natural order," in much the same way that Lakatos talks about the "hard core" of a research program.

methodological hardness; it is assured by the program's *negative heuristic*, i.e., the methodological rule that criticism be directed away from the hard core of the program.[13] The program's *positive heuristic*, by contrast, prescribes the construction of a "protective belt" of auxiliary assumptions, hypotheses, etc., which serves to protect the program's hard core. "It is this protective belt," Lakatos says, "which has to bear the brunt of tests and get adjusted and re-adjusted, or even completely replaced, to defend the [hard] core. A research program is successful if all this leads to a progressive problem-shift; unsuccessful if it leads to a degenerating problem-shift" (1970, p. 133).[14] We gauge the progressiveness of a research program by looking at the character of the adjustments made in its protective belt:

Let us take a series of theories T_1, T_2, T_3, ... where each subsequent theory results from adding auxiliary clauses to (or from semantical reinterpretations of) the previous theory in order to accommodate some anomaly, each theory having at least as much content as the unrefuted content of its predecessor. ... [A] series of theories is *theoretically* progressive (or "constitutes a theoretically progressive problem-shift") if each new theory has some excess empirical content over its predecessor, that is, if it predicts some novel, hitherto unexpected fact. ... [A] theoretically progressive series of theories is also *empirically progressive* (or "constitutes an empirically progressive problem-shift") if some of this excess empirical content is also corroborated, that is, if each new theory leads us to the actual discovery of some *new* fact. Finally, ... a problem-shift [is] *progressive* if it is both theoretically and empirically progressive, and *degenerating* if it is not. We "accept" problem-shifts as "scientific" only if they are at least theoretically progressive; if they are not, we "reject" them as "pseudoscientific." Progress is measured by the degree to which a problem-shift is progressive, [i.e.] by the degree to which the series of theories leads us to the discovery of novel facts. We regard a theory in the series "falsified" when it is superseded by a theory with higher corroborated content (Lakatos, 1970, p. 118).

Theories are, then, never falsified absolutely but only relatively, i.e., they are superseded by better theories. As Lakatos puts it: "There is no falsification before the emergence of a better theory" (1970, p. 119).

[13] Lakatos' point—despite the forbidding jargon in which it is expressed—is essentially a simple and commonsense one. It is that we can never get anywhere if we dwell always upon the "fundamental assumptions" of a theory (or series of theories), instead of its "payoff." The "hands-off" policy prescribed by the negative heuristic allows the scientist to get on with his work without having to constantly defend his core assumptions.

[14] Although never explicitly defined, a problem-shift is a change in directions (or directives) for research. A change is fruitful, promising—"progressive"—if it permits the prediction of new facts even as it accounts for old anomalies, and "degenerating" if it resolves old difficulties by means of verbal and/or ad hoc strategems which do not point out new directions for research.

By way of illustration Lakatos cites "the most successful research programme ever"—Newton's gravitational theory. "In Newton's programme the negative heuristic bids us to divert the *modus tollens* from Newton's three laws of dynamics and his law of gravitation. This 'core' is 'irrefutable' by the methodological decision of its protagonists: anomalies must lead to changes only in the protective belt ..." Newton and the Newtonians did just that. From the beginning Newton's gravitational theory

was submerged in an ocean of "anomalies" (or, if you wish, "counterexamples"), and opposed by the observational theories supporting these anomalies. But Newtonians turned, with brilliant tenacity and ingenuity, one counterinstance after another into corroborating instances, primarily by overthrowing the original observational theories in the light of which this "contrary evidence" was established. In the process they themselves produced new counterexamples which they again resolved. They "turned [as Laplace said] each new difficulty into a new victory of their programme" (Lakatos, 1970, p. 133).

The lesson to be learned from this, and a myriad of other historical examples, is twofold. It is first of all a lesson in *tenacity*: the task of keeping a theory (or series of theories) afloat in the ocean of anomalies requires dogged persistence and ingenuity on the part of its defenders. The second lesson is one of *tolerance*: critics should be tolerant of attempts to "save" theories from "refutation." Neither lesson is taught by dogmatic and/or methodological falsificationists; quite the contrary, both are alike in holding that tenacity in defending a theory is very nearly a crime against science. Against this view Lakatos argues that the history of science is the story of bold conjectures boldly—and tenaciously—defended against apparently "decisive" counterevidence.

This does not mean that *theories* cannot be criticized and even, eventually, falsified. It means, rather, that criticism must be directed against successive adjustments in the protective belt surrounding the hard core of that series of theories which constitutes a research program. The critic must ask: Are these adjustments "progressive" or "degenerating" ones *within the context of this particular research program*? That is, are these adjustments content-increasing or content-decreasing ones? Do these adjustments enable us to predict novel facts even as they explain old anomalies?

A good research program is a good swimmer—mainly because its "protective belt" serves as a life belt, keeping the hard core afloat on an ocean of anomalies. So long as this belt can be adjusted in "progressive" (i.e. content-increasing) ways, the research program is in no danger of sinking. But, by the same token, a research program begins to list and take on water when its protective belt can no longer be adjusted in progressive ways—when, that is, adjustments amount to no more than content-decreasing semantical ones and/or when they fail to anticipate new facts. Only then is the research program itself—hard core and all—in any danger of sinking. But no matter how waterlogged it is, a research program will not sink and have to be abandoned until a better, more buoyant one comes along to replace it. In any case, the decision to abandon one research program in favor of another is not taken lightly (contra earlier falsificationists), nor is it nonrational (contra Kuhn); it is at every step a critical, considered decision in the light of available alternative theories against which the progressiveness (or degeneration) of successive problem-shifts is gauged. Science is, then, both rational and progressive.

But—to ask an old question in a new and different light—is political science such a science? Is it, or can it be, rational and progressive? Are there, or might there one day be, research programs in political science? On these questions Lakatos' methodology of scientific research programs sheds some interesting light.

Research Programs in Political Science

My discussion has so far focused upon a number of interrelated problems in the history and philosophy of science—in particular, problems of commensurability and criticism, falsification and scientific progress. Since the practicing political scientist is likely to wonder what all this has to do with his inquiries, let me enumerate some of the advantages to be gained by viewing political-scientific inquiry through Lakatosian lenses.

The first advantage—alluded to already—is that political science can now dispense with its pseudo-Popperian, or "dogmatic," conception of falsifiability.[15] That is, we can leave behind us the outmoded and untenable view that a theory can be tested directly against *facts* which are wholly independent of the theory under test, and which, if they do not *correspond,* require us to abandon the theory as *falsified.* We can, with Lakatos' aid, see immediately what is wrong with such claims as these: "Whether [an empirical] proposition is true or false depends on the degree to which the proposition and the real world correspond" (Dahl, 1963, p. 8). "If no evidence about the real world can possibly disprove a proposition, it can hardly be called scientific or empirical in character" (Polsby, 1963, p. 5). These claims exhibit both of the

---

[15] I say pseudo-Popperian because Popper never was—despite many social scientists' misreading of him—a dogmatic falsificationist; he is, rather, a methodological falsificationist, though not a "sophisticated" one (Lakatos, 1970).

mistakes made by dogmatic falsificationism, viz., the mistake of supposing that there is a "real world" completely *independent of* but *comparable with* our theories; and the *logical* mistake of believing that *facts* can "disprove" *propositions*.

A Lakatosian perspective also throws a kinder light upon attempts to save a research program from criticism by means of various adjustments to its protective belt. Indeed, a scientist operating within the assumptions of a research program will—quite rightly—spend much of his time and effort in strengthening this protective belt, so as to better protect the program's hard core. That is *not* to say that the hard core is not itself "falsifiable," nor that it is to be protected at *all* costs by making just *any* sorts of theoretical adjustments in the protective belt. Not all adjustments are equally acceptable; some represent the "progress," others the "degeneration" of a research program. If an adjustment is a "content-increasing" one, it is progressive. But if an adjustment is merely ad hoc—consisting, e.g., of a redefinition of terms, or the addition of some hypothesis which "explains" an old anomaly but fails to lead to the discovery of new facts—then that adjustment represents a content-decreasing or "degenerating" problem-shift. Lakatos' conception of progressive and degenerating problem-shifts can be made clearer—and brought closer to home—by means of an example drawn from contemporary political science.

There is at least one well-articulated research program in political science, viz., the "rational choice" approach of Downs, Olson, Riker and others (Moon, 1975, p. 195). The hard core of this program consists—as programs in the *social* sciences must—of a certain "model of man," i.e., a "fundamental conceptualization of what it is to be a person, including not only an account of human needs and capacities, but also a view of how a person is related to others" (Moon, 1974, p. 1). The rational choice program's model of man— which may be traced back to Hobbes—views men as rational self-interested calculators. Men are assumed to be rational, and rationality is in turn defined in instrumental terms: to be rational is to choose that course of action (policy, state of the world, etc.) which will be most efficient in satisfying one's own ordered preferences. The objection that these basic assumptions are themselves "unrealistic" or are "refuted" by the "facts" of human behavior in the "real world," carry little weight with contemporary "positive" theorists (Friedman, 1953, ch. 1; Riker and Ordeshook, 1973, ch. 2). To admit as relevant any direct criticism of the "hard core" would be to violate the "negative heuristic," i.e., the methodological rule that criticism be directed away from the hard core and toward the program's protective belt.

The idea of progressive and degenerating problem-shifts in the rational choice program is especially well illustrated in the various recent attempts to resolve the "paradox of voting."[16] This paradox arises when one attempts, as Downs did in *An Economic Theory of Democracy*, to explain political participation in terms of a utility-maximizing model of rational choice and behavior. Downs' theory predicts that a rational agent would not vote, inasmuch as his single vote would not appreciably alter the probability of his getting what he wants (in this case, his preferred candidate's winning); hence he will not "spend"the time and effort to "buy" what he can get for "free." The paradox stems not from the fact that people do nevertheless vote—theories are not confuted by facts, *simpliciter*—but from several "internal" or "theoretical" anomalies. For consider: a rational agent will "pay the cost" of voting only if, as a result, *he* stands a better chance of getting what he wants for himself. Now in a two-candidate race in which many votes are cast, one voter's chance of affecting the outcome is insignificant; therefore it will not "pay" him to vote. But then (each rational calculator will reason) other rational agents will reach the same conclusion, and so no one will vote. In that case he should vote, since the election will end in a 1—0 victory for his candidate. Presumably, however, each rational agent will reach a similar conclusion about the value of his single vote, and so everyone will vote. In that case, however, each voter's chance of affecting the outcome of the election will be negligible and so—again—no one will vote. This circle, if not vicious, is at least dizzying. It poses, at the very least, a problem for Downs' theory. But—more than that—if it cannot be resolved by means of one or more theoretical adjustments, the hard core of the rational-choice program itself may be in jeopardy.

Such "adjustments" have been proposed, first by Downs himself and later by Riker and Ordeshook. It may be shown, however, that these adjustments represent content-decreasing or "degenerating" problem-shifts.

Downs attempts to resolve the paradox (or rather anomaly) of voting by means of the following adjustment. A rational citizen, he argues, will pay the cost of voting, even if he thereby gains nothing, because he derives satisfaction from "do[ing] his share in providing long-run benefits" for himself and others, through helping to maintain the democratic system (Downs, 1957, p. 270). But then, as Barry notes (1970, p. 20):

"Doing his share" is a concept foreign to the kind of "economic" rationality with which Downs is working. It requires our citizen to reason that since the benefits he gets depend

[16] The following "Lakatosian" analysis of the paradox of voting was first suggested to me by Donald Moon. I have followed closely—indeed purloined—the account of it given in Moon (1975, pp. 196—204).

on the efforts of others, he should contribute too. This may be good ethics, but it is not consistent with the assumptions of the model, which require the citizen to compute the advantage that accrues to him from his doing *x* rather than *y*; not the advantage that would accrue to him from *himself and others* doing *x* rather than *y*, unless, of course his doing it is a necessary and sufficient condition of the others doing it.

Or, to say the same thing in Lakatosian language: Downs' proposed adjustment violates the negative heuristic of the rational choice program, inasmuch as it calls into question the hard-core tenet of instrumental rationality itself. The hard-core assumption is that a rational agent will not "pay" for something if he can get it for nothing. That, after all, is why he will not vote: given that he prefers *A* to *B*, and that many people prefer either *A* or *B* and will vote accordingly, then the probability that *his* voting for *A* will result in *A*'s winning, is very small indeed; and so long as there are *any* "costs" accruing to him from voting, he will not vote. If his candidate wins he can enjoy the fruits of victory without having to pay for them. But then, extending this logic to the long-term rewards accruing to himself and others from maintaining the democratic system, one has to admit—as Downs does—that "he will actually get this reward [too], even if he himself does not vote" (1957, p. 270). Therefore it is *still* irrational for him to vote. To argue otherwise—as Downs insists upon doing—is to reject the hard core of the rational choice program's tenets of self-regardingness and instrumental rationality. Downs' proposed adjustment is therefore impermissible, representing as it does a degenerating problem-shift in the rational choice program.

Another sort of adjustment is proposed by Riker and Ordeshook (1968). Rejecting Downs' introduction of other-regarding (or even altruistic) motives into the calculus of voting, they attempt to resolve the paradox of voting in terms consistent with the program's assumption of self-regardingness. A rational person does stand to gain from voting, they argue, even if those gains be such nonmaterial psychological "satisfactions" as those stemming from "affirming allegiance to the political system," "affirming a partisan preference," and even "compliance with the ethic of voting" (Riker and Ordeshook, 1968, p. 28). This adjustment is, however, sadly ad hoc. As Barry remarks (1970, p. 15):

Now it may well be true that much voting can be accounted for in this way, and one can of course formally fit it into an "economic" framework by saying that people get certain "rewards" from voting. But this *is* purely formal. And it forces us to ask what really is the point and value of the whole "economic" approach. It is no trick to restate all behaviour in terms of "rewards" and "costs"; it may for some purposes be a useful conceptual device, but it does not in itself provide anything more than a set of empty boxes waiting to be filled. . . . Insofar as it includes voting as a purely expressive act, not undertaken with any expectation of changing the state of the world, it fails to fit the minimum requirements of the means-end model of rational behaviour.

Riker and Ordeshook's adjustment is, then, merely a semantical one: they implicitly redefine the concept of "reward" to include any and all sorts of "satisfactions." But then, broadening the concept of reward in this way, and in this direction, represents a degenerating problem-shift, inasmuch as it resolves a *theoretical* anomaly by means of a *verbal* or terminological adjustment.

If these were the only sorts of adjustments to be made in the protective belt of the rational choice program, we might well wonder whether that program itself—"hard core" and all—is salvageable or even worth saving. However, Ferejohn and Fiorina (1974) have proposed a solution to the paradox of voting which constitutes a genuinely progressive problem-shift in the rational choice program. Their proposed adjustment is easily summarized. Rational choice theorists took a wrong turn, they argue, in "equating the notion of rational behavior with the rule of maximizing expected utility" (1974, p. 535). Their solution is to assume not that voters are expected-utility maximizers but that they are instead maximum-regret minimizers; that is, instead of maximizing gains, they minimize their maximum loss, interpreted as "regret." Their "minimax regretter" votes, not because he expects to increase significantly the probability of his candidate's winning, but because he wishes to avoid the most regretful possible outcome, viz., his candidate's losing by one vote. In contrast with the expected-utility maximizer,

The minimax regret decision maker uses a simpler rule. He imagines himself in each possible future state of the world and looks at how much in error each of his available actions could be, given that state. Then he chooses that action whose maximum error over the states of nature is least. If asked why he voted, a minimax regret decision maker might reply, "My God, what if I didn't vote and my preferred candidate lost by one vote? I'd feel like killing myself." Notice that for the expected-utility maximizer the probability of such an event is very important, whereas for the minimax regret decision maker the mere logical possibility of such an event is enough (Ferejohn and Fiorina, 1974, p. 535).

Assuming, then, that voters are indeed minimax regretters rather than expected-utility maximizers, it *is* rational for them to vote. Given this assumption, we can now predict higher levels of voter turnout. Thus the paradox of voting is solved, or rather, dissolved.

The "adjustment" proposed by Ferejohn and Fiorina is quite consistent with the rational choice program's hard core (contra Downs); and it is not merely an ad hoc verbal strategem designed to rid the program of a persistent anomaly (contra Riker and Ordeshook). Their adjustment leaves the hard core untouched, and even strengthened, inasmuch as the newly renovated protective belt now affords even better protection than before. Their adjustment is, moreover, a content-increasing or "progressive" one, in that it leads to the prediction of new and unforeseen facts. For example, it predicts that in a three-candidate race a minimax regretter will not vote for his second choice, even when his most preferred candidate is likely to lose and his least preferred one likely to win. And this, in turn, suggests some promising lines of research into voter choice in multiparty systems.

Of one thing we may be sure: Ferejohn and Fiorina's adjustment in the protective belt of the rational choice program will lead sooner or later to other troubling anomalies which will require further adjustments in the program's protective belt. Just what these anomalies and adjustments will be—and whether these will in their turn represent progressive or degenerating problem-shifts—cannot be predicted, but can only be seen retrospectively with the wisdom of hindsight (Lakatos, 1971). Minerva's owl, as Hegel reminded us, takes flight only at dusk.

How to Be a Good Political Scientist:
A Plea for Tolerance in Matters Theoretical[17]

In dwelling at some length upon the rational choice program I have not meant to imply that political science has at present only one genuine research program. Quite the contrary: I should rather say that political science has now, or has had, a number of promising research programs. I am thinking particularly of two prominent and late-lamented programs—Marxism and functional analysis. In concluding, I want to suggest—perhaps a bit tendentiously—that these programs might have been killed off prematurely. Their protagonists lacked the necessary *tenacity,* their critics the necessary *tolerance,* required to give these programs a fighting chance. Of course their demise may, upon examination, be shown to be no more than just; nevertheless they were rather harshly treated. Never having been adequately protected, they were (in Lakatos' phrase) sitting ducks for the dogmatic falsificationists. These (and perhaps other) downed ducks should be retrieved and their life histories reconstructed and examined with care. We should, in other words, ask ourselves: Were they given a fighting chance? Were their hard cores given adequate protection? Which (if any) of the adjustments in

---

[17] Title borrowed, with amendment and apologies, from Feyerabend (1963).

their protective belts were content-increasing, and which content-decreasing ones?

Of course critics can, and should, criticize. But how much credence should be given to criticisms of budding research programs? While defending the criticizability of all research programs, Lakatos remarks:

> ... criticism does not—and must not—kill as fast as Popper [and other falsificationists] imagined. Purely negative, destructive criticism, like "refutation" or demonstration of an inconsistency, does not eliminate a programme. Criticism of a programme is a long and often frustrating process, and one must treat budding research programmes leniently.

Lakatos adds—with a sympathy for the social sciences rare among philosophers of science—a further warning about "the destructive effect of naive falsificationism upon budding research programs [in the social sciences]" (1970, p. 179).

We political scientists have not, I fear, treated our budding research programs leniently. We have, on the contrary, made them into sitting ducks; and in a discipline which includes many accomplished duck hunters, this has often proved fatal.[18] If we are to be good sportsmen we need to take Lakatos' methodology seriously. This involves a number of moves. It requires, first of all, that we give up our long-held dogmatic falsificationist views; secondly, that we be tenacious in defending and tolerant in criticizing research programs; thirdly, that we distinguish between "hard core" and "protective belt," and direct our defenses and/or criticisms accordingly; fourthly, that our criticisms be retrospective, and directed against adjustments in the protective belt of the program in question; and finally, that we judge the success-to-date of a research program in terms of the "progressiveness" or "degeneration" of its successive problem-shifts.

Consider, for example, the case for "scientific" Marxism. Is Marxism, as one of its defenders (Ollman, 1973) has recently claimed, the best (if not perhaps the only) basis for a genuinely scientific social science? If we are to answer that question we must begin by demarcating between science and nonscience (or pseudoscience). And this—following Lakatos—requires that we be able "to demarcate between scientific and pseudoscientific *adjustments,*

---

[18] Among those who have hunted—and presumably killed—structural-functional ducks are Gregor (1968) and Flanigan and Fogelman (1967). And prominent among those who have stalked Marxian ducks are Acton (1957), Plamenatz (1963, vol. II, ch's. 5, 6), Popper (1963, vol. II, ch's. 18–21), and Gregor (1965, ch's. 4, 5). All are superb critics, but poor sportsmen: they went duck hunting with antiaircraft guns. Their sort of falsificationism virtually guarantees success in hunting. Is it then any wonder that we look, usually in vain, for new "paradigms" in our discipline? No duck in its right mind would fly into our sights.

between rational and irrational changes of theory" (1970, p. 117). We need, in other words, to rationally reconstruct the history of Marxism, and then to determine whether successive adjustments have not only taken care of old anomalies but have, at the same time, predicted new facts; that is, we need to know whether successive adjustments in the Marxian research program represent content-increasing problem-shifts, or content-decreasing ones. (For example: Does Lenin's theory of imperialism represent a progressive or degenerating problem-shift within the Marxian research program?) Obviously I cannot undertake that task here. I raise this issue only to indicate a promising line of inquiry and to plead for tolerance in matters theoretical.

Lakatos' theory of scientific progress has wide-ranging implications for the social sciences, and political science in particular. Perhaps one of the most striking of these implications is that the putative gap between "traditional" or "normative" political theory and political science is now narrowed considerably. Indeed, the "normative" theories of yesteryear may now be viewed as methodological prescriptions in Lakatos' sense. For what they "prescribe" or "recommend" is that we view man and society in certain ways and not in others.[19] Thus Hobbes, for example, commended to us the model of man as a rational self-interested calculator; and modern "positive" theorists follow in his footsteps. And Rousseau—arguing against Hobbes—commended to us the view that man is an other-regarding social being, his wants and aspirations being a product of his education and upbringing; and students of "political socialization" and "civic culture" follow in his footsteps. What each of these "normative" theorists did, in other words, was—firstly—to propose a research program consisting of a not-directly-criticizable set of basic assumptions about human nature and society, and—secondly—to construct a crude protective belt of auxiliary hypotheses designed to insulate the hard core from a direct hit. In any event, the relationship between normative political theory and political science is, from a Lakatosian perspective, very nearly symbiotic. The "oughts" of "normative" theory are as much methodological as moral. Thus it appears that the history of political thought is central to the enterprise of political science. For it is only with the wisdom of hindsight that we rationally reconstruct, examine, and criticize our research programs. There is no other way of gauging the progress of this, or any other, scientific discipline.

Manuscript submitted April 30, 1975.
Final manuscript received June 20, 1975.

[19] Of course that is not what they *intended* to recommend, nor is that *all* they did. For lucid and suggestive discussions of these matters, see Wolin (1968) and Moon (1975, pp. 209–216).

REFERENCES

Acton, H.B. 1957. *The Illusion of the Epoch.* Boston: Beacon Press.

Almond, Gabriel A. 1966. "Political Theory and Political Science," *American Political Science Review,* December 1966, pp. 869–879.

Austin, J.L. 1970. *Philosophical Papers,* 2nd ed. Oxford: Clarendon Press.

Barry, Brian. 1970. *Sociologists, Economists and Democracy.* London: Collier-Macmillan.

Beardsley, Philip. 1974. "Political Science: The Case of the Missing Paradigm," *Political Theory,* February 1974, pp. 46–61.

Boneau, C.A. 1974. "Paradigm Regained: Cognitive Behaviorism Restated," *American Psychologist,* May 1974, pp. 297–310.

Buck, Roger C., and Cohen, Robert S., eds. 1971. *Boston Studies in the Philosophy of Science,* Vol. VIII. Dordrecht: D. Reidel.

Burtt, E.A. 1954. *The Metaphysical Foundations of Modern Science,* 2nd rev. ed. (first publ. 1924). New York: Anchor Books.

Coats, A.W. 1969. "Is There a 'Structure of Scientific Revolutions' in Economics?," *Kyklos,* Fasc. 2, 1969, pp. 289–296.

Collingwood, R.G. 1940. *An Essay on Metaphysics.* Oxford: Clarendon Press.

Dahl, Robert A. 1963. *Modern Political Analysis.* Englewood Cliffs, N.J.: Prentice-Hall.

Downs, Anthony. 1957. *An Economic Theory of Democracy.* New York: Harper & Row.

Euben, J. Peter. 1969. "Political Science and Political Silence," in Philip Green and Sanford Levinson, eds., *Power and Community.* New York: Pantheon, pp. 3–58.

Eulau, Heinz. 1964. *The Behavioral Persuasion in Politics.* New York: Random House.

Ferejohn, John A., and Fiorina, Morris P. 1974. "The Paradox of Not Voting: A Decision Theoretic Analysis," *American Political Science Review,* June 1974, pp. 525–536.

Feyerabend, Paul K. 1963. "How to be a Good Empiricist–A Plea for Tolerance in Matters Epistemological," in Bernard Baumrin, ed., *Philosophy of Science: The Delaware Seminar,* Vol. II. New York: Wiley.

_____. 1970. "Problems of Empiricism II," in Robert G. Colodny, ed., *The Nature and Function of Scientific Theories.* University of Pittsburgh Series in the Philosophy of Science, Vol. IV. Pittsburgh: University of Pittsburgh Press.

Flanigan, William, and Fogelman, Edwin. 1967. "Functional Analysis," in James C. Charlesworth, ed., *Contemporary Political Analysis.* New York: Free Press, pp. 72–85.

Friedman, Milton. 1953. *Essays in Positive Economics*. Chicago: University of Chicago Press.

Friedrichs, Robert. 1971. "Sociological Paradigms: Analogies of Teleology, Apocalypse, and Prophecy," *Sociological Analysis*, Spring 1971, pp. 1–6.

Gregor, A. James. 1965. *A Survey of Marxism*. New York: Random House.

_____. 1968. "Political Science and the Uses of Functional Analysis," *American Political Science Review*, June 1968, pp. 425–439.

Gunnell, John G. 1968. "Social Science and Political Reality: The Problem of Explanation," *Social Research*, Spring 1968, pp. 159–201.

_____. 1969. "Deduction, Explanation, and Social Scientific Inquiry," *American Political Science Review*, December 1969, pp. 1233–1246.

Hanson, Norwood Russell. 1958. *Patterns of Discovery*. Cambridge: Cambridge University Press.

Holt, Robert T., and Richardson, John M., Jr. 1970. "Competing Paradigms in Comparative Politics," in Robert T. Holt and John E. Turner, eds., *The Methodology of Comparative Research*. New York: Free Press, pp. 21–71.

Kuhn, Thomas S. 1962. *The Structure of Scientific Revolutions*. Chicago: University of Chicago Press.

_____. 1970a. "Postscript" to the 2nd ed. of Kuhn (1962), pp. 174–210.

_____. 1970b. "Reflections on My Critics," in Lakatos and Musgrave, 1970, pp. 231–278.

_____. 1974. "Second Thoughts on Paradigms," in Frederick Suppe, ed., *The Structure of Scientific Theories*. Urbana: University of Illinois Press.

Lakatos, Imre. 1970. "Falsification and the Methodology of Scientific Research Programmes," in Lakatos and Musgrave, 1970, pp. 91–196.

Lakatos, Imre, and Musgrave, Alan, eds. 1970. *Criticism and the Growth of Knowledge*. Cambridge: Cambridge University Press.

_____. 1971. "History of Science and Its Rational Reconstructions," in Buck and Cohen, 1971, pp. 91–136.

Landau, Martin. 1972a. *Political Theory and Political Science*. New York: Macmillan.

_____. 1972b. "Comment [on Miller, 1972]," *American Political Science Review*, September 1972, pp. 846–856.

Lebowitz, Barry. 1971. "Paradigms in Sociology: Some Thoughts on an Undebated Issue," a paper read at the 1971 American Sociological Association meetings.

Machamer, Peter K. 1971. "Observation," in Buck and Cohen, 1971, pp. 187–201.

_____. 1973. "Feyerabend and Galileo: The Interaction of Theories, and the Reinterpretation of Experience," *Studies in History and Philosophy of Science*, May 1973, pp. 1–46.

Masterman, Margaret. 1970. "The Nature of a Paradigm," in Lakatos and Musgrave, 1970, pp. 59–90.

Miller, Eugene F. 1972. "Positivism, Historicism, and Political Inquiry," *American Political Science Review*, September 1972, pp. 796–817.

Moon, J. Donald. 1974. "Models of Man in Hobbes and Rousseau: On Political Philosophy and the Study of Politics," a paper presented to the Foundations of Political Theory group, at the Seventieth Annual Meeting of the American Political Science Association, Chicago, August 28–September 2, 1974.

_____. 1975. "The Logic of Political Inquiry: A Synthesis of Opposed Perspectives," in Fred I. Greenstein and Nelson W. Polsby, eds., *Handbook of Political Science*, Vol. I. Reading, Mass.: Addison-Wesley, pp. 131–228.

Ollman, Bertell. 1973. "Marxism and Political Science: Prolegomenon to a Debate on Marx's Method," *Politics and Society*, Summer 1973, pp. 491–521.

Palermo, David. 1971. "Is a Scientific Revolution Taking Place in Psychology?," *Science Studies*, 1971, pp. 135–155.

Polsby, Nelson W. 1963. *Community Power and Political Theory*. New Haven: Yale University Press.

Popper, Karl R. 1962. *Conjectures and Refutations*. New York: Basic Books.

_____. 1963. *The Open Society and Its Enemies*, two vols. New York: Harper Torchbooks.

_____. 1970. "Normal Science and Its Dangers," in Lakatos and Musgrave, 1970, pp. 51–58.

_____. 1972. *Objective Knowledge*. Oxford: Clarendon Press.

Riker, William H., and Ordeshook, Peter C. 1968. "A Theory of the Calculus of Voting," *American Political Science Review*, March 1968, pp. 25–42.

_____. 1973. *An Introduction to Positive Political Theory*. Englewood Cliffs, N.J.: Prentice-Hall.

Rudner, Richard. 1972. "Comment [on Miller, 1972]," *American Political Science Review*, September 1972, pp. 827–845.

Ryan, Alan. 1972. " 'Normal' Science or Political Ideology?," in Peter Laslett, W.G. Runciman, and Quentin Skinner, eds., *Philosophy, Politics, and Society*, fourth series. Oxford: Blackwell, pp. 86–100.

Shapere, Dudley. 1964. "The Structure of Scientific Revolutions," *Philosophical Review*, July 1964, pp. 383–394.

_____. 1966. "Meaning and Scientific Change," in Robert G. Colodny, ed., *Mind and Cosmos: Essays in Contemporary Science and Philosophy*, University of Pittsburgh Series in the Philosophy of Science, Vol. III. Pittsburgh: University of Pittsburgh Press.

Smolicz, Jerzy. 1970. "Paradigms and Models," *Australian and New Zealand Journal of Sociology,* October 1970, pp. 100–119.

Spector, Marshall. 1966. "Theory and Observation," *British Journal for the Philosophy of Science,* May–August 1966, pp. 1–20, 89–104.

Stanfield, J.R. 1974. "Kuhnian Scientific Revolutions and the Keynesian Revolution," *Journal of Economic Issues,* 1974, pp. 97–109.

Stephens, Jerone. 1973. "The Kuhnian Paradigm and Political Inquiry: An Appraisal," *American Journal of Political Science,* August 1973, pp. 467–488.

Toulmin, Stephen. 1963. *Foresight and Understanding.* New York: Harper Torchbooks.

_____. 1967. "The Evolutionary Development of Natural Science," *American Scientist,* December 1967, pp. 456–471.

_____. 1970. "Does the Distinction Between Normal and Revolutionary Science Hold Water?" in Lakatos and Musgrave, 1970. pp. 39–48.

_____. 1972. *Human Understanding,* Vol. I. Oxford: Clarendon Press.

Truman, David B. 1965. "Disillusion and Regeneration: The Quest for a Discipline," *American Political Science Review,* December 1965, pp. 865–873.

Welmes, W.B. 1973. "Paradigms and Normal Science in Psychology," *Science Studies,* 1973, pp. 211–222.

Wittgenstein, Ludwig. 1968. "Wittgenstein's Notes for Lectures on Private Experience and 'Sense Data,' " transcribed and annotated by Rush Rhees, *Philosophical Review,* July 1968, pp. 271–320.

Wolin, Sheldon S. 1968. "Paradigms and Political Theories," in Preston King and B.C. Parekh, eds., *Politics and Experience: Essays Presented to Michael Oakeshott.* Cambridge: Cambridge University Press, pp. 125–152.

_____. 1969. "Political Theory as a Vocation," *American Political Science Review,* December 1969, pp. 1062–1082.

CHARLES O. JONES

Doing Before Knowing: Concept Development in Political Research

This paper discusses problems of concept development, utilization, and modification in political research. Though lacking a paradigm, political scientists still must develop concepts as guides to data collection—essentially an exercise in "doing before knowing." Three cases of concept development are introduced: concepts for general understanding, concepts for research design, and classification of empirical findings. Each of these cases is illustrated from the author's research—with special emphasis on conceptual development and modification for analysis of air pollution policy action.

Yossarian looked at the professor soberly and tried another approach. "Does Orr have a theory?"

"He sure does," Prof. Daneeka responded.

"Then can you approve his dissertation?"

"I sure can. But first he has to make his concepts explicit. That's part of the rule and we follow it scrupulously."

"Then why doesn't he?"

"Because he has a theory," Daneeka said calmly, "and you can't start with a theory."

"I see. He should have started with a set of concepts."

"That's right. As Abraham Kaplan puts it: 'Proper concepts are needed to formulate a good theory.'"

"Well," Yossarian sighed, "all he has to do is turn things around and then you can approve his dissertation."

"No. Then I can't approve his dissertation."

"You mean there is a catch?"

"Sure there is a catch," the professor replied. "Catch-23. Anyone needs a good theory to arrive at the proper concepts."

[with apologies to Joseph Heller, author of the brilliant *Catch-22* (New York: Simon and Schuster, 1961).]

Reprinted from AMERICAN JOURNAL OF POLITICAL SCIENCE, Vol. XVIII, No. 1, February 1974, pp. 215-228, Charles O. Jones, "Doing Before Knowing: Concept Development in Political Research," by permission of the University of Texas Press.

Catch-23 is identified by Kaplan as the "paradox of conceptualization,"[1] and it may be expected to have variable effect among scientific disciplines. The more mature sciences will be less troubled. As Kuhn points out: "normal scientific research is directed to the articulation of those phenomena and theories that the paradigm already supplies."[2] The more pubescent sciences, which surely includes political science, should also be less troubled but for far different reasons. "Good theory," a "disciplinary matrix," "the paradigm"— these are simply not available in political science. Therefore a great deal of improvising, exploration, and experimentation can be justified. The fact is, however, that even scholars of politics have scientific pretensions and thus cannot escape the frustrations of the paradox. Justified or not, and it typically is not, Catch-23 is frequently employed in the many processes by which political scientists judge each other and their students.

The effect of the paradox on political research is of special interest here. Super concern with the dilemmas posed by the paradox can be paralyzing, actually preventing research. Since the search for "good theory" is likely to be unrewarding, one may simply feel too insecure in proceeding any further. And some of our colleagues do, in fact, remain highly theoretical, seeking to develop a suitable paradigm.

But even if one is bold enough to proceed without an overarching paradigm, getting under way is no simple matter if one believes that theory building is a significant enterprise. As Kaplan notes:

Every taxonomy is provisional and implicit theory (or family of theories). As knowledge of a particular subject matter grows, our conception of that subject matter changes; as our concepts become more fitting, we learn more and more. Like all existential dilemmas in science, of which this is an instance, the paradox is resolved by *a process of approximation:* the better our concepts, the better the theory we can formulate with them, and in turn, the better the concepts available for the next, improved theory.[3]

It is understandably distressing for scholars to begin research knowing they must engage in "a process of approximation," for it challenges the mind and risks the ego. In a sense, political scientists must plunge into the dim, dark recesses of the discipline as though they really knew where they were headed. Only a fool (and we have a few) would do so without guidelines, however, which, at minimum, permit a strategic withdrawal.

[1] Abraham Kaplan, *The Conduct of Inquiry* (San Francisco: Chandler, 1964), p. 53.
[2] Thomas S. Kuhn, *The Structure of Scientific Revolution* (Chicago: University of Chicago Press, 2d ed., 1970), p. 24.
[3] Kaplan, *The Conduct of Inquiry,* pp. 53–54. Emphasis added.

I call this form of research entry "doing before knowing," and given the status of our scientific development, it is essential to the research enterprise in political science. "Doing before knowing" is really an exercise in concept development and modification. It is necessary in political research because we have not resolved the paradox—or possibly even approached it as yet. We do not have the paradigm of Kuhn's "normal science." But neither do we have the commitments. Therefore we are really free to draw on many sources for conceptualization. And, fortunately, in my judgment, we are concept rich, if paradigm poor.

The Role of Classification

"Doing before knowing" in research involves concepts before paradigms. It does not suggest data collection before concepts, however. It is an advisory on data collection which asks the scholar to project by responding to the following questions: What is likely to be found? To what does it relate? Why is it important? Having to respond to these questions in advance should force consideration of a set of flexible, interrelated concepts as guides to data collection.

The interrelatedness criterion suggests the need for a classification scheme that is less than a paradigm but considerably more than a random set of concepts, or data collection for its own sake. Classification is, of course, recognized by all as a key process in research, but it is normally discussed as a data analysis process. It is equally significant, in my judgment, in the research design stage.

This can be understood by thinking about the ways one uses concepts. The first is *classification for general understanding*—ordering a universe of discourse with a set of concepts so as to state one's own best understanding of that subject matter and to be able to communicate with others about it. We do this whenever we write about a subject, whether we intend to do research about it or not. The second is *classification of research expectations*—projecting what is to be found. The concepts used here may be identical with or logically derived from the preceding, and aid one in designing a specific research project. The third is *classification of empirical findings*—ordering findings so as to add to, modify, or reject the expectations. At this point, the set of concepts will bear some resemblance to those used earlier to articulate research expectations, but some concepts may be discarded, others modified, and some concepts introduced *de novo* for further research.

It should be pointed out that the effort to classify expectations may be unsuccessful. Much political research will therefore be exploratory in whole or in part. As Lazarsfeld and Barton have observed:

> It happens that research does not always begin with general theoretical categories and theoretically prescribed relations among them. At the present stage of the social sciences a great deal of research must be of an *exploratory* nature, aiming at qualitative answers to . . . questions [calling for simple descriptive data].[4]

There is nothing wrong with exploratory research. It is obviously as important for the pubescent science as it is for the maturing teenager. But it can also become an excuse for some very sloppy scholarship. And, of course, exploration too must eventually be classified if it is to benefit the discipline. The task is particularly difficult because one is not equipped with a set of coherent and integrated expectations. As Selltiz, *et al.,* point out:

> The establishment of principles of classification is especially difficult in exploratory studies, since such studies . . . do not start with explicit hypotheses. At the time of data collection, the investigator does not know which aspects may turn out to be most important. Therefore he must usually collect a large amount of data; thus, in the analysis, he has the problem of dealing not only with unstructured material but also with a vast quantity of it, much of which may prove irrelevant to his purpose.[5]

The Practice of Classification

How does one go about classifying in political research? Having been asked to think about that question for this essay, I can report that it is an uncommonly difficult process to describe. I was relieved to find that others agree. Lazarsfeld and Barton note:

> It can properly be argued that one cannot lay down a set of handy instructions for the categorization of social phenomena: such instructions would be nothing less than a general program for the development of social theory [perhaps a Kuhn-type paradigm]. One cannot write a handbook on "how to form fruitful theoretical concepts" in the same way that one writes handbooks on how to sample or how to construct questionnaires.[6]

Perhaps the most one can do is reconstruct cases of concept development and classification for whatever lessons might be transferable. I propose

[4] Paul F. Lazarsfeld and Allen H. Barton, "Qualitative Measurement in the Social Sciences: Classification, Typologies, and Indices," in Daniel Lerner and Harold D. Lasswell, eds., *The Policy Sciences* (Stanford: Stanford University Press, 1951), p. 156.

[5] Claire Selltiz, *et al., Research Methods in Social Relations* (New York: Holt, Rinehart and Winston, 1964), p. 399.

[6] Lazarsfeld and Barton, "Qualitative Measurement in the Social Sciences," p. 156.

reviewing three cases from my own research. First is the attempt to classify policy processes in *An Introduction to the Study of Public Policy*[7] (a case of classification for purposes of general understanding). Second is the effort to use this framework to classify research expectations on air pollution policy development and implementation. I sought to project from the policy process model to what would likely be found in actual decision making. Third, it became necessary to develop new concepts when those in the model proved inadequate—a classification of empirical findings. In each of the cases described below I attempt to answer the following questions: What is the source of the concepts employed? What functions do these concepts perform? How are they interrelated?

Classification for General Understanding

Even general understanding has to have an object to be purposeful. In the case discussed here, my previous research on institutional processes, principally those in Congress, convinced me of the need to study more carefully the presumed stimulus for government action—*i.e.,* public problems—and the governmental processes for responding. I came to believe that the more institution-bound research overstated the importance of certain institutional mechanisms and, quite simply, failed to provide a very realistic perspective for understanding what happens in government on specific public problems. Therefore I wanted to conceptualize a set of policy processes that were not presumed in advance to be based in a single institution. Put another way, I sought concepts useful in tracing and analyzing public problems from their emergence to and through the effects of government policies. If successful, this framework would assist in integrating the work of other policy scholars, designing research, and teaching policy courses.

I did my shopping for these concepts from the research and theoretical offerings of my colleagues. I found it necessary, however, to select carefully among those wares—choosing those items which suited my purpose without in any way feeling bound to accept a whole line of goods from one producer. As noted above, I had definite explanatory goals in mind. While many of the scholars cited below had something to contribute to those goals, most had other purposes in mind as well. Thus, I felt no compunction about taking what I thought I needed from one scholar and scrapping the rest (or, less bluntly, holding the rest in reserve).

I had need for two sets of concepts in this exercise—those more abstract

---

[7] (Duxbury, Massachusetts: Duxbury Press, 1970).

concepts relating to the nature of a democratic public policy system and a more specific set relating to the structure of the American political system. For the first I relied heavily on John Dewey, David Easton, David B. Truman, Robert A. Dahl, Charles E. Lindblom, and Harold D. Lasswell. As I melded extracts from the works of these men, a network of concepts emerged that performed the function I wanted—*i.e.*, providing a set of general expectations of the "normal" operations of a democratic public policy system. Describing what I extracted from the writings of these several scholars and for what purpose, would take more space than can be allocated for a short paper. Suffice it to say that Dewey's concept of the public, Easton's use of "system," Dahl's "minorities rule," Lindblom's "disjointed incrementalism," and Lasswell's decision categories prepare one for a "problem through policy" system which is highly pluralistic (sometimes brutally so), features bargaining for coalition building, and thus produces incremental output. One is also led to expect a variety of subsystems and processes not necessarily coincident with institutional groups. At least, both Easton and Lasswell encourage us to look outside and between institutions for interactive patterns in politics.

Other, more specific conceptual guidelines were drawn from scholars studying American institutions, intergovernmental relations, and various electoral and policy processes. Some of the scholars relied on here include Morton Grodzins and Daniel Elazar on federalism; J. Leiper Freeman on cross-institutional systems; Aaron Wildavsky on budgeting and planning; Anthony Downs on bureaucracy; V. O. Key, Jr. on public opinion; Murray Edelman on symbolism in administration; Theodore J. Lowi on policy outputs; David B. Truman on group processes. Each of these men has produced works rich in concepts for public policy analysis. Together they prepare one for a complex of governmental units at all levels that share authority, function across institutional barriers, develop means for expansion and survival, respond to (and are biased toward) clearly articulated group interests, adjust to changes in political environment, and seldom measure the social effects of public policy.

The next task was to establish categories useful for understanding public policy processes. With Lasswell, Yehezkel Dror, and others, I proposed a logical sequence of action—from problem identification and representation through formulation, legitimation, implementation, and evaluation. I expected that these functional activities would be characterized by the concepts identified above—some would characterize action throughout, others would be specific to a particular functional activity. If not, then the democratic policy process failed to operate as expected, which in itself might explain subsequent policy action in an issue area.

The purpose of developing this sequence was heuristic, not prescriptive. For example, I had no reason to presume in advance that problems had to be defined in a particular way, or at all for that matter, for policy to be developed and implemented. I sought merely to provide a framework based on a logical ordering of the policy process that reflected concepts drawn from existing scholarship and yet was flexible enough to permit adjustments in light of unexpected findings, new interpretations, and reformulated concepts.

Classification of Research Expectations

It is possible to be more explicit in describing concept classification and development when discussing a specific research application. The case presented here is that of an analysis of air pollution policy development and implementation at the federal level and in Pennsylvania and Allegheny County (in which Pittsburgh is located). If functioning properly, the general classification scheme cited above should facilitate the development of durable expectations about specific policy areas. If the framework is powerful enough, research will simply confirm the expectations. Seldom do we have this advantage in political science, however.

Chart 1 illustrates a set of specific conceptual expectations to guide policy research. For purposes of this exercise, I have limited the projections to the formulation, legitimation, and application stages. It is expected action will occur in the sequence indicated, since logic suggests the stages are consecutive—each dependent on the output of the previous stage. I assume that one can identify patterned and persistent goal-oriented activity within each stage and therefore have ordered the concepts accordingly. As indicated, I propose conceptual expectations for three principal elements of a system—goal, process, and output.[8] The concepts themselves are no more than expressions of what scholars have told me to expect.

Thus, I propose looking for a policy formulation system for air pollution which, in good pluralistic form, seeks to articulate the proposals of those who perceive themselves affected by this issue to such an extent that they gain access to decision makers. And I expect bargaining and compromise to characterize efforts in the legitimation system to develop an insured majority

---

[8] I have not included a set of input categories for this exercise. These were omitted primarily because of space limitations.

CHART 1

Conceptual Expectations of Air Pollution Policy Development and Implementation

Expected Sequence of Activities →	DEVELOPMENT		IMPLEMENTATION
System	→ 1. *Formulation* →	2. *Legitimation* →	3. *Application* →
Goal	Articulation	Insured majority	Contextual change
Process	Access Representation	Compromise Bargaining	Adaptation through mutual role taking
Output	Proposal	Policy increment	Rule (adjustment)

(one which typically would be greater than 50 percent plus 1) for policy increments. Finally, scholars of administration suggest that applying these increments is normally a continual process of adjustment—principally through mutual role taking—so that social change is contextual and not abrupt.

All of this seems a straightforward conversion of the general to the specific—of the policy framework designed for general understanding to a specific instance of policy development and implementation. How did it work out in practice? That brings us to the third case.

Classification of Empirical Findings

The conceptual expectations identified in Chart 1 provided a reasonably close approximation of what in fact happened on this issue in Washington, Harrisburg, and Pittsburgh, before 1969–1970. Least durable, perhaps, were the expectations regarding policy formulation—which proved to be less pluralistic than predicted. But the modifications necessary were inconsequential and hardly deserve explication here.

In 1969–1970, however, the remarkable rise in public concern for the environment made the framework in Chart 1 much less applicable. Chart 1 is based on highly pluralistic assumptions. General public involvement is not predicted or accounted for. For reasons that cannot be analyzed here, however, millions of Americans began to express themselves on environmental decay late in 1969. Public opinion polls, street demonstrations, and media forcefully transmitted demand messages ("clean the water," "clean the air," "save the earth") to generally receptive public officials from the President to the Allegheny County Commissioners.

My findings (developed principally from interviews with approximately 60 federal, state, and local officials, and the voluminous documents available on this issue) suggested that no mere increment in policy would be acceptable in 1969–1970. The general public was perceived by decision makers as supporting dramatic policy change whether or not it could be justified in terms of existing knowledge, technology, or administrative capabilities. Thus it was necessary to search for and invent new concepts. Those which emerged are listed in Chart 2.

A fundamental difference between the expectations and reality in 1969– 1970 is revealed in the altered sequence of activities. Legitimation *preceded* formulation. The widespread public concern resulted in legislative majorities prepared to endorse large, though unspecified, change. The process for developing these majorities was not that of bargaining and compromise but of

CHART 2

Empirical Classification of Air Pollution Policy Development and Implementation (1969–1970)

Sequence of Activities	DEVELOPMENT		IMPLEMENTATION
System	→ 1. *Legitimation* →	2. *Formulation* →	3. *Application* →
Goal	Unspecified change	Satisfy the majority	Determine limits
Process	Demonstration democracy	Escalation	Mutual risk taking
Output	Indeterminate majority	Speculative augmentation	Rhetorical goals

"demonstration democracy."[9] Public officials were encouraged to develop policy beyond capability and warned to ignore pressures to temporize. The legitimation system itself was untidy—involving communication of symbols between the mass public and elected officials. No one knew for certain what was publicly acceptable, however. The message itself was unambiguous: "clear the air." But did the public, or elected officials, fully comprehend what is involved in purifying the air in, for example, Pittsburgh, Pennsylvania, or Los Angeles, California? And were they willing to pay the costs and make the necessary sacrifices in life style? The evidence suggests not and therefore I suggest the term "indeterminate majority" as descriptive of what legitimation had produced in this case.

Those uncertainties plagued both policy formulators and implementors. The formulators had to estimate what might satisfy this indeterminate majority. Instead of seeking to articulate existing knowledge about the problem, feasible solutions, and government regulatory experience, formulators sought to outdo one another. Temporization, so characteristic of bargaining, was supplanted by escalation, with policy augmentation beyond capability the result.

For example, at the national level, the proposed changes in the Clean Air Act by the Nixon Administration were more stringent than those originally offered by Senator Edmund S. Muskie (D—Maine); the amendments passed by the House more stringent yet; and Senator Muskie's Subcommittee on Air and Water Pollution eventually proposed the toughest standards of all.[10]

No set of policy activities may be expected to escape the effects of having ignored the limitations of the knowledge base in a policy area. Thus, administrators too must participate in the guessing game as to what the "public" had in mind in the first place. Complicating their analysis are the commitments made by elected officials, who, presumably, will continue to monitor public attitudes in order to assess whether and how the law should be implemented. Mutual role taking between the regulator and the regulated is clearly less applicable under these conditions (though it will occur). I suggest "mutual risk taking" is more descriptive under these circumstances. Not knowing what the limits are, regulators take almost daily risks in determining what is acceptable. The regulated also take risks—*e.g.,* if they ignore the law, they may be forced to pay heavy penalties, even close down; if they seek to meet

[9] I borrowed this useful concept from Amitai Etzioni—see *Demonstration Democracy* (New York: Gordon and Breach, 1970).

[10] I discuss this process in more detail in "Incrementalism Versus Speculative Augmentation in Federal Air Pollution Policy Making," to appear in a forthcoming issue of the *Journal of Politics.*

impossible standards, they may face economic collapse, particularly if competitors fail to comply and get away with it. The result of mutual risk taking
in the short run may only be a set of rhetorical goals which represent no more
than estimates of what the public wants to hear—presumably, in functional
terms, as a test for defining the real limits of policy application.

What was the source of the concepts in Chart 2? The short answer is that I
applied a little common sense and a good thesaurus to large quantities of data
drawn primarily from documents and interviews. Applying common sense
involves comparing findings with the expectations drawn from the framework
to determine the fit. Perhaps only a slight modification is necessary, and
therefore one can append a branch to the base concept which identifies
special conditions for the variation. If the concepts from the framework
prove unserviceable, as in the case presented in Chart 2, then classification
must begin again.

The principles of coding can be employed if the data are highly structured
(*e.g.*, as with survey data). If the data are unstructured, as in the case here
(and with much policy data), then the task is complicated by a lack of clearly
prescribed rules. Lazarsfeld and Barton do provide one general rule which I
have found useful, however:

The classification should be based on a comprehensive outline of the situation as a
whole—an outline containing the main elements and processes in the situation which it is
important to distinguish for purposes of understanding, predicting, or policy making.[11]

One can see the importance of the general framework at this point. Having
determined that the more specific expectations of Chart 1 were not applicable to the new situation, I reviewed the broader concepts of the general
framework. As noted, when I determined the predicted sequence of action—
formulation-legitimation-application—was not descriptive of events in 1969–
1970, I discovered what I thought to be a fundamental change which
challenged the theoretical basis of the framework.

Altering the sequence—legitimation-formulation-application—provided "a
comprehensive outline of the situation as a whole" and greatly facilitated
establishing the necessary concepts for the several categories identified in
Chart 2. From that point, it was necessary to review the data available for any
one cell (*e.g.*, legitimation system—goal; formulation system—process, etc.),
summarize those data, search for characterizations of the data, and test
specific concepts for their utility as "an abstraction from observed events."[12]

---

[11] Lazarsfeld and Barton, "Qualitative Measurement in the Social Sciences," p. 157.
[12] The definition of concept suggested by Selltiz, *et al.*, *Research Methods in Social
Relations*, p. 41. This book also contains a useful, but brief, section on classifying
unstructured material. See pp. 399–401.

(Parenthetically, a good way to test the appropriateness of a concept is to ask colleagues from other disciplines for their understanding of a term in the context of its use. For example, "What does 'speculative augmentation' suggest to you in reference to policy output?" If they stare at you dumbfoundedly, you may have to return to your desk.)

One should not overemphasize being close to the data in developing concepts. There is a point at which data can no longer speak for themselves, regardless of the amount of shuffling and prodding. One must be sensitive to that fact and once more engage in a little "doing before knowing." I highly recommend pushing aside the interviews, coding categories, summaries of documents, or whatever material one is working with, and engaging in contemplative reflection. Vernon Van Dyke points out that "the development of a desirable classification scheme often requires insight or perceptivity; creative and imaginative thought, and even a sense for the aesthetic, may well be very helpful."[13] And there I must take leave. No one can prescribe how to be creative—least of all someone named Jones.

Concluding Observations

First I must acknowledge what you all surely know. Writing about research methods always makes them sound more rational and systematic than they ever are in fact. In this case what is described as the simple application of concepts to data, with the development of new concepts where needed was, in practice, a lengthy and none-too-systematic process of accommodation between framework and findings. It was anything but a tidy and confident procedure. We are still very much a "do as I say, not as I do" discipline when it comes to research methods.

Second, I would emphasize again that given the primitive state of political "science," one really should not be deterred by the paradox of conceptualization—Catch-23. Kaplan tells us that: "the creative genius works with more than he knows."[14] But so must we more ordinary mortals, and that is why I subscribe to "doing before knowing." As I understand classification and its functions, it demands this measure of boldness from the scholar.

Third, I would argue for greater attention in political research to our inventory of concepts. I believe strongly that, as a discipline, we know more than we know (or use). Personal discovery of a phenomenon does not perforce mean that no one else has encountered it. If we are ever to develop a

[13] Vernon Van Dyke, *Political Science: A Philosophical Analysis* (Stanford: Stanford University Press, 1960), p. 73.

[14] Kaplan, *The Conduct of Inquiry*, p. 269.

"disciplinary matrix," our research must be more cumulative and integrative. That can only happen if new inquiry begins where previous scholarship has ended. Kaplan makes this point differently, and more profoundly, in justifying the use of models.

... we ordinary mortals often know less than we think. The model saves us from a certain self-deception. Forced into the open, our ideas may flutter helplessly; but at least we can see what bloodless creatures they are. As inquiry proceeds, theories must be brought out into the open sooner or later; the model simply makes it sooner. ... The creative imagination, in both scientist and artist, takes the form of a vigorous discussion with the boys in the back room; and there inevitably comes a time when someone says, "Put up or shut up!" It is at this moment that models are brought forward.[15]

While agreeing with Kaplan, I would simply add that in political science the very process of model building itself is likely to increase knowledge and improve research by forcing greater attention to the available stock of classifiable concepts and providing the basis for integrating empirical findings.

[15] *Ibid.*

Formal Theory

MORRIS P. FIORINA

*Formal Models in Political Science**

In recent years the journals have published an increasing number of articles which present or utilize formal models of political behavior and political processes. At present, however, this research probably reaches only a small audience. In an effort to broaden that audience this paper attempts (1) to describe and illustrate the use of formal models, (2) to explain why some believe that the construction of models is a useful research method, (3) to identify subfields in which models exist and suggest others where models should exist, (4) to discuss various types of existing models, (5) to offer some basic critical standards according to which research which involves models can be judged.

During the past decade political scientists have made increasing use of a new method, a method in which political behavior and political processes are studied by constructing formal models of such behavior and processes. Looking back on this development it is clear that Anthony Downs (1957) precipitated it, although some earlier efforts at formalizing the study of politics exist (Richardson, 1939; Black, 1948; Shapley and Shubik, 1954). Downs' work differed from then-prevailing studies in that it was neither a description of a particular real-world democracy nor a portrait of some normatively ideal democracy. Nor did Downs compare and contrast the actual with the ideal, a common practice in the democratic theory of the period. Rather, Downs' book was an attempt to model the central processes of any democratic political system.

Although Downs took pains to explain his intent, the idea of constructing and applying a model was discomforting to many political scientists (Rogers, 1959). In the years since, however, both the use of models and the appreciation of that use has increased. Many graduate programs include courses in formal theory, analytical theory, mathematical models, or the like, and examples of such work increasingly win space in the pages of our journals (Polsby-Riker, 1974). Still, there exists much less of a general understanding of the role of formal models in our discipline than of the role, say, of survey

*I wish to thank Ken Shepsle, Robert Bates, and three anonymous referees for their comments on an earlier version of this paper.

Reprinted from AMERICAN JOURNAL OF POLITICAL SCIENCE, Vol. XIX, No. 1, February 1975, pp. 133-159, Morris P. Fiorina, "Formal Models in Political Science," by permission of the University of Texas Press.

67

research or statistical methods. In this *Workshop* article I propose to examine the place of formal models in political science. My discussion will be concerned less with abstract philosophy of science considerations than with an attempt to convey the perceptions, goals and standards of those who construct or employ formal models in their research.

The Nature of Models

Putting first things first, what is a model? From graduate school scope and methods courses we remember that philosophers of science advance rather precise definitions and invariably bemoan the failure to differentiate models from theories, analogies, and metaphors (Brodbeck, 1959). But rather than engage in a technical definitional exercise I will take the course of describing what political science model builders mean by the term *model.*

All of our models have in common at least three elements. First, they contain a set of primitives or undefined terms. Second, they contain additional concepts defined with the aid of primitives or other previously defined terms. Third, they contain assumptions of various types. These assumptions include those underlying the particular language in which the model is formulated (e.g., calculus, set theory, propositional logic, English) and usually others of a behavioral and institutional nature.[1] Some colleagues would also include in the model proper all statements logically implied by the basic three elements. Others would consider such statements the theory generated by the model. For ease of exposition I shall adopt the former viewpoint in this paper.[2]

Perhaps an examination of a specific model would be a useful supplement to the ostensive definition in the preceding paragraph. Consider for example one of the simple models constructed by Duncan Black (1958, ch. 4) in *The*

---

[1] I wish to emphasize that a formal model need not be a mathematical structure, although many are. Fenno (1973) employs a very specific model even though his book is devoid of mathematical or logical symbols. Of course, a well-developed verbal model should be amenable to restatement in more abstract terms.

[2] A few additional comments on terminology. In contemporary political science the terms "formal model," "formal theory," and "analytical theory" are used more or less interchangeably. Although I recognize the ambiguity inherent in such a situation, one-man attempts to enforce terminological conformity invariably fail. Therefore, in this article I will tolerate the ambiguity. In personal usage I tend to use the term, model, without modifiers like "mathematical" and "formal," and to reserve the term, model, for the abstract logical structure, then switch to the term, theory, when I interpret real politics with the help of the model.

Theory of Committees and Elections, a model which produces Black's well-known "median dominance" theorem.

The primitives in Black's model include terms such as *committee member, proposal,* and *preference.* The defined concepts include *committee, motion, single-peaked curve,* and *optimum.* The assumptions include an infinite (not essential) number of motions, a_i, arranged along some dimension, X, sincere voting (i.e., voting for the motion which stands highest in one's preference ordering), single-peaked preference curves (i.e., a preference curve which changes direction at most once as we traverse the dimension at issue), and no abstention. For ease of exposition consider only the case of a committee with an odd number of members. Given the basic structure outlined, a committee preparing to make a decision can be represented as in Figure 1, where the particular arrangement and number (odd) of preference curves is unimportant.

Now, it is immediately apparent that Black's simple model implies at least one statement about the committee decision process, namely that the motion which is the optimum of the median member (a_3 in this case) can defeat any other motion in pairwise voting. To see that this is so, note that any motion to the left of the median optimum (say a_1) can be defeated by a motion located between it and the median optimum (say a_2). This is true because by the assumptions of single-peakedness and sincere voting, the new motion receives at least the votes of the median member and everyone to his right—by definition of the median, a majority. A similar argument holds for motions to the right of the median. Only the optimum of the median member

FIGURE 1
Representation of a Five-Man Committee

order of
preference

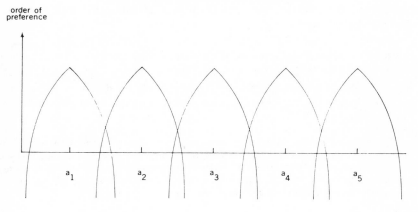

can defeat every other motion: it receives the votes of the median member and everyone on the side opposite the challenging motion.

Thus, Black's model produces an empirically testable proposition, a theory of committee decisionmaking. Given a (majority rule) collective decision process in which pairwise voting occurs, and in which the median alternative enters the voting at some point, then the optimum of the median member is the decision of the committee.[3] Failure to confirm that proposition casts doubt on the assumption of single-peaked preferences, unidimensionality, sincere voting, universal voting, or some combination of these.

Why Models?

Given some agreement on what a model is, the obvious next question is why bother? Does the use of a formal model provide scientific benefits greater than the evident intellectual costs of that use? Do models like Black's contribute to our knowledge over and above traditional wisdom based on empirical observation of the compromise decisions made by many real committees? To me the main advantages of model building lie in considerations of precision of thinking and clarity of argument. These considerations enter on several levels.

First, formulating a model forces precision in the terms of one's argument. In everyday discourse we use words with multiple or ambiguous meanings. But to employ a concept like "group strength" or "issue salience" in a formal model invariably necessitates careful thinking about the precise sense in which we wish to use it. Downs, for example, adopted a very specific, though restrictive definition of a political party. Riker (1962) refined the concept of coalition. Axelrod (1970) formulated a precise notion of conflict of interest. Clearly, one can tolerate more conceptual ambiguity in an informal argument than in a formal one.

A second level on which model building contributes to clarity of thought is on the level of assumptions. The assumptions "drive" a model; they determine the deductions one can make. As such they obviously are crucial. Yet in casual arguments assumptions not only may be stated rather loosely, they often are not stated at all. In working through a formal argument,

---

[3] Experiments Charles Plott and I have conducted reveal the crucial importance of insuring that the median optimum *does* enter the voting, which, in turn, suggests the empirical significance of any institutional rules and procedures which affect committee agenda. Similarly, experiments show that if voting is not pairwise, the median can be consistently eliminated from consideration by choice of a suitable agenda.

however, imprecise or missing assumptions have a way of becoming painfully obvious. The "way" is that one cannot logically draw the conclusions one might have wished (or if one does anyway, the illogic is clearly apparent to one's colleagues). For example, I doubt that the importance of the assumption of single-peaked preferences would have emerged as clearly in a verbal discussion of committee decisionmaking as it did in Black's graphical arguments. Take another case. In decades of discussion of the "centrist" nature of American electoral politics, few imagined the restrictive assumptions that might be necessary to assure that convergence takes place in formal models of the American electoral process (Riker and Ordeshook, 1973, chs. 11–12). Numerous other examples could be cited. In a carefully formalized model all the cards are on the table. Scholarly disagreement can focus quickly where it often belongs: on the different basic assumptions with which the contending sides approach the subject.

A third way in which formal models contribute to clarity of thought is closely related to the clarity and completeness of definitions and assumptions. A formal argument is by far the easiest to check for logical validity (provided one understands whatever abstract reasoning which may be involved). We have all had the experience of reading and rereading a discursive essay and remaining undecided as to whether or not the conclusions hold. Far less often will such uncertainty remain after studying a formal argument. Given the definitions and assumptions, a conclusion is either valid or invalid. Moreover, if an argument is invalid, the location of the invalidity often suggests what modifications or additions are necessary in order to produce logical validity. On occasion I have believed that a given proposition would hold in a model with which I was working, only to work it out and find that I was in error. Sometimes a more specific assumption was needed, sometimes a concept was imprecise, and sometimes my common sense simply was wrong. But in each case the shortcoming was one which did not become apparent so long as everyday English was the language of the argument.

A further advantage of model building lies in the penetration of argument which models allow. From the assumptions one deduces some conclusions. From these and the assumptions one produces further conclusions. From these ... and so forth. Everyday language is not well suited to carrying out these second and higher order arguments. The scholar does not himself see the fullest implications of his argument, nor can his audience follow him very far before confusion arises. Formal models greatly facilitate carrying an argument to its logical end—bleeding a set of assumptions dry, so to speak. One's previous conclusions are at hand in the form of compact theorems, equations, or the like. These in turn suggest new directions or stages for the argument. Sometimes one's results "link up" with those in another model so that a large theoretical jump can occur very quickly. Recasting the spatial model in game-theoretic form is one example of such a link-up (Hinich, Ledyard, Ordeshook, 1973). The convergence of some aspects of game theory with social choice theory is another (Wilson, 1971).

In sum, I would argue that the major advantage of using formal models is the precision and clarity of thought which these models require, and the depth of argument which they allow. Yet I recognize that many are skeptical of the position just presented. Doubters would argue that intellectual clarity is purchased at too dear a price, that it involves simplifying social reality beyond all recognition, that formal models are "elegant models of irrelevant worlds." The charge is not uncommon, nor altogether unwarranted, so I will attempt to answer it.

The contention that mathematical models are hopelessly unrealistic is a difficult one to deal with, for it raises a question of degree rather than one of kind. How unrealistic is hopelessly unrealistic? By their very nature models are abstractions. One ignores many variables in an attempt to isolate a few important ones which largely account for the patterns in our empirical observations. Ashby (1970, pp. 94, 96) makes the point nicely:

I would like then to start from the basic fact that every model of a real system is in one sense second rate. Nothing can exceed, or even equal, the truth and accuracy of the real system itself. Every model is inferior, a distortion, a lie. . . .

No electronic model of a cat's brain can possibly be as true as that provided by the brain of another cat; yet of what *use* is the latter as a model? Its very closeness means that it also presents all the technical features that make the first so difficult. From here on, then, I shall take as a basis the thesis that the first virtue of a model is to be useful.

Physical scientists are aware that numerous mathematical functions fit any set of observed data. Each of these, when suitably interpreted, provides an alternate explanation of the data. Similarly, a modeler does not believe (at least he is not justified in believing) that his model is *the* explanation, only that it is one of many. Given this relatively modest view of his intellectual product, a modeler tends to brush off criticisms that his models are hopelessly unrealistic. With no real expectation of finding the one, true explanation, he settles for one which works, i.e., predicts more accurately than anything else available.

The preceding point of view has found its most popular expression in Milton Friedman's (1953) "as if" argument. Briefly, judge a model not by the realism or plausibility of its assumptions, but rather by the accuracy of its predictions. If the model works, say that people behave *as if* the model underlies their behavior.

The *as if* argument can be carried too far, I think, especially by new converts to formal modeling who show a tendency to elevate Friedman's dictum to 11th Commandment status. In some circles the *as if* argument is known unsympathetically as the "F-twist" (Samuelson, 1963), and at least one skeptic has dubbed it "Friedman's principle of unreality" (Simon, 1963). The difficulty that can arise stems from the role of basic assumptions in specifying the empirical situations to which the model applies. If the assumptions are wildly inaccurate, the model applies nowhere and its implications become nonfalsifiable. Nevertheless, because theoretical assumptions are never literally true, they all are inaccurate to some degree, and we tend back to the position that the primary test of the adequacy of the assumptions must lie in the accuracy of the predictions. Thus, if what seems like a hopelessly simplified theory predicts quite well, we may judge the theory as sufficiently accurate for our purposes, regardless of its appearance of unrealism. If it is hopelessly unrealistic, surely it will not stand the test of time. If it does, perhaps our initial notions of realism were in fact unrealistic. Other things equal, I will opt for more accurate assumptions over less accurate ones, but other things are seldom equal.

As a postscript to this section I venture the opinion that modelers make no more hopelessly unrealistic assumptions about reality than do the practitioners of other techniques; they are just more explicit about doing so. Statistically inclined political scientists begin articles with innocent sounding statements like "Factor analysis is a technique . . . ," leaving the unwary in the dark about the numerous special assumptions which underlie the technique. Years ago Donald Stokes (1963) published an excellent critique of the Downsian spatial model. He pointed out that it was a serious oversimplification to assume that an issue space remained constant over time, to assume that voters perceive the space identically, and to assume that voters agree upon the actual candidate locations and vice versa. All very true. But how many of those occasionally engaged in multidimensional scaling (and how many more of those who read such research) are fully aware that these techniques typically make corresponding assumptions about the manner in which the data are generated?[4] The point is simple. Even those whose hands are buried deepest in the data make very big and questionable assumptions in their research. Many who throw stones at formal models reside in glass houses themselves.

---

[4] Happily, in a recent Workshop article Herbert Weisberg (1974) brightly illuminates the foundations and procedures of such techniques.

An Illustrative Example

Having asserted that formal models force precision in the use of concepts, candor about analytical assumptions, and clarity in one's arguments, I now will try to illustrate these processes by showing them at work in a specific model.[5]

Consider the question of constituency influence on legislative roll call voting behavior. From empirical studies we know that representatives are not highly visible (Stokes and Miller, 1962); they are not bombarded with instructions from hordes of issue-conscious constituents. Thus, let us assume that representatives view their districts in rather simple group terms (e.g., the labor vote, the black vote, the sportsmen's vote, etc.). What is it about such groups that interests the representative? Plainly, their votes, money, and other resources which might affect his reelection are foci of his attention. Moreover, for any group influence to operate, the representative must perceive some causal relation between his voting record and the application of group political resources.

Can one formulate a measure of group political resources? Let us assume that representatives have subjective estimates, p, of their probability of reelection, and that they would like these estimates (which reflect reality, we presume) to be as high as possible. Given this assumption, it is natural to assume further that the representative translates gains or losses in group support into increments and decrements in his subjective probability of reelection. Specifically, consider a group, G_j. Define the *strength*, S_{jk}, of G_j on issue k as $(x_{jk} + z_{jk})$, where x_{jk} is the amount the group could increase the representative's probability of reelection in grateful response to a favorable vote on issue k, and z_{jk} is the amount the group could decrease p in antagonistic response to an unfavorable vote. Thus, the strength of a group reflects its raw capability of affecting the representative's probability of reelection. As mentioned, this capability may reflect numbers, money, or other resources possessed by the group. Groups for whom $S_{jk} > 0$ for issue k are termed "significant" groups: they must be included in the decision problem for issue k. Groups for whom $S_{jk} = 0$ are termed "insignificant": the representative ignores them in making his voting decision on issue k.

In addition to their strength, a second dimension along which district

---

[5] The model is presented at length in my book (Fiorina, 1974a) and extended in a later paper (Fiorina, 1974b). Somewhat immodestly, I might observe that the book is a good beginning for someone interested in formal modeling, since the level of analysis is very simple and the style is that of an essay rather than the Teutonic style of axiom-theorem-proof.

groups will differ is whether or not they are in the representative's electoral coalition. Has he won with their aid, or in spite of their opposition? Define two additional concepts:

Friendly group: $z_{jk} \geqslant x_{jk} \geqslant 0$

Unfriendly group: $x_{jk} \geqslant z_{jk} \geqslant 0$

If, on balance, a group currently supports a representative, he has more to lose by alienating them than he has to gain by pleasing them further. In contrast, for unfriendly groups he has less to lose by alienating them further than he has to gain by winning their support. I assume that representatives view the groups in their districts in these terms.

Earlier I noted that when representatives make their voting decisions, they generally will be uncertain about the consequences of those decisions. That is, while a representative may have little difficulty in calculating how much a group could help or hurt him in his reelection battle *if* it entered the fray, what is the *likelihood* that the group actually will do so? Here the model relies heavily on the mechanism of anticipated reactions. Define c_{jk} as the probability that a vote on issue k will draw G_j into the next campaign. The representative uses c_{jk} to discount S_{jk} in the voting decision.

The alternatives available to a representative are simple to enumerate. He may vote aye, abstain, or vote nay. For simplicity's sake order the groups in each voting decision according to their respective strengths (i.e., $S_1 \geqslant S_2 \geqslant \ldots \geqslant S_n$), then identify the voting strategies as a_1—vote with S_1 (and allies, if any), a_2—abstain, and a_3—vote against S_1 (and allies, if any). As yet no payoff to the abstention strategy has been specified. Assume that an abstention on issue k arouses an unfavorable reaction, y_{jk}, for a significant group, G_j, where $0 \leqslant y_{jk} \leqslant z_{jk}$. That is, an abstention on an issue touching a group's interests has the potential to cost the representative something, but certainly no more than an unfavorable vote.

Note the implicit assumption that representatives have a very limited time horizon. I would argue that representatives have only the vaguest idea of the number and kinds of bills they will vote on between campaign periods. Thus, they make decisions one at a time, day by day. They do *not* take risks now with the intention of making it up later. Essentially, then, the model has no future (of course, the past is reflected in changing estimates of p, S_j and c_j as the legislative session proceeds).

Putting all of the foregoing together, one can construct and analyze simple decision problems. Figure 2 illustrates the decision when only one group has a

FIGURE 2

Voting Decision for Consensual Case

	States	
Vote	S_1 G_1 Enters Campaign	S_2 G_1 Does Not Enter Campaign
With G_1	x_1	0
Abstain	$-y_1$	0
Against G_1	$-z_1$	0

nonzero probability of reacting to the vote. To elaborate, the representative's vote draws G_1 resources into the campaign with probability c_1. Depending on how he votes he receives x_1, $-y_1$, or $-z_1$, in such a case. With probability $(1 - c_1)$ the representative's vote goes unnoticed and has no electoral impact.

At this point an implicit assumption becomes suddenly explicit. I have assumed that the probability a group reacts to an issue is independent of how the representative votes. In symbols, $Pr(S_1 /with) = Pr(S_1 /abstain) = Pr(S_1 / against) = c_1$. Elsewhere (Fiorina, 1974b), I have built an "ungrateful electorate" notion into the model by assuming that groups are more likely to enter a campaign when a representative votes against them than when he abstains or votes for them. For present purposes, however, let us simply note the assumption and proceed.

What does the analysis of Figure 2 reveal? The expected return from voting with the group is $c_1(x_1) \geqslant 0$, from abstaining $(-c_1 y_1) \leqslant 0$, and from voting against the group, $(-c_1 z_1) \leqslant 0$. Thus, to maximize his subjective probability of reelection a representative facing such a decision always votes with the group. If a representative typically faces such decisions, he will end up with a very high probability of reelection (barring stupidity and mistakes).

Before proceeding, one might take note of two further implications of the analysis. First, voting with the district group is the representative's optimal strategy whether c_1 is large or small. In this simple model the representative votes in accord with the group's wishes whether he believes they are certain to react to his vote or only believes that they are not certain not to. Of course, a more complex model might change this conclusion. Second, the representative votes in accord with group wishes whether the group is friendly or unfriendly. Our distinction as yet makes no difference.

Admittedly, the political world is seldom so simple as that pictured in Figure 2. Real representatives find cleavages within their districts: Republican-Democratic, black-white, urban-rural, business-labor. What happens when we put conflict into the model? Figure 3 illustrates the decision problem for a conflict situation. Thus, if a representative votes with the stronger group, and S_1 holds, he receives $(x_1 - z_2)$. If S_4 holds, the vote goes unnoticed and has no electoral consequences.

Immediately upon attempting to analyze Figure 3 we discover the need for an additional assumption. Are the probabilities c_1, c_2, that groups enter the campaign independent? If so, then the probabilities of S_1, S_2, S_3, S_4 are $(c_1 c_2)$, $c_1(1 - c_2)$, $(1 - c_1)c_2$, $(1 - c_1)(1 - c_2)$, respectively. The independence assumption would appear to require that the groups be mutually exclusive. But, if not independence, what? We have no theory which would specify how the probabilities of S_1, S_2, S_3, S_4 would depend on c_1, c_2. So, let us make the restrictive assumption and proceed. We can take some consolation in the fact that without constructing the model we might never have realized the question existed.

From Figure 3 the expected value of voting with the stronger group is

$$c_1 x_1 - c_2 z_2 \text{ which may be} > = < 0.$$

The expected value of abstaining is

$$-c_1 y_1 - c_2 y_2 \text{ which is} \leqslant 0.$$

The expected value of voting against the stronger group is

$$c_2 x_2 - c_1 z_1 \text{ which may be} > = < 0.$$

FIGURE 3

Voting Decision for Conflictual Case

	States			
Vote	S_1	S_2	S_3	S_4
With G_1	$x_1 - z_2$	x_1	$-z_2$	0
Abstain	$-y_1 \quad -y_2$	$-y_1$	$-y_2$	0
Against G_1	$-z_1 \quad +x_2$	$-z_1$	x_2	0

Where S_1: Both groups react to the vote
S_2: G_1 reacts, but not G_2
S_3: G_2 reacts, but not G_1
S_4: Neither group reacts

Thus, comparing expected values we see that a representative favors the stronger group rather than the weaker if

$$c_1(x_1 + z_1) \geqslant c_2(x_2 + z_2) \tag{1}$$

and if (1) holds, he votes with the stronger group, G_1, rather than abstain if

$$c_1(x_1 + y_1) \geqslant c_2(z_2 - y_2) \tag{2}$$

while if (1) fails to hold, he votes with the weaker group, G_2, rather than abstain if

$$c_2(x_2 + y_2) \geqslant c_1(z_1 - y_1) \tag{3}$$

Several points of interest are evident. First, note that abstention *never* yields a positive payoff. If a representative finds it in his best interest to abstain, this only illustrates the difficulty of the situation: voting would be even worse. In other words, in the conflictual case, representatives may face situations in which their probability of reelection falls no matter what they do. Thus, the model clarifies the theoretical rationale for the empirical correspondence between the homogeneity-heterogeneity of a district and its electoral safety or marginality. Homogeneous districts serve up consensual decision problems which a representative can handle easily and profitably. Heterogeneous districts produce conflictual decision problems. And, depending on the variables contained in (1) to (3), the representative may be unable to make such decisions without suffering. Heterogeneity makes marginality more likely.

In fully analyzing conditions (1) to (3), four logical configurations are relevant.

  a. Stronger and weaker groups friendly.
  b. Stronger group friendly, weaker unfriendly.
  c. Stronger group unfriendly, weaker friendly.
  d. Stronger and weaker groups unfriendly.

But space precludes my carrying this example so far. I will conclude by mentioning one conclusion which I could *not* find in the model. When I began this work I carried along numerous suggestions from the literature. One of these was that representatives from marginal (i.e., heterogeneous) districts are more subject to constituency influence than those from safe (i.e., homogeneous) districts. A second was that representatives from marginal districts adopted compromise, middle-of-the-road roll call voting strategies. In the model I constructed, however, such conclusions did not follow. In fact, on a theoretical level I was led to believe the opposite of the second, an expectation since verified (Fiorina, 1974, pp. 100–108). In other words, working with the model disabused me of some notions that both casual argument and earlier studies seemed to support.

The preceding example illustrates, I hope, the points made in response to the question, why models? Definition of concepts, choice of initial assumptions, discovery of additional implicit assumptions, reasoning according to fixed, objective procedures—all of these are fostered by the process of formalizing an argument. Whether one chooses mathematics or precise, careful English as the language of one's model, would anyone really find fault with the logical rigor entailed by model construction?

When Are Formal Models Most Useful?

As with any other technique, the construction or application of a formal model is sometimes more appropriate for a given research area and other times less so. In this section I will offer some opinions about research areas ripe for modeling. First, consider the descriptive or explanatory use of models.

If our purpose is to explain observable political behavior in a given context, then it seems to me that models can be used most advantageously where there exists a body of accepted empirical findings about political behavior in that context. After all, how does one go about choosing concepts, defining them precisely, and making appropriate assumptions in a substantive vacuum? Consider for a moment the empirical process of constructing explanatory models, a process Arthur Goldberg (1968) terms "retroduction."

Given some empirical finding(s), X, one poses the question, "How might the world be structured such that X holds, occurs, or is true?" The answers to this question are models, all of which have in common that they assume or imply X. To be worthy of consideration a model must have at least this one tie (X) to the empirical world. For example, Downs appears to have had several "facts" in mind when he formulated his theory—that parties in a two-party system are alike but in a multiparty system distinct; that many citizens are ill-informed and vote on the basis of shortcuts such as party ID and ideology; that democratic governments do "too little;" and no doubt several others. A second example is John Ferejohn's (1974, ch. 7) model of the congressional conference committee bargaining process. Ferejohn requires that his model be consistent with two seemingly inconsistent findings: (1) that interview evidence suggests that the House has a stronger position in the conference than the Senate; (2) that examination of conference outcomes suggests that the Senate is more successful in conference. Another example is Shepsle's (1974) model of the House committee assignment process. Rather than construct a highly abstract general model of how party leaders and the Committee on Committees distribute committee posts, Shepsle incorporates in the model the detailed rules currently prevailing in the House (e.g., only one assignment if to an exclusive committee, no more than one assignment to a semiexclusive committee, etc.), as well as other empirical findings about the committee assignment process. In each of these examples empirical facts establish constraints on the models constructed; one requires a priori that the model be consistent with these facts.

The value of "retroduction" is self-evident. Innumerable models are conceivable; far fewer are interesting. The size of the interesting class will partially be determined by what we know in a given area. Many, many models will imply X; somewhat fewer will imply both X and Y; fewer still will imply all of X, Y, and Z; and so forth. The more we know, the more restrictions we can place on our models, and the less likely will our models be serious misrepresentations of the empirical world.

With the preceding comments in mind, I will suggest various areas ripe for the application of formal models. As one would expect, the first is where some modeling has already occurred—the electoral process. We have great quantities of data, mostly American, but increasingly foreign as well. Numerous capable researchers are mining these data, and some generalizations are beginning to emerge. Such a situation is close to ideal.

Consider what has already occurred. Building on traditional wisdom and early voting studies, Downs presented a model of party competition in a democratic system. Authors such as Garvey (1966), Davis, Hinich, and Ordeshook (1970), Shepsle (1972), and McKelvey (1972) refined various aspects of the Downsian model. These efforts directly influenced some empirical research (Shapiro, 1969; Rabinowitz, 1973; Page and Brody, 1972) and perhaps indirectly provided some of the impetus for the upsurge of research on issue voting (see Kessel, 1972, for citations). Aranson and Ordeshook (1972), Coleman (1971), and Black (1975) extended the earlier simple models to take into account empirical research on party activists. Inconsistencies between the Downsian voter model and empirical turnout levels motivated Riker and Ordeshook (1968) and Ferejohn and Fiorina (1974a) to try new theoretical avenues, which in turn led to new hypotheses to be tested (1974b). And in a related area of research, findings about the correlates of political participation led to additional theorizing about the nature of the participation decision (Tollison and Willett, 1973). In the area of voting behavior and electoral process I believe it fair to conclude that there has been considerable interchange between empirical research and formal models, and that both have profited from it.

A second area in which formal models almost certainly will prove valuable is the legislative process. Again, there exist numerous informative empirical studies ranging from detailed interview materials to highly quantitative roll call studies. Aspects of the legislative process that have been modeled thus far include coalition formation (Koehler, 1974), roll call voting (Fiorina, 1974, 1975; Gilbert, 1973) conference committee decisionmaking (Ferejohn, 1974), and committee assignments (Shepsle, 1974). This first generation of models has not as yet had much impact on empirical research, however.

The study of the judicial process presents virtually the same picture as that of the legislative process. Again, there are numerous high quality empirical studies in which to ground formal models. Already Rohde (1972a,b) has applied Riker's (1962) and Axelrod's (1970, ch. 8) theories of coalition formation to the study of opinion coalitions on the Supreme Court. In the future I expect that formal models will appear quite frequently in studies of the legislative and judicial processes.

By implication, formal models are not so usefully applied where little is known about the behavior of interest. I will not be so foolish as to name any areas of the discipline which fit that category, but certainly in some subfields there is little agreement even on what should be studied and how, let alone on what is known. Possibly, by adopting the categories and approach of one of the contending sides, a researcher could build a model which would bring order out of chaos, but I would not be optimistic about the possibility.

Thus far I have discussed the use of models to explain political behavior, and the conditions under which that use is most appropriate. But there exists another type of research question for which formal models are quite appropriate. That question involves the abstract properties of alternative institutional arrangements. Formal analysis of political institutions and "rules of the game" are very revealing.

With no more than simple arithmetic Duncan Black (1958) suggested effects and properties of various voting schemes, e.g., pairwise voting (exhaustive and not), rank-order voting, and extraordinary majorities. He also clarified and carried forward the analysis of single-member district, multimember district, plurality winner, and proportional representation systems. Many political scientists are familiar with the interesting institutional analyses in Buchanan and Tullock's *The Calculus of Consent* (1962). But scores of other studies can be cited. May (1954), Murikami (1968), Rae (1969), Plott (1967), and numerous others have examined majority rule. Ferejohn and Grether (1974) have probed into the rule of extraordinary majorities. Fishburn (1971), Murikami, and Fine (1972) have attempted to formalize and analyze what it means to have a representative system. Institutional analysis virtually demands a formalized study; the effects of rules and procedures can be extremely subtle. Formal analyses reveal possibilities that verbal discussions anticipate only vaguely, if at all (Fishburn, 1974).

From institutional analysis it is but a short step to political philosophy. Why should majority rule be adopted? Which institutions are the fairest or most just? Ironically, here, where formal models have had little impact, is where they profitably could be applied. Broadly construed, the abstract analyses in modern social choice theory focus on the same questions (albeit more narrowly) as does classical political theory (Shepsle, 1974b; Plott, 1972). I find it very interesting that John Rawls' (1971) prize-winning book, *A Theory of Justice,* contains ample documentation of the influence of various individual and social choice models; moreover the book recently has been critiqued by formalizing its argument and examining its consequences (Plott, 1974). In 1968 Riker and Shapley pointed to the relevance of formal models for normative analysis. I would reemphasize their observation here. Perhaps an unforeseen byproduct of the development of formal models will be a renewed interest in the study of institutional and normative political science, areas which have fallen into relative neglect during the behavioral era.

As the preceding pages make evident, I have no simple answer to the question which leads off this section. When are formal models most useful? If I were allowed only one sentence in which to provide an answer, I would probably focus less on the inappropriateness of a given subject than on the inappropriateness of given models. Tailor the model to the research question, not vice versa. Models become inappropriate when they cease to be tools and become ends. Just as there are a few individuals who see the political world only as an arena for the application of some cherished statistical method, so there are people who see the world as something to be twisted and bent to fit some particular model. We can only hope that their tribe does not increase.

Kinds of Models

Existing formal models can be classified in various ways, but before suggesting several possible categorizations I will argue against one which rears its head far too often: normative vs. positive, or normative vs. empirical.[6] In my opinion this distinction serves no useful purpose. It has wasted far too much scholarly time and energy in the past, and unfortunately it shows a recent tendency to become the last refuge of formal modelers reluctant to confront the real world.

Theories are theories. The structure of a normative theory looks no different from that of a positive theory. Sometimes it is claimed that the premises of a normative theory contain imperatives, whereas the premises of a positive theory contain only declaratives. But I suggest that such distinctions do not lie in the theory or model itself, but rather in the mind of the theorist, in his attitude towards the theory. Let me elaborate.

The "normative theorist" regards certain axioms of his theory as true, as nonfalsifiable, whether this status stems from revelation, intuition, natural law, or whatnot. Given this attitude it is clear that the implications of these axioms are similarly nonfalsifiable; they are prescriptions, not hypotheses. If the real world does not conform to these prescriptions, the response of the theorist is to censure the behavior, to recommend that the world should change.

In contrast, the positive theorist regards the axioms of his theory as approximations to behavioral laws and characteristics of the situation being modeled. Given this attitude, the implications of the axioms are propositions subject to falsification, hypotheses about what is present in the real world. If the world does not conform to the hypotheses, the hypotheses must give way. The theorist goes back to the drawing board to revise or abandon some of the axioms.

For the positive theorist the model must accommodate the world. For the normative theorist the world must conform to the model. To see that the distinction is purely one of attitude, consider how the same model can be used in both ways.

Take some economic model which posits that atomized individuals interact under perfectly competitive conditions. Such a model can illuminate some spheres of economic activity even today—it has some exploratory power. Yet note that libertarians take that same model as a norm. If the model does not describe behavior in some sectors of the economy (because of statist or

---

[6]Sometimes one sees a trichotomous classification of theories into normative-positive-descriptive, or normative-positive-empirical. In my own usage I do not differentiate between a positive and a descriptive theory; a positive theory is intended to explain and describe behavior. A poll of my colleagues in the field of economics elicited the same point of view. Thus, I consider only the proposed dichotomy referred to in the text.

do-gooder interference with the market), the libertarian does not switch to a new model (monopoly, oligopoly, central planning, etc.). Rather, he condemns the conditions which prevent the model from being descriptive.

A second example is perhaps more compelling. Take the theory of subjective expected utility (Savage, 1954). Howard Raiffa (1968) and his associates at the Harvard Business School teach this theory to their students, but they teach it as a "normative" theory. Through proof, paradox, and case study, Raiffa attempts to convince decisionmakers that to act in their own best interests, they *should* act so as to maximize subjective expected utility. But note that if a student learns well and uses the theory in making decisions, the theory will predict, explain, and describe his decisions. The same theory is normative to Raiffa, positive to the scholar studying the decisions of Raiffa's students, and *both* to those making the decisions. Enough said.

Turning to the constructive side, I will suggest three somewhat useful classifications of existing formal models. These are not meant to be mutually exclusive or exhaustive. They simply convey some general information about the model under consideration.

One way of classifying models is according to the general theory (paradigm?) of human behavior which underlies them. That is, models used in political science are examples or applications of more general models. These general models in turn reflect certain basic beliefs about the nature of human behavior.

Most formal models in political science are examples of rational-choice models, a class of models which dominates economics. Such models reflect a view of man as a purposive being: individual behavior is seen as an attempt to maximize individually held goals. Decision theoretic models, game theoretic models, spatial models—all are examples of this basic class of models. Several attempts to analyze the individual voting decision (Riker and Ordeshook, 1968; Ferejohn and Fiorina, 1974a) illustrate very clearly the basic elements of a rational-choice model.

Other models of individual behavior have been developed in psychology and sociology. These models generally emphasize the responsive side of man rather than his purposive side. There are various mathematical learning models (Estes, 1964) which grew out of the basic stimulus-response-reward paradigm. But to the best of my knowledge there are as yet no literal political applications of such models. The leading model in sociology—the role model—similarly reflects a view of human behavior as primarily responsive.[7] Behavior

---

[7] Ralf Dahrendorf (1968, pp. 90–91) writes:

With the existence of these few categories (e.g., expectations, social role, sanctions—M.F.) . . . we may formulate the proposition that implicitly or explicitly

is seen as a response to internalized norms and the expectations of significant others. Obviously, political science has been strongly influenced by the sociological paradigm (e.g., social determinist model of voting behavior, political socialization studies, legislative role studies). But there are not many formal models which reflect the sociological paradigm.[8] One exception occurs in the work of Wayne Francis (1965). Also, in McPhee and Glaser (1962) there are a number of interesting political applications of models set within the sociological tradition.

A second dimension along which to array models is micro-macro. Are individuals the basic unit of analysis, or are groups, classes, nations, etc. the basic analytic unit? Those who employ individualistic models frequently hold the view that macro phenomena should be completely explainable in micro terms. For example, in macroeconomics the aggregate supply and demand relationships should be built up from individual demand and supply curves (easier to believe than to demonstrate, incidentally). Or in political science, some analysts maintain that an election is no more than the sum of numerous citizen, activist, and candidate decisions. Others, however, would dispute this position. Some argue that modeling macro events is simply much easier if individual behavior is not considered explicitly. Others (Przeworski, 1973) argue that individual behavior is affected by contextual influences that individualistic models do not capture. At any rate, one can find examples of models which cut into the micro-macro continuum at various points. Whether one chooses to analyze the behavior of unified collective actors (Richardson, 1960), atomized individuals, or something in between depends mostly on what one wishes to explain, how soon one wishes the answer, and what one wishes to do with it. Depending on the answers, either individualistic or macromodels might be more appropriate.

Finally, one might differentiate among models according to their static or dynamic nature.[9] Our present applications of decision and game theoretic

---

underlies all research and theoretical work in modern sociology. *Man behaves in accordance with his roles.* Thus man basically figures in sociological analyses only to the extent that he complies with all the expectations associated with his social positions. This abstraction, the scientific unit of sociology, may be called *homo sociologicus.*

[8] William Mitchell (1969) remarks that political sociologists are particularly reluctant to sacrifice realism for analytical simplicity. Such an attitude obviously is not conducive to formal modeling. Of course, the "to hell with realism" attitude shown by some political economists is not conducive to *useful* formal modeling.

[9] Here is an appropriate spot to make an observation about simulation models (which are not automatically dynamic as is sometimes believed—see Pool, Abelson, and Popkin, 1964, for example). In the natural sciences, if one's model contains so many variables

models are static. One seeks to find an optimal choice or equilibrium outcome, given an unchanged set of initial parameters (e.g., the strategy set, payoff functions, etc.). In contrast there are models whose basic concern is representing change. The collection of articles in McPhee and Glaser's *Public Opinion and Congressional Elections* (1962) contains several such models. Models have been constructed to predict attitude change (Kreweras, 1966), the spread of rumors, arms races, and other dynamic phenomena (Boulding, 1962, chs. 2, 6, 7; Rapoport, 1960, part 1). Again, the type of model which is appropriate depends on the questions one is asking. A priori there is no reason to prefer micro or macro, static or dynamic, purposive or responsive. The important question is what model best answers the questions of concern.

Critical Judgment of Models

When reading about the construction of a new model or the application of an old one, what should one look for? What are some criteria of judgment that one might apply?

If the model is intended as an explanation of some political phenomenon, then the critical question is just what is the model intended to explain? Banal? Not at all. Identification of the primary research question(s) enables one to bring to bear one's critical acumen (and personal biases) on several major questions: should the model be micro or macro? Static or dynamic? Rational choice or sociological? Identification of the primary research question enables one to make an initial judgment about the appropriateness of the model. For example, early spatial models (Davis, Hinich, and Ordeshook, 1970) are static, micro, rational choice models.[10] If one views the electoral process as quintessentially a dynamic, macro process, one might simply reject out of hand spatial models of the electoral process.

Turning to more specific matters, one should carefully study the assumptions of the model. Are they reasonable attempts to approximate aspects of the situation under study, or are they made in the spirit of "This assumption

---

and relationships that a paper and pencil analysis is impractical, one turns it loose on the computer. In political science, however, even very simple models sometimes get put on the computer because they are used to manipulate large amounts of data (Pool, Abelson, and Popkin, 1964; Matthews and Stimson, 1974). At any rate, simulation models should be evaluated in the same fashion as other formal models, with the exception that repeated runs and sensitivity testing typically will replace logical proofs.

[10] Later developments of the model (McKelvey, 1972) relax the rational choice part by representing citizen behavior by aggregate "support functions" rather than individually rational decision rules.

is crazy, but I can't get any results without it"? If the latter, beware. All modeling involves a trade-off between simplicity and realism. But one must take care not to trade away the problem in order to get enough simplicity to analyze it. Consider the model proposed by Robert Barro (1973) to analyze the electorate's control of their representatives. Barro whets our interest when he writes (1973, p. 19):

> The model focuses on the division of interest between the public and its political representatives. The division of interest arises because the public officeholder is assumed to act to advance his own interests, and these interests do not coincide automatically with those of his constituents. The electoral process and some elements of the political structure are then analyzed as mechanisms which can be used to move the officeholder toward a position where the advancement of self-interest approximates the advancement of the interests of his constituents.

But upon reading further we learn that:

> *In order to facilitate the analysis* of political control, the theoretical model incorporates an extremely simplified version of the underlying "public interest." In section I *an assumption of common tastes on private goods versus the single type of public good insures unanimous agreement among individuals on the ideal aggregate level of governmental activity.* Given this unanimity, the model abstracts from differences of opinion among the public and focuses on the problem of the public's control over its political representatives. (Emphasis mine.)

Barro remarks that his model complements other work which allows divergent tastes, but I remain skeptical.

Given that the assumptions of a model capture the essential aspects of the situation under study, one should ask an additional question. Are some assumptions so specific that the model lacks robustness? If certain variables are assumed to follow particular probability distributions, or if variables are assumed to be related via specific functional forms, then hard questions should be asked. Do we have evidence (either empirical or as the conclusions of other accepted models) that the specific distributions or functional forms are justified? If not, we should be skeptical of the conclusions of the model, for they may be totally dependent on the distributions or functional forms assumed. Slight perturbations of the assumptions could alter the conclusions drastically.

For example, the Brams-Davis (1974) model of campaign resource allocation depends critically on the assumption that candidates expend exactly the same amount of resources in each state. The Gilbert (1973) model of roll call voting assumes that representatives strive for 50% + 1 votes. If some recalcitrant representative wishes 55% of the vote, the conclusions of the model may not hold for him. In my book (Fiorina, 1974) I assume that a roll call vote against a constituency group always hurts a representative more than a vote for them helps.

I hasten to emphasize that such specific assumptions by no means make a model useless. After all, they may be exactly correct. Highly specific assumptions simply raise a caution flag. The implications of the model may result directly from the specificity assumed, so examine it carefully.

Even if the model is not intended as explanatory, one still must pay careful attention to the assumptions. In analyses of institutional arrangements, one will come across abstract axioms labeled "anonymity," "positive responsiveness," "liberalism," "nondictatorship," etc. Do such axioms capture the essence of such concepts? If not, there is uncertainty about the meaning of the model's implications. An example is an impossibility theorem proved by Sen (1970). Loosely speaking, Sen shows that under certain general conditions an additional condition he calls liberalism is incompatible with the existence of a collective choice rule which designates a best alternative from every subset of alternatives. The essence of Sen's "liberalism" is that for every individual there is at least one pair of alternatives for which his preference alone determines the social choice (e.g., pink walls in his bedroom rather than white walls). As Sen recognizes, however, liberalism can be defined in various ways. An alternative formulation might be to designate some subset of alternatives as simply outside the domain of feasible alternatives ("Congress shall make no law. . . .").

The essence of the preceding discussion is simple. Do not skip over the technical portion of a formal model and go directly to the conclusions. Rather, examine carefully the definitions and assumptions of the model. The model's conclusions are implicit in the definitions and assumptions. Scrutinize the latter as well as the former.

Finally, examine the correspondence between the conclusions of a formal model and the researcher's interpretations of them. Theorems sometimes may be terribly abstract. And (down deep) many formal modelers are just as concerned over the relevance of their work as are more empirically oriented researchers. Thus, a little wishful thinking sometimes can creep in between theorem and interpretation. The consumer of such work should be aware of the possibility.

Otherwise, judge work involving models as one would judge any other work. Is it careful, insightful, and does it advance our understanding? In the end every study must be judged against those standards.

Manuscript submitted May 13, 1974.
Final manuscript received September 10, 1974.

REFERENCES

Aranson, Peter, and Ordeshook, Peter. 1972. "Spatial Strategies for Sequential Elections," in Richard Niemi and Herbert Weisberg, eds., *Probability Modeling in Political Science.* Columbus: Merrill.

Ashby, W. Ross. 1970. "Analysis of the System to be Modeled," in Ralph Stogdill, ed., *The Process of Model-Building in the Behavioral Sciences.* New York: Norton, pp. 94–114.

Axelrod, Robert. 1970. *Conflict of Interest.* Chicago: Markham.

Barro, Robert. 1973. "The Control of Politicians: An Economic Model," *Public Choice,* Spring 1973, pp. 19–42.

Black, Duncan. 1948. "On the Rationale of Group Decision Making," *Journal of Political Economy,* February 1948, pp. 23–34.

——. 1958. *The Theory of Committees and Elections.* Cambridge: Cambridge University Press.

Black, Gordon. 1975. *Parties and Elections.* San Francisco: Freeman.

Boulding, Kenneth. 1962. *Conflict and Defense.* New York: Harper.

Brams, Steven, and Davis, Morton. 1974. "The 3/2's Rule in Presidential Campaigning," *American Political Science Review,* March 1974, pp. 113–134.

Brodbeck, May. 1959. "Models, Meaning, and Theories," in Llewellyn Gross, ed., *Symposium on Sociological Theory.* New York: Harper.

Buchanan, James, and Tullock, Gordon. 1962. *The Calculus of Consent.* Ann Arbor: University of Michigan Press.

Cherryholmes, C., and Shapiro, M. 1968. *Representatives and Roll-Calls: A Computer Simulation of Voting in the Eighty-Eighth Congress.* Indianapolis: Bobbs-Merrill.

Coleman, James. 1971. "Internal Processes Governing Party Positions in Elections," *Public Choice,* Fall 1971, pp. 35–60.

Dahrendorf, Ralf. 1968. "Sociology and Human Nature," in *Essays in the Theory of Society.* Stanford: Stanford University Press, pp. 88–106.

Davis, O.; Hinich, M.; and Ordeshook, P. 1970. "An Expository Development of a Mathematical Model of the Electoral Process," *American Political Science Review,* June 1970, pp. 426–448.

Downs, Anthony. 1957. *An Economic Theory of Democracy.* New York: Harper and Row.

——. 1959. "Dr. Rogers' Methodological Difficulties—A Reply to His Critical Note," *American Political Science Review,* December 1959, pp. 1094–1097.

Estes, William. 1964. "Probability Learning," in A. W. Melton, ed., *Categories of Human Learning.* New York: Academic Press.

Fenno, Richard. 1973. *Congressmen in Committees.* Boston: Little, Brown.

Ferejohn, John. 1974. *Pork Barrel Politics.* Stanford: Stanford University Press.

Ferejohn, John, and Fiorina, Morris. 1974a. "The Paradox of Not Voting: A Decision Theoretic Analysis," *American Political Science Review,* June 1974, pp. 525–536.

_____. 1974b. "To p or Not to p," Caltech Social Science Working Paper No. 53, Pasadena, California, September 1974.

Ferejohn, John, and Grether, David. 1974. "On a Class of Rational Social Decision Procedures," *Journal of Economic Theory,* in press.

Fine, Kit. 1972. "Some Necessary and Sufficient Conditions for Representative Decision on Two Alternatives," *Econometrica,* November 1972, pp. 1083–1090.

Fiorina, Morris. 1974. *Representatives, Roll Calls and Constituencies.* Lexington, Massachusetts: Heath.

_____. 1975. "Constituency Influence: A Generalized Model and Implications for Quantitative Studies of Roll Call Behavior," *Political Methodology,* forthcoming.

Fishburn, Peter. 1971. "The Theory of Representative Majority Decision," *Econometrica,* March 1971, pp. 273–284.

_____. 1974. "Paradoxes of Voting," *American Political Science Review,* June 1974, pp. 537–546.

Francis, Wayne L. 1965. "The Role Concept in Legislatures: A Probability Model and a Note on Cognitive Structures," *Journal of Politics,* August 1965, pp. 567–585.

Friedman, Milton. 1953. "The Methodology of Positive Economics," in *Essays in Positive Economics.* Chicago: University of Chicago Press, pp. 3–43.

Garvey, Gerald. 1966. "The Theory of Party Equilibrium," *American Political Science Review,* March 1966, pp. 29–38.

Gilbert, Jane. 1973. "Constituent Preferences and Roll Call Behavior" (unpublished paper).

Goldberg, Arthur. 1968. "Political Science as Science," in Robert Dahl and Deane Neubauer, eds., *Readings in Modern Political Analysis.* Englewood Cliffs, New Jersey: Prentice-Hall, pp. 15–30.

Hinich, Melvin; Ledyard, John; and Ordeshook, Peter. 1973. "A Theory of Electoral Equilibrium: A Spatial Analysis Based on the Theory of Games," *Journal of Politics,* February 1973, pp. 154–193.

Kessel, John. 1972. "The Issues in Issue Voting," *American Political Science*

Review, June 1972, pp. 459–465.

Koehler, David. 1974. "A Theory of Legislative Coalition Formation," a paper presented at the MSSB Workshop on Mathematical Models of Congress, Aspen, Colorado, June 1974.

Kreweras, Germain. 1968. "A Model for Opinion Change During Repeated Ballotting," in Paul Lazarsfeld and Neil Henry, eds., *Readings in Mathematical Social Science.* Cambridge: M.I.T. Press, pp. 174–191.

Lipset, S.M., ed. 1969. *Politics and the Social Sciences.* New York: Oxford University Press.

Matthews, Donald, and Stimson, James. 1974. *Yeas and Nays: Normal Decision Making in the House of Representatives.* New York: Wiley.

May, K. O. 1954. "Transitivity, Utility and Aggregation in Preference Patterns," *Econometrica,* January 1974, pp. 1–13.

McKelvey, Richard. 1972. "Policy Related Voting and its Effects on Electoral Equilibrium," a paper presented at the American Political Science Association Meeting, Washington, D.C., September 1972.

McPhee, William, and Glazer, William. 1962. *Public Opinion and Congressional Elections.* New York: Free Press.

Mitchell, William. 1969. "The Shape of Political Theory to Come: From Political Sociology to Political Economy," in S. M. Lipset, ed., *Politics and the Social Sciences.* New York: Oxford University Press, pp. 101–136.

Murakami, Y. 1968. *Logic and Social Choice.* New York: Dover.

Niemi, Richard, and Weisberg, Herbert, eds. 1972. *Probability Models in Political Science.* Columbus: Merrill.

Page, Benjamin, and Brody, Richard. 1972. "Policy Voting and the Electoral Process: The Vietnam War Issue," *American Political Science Review,* September 1972, pp. 979–995.

Plott, Charles. 1967. "A Notion of Equilibrium and its Possibility under Majority Rule," *American Economic Review,* September 1967, pp. 788–806.

_____. 1972. "Ethics, Social Choice Theory, and the Theory of Economic Policy," *Journal of Mathematical Sociology,* July 1972, pp. 181–208.

_____. 1974. "Rawls' Theory of Justice: An Impossibility Result," Caltech Social Science Working Paper No. 49, Pasadena, California, August 1974.

Polsby, Nelson, and Riker, William. 1974. "New Math," *American Political Science Review,* June 1974, pp. 733–734.

Pool, Ithiel; Abelson, Robert; and Popkin, Samuel. 1964. *Candidates, Issues and Strategies.* Cambridge, Massachusetts: M.I.T. Press.

Przeworski, Adam. 1974. "Contextual Models of Political Behavior," *Political Methodology,* Winter 1974, pp. 27–61.

Rabinowitz, George. 1973. "Spatial Models of Electoral Choice: An Empirical Analysis." Institute for Research in Social Science Working Paper in Methodology No. 7, Chapel Hill, North Carolina.

Rae, Douglas. 1969. "Decision Rules and Individual Values in Constitutional Choice," *American Political Science Review,* March 1969, pp. 40–56.

Raiffa, Howard. 1968. *Decision Analysis.* Reading, Massachusetts: Addison-Wesley.

Rapoport, Anatol. 1960. *Fights, Games, and Debates.* Ann Arbor, Michigan: University of Michigan Press.

Rawls, John. 1971. *A Theory of Justice.* Cambridge: Harvard University Press.

Richardson, L. F. 1939. "Generalized Foreign Policy," *British Journal of Psychology Monographs Supplements.*

_____. 1960. *Arms and Insecurity.* Chicago: Quadrangle.

Riker, William. 1962. *The Theory of Political Coalitions.* New Haven: Yale University Press.

Riker, William, and Ordeshook, Peter. 1968. "A Theory of the Calculus of Voting," *American Political Science Review,* March 1968, pp. 25–42.

_____. 1972. *An Introduction to Positive Political Theory.* Englewood Cliffs, New Jersey: Prentice-Hall.

Riker, William, and Shapley, Lloyd. 1968. "Weighted Voting: A Mathematical Analysis for Instrumental Judgments," in Roland Pennock and John Chapman, eds., *Nomos X: Representation.* New York: Atherton, pp. 199–216.

Rogers, W. Hayward. 1959. "Some Methodological Difficulties in Anthony Downs' *An Economic Theory of Democracy," American Political Science Review,* June 1959, pp. 483–485.

Rohde, David. 1972a. "A Theory of the Formation of Opinion Coalitions in the United States Supreme Court," in Richard Niemi and Herbert Weisberg, eds., *Probability Models of Collective Decision Making.* Columbus: Merrill.

_____. 1972b. "Policy Goals and Opinion Coalitions in the Supreme Court," *Midwest Journal of Political Science,* May 1972, pp. 208–224.

Savage, Leonard. 1954. *The Foundations of Statistics.* New York: Wiley.

Sen, Amartya. 1970. "The Impossibility of a Paretian Liberal," *Journal of Political Economy,* January–February 1970, pp. 152–157.

Shapiro, Michael. 1969. "Rational Political Man: A Synthesis of Economic and Social-Psychological Perspectives," *American Political Science Review,* December 1969, pp. 1106–1119.

Shapley, L. S., and Shubik, M. 1954. "A Method for Evaluating the Distribution of Power in a Committee System," *American Political Science Review*, September 1954, pp. 787–792.

Shepsle, Kenneth. 1972. "The Strategy of Ambiguity: Uncertainty and Electoral Competition," *American Political Science Review*, June 1974, pp. 555–568.

_____. 1974a. "A Model of the Congressional Committee Assignment Process: Constrained Maximization in an Institutional Setting," *Public Choice*, in press.

_____. 1974b. "Theories of Collective Choice," in Cornelius Cotter et al., eds., *Political Science Annual V: Collective Decision Making*. Indianapolis: Bobbs-Merrill, pp. 1–87.

Simon, Herbert, and Samuelson, Paul. 1963. "Problems of Methodology— Discussion," *American Economic Review* (supplement), May 1963, pp. 229–236.

Stokes, Donald E. 1963. "Spatial Models of Party Competition," *American Political Science Review*, June 1963, pp. 368–377.

Stokes, Donald E., and Miller, Warren. 1962. "Party Government and the Saliency of Congress," *Public Opinion Quarterly*, Winter 1962, pp. 531– 546.

Tollison, R. D. and Willett, T. D. 1973. "Some Simple Economics of Voting and Not Voting," *Public Choice*, Fall 1973, pp. 59–71.

Weisberg, Herbert. 1974. "Dimensionland: An Excursion into Spaces," *American Journal of Political Science*, November 1974, pp. 743–776.

Wilson, Robert. 1972. "The Game-Theoretic Structure of Arrow's General Possibility Theorem," *Journal of Economic Theory*, August 1972, pp. 14–20.

CHARLES R. PLOTT

Axiomatic Social Choice Theory: An Overview and Interpretation*

Normative concerns are central to the study of democratic theory and the policy-relevant areas of political science and economics. The same normative concerns are central to the study of axiomatic social choice theory. Despite similarities in origin and in underlying philosophical orientation, the fields have evolved separately and within different methodologies. This paper attempts to survey the most recent major results in axiomatic social choice theory within a unifying interpretation accessible to nonspecialists.

Why should a political scientist be interested in something like social choice theory? At this early stage of the subject's development, studying it will be of little help to those who want to understand broad questions about the evolution of institutions. It might be of limited help to those who study narrow questions about behavior, but only because of a close relationship between social choice theory and theories of strategic behavior. Political scientists interested in the normative aspects of systems are the potential customers, for it is out of concern for their problem, at least their problem as seen through the eyes of two economists, K. J. Arrow and Duncan Black, in the 1940s, that the field seems to have been born.

The subject began with what seemed to be a minor problem with majority rule. "It is just a mathematical curiosity," said some (Dahl and Lindbloom, 1953, p. 422). But intrigued and curious about this little hole, researchers, not deterred by the possibly irrelevant, began digging in the ground nearby as described below in the first section. What they now appear to have been uncovering is a gigantic cavern into which fall almost all of our ideas about

*Financial support supplied by the National Science Foundation is gratefully acknowledged. An early draft of this paper was presented at an MSSB conference on Democratic Theory and Social Choice Theory, Key Biscayne, 1975. The comments by participants have led to several changes. W. T. Jones and Paul Thomas provided many helpful editorial comments, and I have enjoyed the benefit of many discussions on this subject with colleagues John Ferejohn, Mike Levine, and Steven Matthews.

Reprinted from AMERICAN JOURNAL OF POLITICAL SCIENCE, Vol. XX, No. 3, August 1976, pp. 511-596, Charles R. Plott, "Axiomatic Social Choice Theory: An Overview and Interpretation," by permission of the University of Texas Press.

social actions. Almost anything we say and/or anyone has ever said about what society wants or should get is threatened with internal inconsistency. It is as though people have been talking for years about a thing that cannot, in *principle,* exist, and a major effort now is needed to see what objectively remains from the conversations. The second section of the paper is an attempt to survey this problem.

Are these exaggerated claims? If this essay serves its purpose we will find out. The theory has not been translated into the frameworks of political and social philosophy with which political scientists are most familiar, so its full implications are yet to be assessed. Perhaps by outlining what seem to be the major results and arguments within a single integrated theme which makes them accessible to such a broad professional audience, new modes of thought can be brought to bear on the problems and we can successfully demonstrate what social choice theorists have been unable to demonstrate—that such claims are in fact exaggerated. If the results go the other way, if the claims are not exaggerated, then perhaps the paper will supply the reader with some new tools and perspectives with which to attack old, but very important problems.

The central result is broad, sweeping, and negative. Paul Samuelson rates it as one of the significant intellectual achievements of this century (Samuelson, 1967). It certainly weighed heavily in the decision to award K. J. Arrow the Nobel prize in economics. Most of the remaining work can be interpreted as attempts to discredit this central discovery. An outline of these attempts following a development of the theorem forms the second section of the paper. The first section is devoted to providing several examples of the types of problems that the major result claims are pervasive. Care must be taken, however, not to confuse the examples with the meaning of the result. They should be taken as symptoms of something much more serious and as examples which bring a little closer to home what is otherwise a very abstract argument.

The third section of the paper sketches what at first amounted to a small offshoot from the effort outlined in the second section but now seems to be becoming a major, independent area of study. Such positive results that we do have are here. Very early in the development of the literature, it was discovered that it is possible to describe certain institutions, processes, and procedures in axiomatic terms, whereby a set of axioms can be viewed as a set of "parts" which taken together "make" the process. For a pure theorist constrained only by his imagination and by logical consistency, several interesting questions immediately occur. What are the axiomatic constructions, the "parts" so to speak, of some of our existing processes? What is the real difference in terms of their "parts" between, say, the Borda count and the Dodgson balloting systems? What difference does it make in terms of axiomatically described process behavior if people vote for their top two candidates rather than only one? Even this type of analysis might provide tools for the practically minded political scientist. We have here a new vehicle through which institutional comparisons can be made, and we have no idea about how far it might carry us. If one can axiomatically describe institutions and processes, then one can use the power of axiomatic methods to examine process behavior and compare processes. In fact, one might even be able to take the desirable (axiomatic) "parts" of several different processes and use the methods to put them together and form a (historically speaking) brand new process with "better" features than any of those from which the "parts" were taken.

Crazy? We really don't know. Perhaps this essay will help someone prove that the whole field is irrelevant and thereby allow existing scholars to rest easily with their work.

PARADOXES OF VOTING

As an introduction to axiomatic social choice theory, let's examine a few paradoxes about voting processes. "Paradoxes" might be the wrong word. In fact one of the real paradoxes is why we regard the following examples as paradoxes. Nevertheless, paradox or not, everyone usually agrees that there is definitely something unintuitive and peculiar going on.

The standard example is the following majority rule cycle. Suppose there are three people $\{1,2,3\}$ and three alternatives $\{x,y,z\}$. The first person feels x is best, y is second, and z is third. The second person thinks y is best and it is followed in order by z and then x. The third person prefers z most with x in second place and y last.

In order to save printing costs, let's adopt the shorthand way of representing such situations used by students of these problems. The notation "P" will mean "preferred" and the notation "I" means "indifferent" and any subscript on the letters simply denotes the name of the person to whom the attitude is ascribed. For example, P_i is the preference of individual i. So we have:

first person	xP_1yP_1z,	(x is preferred to y is preferred to z)
second person	yP_2zP_2x,	(y is preferred to z is preferred to x)
third person	zP_3xP_3y.	(z is preferred to x is preferred to y)

Now which alternative should this society get? Naturally, it should get what it wants. Which alternative does it want? Naturally, it wants what the majority prefers. But then the social preference, P_s, looks like this:

$$xP_syP_szP_sx$$

since 2 and 3 prefer z to x, 1 and 2 prefer y to z, and 1 and 3 prefer x to y. This result is called a *majority rule cycle* or *majority preference cycle*.

There are four standard responses to this. The first is "ugh!" which requires no elaboration. The second response amounts to throwing out the implied definition of social preference. "This cycle doesn't mean anything; the group will choose the best thing when they meet—just let them vote and things will be OK as long as they come to *some* agreement." The trouble is that the outcome depends only upon the voting sequence. The outcome is y, x, or z, depending only upon whether the agenda sequence A, B, or C, respectively is adopted. This is true in theory and in fact (Plott and Levine, 1975). Now, what kind of social philosophy should depend upon that?

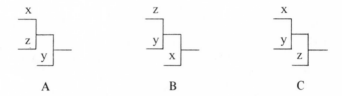

The third reaction amounts to a denial that the phenomenon exists. "Well, you pulled that one out of a hat, but how often will such a crazy case occur?" If everything is random, the answer is not what the asker expected to hear. In this case the answer is simply *"almost* always." The probability of this event approaches *one* as the number of alternatives approaches infinity and it approaches it *very* rapidly. In this sense the cycle is *the* case and *not* the exception.

But, one might argue, everything is not random—people have similarities in preferences. How does that affect the probabilities? A considerable amount of work has been exerted in an effort to characterize the types of individual preference configurations for which the majority rule process does not have this cyclical property. What has been learned will be outlined below, but in general, the results have not been encouraging. This line of questioning, if anything, has supported the view that the phenomenon is pervasive.

The fourth reaction is a claim that there is no paradox at all. "When the majority rule cycle occurs, then society is simply indifferent—any of the alternatives in the cycle is as good as any other." Now this is a rather clever position but there are still problems. Consider the following example, this time with three people and four options.

first person $yP_1 xP_1 wP_1 z$,
second person $xP_2 wP_2 zP_2 y$,
third person $wP_3 zP_3 yP_3 x$.

Now suppose first, that w is the status quo—the alternative which involves "doing nothing"—and second, that the following sequence of votes occurs.

As the reader can see if he traces out the process, the ultimate choice is z. But *everyone* prefers w, the status quo, to z, the option finally chosen. So, here we have a majority rule cycle that contains two options, one of which is unanimously preferred to the other. That means that proponents of this idea would have society be indifferent between two alternatives even though one was unanimously preferred to the other. Process behavior like this would violate even a minimal concept of efficiency. An economist would ask: "Why should a society accept one alternative when another alternative exists which would make *everyone* better off?" Almost all social philosophers would agree that all concepts of sovereignty require that a people *unanimous* should not be refused.

"Well," says the skeptic, "that's easy to cope with. Simply find some way to first eliminate the Pareto dominated options, those which are unanimously beaten by some other option, and then apply majority rule to what remains." For lack of a better term call this "modified majority rule."

The problem with this line of argument is that it does not sit well with the concept of a social preference. To see this, suppose people have the preferences as listed in the example immediately above and that z and y are the only options open. By majority rule, z will be chosen, and we would conclude that society prefers z to y, or more strongly, we would conclude that z is better than y. Now suppose the options are expanded to the set $\{w,x,y,z\}$. Using the process proposed above we eliminate z from consideration, since everyone prefers w to z, and declare w, x, and y all "equally good" or all "equally preferred." They are all in the majority rule cycle, and all are better than z. But notice this is in flat contradiction to the conclusion above, that z was socially preferred to y. Even though we have not formally defined a concept of social preference, most people would intuitively object to this type of inconsistency. We must abandon either this skeptic's idea, and thus majority rule, or our intuitive ideas about social preference.

Let's try the former. After all, there are lots of processes other than majority rule and many of them are successfully used. A prime example is the Borda count, or point voting system, described as follows. Each person ranks the options under consideration and assigns each a number in accord with its level in the ranking. That is, the least preferred gets 1 point, the next least gets 2 points, etc. Points are all totaled and the option which receives the greatest number of points is chosen. Consider the four-option, seven-person example, first discovered by Fishburn (1974b), given in Table 1. The point totals are shown in the box. Clearly y is best, and it is followed in ranking by x, w, and z in order. But, suppose z was eliminated from early consideration (if not by some natural cause) since it gets the least points, and besides it is

TABLE 1

Borda Count: A Four-Option,
Seven-Person Example

Individual Rankings						
Mr. 1	Mr. 2	Mr. 3	Mr. 4	Mr. 5	Mr. 6	Mr. 7
w	x	y	w	x	y	w
x	y	z	x	y	z	x
y	z	w	y	z	w	y
z	w	x	z	w	x	z

	Total Points	
w	18	15 ←
x	19	14
y	20 ←	13
z	13	

Pareto-dominated by y. With z gone there are only three options, so points are assigned to $\{$w,x,y$\}$ in magnitude from 1 to 3 rather than 1 to 4 as before. With this done, the result on the right is discovered. Now the social ordering w, x, and then y. This is exactly the *inverse* of what it was in the first set of circumstances.

The social preference, as defined through the Borda count, certainly goes against intuitive ideas about how a concept like social preference should behave. So, we are back to a junction we have visited before. Either we must abandon our intuitive ideas about social preference—and perhaps, as will be considered below, with this goes much of our heritage, centuries of work and reasoning in the field of social philosophy—or we must examine additional processes.

We will take the latter route first, since the former route would be presumptuous, at best, and perhaps grossly wasteful of perfectly good ideas. Having taken it, however, we will be forced to return to this junction again and begin to slowly and painfully seek where the first route leads. That is the current state of the theory. Some are still edging along the sides of the cavern following the difficult paths that remain from the optimistic route, while others have already accepted a position at the bottom of the hole and are trying to construct some stairs which might lead out.

THE GENERAL POSSIBILITY THEOREM

Problem Formulation

At this point everyone should agree that something strange and perhaps unexpected is going on. Furthermore, the possible ramifications are very broad. If the concepts, which help us speak about how we feel whole societies, polities, and even worlds should behave, do not work at all for the simple case of a society with a handful of people with just a few alternatives, then perhaps we apply them at the global level only because we do not really understand them. The simple cases are a natural proving ground for any tools which might be applied to the more complicated.

Now exactly what are the facts and what is being called into question? The facts are that several commonly accepted means of providing social choices from among a field of contenders have some unusual properties. The behavior of these methods does not sit well with our intuitive notions of social preference, and we wish to know what type of system, if any, would sit well with us.

Social Preference

Perhaps the first step is to try to provide a precise statement of our intuition. At the base is some concept of social preference. Any method of social choice should yield the socially most preferred alternative—the "best" option in the eyes of society as a whole. The immediate temptation is to begin to define the social preference directly: what determines the list of priorities, what special considerations need to be included, etc. Such arguments and discussions are enlightening and useful, but anyone who has ever engaged in such a discussion knows that for some reason they never end. Perhaps by using a very clever insight first used by Arrow, we can avoid all of that. Without agreeing on whether society prefers x to y or not, we can all agree on the following *principles* of social preference.[1]

    I. *Preference Transitivity.* If society prefers option x to option y, and it prefers option y to option z, then option x is preferred to option z (assuming of course that no relevant consideration has changed in the interim).

    II. *Indifference Transitivity.* If society is indifferent between option x and option y, and it is indifferent between option y and option z, then it is indifferent between option x and option z.

    III. *Value/Feasibility Separation.* The social attitude, preference or indifference, between x and y does not depend upon what other options are feasible.

    IV. *Universal Domain.* The social attitude, preference or indifference, between every pair of options is always defined, even though there may be a great deal (all possible) of conflict among the opinions (rankings of options) of individual members of the society.

Thinking about the examples we have already reviewed will help us begin to understand these principles. The first example shows that majority rule as a way of determining the social preference violates the first principle. The "modified majority rule" and the Borda count examples violate the third principle. The fourth principle simply says that we expect the concept of social preference to make sense in the particular cases (and other cases as

---

[1] Formally speaking, we need more principles than the ones listed (which the reader will probably implicitly assume anyway): (i) for all x, xI_Sx; (ii) for all x and y, xI_Sy implies yI_Sx; (iii) xP_Sy and yI_Sz implies that xP_Sz; (iv) for any x and y we have one of xP_Sy or yP_Sx or xI_Sy. We also need an important Principle 0 which states that a social preference exists.

well) where individual members of the society have the rankings as given in the examples. More specifically, it means that we expect the social preference to be defined for every array of individual rankings. If you don't like the implicit assumption of individual transitivity, we can expand the domain to include the cases where individual preferences can be intransitive as well.

As it turns out, these are very strong principles. We will ultimately consider doing away with all of them. But, before that happens, let's show why they are intuitively reasonable and how they are implied by the way we normally think about normative social philosophy.

The first three principles are usually accepted as reasonable at the individual level of cognition. Instances of cyclical individual preference or indifference are items of great curiosity (Tversky, 1969; Lichtenstein and Slovic, 1971), especially if the individual exhibiting the cycle is willing to accept it. Violations of these principles are considered unusual and rare at best. The third principle simply demands that the *concept* of social preference between alternatives has an existence independent of the concept of feasibility of alternatives. It says we do *not* have to be aware of what we are *able* to do *before* we can even discuss what we would like to do. The fourth principle forces us to take a stand on behalf of society as a whole, even though individuals within society have conflicting desires.

Some see the first three principles as following almost axiomatically from the word "best." They would maintain that society should have what is best and that if x is better than y and y is better than z, then it follows that x is "best," clearly better than both y and z. Here we have the first principle with the concept "better" substituted for the word "preference" in the principles.

Concepts of social welfare similarly imply such principles. If the social welfare is greater with option x than with option y, and if social welfare is greater with option y than with option z, then it follows from the concept "greater" that social welfare is greater at x than at z. We thus have derived Principle I, Preference Transitivity. Principle II, Indifference Transitivity, is similarly trivial. Principle III, Value/Feasibility Separation, follows since the level of social welfare generated with option x is generally considered to be independent of whether option y was or was not feasible. So we can see that concepts of social welfare necessitate acceptance of these principles.

The list can be multiplied. Most concepts regarding the normative aspects of social choices utilize these principles *plus* many more. To reject these three would be equivalent to rejecting any social philosophy which implies them. So, it would seem that if we adopt at least these we can proceed. But recall we have already been warned that the analysis below will strongly suggest that these three principles are exactly what we cannot accept. Even though it may *seem* as though we have said nothing but the obvious, we have already descended into the cavern.

Normative Content of Social Preference

So far we have said very little of a normative nature. We have said that we are willing to channel normative demands through a concept of social preference, but we have not made any normative demands. For example, should the social preference have anything to do with individual preferences? How should the social preference be defined?

Almost any libertarian philosopher would demand that if a concept like social preference is to be used, then it should have some systematic connection with individual attitudes. For example, if *everyone* preferred option x over option y, then at least some would maintain, society should not be indifferent between the two options or perversely prefer y to x. That is the famous Pareto Principle. It is actually stronger than the principle we will use.

> V. *Responsive.* For each pair of alternatives, x, y, there is a pattern of attitudes, ranking R_1 for person number 1, ranking R_2 for person number 2, etc., such that y is not preferred by society to x, given that the pattern of attitudes $(R_1, R_2, \ldots, R_n)$ prevails.

For some this would seem to be a very minimal sovereignty condition. Most of us would readily demand much more. It simply says that no option is preferred by society to any other option, regardless of the pattern of individual rankings. People's preferences prevail over all other considerations. The social preference is "responsive" to individual citizens. If one accepts the Pareto Principle, then one clearly accepts this principle, since the Pareto Principle states one of the circumstances, unanimity, when the pattern of preferences necessarily outweighs other considerations.

Process

Before continuing let's check our location. We are attempting to understand the paradoxes above and see if we can find a process, a method of making group decisions, which does not have such paradoxical results. Our first principles attempt to make clear what constitutes "paradoxical behavior." The principles are a type of *minimal* expectation about system performance. The strange behavior of the examples above is in violation of these principles.

How can we find those processes which do not have paradoxical properties? There are literally millions of processes. In fact, by making small alterations in procedures, there are literally millions of variations of any one process. How can we hope to even *list* them all, much less examine the behavior of each under a variety of circumstances?

This almost overwhelming task can be solved by a two-step approach. The first step is to consider processes only in terms of behavior patterns. If many different systems of institutions always behave identically under identical circumstances, then there is no need to study them all. We need only study one from the set, recognizing that all others in the set are behaviorally equivalent. So the idea is to solve first the simpler problem of finding behavior patterns consistent with our principles. Then, having identified the behavior we want, we can attempt to find institutions and rules which induce that behavior.

Consistent with this plan, the first step is to identify what types of behavior are common to all systems. For example, if we define the outcome or outcomes in case of a tie to be the *choice* of the system, then the following two properties seem sufficiently obvious. (1) The *choice* resulting from any system must be one of the feasible options. (2) The *choice* resulting from any system depends in part on the attitudes, preferences, and wants of the people in the system. All systems have both properties.

A third property, which appears to be common to all processes, deserves the status of a principle. People's attitudes about the infeasible alternatives do not affect the outcome of the process, the *social choice,* unless they affect their attitude about the feasible. The choice, at this point, need have nothing to do with a social *preference.* We will name the principle accordingly Independence of Infeasible Alternatives.

Notice that some new concepts have formally entered with this and the last postulate: (1) the set of feasible options, and (2) social choice. There are two different concepts of "feasible set" floating about. The first comes from economics and is based upon physical and technical considerations. The infeasible options are those which one can imagine, but are impossible given the resource base and technology. The second is more akin to parliamentary processes whereby the "feasible" alternatives are those which are in some sense under consideration. The first type of set will be called the *feasible set* and the second type will be called the *contender set.*

The *social choice* is the option that results from the process. Naturally any chosen option must be a feasible option. We can avoid many problems later if we adopt a convention now regarding ties, ill-defined procedures, and even perhaps uncertainty of outcome. To allow for all these possibilities, we do *not* demand that the social choice necessarily be a single option. We can say the choice is a *set* of options as long as we understand that this means one option from the chosen set will ultimately be the outcome, and we need not even develop a term for the latter.

With these ideas in mind we can talk about a *social choice function,* denoted as $C(v,R_1,\ldots,R_n)$. For any actual or imaginary process it designates, for each feasible set v and each array of individual rankings $(R_1, \ldots,R_n)$, the set of options that are outcomes (the "chosen" outcomes). With this notation we can now formally state the principle.

VI. *Independence of Infeasible Alternatives.* Suppose, where $(R_1,\ldots, R_n)$ is an array of rankings, one for each individual, and $(R'_1, \ldots, R'_n)$ is a different array such that for each individual i = 1,2,\ldots,n, R_i and R'_i are identical over all options in the feasible set v, then

$$C(v,R_1,\ldots,R_n) = C(v,R'_1,\ldots,R'_n).$$

The principle says that if the feasible set remains the same and the outcome changes, then the change in outcome must have been due to a change in someone's attitude about some of the *feasible* options. We used the Borda count example. If only $\{w,x,y\}$ are feasible, the points one through three are assigned. If someone's preference for the fourth option, z, changes, it does not affect the numbering of the three feasible alternatives, and thus the social choice is not affected. Furthermore, if the social choice over the feasible set $\{w,x,y\}$ changes, it could be due only to a change in assigned numbers, and thus be due to an altered ranking.

This axiom, which Arrow called Independence of Irrelevant Alternatives, is, historically speaking, the most controversial of all the postulates listed. Much of this controversy is due to a mistake in Arrow's own explanation and defense of the axiom, which differs from the one we are using here.[2] It would be grossly misleading to indicate that all of the controversy is over. For example, we can easily think of procedures which violate the axiom. How then can we say in seemingly bold contradiction that all processes satisfy it?[3]

---

[2] Arrow incorrectly claims that the Borda count *violates* the axiom. The mistake, which was first discovered by Plott (1971), was based on a confusion of this axiom with Principle III above which is, as we have already seen, violated by the Borda count.

[3] Suppose only those who prefer Lincoln to Johnson (neither is feasible), get to vote in the next election. If preferences for these infeasible alternatives change, then the voting population and thus the outcome changes, even though no one's ranking of the feasible options changes. This process does not satisfy Principle VI.

Rather than follow this interesting argument here, we will postpone the discussion for a special section later.

Rational Social Choice

Perhaps it is so trivial that it need not be mentioned that any normative theory of social choice demands a correspondence between what society prefers and what is actually chosen. But if there has been truth in advertising and we are now going down a dead-end road, then we had better be clear about what we have done so we can find our way back.

The principle states that the option that results from the operation of the social process is the socially most preferred of the feasible options, and if there are several options feasible and equally good at the top of the social ranking, then any one of them can result.

VII. *Rational Choice.* If v is the set of feasible options $(R_1, \ldots, R_n)$ are the individual rankings and if $C(v, R_1, \ldots R_n)$ is the resulting social choice, then $C(v, R_1, \ldots, R_n) = \{$the set of options in v which are best, or tied for best, according to the social preference$\}$.

The Problem

Is there a process which does not behave in a paradoxical way? Is there a process that chooses in accord with some conception of a social preference? The answer is yes, but *all* examples are of a particularly distasteful sort. In order to be clear we need to add some summary definitions.

Theorem Statement

Let E be a *universal set of options*. These are all the options you can imagine, whether feasible or not. Just put them together and call them a set. Clearly it is going to be big, but that is OK.

A *social preference definition* is a function which attaches to each pattern (n-tuple) of rankings of E, one ranking for each of the n individuals, a single ranking of the options of E for society. From the first four principles, Preference Transitivity, Indifference Transitivity, Value/Feasibility Separation, and Universal Domain, it makes sense to talk about a social ranking over all of the options of E. Principle V, Responsive, indicates that its particular form is going to be functionally dependent upon individual rankings. Thus, how we define the social preference depends, in part, upon the pattern of individuality preferences, and Principle VI will assure that these are all that count.

A social preference definition is *dictatorial* in case there is an individual i_0 such that either $\{xP_{i_0} y$ implies $xP_s y$ for all x,y and regardless of the rankings of the other individuals$\}$ or perversely $\{xP_{i_0} y$ implies $yP_s x$ for all x,y and regardless of the rankings of the other individuals$\}$. A dictator is an individual whose preference dictates the social preference. By checking his preference *alone* you can determine the social preference. The implication of the dictator's ranking can be either positive or negative. If the implication is positive, then when he ranks any x over any y, the options are ranked the same way in the social preference. If the implication is negative, then whenever he ranks any x over any y, the social ranking between the two options is the *opposite*.

We can now state a theorem based upon Wilson's (1972a) version of the famous *Arrow General Possibility Theorem*.

Theorem. If E has at least three options and $C(v, R_1, \ldots, R_n)$ is the choice function of some process (thereby satisfying Principle VI, Independence of Infeasible Alternatives) and if $C(v, R_1, \ldots, R_n)$
   i) is defined for all finite subsets of E (any subset of E can be a feasible set);
   ii) is connected through Principle VII, Rational Choice, to a social preference definition;
   iii) the social preference definition satisfies Principles I, II, III, (the preference axioms) IV, Universal Domain, and V, Responsive;
then either
   iv) the social preference definition is dictatorial, or
   v) for all x and all y, $xI_s y$ regardless of individual rankings.

That is a mouthful, but what does it mean? It probably means that if you are in agreement with Principles I through VII, then you necessarily have what some would regard as a strange definition of social preference. Either you have defined society to be always indifferent, or your conception of the social preference is defined in terms of the attitude of a single individual who is either always favored, since if he ranks x over y so does society, or always disfavored, since if he ranks x over y society ranks y over x.

There is no question about the validity of this result. The theorem is true. All of our principles seemed reasonable enough, so what is the trick? The answer to that question is simply not in. Each step of the argument must now be retraced with a great deal of care. This reexamination process has been the subject of a great deal of attention.

Implications

Before we go to all that trouble, however, let's look at the stakes. Some, like myself (Plott, 1972) would claim that the concept of social preference itself must go. Buchanan (1954a, b) was right in his original criticism of Arrow, that the concept of social preference involves an illegitimate transfer of the properties of an individual to the properties of a collection of individuals. For me, the Arrow theorem demonstrates that the concept of social preference involves the classic fallacy of composition, and it is shocking only because the thoughts of social philosophers from which we have developed our intuitions about such matters are subject to the same fallacy.

In order to see how extreme this position is, we should investigate first how broadly the theorem can be interpreted, and investigate second the various implicit ways in which our principles of preference can appear. The first problem, that of interpretation, shows up in the following criticism:

A theory of committees and vote tabulation processes has nothing to do with a whole society, with its history, heritage, legal system, rights, etc. It is to whole societies and social systems that the concept of social preference applies.

There is a two-headed answer to this. First, one would expect that concepts like social preference applicable to large complex societies are also applicable in the special case of a simple one. If your ideas get you into trouble in the special case of a small uncomplicated society such as a committee with well-defined options, they will by definition get you into trouble in the general case.

Secondly, the charge is based upon an unnecessarily narrow view about what has been demonstrated. To be sure, the examples involved committees and committee processes, but nothing about the formulation limited the interpretations to these. An option or social alternative could be a complete description of the amount of each type of commodity, the amounts of various types of work done by each individual, the amount of each type of resource used by each firm, the production level of each firm, the type of government agencies and the services provided by each, etc. An option can be a very complicated thing, but its degree of complexity negates none of the arguments above unless it bears on the interpretation of one or more of the principles.

The set of feasible options could be a *consumption possibilities set* and the process could be a competitive process, a capitalistic process, a socialistic process, or any other kind of process.[4] There is no need, for example, for the process to be directed in that some judge, administrator, or planner uses the defined social ranking to determine the best option and then directs its implementation. The process could be any type of game, voting process, market process, political process, etc., as long as the institutions are designed so that the resulting outcomes, equilibriums, winners, etc. are always, as dictated by Principle VII, Rational Choice, "best" according to the social preference ranking. We conclude that there is nothing about the analysis which precludes the application of our results to whole societies.

"Even if the framework does apply to whole societies, what difference does it make? No one really accepts or uses the idea of a social preference anyway, so no one cares if there are deep logical inconsistencies. The whole enterprise is simply an exercise in logic." It is this line of criticism that we will now attempt to refute by demonstrating that many commonly used concepts are equivalent to the concept of a social ranking.

One does not have to look far to find concepts like social needs, group wants, etc. These are simply expressions of priorities and are thus rankings of options. In other words, they all imply the same technical properties as preference. Ideas about what is good for society are no different. If option x is better for society than option y and option y is better for society than option z, then option x is better than option z. The word "preference" does not appear, but this is clearly a statement of Principle I with "better" replacing "preference." All of the arguments apply without modification. The key observation here is that possibly different substantive concepts, e.g., the "preferred" as opposed to the "best," have the same technical properties, and these technical properties cause the problem.

Even more formalized concepts suffer from the same difficulty. Take for example the concept of economic welfare. To different options one attaches a number, perhaps computed from certain types of economic considerations, indicating the level of economic welfare. Certain forms of cost-benefit analysis are attempts to operationalize such a formula. But indicators of social welfare clearly imply a ranking of social options according to the numbers which indicate the levels of welfare. The ranking satisfies all of our principles of social preference, and thus the theorem stands as a criticism of any such

[4] The term comes from economics. It refers to all possible ways in which final consumption goods can be distributed among members of society, given that the only limitations are resources and the production capacity of the society.

formula. The only admissible definitions of welfare are those which are dictatorial.

Rawls (1971) has diagrams which give rather explicit shapes to the social ranking. Society is better off with one distribution of primary goods over another if the worst-off person is better off. Since this ranking satisfies all of our principles of social preference it follows that, if he is theorizing about processes, thereby picking up the remainder of our principles, his system has the same problems as do all others. In this particular case it seems as though the only admissible definition of the worst-off person, a definition which he does not supply, is that the worst-off person always remains the same person, even in the extreme case in which he has acquired all the primary goods in society (Plott, 1974).

So, we can see that social choice theorists have a potential audience larger than themselves. The major results do have profound and broad implications. Let's turn now to a detailed discussion of the principles.

The Analysis: An Overview

The problem was, and is, that when we are precise and clear about our intuitive notions about social actions, we discover delicacies and inconsistencies which we had no idea existed. Is the problem that our precise statements fail to capture our notions? Or, are our notions actually wrong? Or, have we simply imposed a technical feature on the analysis which, once modified, will eliminate all the problems?

How one proceeds on these questions, what principles are first examined and how they are modified, is heavily dependent upon the idiosyncracies and philosophical persuasions of the investigator. The analysis has different implications for different philosophies. Moreover, the formal statements of the principles can be interpreted in a variety of different ways. For example, the Independence of Infeasible Alternatives can be interpreted as a normative statement which *should,* according to some, be embodied in any social preference definition; it can be interpreted as defining a type of binary voting process only (Pattanaik, 1971); it can be interpreted as a type of information conserving process (Brown, 1973a); it can be viewed as a principle which prohibits intensity considerations (Sen, 1970a); it can be confused with Principle III (Ray, 1973); it can be modified to imply Principles I and II (Hansson, 1969a; 1973); it can be interpreted as above, etc., etc., etc. So, a conclusion that "Principle X is the real problem" must always be relative to some particular interpretation of the whole set of principles and the purpose of the enterprise. Principles which can be disregarded on one interpretation, and thus "solve" the dilemma, are absolutely essential to some other interpretation. So, by the time we take all the possible philosophies together with all the possible interpretations of the principles, we have a very large number of possible implications of the analysis.

As we proceed then, to survey some of the known results, we must be careful not to judge them from one point of view alone. Furthermore, as the reader probes deeper into the papers referenced here, he should not expect to find other authors motivated by the interpretations I have developed; or by some single interpretation; or indeed by any interpretation at all. Many believe that a deeper understanding of how the simple mathematical logic itself works may be the very thing we need to remove the paradoxes; so they legitimately analyze the mathematics involved without regard for interpretations.

The Pareto Principle

The Pareto Principle comes in two forms. One is a statement of a normative position, while the other is a statement of a possible behavioral law. The normative version is:

VIII. *Pareto Principle.* If x is available and everyone ranks x above y, then y should not be chosen.

This axiom was part of the original Arrow system of axioms. Within a social preference framework where choice is necessarily generated by a preference, it would be stated "If everyone prefers x to y, then society prefers x to y."

There has been a great deal of unnecessary confusion about this axiom. Contrary to what many think, the axiom does *not* demand unanimity as a condition for the determination of social preference. It does *not* say "If society prefers x to y, then everyone prefers x to y." It only says that *when* there is unanimity the social preference is determined, and it may also be determined in many other cases as well. To deny the axiom would be to accept the position that there are cases in which everyone in the society prefers x to y but society does not. Put this way, the axiom would seem to be part of any libertarian philosophy and could be listed along with Principle V as part of the normative structure of a social preference definition.

The second statement of the axiom is a statement along behavioral lines: "If everyone ranks x over y and x is feasible, then y *will not* be chosen." This is a hypothesis about the possible long-run tendency of social systems. Postulates like this are frequently found in coalition theories, for example.

Any system that consistently violated this principle, the thesis maintains, would soon evolve into a different system. Institutions which induce prisoner's dilemmas and the resulting inefficiencies for societies as a whole are not viable and will soon be transformed.[5] The boundaries of this thesis are still under investigation, but if it is thought to be generally correct, then it should be listed along with the Independence of Infeasible Alternatives as a natural property of processes.

Regardless of how this axiom is interpreted we know one thing for sure. It is not the cause of the problem outlined above, since it was *not* part of our formulation even though it was part of Arrow's. Our principles imply that there must be either a "positive" dictator who always gets what he wants most or a "negative" dictator who always gets what he wants least. If we add the Pareto Principle then, due to a theorem proved by Wilson (1972a), the *only* change is the removal of the latter "negative" dictator.

So regardless of the interpretation of the Pareto Principle, it can hold all of the time, part of the time, or never; its acceptance, rejection, or modification does nothing to help us out of the dilemma with which we started.

The Domain of Social Preference

Somehow we got from a lot of principles to a position where we are expecting our social preference definition and social choice process to do a lot for us. In particular, we expect our social preference definition to handle every pair of options, regardless of the pattern of conflict (Principle IV, Universal Domain).[6] Secondly, we expect our social choice process to yield a result when *any possible* subset of options is feasible, and regardless of the pattern of conflict (Principle VII, Rational Choice). Have we been unrealistic and demanded more than is necessary here? It would be easy to say yes if some reasonable consequences followed from relaxing these principles.

Notice, now, that to play this tune, we have a lot of strings to touch. We can say that the social ranking need not be defined over every pair of options, or we can say that it need not be defined for every pattern of conflict, or we can use some combination of the two. We can alter Principle IV, Universal Domain, and a "technical" requirement buried in a footnote, and say that for

---

[5] For definitions and examples of prisoner dilemma games see Luce and Raiffa (1957).

[6] The reader will recall that we had some additional "technical" requirements listed in footnote 1. The important thrust of those assumptions was completeness. For *every* pair of options we had either preference or indifference.

certain special options, the social ranking need not be defined.[7] The social preference would be "incomplete." Alternatively, we can say that for certain patterns of conflict, certain configurations of individual rankings of the options, the social ranking need not be defined for *any* pair of options. That is, society would not be indifferent but neither would it have a ranking. The idea, then, is to limit the patterns of conflict for which the definition applies. Of course we have to worry about Principle VII, since it demands that the social choice be "preference based" regardless of the pattern of conflict, but perhaps we can take care of that.

So basically, the idea is to either allow the preference definition to be incomplete over pairs, or limit the pattern of individual rankings that we wish to consider, or both. The former route begins to raise rather serious problems, both technical and philosophical, with our original formulations. It requires a reformulation of our original demands, the full consequences of which are currently unknown. What does it mean to say, on some occasion when society by definition prefers x to y and y to z, that the ranking between x and z is undefined? From a technical and mathematical point of view, there is no problem with this, but the interpretation, relative to our original examples, has yet to be thrashed out. See Fishburn (1973b, 1974d).

The second route, placing limitations on the pattern of conflict, is also difficult, but here there has been some advanced scouting. In some sense we would like to know over what domain, what patterns of individual rankings or what patterns of conflict, do we not get "impossibility results." Unfortunately, that problem has not even been well formulated, much less answered, but we do have answers to some "closely related" questions which seem to indicate that this whole line of questioning is not the path to follow.

Theorem. If all our principles were modified to operate over certain limited patterns of rankings across the set of individuals, then there is a dictator over every "free" triple of alternatives.

A *"free" triple* is a set of three alternatives for which the social preference is defined for all patterns of rankings of the three alternatives across individuals. The theorem, due to Murakami (1961), says that for every three-element set over which we fail to restrict the patterns of conflict and on which the social preference is defined, we pick up a dictator. This dictator of the social preference over a three-element set may also necessarily be a dictator over

---

[7] Footnote 6 applies here also.

some other three-element set as well—it depends upon the general pattern of restrictions. So, even if you are willing to live with dictators over three-element sets, you must strategically choose the patterns of conflict you are willing to consider; otherwise you will end up with only one dictator, and the process of picking these conflicts is going to be tedious and perhaps without motivation or interpretation. Of course we will know a lot more once the pure mathematical problem is solved.

Other studies have taken the more indirect route of studying particular processes. The process of simple majority rule has received the most attention, with the outstanding question being: Over what patterns of conflict does majority rule cycle? There are two answers, depending upon how one interprets the term "patterns of conflict."

The Inada-Pattanaik-Sen approach has been to try to isolate a set of rankings of the alternatives such that if each individual in society has a ranking which is a member of this set, then the majority rule preference would be transitive.[8] As a trivial application of the approach, take a set which has only two rankings. If every individual in society has one of these two rankings, then there can be no majority rule cycle (the reader is invited to try to find one). The mathematical problem is to get the set as "big" as possible, and the interpretive problem is to see if there is any reason to believe that individual ranks would, or perhaps should, be restricted to such a set.

Now that the mathematical part has been answered, the answer to the interpretive part appears to be "no." We have now, as a result of recent research, a set of axioms with the properties:

i) If a set of rankings satisfy these axioms and if each individual has a ranking from the set, then the majority preference is transitive.

ii) If a set of rankings does not satisfy the axioms, then there is a pattern of conflict, such that the ranking of each individual is in the set and the majority preference cycles.

The set of axioms is very restrictive and to date has not been successfully applied at either the behavioral level or normative level. For an excellent, detailed analysis of the extremely restrictive nature of the complete set of axioms relative to usual assumptions in behavioral models regarding the form of individual preferences, the reader should consult Kramer (1974). When the number of alternatives is large, using this axiom set is almost like assuming unanimity.

---

[8] For a good summary see Fishburn (1973) or Sen (1971).

The second approach is to try to place restrictions on the patterns of conflict directly. In the case of majority rule, what patterns of conflicts cause cycles? The news is bad. Essentially, all patterns for which there is no indifference cause problems. Studies which examined the probability of the Paradox (DeMeyer and Plott, 1970; Garman and Kamien, 1968; Niemi and Weisberg, 1968; Pomeranz and Weil, 1970; Gehrlein and Fishburn, 1975) have found that when indifference is not allowed and all individual rankings occur at random, the probability of a cycle becomes *one* as the number of alternatives grows large. The approach is also very rapid.

So the news shapes up as follows. Patterns of conflict which do not cause problems form a set of measure zero in the set of all possible conflicts. In a sense, the set of "trouble free" patterns of conflict is "infinitely small" when put against the background of all possible patterns of conflict. If we are to follow this route, we need some justification for focusing on this very small (relative to the whole set) pattern of conflicts. Suppose, for example, people always have "similar" attitudes. What happens then? If one defines "similar" to mean the proportion of people whose preferences can be put on a single "scale" the answer can be found in Niemi (1969). A measure of "social homogeneity" is developed by Fishburn (1973b) and another by Jamison and Luce (1973). An index of "voter antagonism," based upon the number of pairs of individuals whose preferences are in conflict, is developed by Kuga and Nagatani (1974) and related to the frequency of cycles. To make a long story short, one can conclude that as similarity among preferences decreases, then the likelihood of a majority cycle increases. Currently we have no theoretical reason to suspect that any of these indexes tend to be "low," but there is some evidence (Jamison, 1975) which suggests that the theory might be overly pessimistic.

What happens if we don't require the majority preference relation to be transitive? After all, it might not hurt if there is a cycle as long as it is not on top. Why not simply demand that there is a majority winner over everything else? This means that we would be willing to accept a case where w is preferred by a majority to x, y, and z, and therefore "wins" even though there is a cycle among x, y, and z. It is a great idea, but it flies directly in the face of Principle I. Furthermore, our willingness to compromise like this buys us very little in the case of majority rule. Conditions on conflicts which assure the existence of such a majority winner were worked out for certain cases by Plott (1967), and for an expanded class of cases by Sloss (1973). In addition, the probability was examined by DeMeyer and Plott (1970). The news remains sad. Our compromise bought us nothing. The theoretical probability of such a majority winner as the number of alternatives grows to infinity is conjectured to be zero. Of course, until someone proves it there is always a ray of hope.

Well, so much for majority rule. What about the existence of *some* preference definition? Can't we at least get away from the impossibility results by limiting the pattern of conflicts? Several results on this broader problem can be found in Fishburn (1973a). The outlook is not good, however. This path has become exceedingly narrow and slippery. Perhaps we had better return to where we started and try another route.

The Number of People

The impossibility theorem stated above made no assumptions about the number of people except that the number is finite. What happens if this assumption is removed? The question is interesting primarily because it gives us insight into the technical structure of the problem. If impossibility problems do not occur when there are infinite numbers of people, perhaps we need to rethink our formulations. After all, many models of social behavior proceed as if the population were infinitely large (Riker and Ordeshook, 1973). When we use proportions and percentages to describe populations and assume these percentages are continuous, we are making an implicit assumption about the size of the population.[9] This would not be the first time that the assumption of a continuum has provided just the proper sloppiness to make a model work, and if it does work then perhaps we should explore those interpretations within which such an assumption might make sense.

Fishburn (1970) posed the problem and provided us with what seemed to be a positive result. If all of our conditions are satisfied and if there is an infinite number of people, then there need not be a dictator.

The optimism generated by the Fishburn result was soon erased by Kirman and Sondermann (1972). In the infinite case, our concepts necessarily generate a peculiar type of "invisible dictator" which can only exist in the infinite case. There always exists a set of individuals which dictates (if this set is unanimous for x over y, then society prefers x over y). Furthermore, *any such set necessarily contains a proper subset which also has dictatorial powers.* So while no single person is dictator, the set of people who have dictatorial powers is "infinitely small." In order to see this, imagine people distributed continuously along a line, with each point representing a person.

---

[9] If there are only ten people, it is impossible for exactly 95 percent of them to have any particular characteristic.

Some dictatorial set then could be taken as an interval. The result says that there is also a proper subset of this set which is also dictatorial.[10]

So, what momentarily appeared to be a trail turns out to be a dead end. Allowing the population to be infinite does not help at all. Let's go back again and pick up another path.

Independence of Infeasible Alternatives

Here we are at the most controversial principle in the whole constitution. As we explore this, the reader should be informed of two related facts. First, there is a great deal of confusion about the axiom, due primarily to Arrow. He chose a poor example to illustrate its meaning. In fact, because of this confusion we have used the word "infeasible," following Fishburn (1973a), instead of Arrow's term "irrelevant" in the axiom's name. Second, the argument and interpretation we will give is "new" in the sense that it is not fully integrated into the literature. Our position was first advanced in Plott (1971) and is followed up in a few places, but it is fair to say that it has not withstood the test of a long period of professional scrutiny.

As it is stated, our axiom says nothing at all about the social preference definition. It operates completely independently of any such concept. It says that *if* the feasible set remains fixed and *if* individuals' preferences over the feasible options remain fixed, *then* the social *choice* remains fixed. This has been a source of great confusion, since many people state the axiom in terms of the social preference definition as opposed to the choice as we have done.[11] Since stating the axiom in terms of a social preference definition would foreclose our freedom of examining the axiom independently of a social preference definition, we wish to avoid any such ties.[12]

---

[10] How could two sets be dictatorial? Notice that the preference of a dictator is *sufficient* to determine a social preference, but it is not *necessary*. If he prefers x to y, then so does society, but if he is indifferent, someone else's preference can prevail. The original theorem is actually that there is a sequence of dictators. The preference determining powers of any one of them would exist only in those cases where those in front of him are indifferent. We should also add, for the mathematically inclined, that the "measure" of such a set may indeed be large. Currently no theorems have exploited the various measure theoretic possibilities.

[11] The axiom would become: "The social preference between x and y depends only upon the pattern of individual preferences for x and y, and not upon any preferences for z." See Mayston (1974).

[12] See Hansson (1973) for an unjustified criticism of our position. The claim there is that Arrow did not do what we are doing. The answer is that if he didn't do it the way

This principle tells us that certain types of model behavior are inconsistent with the behavior of any possible real system. It is based on a presumption that there are (natural) behavioral principles (laws) which govern the behavior of all social systems. If such laws exist, they carry implications for the normative problem of finding a social preference definition. We are, after all, fundamentally interested in finding an acceptable decisionmaking system, and our search for a social preference definition is a means to that end. If the implementation of a social preference definition requires system behavior in violation of such laws, then we would reject the definition on practical grounds, if not moral grounds as well ("ought" implies "can").

Where are such general behavioral principles to be found? The one we use is a property of *all* of our current societal models. It is a property of general economic models, spatial models of politics—any of our current game theoretic, cooperative or noncooperative models. Whether or not one can design systems that both work and violate the proposed law remains to be seen.

Remember, the principle says that preference changes for infeasible options will not change the social choice—the process outcome (unless preferences change for the feasible as well). Let's take, as an example of a proposed process that violates the principle, a process similar to the Borda count, and see why we think it (as a process) will not work. Suppose we are choosing from a list of candidates $\{w,x,y,z\}$, who will receive an offer as full professor. To this list is added a set of four infeasible candidates, James Madison, Thomas Jefferson, J. S. Mill, and Karl Marx, giving a total list of eight candidates. Each member of the appointment committee is to rank all eight candidates according to his evaluations and assign each candidate the value of his rank, with the lowest ranked receiving the number 1. If, for example, your ranking, R, from first to last was Madison, Jefferson, feasible candidates w, x, y, then Mill, feasible candidate z, and Marx, you would assign them the numbers 8, 7, 6, 5, 4, 3, 2, and 1, respectively. Now the *feasible* candidate with the highest total score will receive the appointment. This process, the argument claims, violates the principle. In order to see this, the argument would go: simply notice that if you changed your mind about Madison and Jefferson, two infeasible candidates, and ranked them just below x, then each of w and x would, in your new ranking, R', receive two points more, which could conceivably be enough to change the total vote outcome, making one of them the winner. Notice now that relative to each other, preferences for feasible alternatives have remained the same between the two situations, but the social choice is (by assumption that this change in total points was enough to change the outcome) different. This is *exactly* the type of behavior our principle declares that no process has, and yet here we see it. The critic would say the principle is wrong and should be discarded.

Have we demonstrated that the principle is wrong and should be discarded? It is not that easy. The justification of the principle against this attack rests on a deeper (game theoretic) principle about the natural strategic behavior of individuals involved in such a process. The situation we have postulated presupposes a type of "honest" reporting of preferences which could not have occurred according to this theory. If you could have been sure of changing the outcome to some more favorable outcome by some slight "misrepresentation" of your preferences, you would have done so. It could never have been to your advantage to "honestly" report your first ranking, R. Since neither Madison nor Jefferson could possibly be chosen, you have nothing to lose by reporting them as being ranked lower than they really are. The consequence of this behavior is to break the ties between your preferences for the infeasible options and what you report. You would report what you see as strategically most advantageous. Since your strategic advantages have nothing to do with your preferences for infeasible options, what you report has nothing to do with such preferences. Consequently, if preferences for the infeasible change (without some change for the feasible) you will not change what you report, and thus the process outcome will not change. But that is exactly what Principle VI, Independence of Infeasible Alternatives, declares. We conclude that the proposed process could not behave as reported, and the principle remains intact.

With the argument above we can begin to get a feeling for what we are up against. We might quibble about whether or not people *always* behave in such a "dishonest" manner, but that would miss the point. In order to use a process which violates Principle VI we must be assured (given our current understanding) that individuals will *never* behave strategically, and that is an entirely different thing.

Well, we can see that we picked a bad example, but how can we generalize Principle VI to *all* processes? That is done by relying on the theory of games. As it turns out, all processes, at least all reported to date, can be modeled within the game theoretic framework. Anything you have seen or can describe can be modeled as a game, or so the game theoretic practitioners would claim. If you have seen it, then they can model it. This is not to say that their job would be easy or practical. It may take them a lifetime or two to do it, but that is due to the current limitations of mathematics, etc., and does not bear upon the validity of principles which may govern their models.

Almost all game theoretic models satisfy our principle. The qualifier "almost" is there for a purpose and signals the existence of a path which might be fruitfully followed. Before seeing where it goes, let's examine the two major categories of the game theoretic models—*noncooperative games* and *cooperative games*. The relationship between our principles and *noncooperative games* was first formally introduced by Plott (1971). In the noncooperative game setup, each individual has partial control over the option resulting from the process. Voting is only one way such controls are manifested. In general, each individual has his own set of feasible actions from which he is free to choose. The social choice is the option which results from any particular pattern of individual actions—each from his own set of feasible actions. Suppose, for example, a group of two people in isolation from all other considerations is to choose the overall room temperature in a room with two heating units, each being controlled by a different individual. Each, then, has a set of feasible actions defined by the technological capabilities of the heater under his control. Each has partial control over the social options (overall room temperature). Game theory seeks an understanding of the choices each individual would make, given his preferences among the various room temperatures, his recognition of the interdependence between the two, etc. There are several competing models, within this general model, which predict the outcome. The most widely accepted is the Nash equilibrium model, which holds that the two will jockey around their individual dials until they reach an overall temperature—a social choice—such that neither, by changing his dial alone, can improve upon the situation according to his own tastes. More complicated theories have each individual maintaining some theory about how the other individual will react to any change he might make, etc. The general and profound message is, however, that none of these theories about what the outcome will be rely upon how either individual feels about room temperatures which cannot be achieved. The choice, then, is independent of preferences for infeasible options.[13]

---

[13] This can be formalized as follows: Let A_i be the set of actions reserved for individual i and let the Cartesian product $E = \prod_{i=1}^{n} A_i$ be the universal set of social actions. If $v \subset E$, let $A_i(v)$ be the projection of v on A_i and let the admissible sets of v be $\left\{ v : \prod_{i=1}^{n} A_i(v) = v \right\}$. The choice function is defined as $C(v, R_1, \ldots, R_n)$ where R_i are rankings of E. The Nash equilibriums can then be defined as $N(v, R_1, \ldots, R_n) = \left\{ (\bar{a}_i, \ldots, \bar{a}_n) \in v : (\bar{a}_i, \ldots, \bar{a}_{i-1}, \bar{a}_i, \bar{a}_{i+1}, \ldots, \bar{a}_n) \, R_i \, (\bar{a}_1, \ldots, \bar{a}_{i-1}, a_i, a_{i+1}, \ldots, a_n) \right.$ for all $a_i \in A_i(v)$ and all i $\}$. If $C(v, R_1, \ldots, R_n) \subset N(v, R_1, \ldots, R_n) \neq \phi$, then C(v,

What about *cooperative games*? The key idea there is the idea of dominance which Wilson (1971a, 1972b), Bloomfield and Wilson (1972), and Bloomfield (1976) have integrated into the social choice framework. An option x is said to *dominate* an option y in case there is some group of people each of whom prefers x to y and who collectively have "the power to implement x over y." Dominance then is the coincidence of "power" and preference.[14]

In order to get from the concept of dominance to the actual outcome of the process, *solution concepts* are used. Solution concepts are models which use the idea of dominance as a basic parameter in predicting which options, from a large set of options, will be the resultant group choice. There are several competing solution concepts. For example, the *core* of a set of feasible options is a set of options, each of which is feasible and each of which is undominated by any other feasible option. An application of the resulting "core model" would be a prediction that the option resulting from the process would be some member of the core.[15]

There are other solution concepts as well, but they all share with the core the property that the predicted outcome depends *only* upon the dominance configuration among the feasible options and not the infeasible options. So as long as the dominance relation does not depend upon individuals' preference for infeasible options, then our Principle VI, Independence of Infeasible Alternatives, is satisfied.

We can now see what a process must look like if Principle VI and the resulting consequences are to be avoided. The "rights and powers" of individuals and groups must be sensitive to and depend upon their opinions about infeasible options. All processes which do not conform to the restrictions imposed by Principle VI can be found among those in which what you can do depends upon what you *would* do in some hypothetical situations. To date no one has found such a process. The focus of the research effort is clear, but the outlook is dim, as will be discovered in the section of *strategyproof processes*.

So here we are. Principle VI has done a pretty good job of surviving. It is

---

$R_1, \ldots, R_n$) satisfies Principle VI. Note there are obvious difficulties with existence, etc., but those are not our concern here.

[14] Let N be the set of individuals and let $\Delta(x,y) = \left\{ C \subset N : C \text{ has the power to implement x over y} \right\}$. We can say that x dominates y in case there is a $C \in \Delta(x,y)$ such that xP_iy for all $i \in C$.

[15] We can say that $C(v, R_1, \ldots, R_n) = \left\{ x \in v : yD(R_1, \ldots, R_n)x \text{ for } no \ y \in v \right\}$.

tarnished and damaged a little, but it is clearly still in the air. Certainly the rubble in this path cannot be removed by simple handwaving. Let's go back.

Cardinal Utilities

This problem is so complicated that it would take a book-length paper simply to explore all of its facets. First, the concept of cardinal utility itself is unclear. Different scholars use the word to mean different things. Secondly, what it means to "compare utilities" across people has not been clearly specified. If we have numbers representing people's attitudes, it is easy to find many nice functions (Hildreth, 1953; Harsanyi, 1955; DeMeyer and Plott, 1971; Sen, 1976), so it is tempting to claim that the "obvious" way around the problem is to allow interpersonal comparison of utilities. Judging from the comments one finds in the literature, the urge to represent individual attitudes by something more than rankings is almost overwhelming. However, the numbers must be interpreted, and close examination suggests that there is nothing simple or obvious about how one might proceed.

Let's digress a little on the meaning of cardinal utility. What does it mean to say that someone has "cardinal utility"? The textbook answer is that he has a utility function unique up to linear (affine) transformations, but that simply induces the same question with "unique up to linear (affine) transformation" substituted for "cardinal utility." What does it mean to have one of those? Unfortunately there are several answers, none of which seem to get to the heart of the ethical question about how society should choose, which we would like answered. We consider only two here.

The first answer comes from the decisionmaking-under-uncertainty literature. Certain preference rankings of lotteries are structured *as if* there is a utility value attached to each lottery outcome and as if each lottery is ranked according to the utility it is expected to yield. For example, consider lottery one, which yields one apple with probability P_A and one orange with probability P_O; and consider lottery two, which yields an apple with probability P'_A and an orange with probability P'_O. Some rankings over these two lotteries, along with others, are structured *as if* the apple would yield a utility (experience?) of magnitude U_A and the orange would yield one of U_O, and lottery one would be ranked over lottery two in case $P_A U_A + P_O U_O > P'_A U_A + P'_O U_O$. Now the words "utility," "experience," and "magnitude" have not been defined. Furthermore, they *have never* been defined and *need not* be defined for this conception of cardinal utility. Any numbers will do for U_A and U_O as long as the resulting expectation calculations yield a ranking of the lotteries identical with the preference ranking under consideration. But wait a minute! Why are there *two* concepts here—expectation *and* preference ranking? The answer is that there aren't. There is only a preference ranking. We just search around for numbers which allow us to express the ranking *as if* expectation calculations were going on.

What do these numbers have to do with our ethical problem? Well, they are "cardinal utilities" in the sense they are "unique to linear (affine) transformations" but they carry no more information at all than the simple ranking of lotteries from which they were derived. Don't they express "intensity of desire"? Only in the same sense that your willingness to pay a maximum of $.25 for an apple and a maximum of $.05 for an orange expresses an "intensity of desire." They only express the fact that you are indifferent among the following three options: (1) you have the $.25 and no apple and no orange, (2) you do not have the $.25 and have no orange but you do have the apple, (3) you have $.20 and the orange but you have no apple. Nothing more than a ranking is involved. This type of intensity was never prohibited by our formulation of the problem (Campbell, 1973). Intensities like this were permissible all along, since they only amount to a ranking and we still obtained an impossibility result.

What happened? Our original problem formulation was much broader than you might have expected, and in addition this conception of "cardinal utility" may have been much narrower than you wanted. By allowing lotteries to be among the options, in the same way that we allow money in hand to be a dimension of options, we have no "external" measure of tradeoffs, and thus are left with rankings alone. This is probably of little consequence, since few would accept "desire to pay" as a measure of intensity on which to ultimately base moral judgments. Our desire to pay is obviously sensitive to income. Likewise, tradeoffs between lotteries are likely to be judged inadequate because they are "sensitive to attitudes towards risk." Judging intensity in terms of the distance one would run in order to have one option over another depends upon "attitude towards running" and judging in terms of the height of a cliff from which one would jump in order to have one option over another depends upon "attitude towards height," etc.

So there are many measures of intensity. They have all been well recognized for years but for some reason none have received universal or even partial acclaim. Why not? Perhaps they do not sit well with our intuitive notions about what an intensity measure should give us. Perhaps we are wanting more information than is contained in a simple ranking, but what could it be?

The leading interpretation of what we are asking is that we want to know for every set of four options, say $\{w,x,y,z\}$, whether an individual's preference for option w over option x is greater or less than his preference for option y over option z (Alt, 1971). The information needed then, in addition to the preference ranking over options, is an additional ranking over pairs of options. By now we are accustomed to roadblocks, so let's see what they look like here.

The first and most obvious problem is one of establishing the existence of the ranking over pairs of options as opposed to simply a ranking over options. A preference ranking over options can be objectively connected to choice behavior through the theory of revealed preference (Richter, 1966, 1971). Another easier, but perhaps more controversial, way is to assume that the word "preference" means something, perhaps even the same thing, to everyone. So, if you simply ask people for their preference, their answer can be taken as meaningful. However, the idea of a ranking over pairs of options does not seem to have this operational support. There are folks out there, e.g., me, who would claim that a ranking over pairs of options has no general, unique meaning. What do you do with a person who, when asked if his preference for w over x is greater than his preference for y over z, responds by saying that he does not understand the question? He may be willing to order "similarity" between pairs of options; he would say, for example, that the similarity between w and x was greater than the similarity between y and z, but is unable to substitute the word "preference" in this context.

The impulse is to probe, using new words like desire, want, strength, and using the fact that almost everyone has some experience to which he will simultaneously attach the words "intense" and "feeling," until you have found a question that he will answer and which does indeed yield an ordering over pairs of options. Thermometer questions, "How warm do you feel toward x?" seem to be of this sort. But once the ordering is obtained by one means or another, we face a new problem even though the intensity data might be used to accurately predict behavior. What moral significance can one associate with it? The very probing required to get the data has created the possibility that the individual has simply substituted for the question one of the measures that we have already rejected (amount he would pay, height of cliff, etc.) as a basis for moral judgments, even though such substitution would make no difference at all for scientific and prediction purposes. How do we guard against that? I don't think the answer is known.

Problems do not stop here. Even if some concept of cardinal utility can be established as a basis for moral judgments, we face some new and different problems. First, there is a problem of constructing an acceptable social preference definition from the cardinal data as opposed to the ordinal data with which we have been attempting to deal, and secondly, there is a problem of designing a system which will be sensitive to these data.

How do we define the social preference to use accepted measures of "utility"? We are facing, of course, the problem here on interpersonal comparisons. It is not a simple job of adding up numbers, since our data are in the form of rankings of pairs of options. We have no "unit" and no "zero" on which to fix a scale. As it turns out, we have just as delicate a problem here as we did with our original problem when we only had rankings of options to work with. A fundamental impossibility result based on cardinal utilities can be found in Schwartz (1970, 1972). The problem is that very reasonable principles regarding how one uses these new data lead immediately to contradictions.

Since the Schwartz result might not be the ultimate impasse, let's continue to look ahead. Suppose we have an acceptable social preference definition based on such data. How are we going to design a process which uses it? Independence of Infeasible Alternatives, Principle VI, tells us that processes in general are not sensitive to rankings of *pairs* of options. They are only sensitive to the rankings of options. For example, one of the major conclusions of nineteenth century economic theorists was that the existence of cardinal utility was unnecessary for an explanation of the workings of an economic system. The system will work the same regardless of the magnitude of cardinal utilities, as long as the ordinal utilities remain the same. Principle VI is telling us that even if the relevant parameters are in the social preference definition, the system will not act on them.

So, we are stuck, even here, with our original impossibility result. Unless we can come up with some new kind of process which systematically uses these "intensity" data, we are blocked. The problem is now one that was discussed earlier. If the process is sensitive to individual rankings of pairs, and if it is not dictatorial, you will report whatever ranking of pairs is to your advantage to report. Your strategic behavior causes the outcome to be something other than what society by definition prefers, thereby causing Principle VII, Rational Choice, to be violated. Since no one else can *see* your ranking of pairs, your strategic behavior cannot be prevented. For an example see Dyer and Miles (1976).

There are even complicating factors. A natural way to proceed is to try to design a two-stage process. The first would systematically entice you to reveal your true ranking of pairs, while the second would use the information about your true preferences, thus obtained, as inputs to determine the social choice. But this direction has been shown by Gibbard (1973) and Satterthwaite (1975) to lead to dead ends. They have concluded that within a wide class of specifications, the necessary initial process does not exist.

So here we are once again facing a return trip. By simply claiming that we plan to use the concept of cardinal utility, we solve no problems at all. Unless one can see how to tiptoe through the objections, this route must be declared a dead end. However, like the other paths, this one does not really end in the middle of space with absolutely no forward alternative left, but what remains is definitely a job for a dedicated creative scout. Let's go back.

The Transitivity Axioms

Well, we've examined most of the principles now, and have failed to discharge or even successfully modify any of them. Only Principles I, II, III, and VII remain. Principles I and II, Preference and Indifference Transitivity, set forth some of the technical properties we might expect a social preference to have. Principles III, Value/Feasibility Separation, and VII, Rational Choice, on the other hand, form the very basis for using a concept like social preference in the first place. If those are removed, then we have really changed the nature of the whole enterprise. Let's try I and II first.

Even in the case of individual choice there is evidence that I and II do not *always* hold. Recall, we obtained these principles by an analogy to individual preference, so we have ample justification for exploring what might result if they are removed or modified.

What happens if we remove condition II, the requirement that the social indifference is always transitive? That means we are willing to live with situations when xI_sy and yI_sz but xP_sz. Society is indifferent between x and y and it is, by definition, indifferent between y and z but, with nothing at all changed, it prefers x to z. The social indifference is no longer required to be transitive, but of course the social preference relation is still transitive. For technical reasons, attitudes with this property are called quasi-transitive.

The answer was supplied in Sen (1970a, pp. 76–77), Mas-Colell and Sonnenschein (1972, Theorem 1).

Theorem. If Principle II is removed, V is replaced by the Pareto Principle, and if all other conditions are retained, then there exists a set of individuals, say c, such that for any pair of options, $\{x,y\}$, if xP_iy for all members i of c, then xP_sy.[16] Furthermore, if xP_iy for some member(s) of c and yP_ix for some other member(s), then xI_sy.

The theorem says that the *only* social preference definitions which are consistent with our set of principles are oligarchies. That is, there must

---

[16] If the group is unanimously indifferent, then there could be a "second order" group which "takes over" in lexicographic fashion, the powers of the first group.

necessarily exist a set of individuals such that when they are united, unanimous in preference, then the social preference is decided, and if they are in conflict, then society is indifferent. If they are not in conflict, then any social "nonindifferences" must be due to unanimity among a second coalition (possibly disjoint from the first) which is unanimous in opinion and which has "powers" which become active only when the first coalition is indifferent.

Though oligarchy is probably better than dictatorship, this type of social preference definition is not likely to win wide acclaim. If one is opposed to oligarchy, then some other principle must be altered. What happens if, in addition to eliminating Principle II, we alter Principle I as follows?

I'. *Acyclicity.* The social preference is not cyclic. That is, for no sequence of options, $x_1, x_2, \ldots, x_m$, do we have $x_1 P_s x_2$ and $x_2 P_s x_3$ and ... and $x_{m-1} P_s x_m$ and $x_m P_s x_1$.

The requirement that the social preference be transitive, i.e., $x P_s y$ and $y P_s z$ implies $x P_s z$, has been dropped. Instead we require that the social preference is *not* cyclic. We rule out behavior like $x P_s y$ and $y P_s z$ and $z P_s x$, so we know that $x P_s y$ and $y P_s z$ imply that either $x I_s z$ or $x P_s z$ is the case. If we make this change, we are no longer free to speak at all of a social preference *ranking.* No longer will it necessarily make sense to talk about the second and third best, etc,, which form the essence of the concept of a ranking.[17] Instead we can speak of a *social acceptability relation,* which will be designated as R_s.[18] By $x R_s y$ we will mean that x is just as acceptable as is y; by $x P_s y$ we will mean $x R_s y$ but *not* $y R_s x$; and by $x I_s y$ we will mean $x R_s y$ *and* $y R_s x$. In this new jargon our Principle I' has the implication that for any finite set of feasible options, there necessarily exist some options that are just as acceptable as any other feasible option in the set (Sen, 1970a, Lemma

---

[17] Suppose we have xIz, xPy, yPz. Now x seems clearly acceptable, since it is just as acceptable as both y and z, but we would probably hesitate to say that it is *ranked* first, since it is not clear what would be *ranked* second. One might argue that y should be ranked second, but notice that there would be some ambiguity, since we would be ranking it above z, which is just as acceptable as the thing ranked first. Thus we can see that in cases like this the concept of a ranking is not really appropriate.

[18] You will not find this term in the literature. Instead, the term social preference relation is generally used, even though the term preference can be confusing because it does *not* mean the P_s we have been using. The P_s is called *strict* preference relation in the literature, and the relation R_s is called the *preference relation.* What we are calling a *social acceptability relation* Sen (1970), for example, would call a *Collective Choice Rule* and if we added the requirement I' it would be called a *Social Decision Function.*

1*1). If we take "optimum" to mean "nothing is better," then only the bare bones of the concept of an "optimum" remains.

What happens now is not completely known. A complete characterization of the social preference definitions consistent with I' and our other principles has not yet been obtained.

The following result is due to Brown (1973a,b, 1974, 1975a,b), who has been seeking to characterize the definition in terms of what he calls a collegium. A collegium is a set of individuals such that any member inside the set has an absolute veto and no member outside the set has a veto. For a motion to carry, the collegium must be unanimous and the motion must also be ratified by some select coalition other than (disjoint from) the collegium.

Theorem. If the social preference definition and process satisfy I', Acyclicity; III, Value/Feasibility Separation; IV, Universal Domain; VI, Independence of Infeasible Alternatives; VII, Rational Choice; and VIII, Pareto Principle, then there exists a special set of individuals C_0 and select sets of individuals $\{C_1, C_2, \ldots, C_k\}$ such that if xP_iy for $i \in \{C_0 \cup C_j\}$ for some C_j from among the select sets, then xP_sy.

This is an illuminating result, but problems remain. If we use a process based on a collegium, then the induced social preference definition may not satisfy I', III, IV, VI, VII, and VIII. Furthermore, the conditions under which the members of the set C_0 in the theorem necessarily have the veto powers of collegium members are still unknown. That is, the social preference may be determined in many instances even though the collegium is not unanimous. Nevertheless, this result and others he provides show that collegiums are in some sense close to forming the only preference definitions compatible with our new principles, but additional work remains.

By replacing V with a different normative principle to be used in addition to I', III, IV, VI, VII, and VIII, we can get another view of what is going on. The following principle says that every individual has a tie-breaking capacity.

IX. *Strong Monotonicity.* If xI_sy, given some pattern of individual rankings $(R_1, \ldots, R_n)$, and one person changes his mind, he either moves from indifference to preference, moves from preference to indifference, or reverses preferences; then society moves from indifference to preference (in the direction of his change).

The following result was presented in Mas-Colell and Sonnenschein (1972).

Theorem. If the process satisfies I', Acyclicity; III, Value/Feasibility Separation; IV, Universal Domain; VI, Independence of Infeasible Alternatives; VII,

Rational Choice; VIII, Pareto Principle; and IX, Strong Monotonicity; then there is an individual i_0 who has veto power over any pair of alternatives. That is, if $xP_{i_0}y$, then either xI_sy or xP_sy.

An interesting breakthrough was provided by Ferejohn and Grether (1974) for the case of a finite number of options. Suppose the number of options is M; the number of people who prefer x to y is $N(x,y)$; and the number who prefer y to x is $N(y,x)$. A social preference definition we will call the FG rule is

$$\text{FG: } xP_sy \text{ if and only if } N(x,y) > \left(\frac{M-1}{M}\right) (N(x,y) + N(y,x)).$$

This rule satisfies all of our principles I' through VI and in a sense is the "best" rule which does so in this finite case.[19] The trouble is that if M is very large relative to the number of people, it is equivalent to unanimity.

That's it. Acyclicity is the weakest condition which we can use and still have the social preference resemble anything like an individual preference. It is as relaxed as we can become and still use the concept of an "optimum." The road is not closed. Acyclicity may provide the answer, but informed observers (Ferejohn, 1976) say that any day now we will find a "collegium-like" structure forming the end of the path. Let's return to the origin.

Responsive

While Principle V and similar axioms such as the Pareto Principle look very innocent indeed, and have never been questioned in this literature, I conjecture that when judged from the broader perspective of the history of ideas, they are the most controversial of them all. They say that the social preference definition should in some sense be based on individual preferences. The definition can never operate in total disregard for all preferences of all individuals.

Before going to what may seem to some to be the heart of the problem, let's dwell momentarily on what could be a misconception about the analysis. "Why should the social preference be sensitive to individual preferences? Individuals are notably misinformed and may indeed be under the influence

---

[19] Among those rules which are symmetric in the arguments, it is the one for which the P relation is the largest.

of something like advertising and therefore unaware of their 'true' preferences." There is a simple answer to this. We have problems even when the data *are* the true preferences. If we had a theory or method to separate out "true" preferences from those "under the influence," and if we would want the social preference to be responsive to the true ones, then we would still have *all* the problems we have been outlining. Simply take the individual preferences we have been using to be the "true preferences" and start from the beginning.

What about social preference definitions which are founded on religious codes and customs? These need not be responsive to individual preferences at all. In fact, one can see much of democratic theory as saying, "If you must go through this exercise of finding a social preference definition, then Principle V should be part of it." Notice that it is here, as opposed to transitivity, that the reference to democratic theory is most useful. So those who reject democratic theory in general are likely to reject this principle also. Such individuals may have problems within whatever system they choose, but they are not going to be troubled by the analysis we are pursuing. In particular, they should not have even found our initial examples paradoxical, and probably stopped reading long before now. For the rest of us, however, the axiom remains, and we must search elsewhere.

Rational Choice

Brian Barry has suggested that the rational choice axiom, VII, may be the problem.[20] Why should we expect the "most preferred" to always be chosen? Perhaps we should define the social preference and then look for processes which come as close as possible to yielding the best outcome. Of course we have to come to grips with what it means to be "close," but the idea seems sound. What happens when we drop axiom VII? It depends upon what we replace it with, but in general the answer is that we currently don't know. The idea should be pursued.

Value/Feasibility Separation

What happens if axiom VII remains? There is only one axiom left—axiom III. Everything else must stay, either because of what nature has done to us or

---

[20] He raised this issue in conversation at a conference on "Social Choice and Democratic Theory," Key Biscayne, 1975.

because of "innocence." Let's examine what this principle says and see where it comes from. Like it or not, the only choice, given what is currently known, is likely to be between this principle and one of the dictator-like social preference definitions.

Principle III says that the social preference definition between any pair of options, say x, y, does not change as the set within which they are being considered changes—all other relevant things being held constant. If we are going to use a concept of preference at the societal level, then we need this principle since it forms a large part of the heart of preference theory. Our recognition within ourselves of the independence of our desires from our opportunities, of our freedom to proceed with value calculations independently of feasibility considerations, serves as a base for much of the theory's appeal. Doing away with this is, in essence, doing away with the concept of a social preference definition altogether.

Well, that takes a little thought. Why did we get into the *social* preference business in the first place, and what are the alternatives? We got here because of our intuition and because of a lot of things we find in books. Of course books can be wrong and our intuition can lead us astray. It would not be the first time that someone illegitimately transferred the principles which govern his own behavior to other things. Human qualities are attributed to plants, automobiles, and computers every day. If we eliminate Principle III, we are admitting, as claimed by Plott (1972) and Schwartz (1972), that we have made the same mistake with groups of individuals.

What are the alternatives? Shouldn't social choices follow some standards? Yes, but standards do not have to look like preferences. They can look like prohibitions against certain events. That is, standards can look like *constraints,* e.g.: "the outcome should not violate anyone's rights"; "Thou shalt not kill"; "No one should starve to death"; "No Pareto dominated option should be chosen"; etc. So, an alternative to the use of a social preference definition is to use constraints. Rather than attempting to find what is *most* preferred or *most* acceptable, we can try to find something which is simply acceptable as opposed to something which is optimal.

Search for Choice Principles

If Principle III is eliminated, then there is no need to think in terms of a social preference definition at all. We can focus directly on the process and inquire about the implications of behavioral constraints. Are various constraints (which carry interesting normative implications) consistent? What kind of process might correspond to certain types of behavior? Can we invent new processes which have those aspects we like about existing processes but do not have some of the more distasteful properties?

This change in focus may involve a subtle change in philosophical position. Perhaps we are no longer attempting to define the good options which would serve as a standard against which process performance is judged. We may have instead begun a search for acceptable processes and procedures which are to be judged in terms of their behavior in general, and not in terms of how well they choose the "proper" outcome. We may have shifted our focus from questions about "substance" to questions about "procedure." In the literature no one takes sides on this issue, so we drop it for now.

How do we proceed without a concept of social preference? We can place our normative demands on the choice function, the process model $C(v,R_1, \ldots ,R_n)$, directly. For example, the Pareto Principle becomes: If everyone ranks x above y and if x is feasible, then $y \notin C(v,R_1, \ldots ,R_n)$; i.e., y does not result from the process. Other norms can be similarly stated. Notice in particular that the statement of this norm does not require a social preference concept. We do not pick up a concept of social preference simply because we want to engage in normative discourse. The point is subtle and is a frequent cause of controversy.

In spite of our declaration that we have done away with the concept of a social preference, it can creep into the analysis through the back door. "O K, so we will no longer attempt to find a social preference definition. We can forget about that as long as we adopt the proper principles to govern the selection of a social choice function. For example, don't you feel there should be some consistency between the outcome which results from small feasible sets and the outcome which results from larger sets?" Our introductory examples can make this argument seem most appealing, but if your answer is yes, then you are in great danger. Certain consistency principles governing choice functions directly carry the implication that society will choose *as if* the choices were generated from some social preference definition. If we subscribe to one of them, we are back where we started.

The classic example is the following, which in the literature is called the Weak Axiom of Revealed Preference.

WARP. Suppose the social choice, when the feasible set is v, is given by $C(v,R_1, \ldots ,R_n)$, and that it is $C(v',R_1, \ldots ,R_n)$ when the feasible set is v'—the rankings of all individuals remaining fixed. If v is a subset of v', then if any option is in both v and $C(v',R_1, \ldots ,R_n)$, the set of options in both v and $C(v',R_1, \ldots ,R_n)$ is exactly equal to $C(v,R_1, \ldots ,R_n)$.

A picture might help. (See Figure 1.) By breaking the axiom WARP into two parts we can understand the diagrams. (i) If two options are tied for a "win" in a contest within a small set, then either they tie again over the larger set or neither is a "winner." (ii) If an option was a winner from a big set, then it should also be a winner in any smaller subset.

If this consistency principle is imposed and if VI is retained (and if v can be any finite subset of E), then the process chooses *as if* we had started with a social preference definition which satisfies I, II, III, IV, V, and VII. The results are all the same as in the social preference case, and we end up with a "dictator."

So, if we accept all of WARP, then we are in trouble. Perhaps by dividing it into "parts," such as in the discussion above, we could keep the "desirable" part and eliminate the rest. In doing so we would have a better understanding of what we want in terms of process performance. This idea has served to motivate much current research.

Of course, the trouble with the approach is that we have no general guidelines for dividing up the axiom and no criterion for "acceptable"

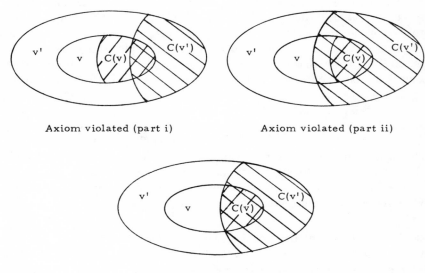

Axiom violated (part i)   Axiom violated (part ii)

Axiom not violated

FIGURE 1

performance other than our own intuition which, as we have seen, is definitely capable of leading us astray. Partial guidelines can come from institutions. Others can come from individual behavioral regularities, as will be seen in the next section, but currently there is no "metaprinciple" which governs this portion of the area. From here the subject also becomes very technical, and since excellent surveys have been provided by Fishburn (1974c), Sen (1976), and Richelson (1975a), we need not cover it.

Summary and Loose Ends

A summary of what we have done would probably be welcome at this point. What seem to be the strong points and the weak points of the formal analysis? Where are the various interpretations of the formalisms likely to hold, and where are they likely to break down?

The analysis started with a few examples of process behavior which serve as convincing demonstrations for most that the world is not at all as we expected. From these we begin to develop an overriding hypothesis about why we regarded the behavior demonstrated in the examples as peculiar or "paradoxical." We found that these examples violate certain principles of preference which are generally present in individual choice behavior. The question then became "What processes do choose in accord with these principles?" The answer which has been slowly seeping in over the past few years is now beginning to take a definite shape. There appear to be none which are free of "dictator-like" features.

This negative answer began with Arrow's General Possibility Theorem. At first, since there were so many abstract and complicated aspects of the argument, the theorem was essentially ignored. Most scholars suspected that buried somewhere in the jargon was a key assumption which, once made explicit, would either make the whole thing go away or at least prove that the result was relevant to only some special and isolated situations. With some justification, they continued to base normative analysis upon concepts which the theorem suggested were inconsistent. After all, analysis must begin somewhere, and if all potential problems had to be solved before beginning, the beginning would never occur. Within just the last three or four years, we have moved ourselves to a much better vantage point from which we can survey what is going on. Most of the obvious potential routes around the result have been tried, and almost every aspect of the technical concepts has been examined in detail.

Table 2 provides a summary of several of the major ideas about how to dismantle the result, and the types of problems they encounter. The com-

TABLE 2

Attempts to Eliminate the General Possibility Theorem

Idea	Answer
Eliminate the Pareto Principle	It was not used, so there is nothing to eliminate. Besides it only seems to provide some "direction" in the theorem.
Reduce the size of the domain	It seems though *very* little conflict is needed to generate negative results. More than an amount adequate to cause problems is likely to naturally exist.
Remove Independence of Infeasible Alternatives	If the discussion is about processes within which individuals are placed in a position where their decisions affect their own total well-being, then the axiom seems to be unavoidable.
Use Cardinal Utilities	a. In the sense of rates of substitution, amounts one would pay, and attitudes toward lotteries, cardinality is not precluded if the options are viewed as social *states.* b. Processes are not sensitive to cardinality of the classical variety so special processes which are influenced by these data need to be invented. Impossibility results about the existence of such processes have been discovered.
Remove Social Indifference Transitivity	It leads only to oligarchies.
Use Acyclicity	It looks as though it will only lead to collegiums.
Remove Responsiveness	This divorces the concepts of social preference and individual preference.
Remove Value/Feasibility Separation	This is equivalent to doing away with the concept of social preference.
Remove Rational Social Choice	The consequences of this are unknown.

ments on the table are generalizations about the state of the art. They are *not* claims that the ideas listed should no longer be pursued. Rather, the comments underline the importance of doing even more research along these lines. That said, however, the generalizations point to a very important conclusion about how this research should be regarded. Until recently it has not been unrealistic to presume that the negative results would be eliminated through one of these paths of analysis. There was really no need for scholars who used concepts like "social preference," the "wants and desires of the people," etc., to justify the use of the concepts prior to application or to establish that the concepts could be consistently applied. The generalizations on Table 2 indicate that it may be time for a shift in the burden of proof. Now it is reasonable to suppose that the negative results should be taken at face value and that our philosophical positions must be altered accordingly.

If we are to take the result seriously, then what are the consequences? In very general terms, it seems that we cannot inquire about what kinds of processes "give people what they want." The concept of "process" seems to be inconsistent with the concept "what the people want." The reason appears to be that the latter concept, which is actually the concept of social preference in disguise, suffers from a type of fallacy of composition. It illegitimately presupposes that a property, preference, of each individual in a group is also a property of the group.

For many scholars, such a conclusion will not be disconcerting at first, since they never thought of a *group* as having a preference anyway. Economists, for example, will usually aggressively avoid any such presupposition. But, the basic problem is not the concept of social preference itself. Rather, the basic problem is the internal consistency of "preference-like" behavior, and this can be induced by a great number of concepts. Any concept which induces at the societal level a consistency between choices over different feasible sets of the type represented by the axiom WARP, is likely to have problems. These include concepts which carry the connotation of "optimum outcome" or the "best outcome" or the "maximum" of anything, since each can be operationally equivalent to a preference. Now it would seem that anyone using these concepts should at least provide the rest of us with some assurance that his analysis does not founder on the most obvious of the inconsistencies.

Are there important areas where the analysis does not apply? The key problem is caused by the consistency induced by preference between choices over different feasible sets. If in some instances and for some reason the concept of a feasible set does not apply, then it may be possible to avoid the difficulties. What, for example, is the feasible set of legislative enactments? Is this set different from the universal set of all conceivable legislative enactments? Does this feasible set change from time to time? If not, then when the options are pieces of legislation the theorem might not apply. What about value judgments? Does there exist a feasible set which differs from the set of all conceivable value judgments? If value judgments are the options and if individuals rank them, then we might be able to talk about a group ranking of value judgments without getting into trouble.[21]

The "process" interpretation of Independence of Infeasible Alternatives also carries another important qualification. There may be a good argument for the axiom if each option is an entire social state. What happens if an "option" is only one component of a social state, as is the case with normal committee processes? Then individuals can bring considerations external to the process—such as bribes, side payments, the external negotiations—to bear in influencing the process. The outcome of the process would seem to be very sensitive to committee members' attitudes toward these external options, and changes in preferences regarding these things may well result in changes in process outcomes. As it stands now, the applicability of the axiom in such situations has not been established.

Perhaps the above arguments will provide the reader with the flavor of the negative results and enable him to explore the possible ambiguities, when examined form this point of view, of the philosophies with which he is familiar. Perhaps someone, when comparing philosophical outlook, will notice the key which will allow us to disregard the negative results completely. [*Editor's note*: The section "Axiomatic Models of Processes, Procedures, and Institutions" (pp. 554–587 of the original) has been deleted here.]

SOME NOTES ON THE OVERVIEW

In closing, a remark or so about our perspective is in order. The reader has been warned at several points that our interpretation is not universally accepted or, in some cases, even recognized. The important turning points should be underlined.

First, our formulation of the impossibility theorem cannot be found explicitly in the literature. Some, following Arrow, formulate the problem as a mapping from individual preferences into a social preference. Others start with a choice function and make no explicit reference to a social preference. We implicitly started with a social preference existence axiom (an implicit Principle 0). From this and other axioms we could *deduce* the Arrow formulation.

---

[21] There is some controversy on this point. Compare Plott (1972) and Sen (1976).

Since our formulation differs, our axioms differ also. The Value/Feasibility Separation axiom is new, for example. Use of the term "social preference" *definition* is new. Our use of the concept of "feasibility," while not new, is certainly wedded to a particular subset of the literature. The same holds for all of our "process" interpretations and even our repeated use of the concept of "intuition" used in motivating the research.

When the reader picks up the challenge with which we began, and if he does indeed demonstrate that the whole field is irrelevant, he should check with the original sources before making his claim. While he may provide me with an incentive to "rest easily" with my work, some of the scholars whose work is referenced here might hesitate to join me. If, on the other hand, the reader has found that this theory provides him with new tools with which to attack old problems, he should definitely consult the papers we have referenced here. In our effort to provide a unified theory, we have only touched upon the many exciting ideas and insights which exist.

Manuscript submitted December 17, 1975.
Final manuscript received March 8, 1976.

REFERENCES

Adelsman, R., and Whinston, A. 1975. "The Equivalence of Three Social Decision Functions," Purdue University, WP-75-155, November 1975.

Alt, Franz. 1971. "On the Measurement of Utility," in J. S. Chipman, et al., eds., *Preference, Utility and Demand.* San Francisco: Harcourt Brace Jovanovich, Inc.

Arrow, K. J. 1963. *Social Choice and Individual Values.* New York: Wiley; 2nd edition 1963.

____. 1959. "Rational Choice Functions and Orderings," *Economica,* 1959, vol. 26, pp. 121–127.

——. 1973. "Some Ordinalist–Utilitarian Notes on Rawls' Theory of Justice," *Journal of Philosophy,* 1973, vol. 70, pp. 245–263.

Atkinson, A. B. 1970. "On the Measurement of Inequality," *Journal of Economic Theory, vol. 2,* pp. 244–263.

——. 1975. *Economics of Inequality,* Oxford: Clarendon Press.

Aumann, Robert J. 1967. "A Survey of Cooperative Games without Side

Payments," in M. Shubik, ed., *Essays in Mathematical Economics.* Princeton: Princeton University Press.

Barbera, S. 1975. "The Manipulability of Social Choice Mechanisms That Do Not Leave Too Much to Chance," mimeographed, Northwestern University, 1975.

Bartoszynski. 1972. "Power Structure in Dichotomous Voting," *Econometrica,* November 1972, vol. 40 pp. 1003–1019.

Batra, R. N., and Pattanaik, P. K. 1972a. "Transitive Multi-Stage Majority Decisions with Quasi-transitive Individual Preferences," *Econometrica,* 1972, vol. 40, pp. 1121–1135.

———. 1972b. "On Some Suggestions for Having Non-binary Social Choice Functions," *Theory and Decisions,* 1972, vol. 3, pp. 1–11.

Black, R. D. 1958. *The Theory of Committees and Elections.* New York: Cambridge University Press.

Blair, D. H.; Bordes, Georges; Kelley, Jerry S.; and Suzumura, Kotaro. 1976. "Impossibility Theorems without Collective Rationality," *Journal of Economic Theory,* forthcoming.

Blau, J. H. 1975. "Liberal Values and Independence," *Review of Economic Studies,* 1975, vol. 42, pp. 395–401.

Blin, J. M. 1973. *Patterns and Configurations in Economic Science.* Cambridge: D. Reidel Publishing Co., Dordrecht, Holland.

Blin, J. M., and Whinston, A. B. 1975. "Discriminant Functions and Majority Voting," *Management Science,* 1975, vol. 21, pp. 557–566.

Bloomfield, S. 1976. "A Social Choice Interpretation of the von Neumann-Morgenstern Game," *Econometrica,* Jan. 1976, vol. 44, pp. 105–114.

Bloomfield, S., and Wilson, R. D. 1972. "Postulates of Game Theory," *Journal of Mathematical Sociology,* 1972, vol. 2, pp. 221–234.

Bowman, V. J., and Colantoni, C. S. 1973. "Majority Rule under Transitivity Constraints," *Management Science,* 1973, vol. 1, pp. 1029–1041.

———. 1974. "Further Comments on Majority Rule under Transitivity Constraints," *Management Science,* 1974, vol. 20.

Brams, Steven J. 1975. *Game Theory and Politics.* New York: The Free Press.

Brown, D. J. 1973a. "Acyclic Choice," Cowles Foundation discussion paper, 1973.

——— 1973b. "Aggregation of Preferences," forthcoming in *Quarterly Journal of Economics.*

———. 1974. "An Approximate Solution to Arrow's Problem," *Journal of Economic Theory,* 1974, vol. 9, pp. 375–383.

———. 1975a. "Acyclic Aggregation over a Finite Set of Alternatives," Cowles Foundation Discussion Paper No. 391, Yale University, 1975.

———. 1975b. "Collective Rationality," Cowles Foundation Discussion Paper No. 393, Yale University, 1975.

Buchanan, J. M. 1954a. "Individual Choice in Voting and in the Market," *Journal of Political Economy,* August 1954, vol. 62, pp. 334–43.

———. 1954b. "Social Choice, Democracy, and Free Markets," *Journal of Political Economy,* April 1954, vol. 62, pp. 114–123.

———. 1968. *The Demand and Supply of Public Goods,* Chicago: Rand McNally.

Campbell, D. E. 1973. "Social Choice and Intensity of Preference," *Journal of Political Economy,* 1973, vol. 81, pp. 211–218.

Coleman, James S. 1973. *The Mathematics of Collective Action,* Chicago: Aldine.

Dahl, R. A., and Lindbloom, C. E. 1953. *Politics, Economics and Welfare,* Harper Torchbook edition. New York: Harper and Row.

DeMeyer, F., and Plott, C. R. 1970. "The Probability of a Cyclical Majority," *Econometrica,* 1970, vol. 38, pp. 345–354.

———. 1971. "A Social Welfare Function Using 'Relative Intensity' of Preference," *Quarterly Journal of Economics,* February 1971, vol. 85, pp. 179–186.

Dyer, J. S., and Miles, R. F., Jr. 1976. "An Actual Application of Collective Choice Theory to the Selection of Trajectories for the Mariner Jupiter/Saturn 1977 Project," *Operations Research* (for theory) 1976.

Farquharson, R. 1969. *Theory of Voting.* New Haven: Yale University Press.

Ferejohn, J. A. 1976. "Brown's Theory of Collective Choice." Social Science Working Paper No. 117, California Institute of Technology, 1976.

Ferejohn, J. A., and Grether, D. M. 1974a. "On a Class of Rational Social Decision Procedures," *Journal of Economic Theory,* 1974, vol. 8, pp. 471–482.

———. 1974b. "Weak Path Independence," Social Science Working Paper No. 80, California Institute of Technology, 1974.

Fine, B., and Fine, K. 1974. "Social Choice and Individual Ranking," *Review of Economic Studies,* 1974, vol. 41, pp. 303–322, 459–475.

Fine, K. 1972. "Some Necessary and Sufficient Conditions for Representative Decision on Two Alternatives, *Econometrica,* November 1972, vol. 40, pp. 1083–1090.

Fishburn, P. C. 1970. "Arrow's Impossibility Theorem: Concise Proof and Infinite Voters," *Journal of Economic Theory,* 1970, vol. 2, pp. 103–106.

———. 1972. "Lotteries and Social Choice," *Journal of Economic Theory,* 1972, vol. 5, pp. 189–207.

142   Charles R. Plott

_____. 1973a. *The Theory of Social Choice,* Princeton: Princeton University Press.

_____. 1973b. "Voter Concordance, Simple Majorities, and Group Decision Methods," *Behavioral Science,* 1973, vol. 18, pp. 364–376.

_____. 1974a. "On Collective Rationality and a Generalized Impossibility Theorem," *Review of Economic Studies,* 1974, vol. 41, pp. 445–457.

_____. 1974b. "Paradoxes of Voting," *American Political Science Review,* 1974, vol. 68, pp. 537–546.

——. 1974c. "Social Choice Functions," *SIAM Review,* January 1974, vol. 16, pp. 63–90.

_____. 1974d. "Impossibility Theorems without the Social Completeness Axiom," *Econometrica,* 1974, vol. 42, pp. 695–704.

_____. 1975. "A Probabilistic Model of Social Choice: Comment," *Review of Economic Studies,* 1975, vol. 42, pp. 297–301.

_____. 1976. "Dictators on Blocks: Generalizations of Social Choice Impossibility Theorems," *Journal of Combinatorial Theory B,* 1976, vol. 20.

Fishburn, P. C., and Gehrlein, W. V. 1975. "Election by Chance in a World of Uncertain Voters," mimeographed, Pennsylvania State University, 1975.

Gärdenfors, P. 1973. "Positionalist Voting Functions," *Theory and Decision,* 1973, vol. 4, pp. 1–24.

Garman, M., and Kamien, M. 1968. "The Paradox of Voting: Probability Calculations," *Behavioral Science,* 1968, vol. 13, pp. 306–323.

Gehrlein, William V., and Fishburn, P. C. 1975. "The Probability of the Paradox of Voting: A Computable Solution," mimeographed, Pennsylvania State University, College of Business Administration, University Park.

Gibbard, A. 1973. "Manipulation of Voting Schemes: A General Result," *Econometrica,* 1973, vol. 41, pp. 587–601.

——. 1974. "A Pareto-Consistent Libertarian Claim," *Journal of Economic Theory,* 1974, vol. 7, pp. 388–410.

Goodman, Leo A., and Markowitz, Harry. 1952. "Social Welfare Functions Based on Individual Rankings," *American Journal of Sociology,* November 1952, vol. 57, pp. 257–262.

Hansson, B. 1969a. "Voting and Group Decision Functions," *Synthese,* 1969, vol. 20, pp. 526–537.

_____. 1969b. "Group Preferences," *Econometrica,* 1969, vol. 37, pp. 50–54.

_____. 1972. "The Existence of Group Preferences," Working Paper No. 3, The Mattias Fremling Society, Lund, Sweden, 1972.

——. 1973. "The Independence Condition in the Theory of Social Choice," *Theory and Decision,* 1973, vol. 4, pp. 25–49.

Harsanyi, J. C. 1955. "Cardinal Welfare, Individualistic Ethics, and Interpersonal Comparisons of Utility," *Journal of Political Economy,* 1955, vol. 63, pp. 309–321.

Herzberger, H. G. 1973. "Ordinal Preference and Rational Choice," *Econometrica,* 1973, vol. 41, pp. 187–237.

Hildreth, C. 1953. "Alternative Conditions for Social Ordering," *Econometrica,* 1953, vol. 21, pp. 81–95.

Hurwicz, L. 1973. "The Design of Mechanisms for Resource Allocation," *American Economic Review,* May 1973, vol. 63, pp. 1–30.

Intriligator, M. 1973. "A Probabilistic Model of Social Choice," *Review of Economic Studies,* 1973, vol. 40, pp. 553–560.

Jamison, Dean T. 1975. "The Probability of Intransitive Majority Rule: an Empirical Study," *Public Choice,* Fall 1975, vol. 23, pp. 87–94.

Jamison, D. T., and Luce, E. 1973. "Social Homogeneity and the Probability of Intransitive Majority Rule," *Journal of Economic Theory,* 1973, vol. 5, pp. 79–87.

Kelly, J. S. 1974a. "Necessity Conditions in Voting Theory," *Journal of Economic Theory,* 1974, vol. 8, pp. 149–160.

_____. 1974b. "Voting Anomalies, the Number of Voters and the Number of Alternatives," *Econometrica,* 1974, vol. 42, pp. 239–251.

_____. 1975. "Strategy-proofness and Social Choice Functions with a Large Image Set," mimeographed, 1975.

Kemeny, J. 1959. "Mathematics without Numbers," *Daedalus,* 1959, vol. 88, pp. 577–591.

Kirman, A. P., and Sondermann, D. 1972. "Arrow's Theorem, Many Agents and Invisible Dictators," *Journal of Economic Theory,* 1972, vol. 5, pp. 267–277.

Kramer, G. H. 1972. "Sophisticated Voting over Multidimensional Choice Space," *Journal of Mathematical Sociology,* 1972, pp. 165–180.

——. 1974. "On a Class of Equilibrium Conditions for Majority Rule," *Econometrica,* 1974, vol. 41, pp. 285–297.

——. 1975. "A Dynamic Model of Political Equilibrium," Cowles Foundation Discussion Paper No. 36, June 1975.

Kramer, G. H., and Klevorick, A. K. 1974. "Existence of a 'Local' Cooperative Equilibrium in a Voting Game," *Review of Economic Studies,* 1974, vol. 41, pp. 539–547.

Kuga, K., and Nagatani, H. 1974. "Voter Antagonism and the Paradox of Voting," *Econometrica,* 1974, vol. 42, pp. 1045–1067.

Levenglick, A. 1975. "Fair and Reasonable Election Systems," *Behavioral Science,* 1975, vol. 20, pp. 34–46.

Lichtenstein, S., and Slovic, P. 1971. "Reversals of Preference Between Bids and Choices in Gambling Decisions," *Journal of Experimental Psychology,* 1971, vol. 89, pp. 46–55.

Luce, R. D., and Raiffa, H. 1957. *Games and Decisions.* New York: Wiley.

Marschak, J., and Radner, R. 1972. *Economic Theory of Teams.* New Haven: Yale University Press.

Mas-Colell, A., and Sonnenschein, H. 1972. "General Possibility Theorems and Group Decisions," *Review of Economic Studies,* 1972, vol. 39, pp. 185–192.

May, K. O. 1952. "A Set of Independent, Necessary and Sufficient Conditions for Simple Majority Decision," *Econometrica,* 1952, vol. 20, pp. 680–684.

Mayston, David J. 1974. *The Idea of Social Choice.* New York: St. Martin's Press.

McFadden, D. 1975. "The Revealed Preference of a Government Bureaucracy: Theory," *The Bell Journal of Economics,* 1975, vol. 6, pp. 409–416.

Merchant, D. K., and Rao, M. R. 1975. "Majority Decisions and Transitivity: Some Special Cases," University of Rochester, Graduate School of Management, Working Paper Series 7506, October 1975.

Murakami, Y. 1961. "A Note on the General Possibility Theorem of the Social Welfare Function," *Econometrica,* April 1961, vol. 29, pp. 244–46.

———. 1968. *Logic and Social Choice.* London: Macmillan.

Nash, J. F. 1950. "The Bargaining Problem," *Econometrica,* 1950, vol. 18, pp. 155–162.

Niemi, R. G. 1969. "Majority Decision-making with Partial Unidimensionality," *American Political Science Review,* 1969, vol. 63, pp. 488–97.

Niemi, R. G., and Weisberg, H. F. 1968. "A Mathematical Solution for the Probability of the Paradox of Voting," *Behavioral Science,* vol. 13, pp. 317–23.

Parks, R. R. 1971. "Rationalizations, Extensions and Social Choice Paths," Washington University, St. Louis, 1971.

———. 1973. "The Bergson-Samuelson Welfare Function: An Impossibility," mimeographed, Washington University, St. Louis, 1973.

Pattanaik, P. K. 1971. *Voting and Collective Choice.* New York: Cambridge University Press.

———. 1973. "On the Stability of Sincere Voting Situations," *Journal of Economic Theory,* 1973, vol. 6, pp. 558–574.

———. 1974. "Stability of Sincere Voting under Some Classes of Non-binary Group Decision Procedures," *Journal of Economic Theory,* 1974, vol. 8, pp. 206–224.

———. 1975. "Strategic Voting without Collusion under Binary and Democratic Group Decision Rules," *Review of Economic Studies,* 1975, vol. 42, pp. 93–103.

Plott, C. R. 1967. "A Notion of Equilibrium and Its Possibility under Majority Rule," *American Economic Review,* 1967, vol. 57, pp. 788–806.

_____. 1971. "Recent Results in the Theory of Voting," in M. Intriligator, ed., *Frontiers of Quantitative Economics.* Amsterdam: North-Holland.

——. 1972. "Ethics, Social Choice Theory and the Theory of Economic Policy," *Journal of Mathematical Sociology,* 1972, vol. 2, pp. 181–208.

_____. 1973. "Path Independence, Rationality and Social Choice," *Econometrica,* 1973, vol. 41, pp. 1075–1091.

——. 1974. "Rawls Theory of Justice: Some Impossibility Results," paper presented at the Public Choice Society Meetings, 1974.

Plott, C., and Levine, M. 1975. "On Using the Agenda to Influence Group Decision: Theory, Experiments and Application," Social Science Working Paper No. 66, California Institute of Technology, April 1975.

Pomeranz, J. E., and Weil, R. L. 1970. "The Cyclical Majority Problems," Communications of the ACM, vol. 13, 1970, pp. 251–254.

Rawls, J. 1971. *A Theory of Justice.* Oxford: Clarendon Press.

Ray, P. 1973. "Independence of Irrelevant Alternatives," *Econometrica,* 1973, vol. 32, pp. 987–991.

Richelson, Jeffrey. 1975a. "Conditions on Social Choice Functions," A. R. Wagner & Co., Beverly Hills, November 1975, mimeographed.

——.1975b. "A Comparative Analysis of Social Choice Functions," *Behavioral Science,* 1975, vol. 20.

Richter, M. K. 1966. "Revealed Preference Theory," *Econometrica,* 1966, pp. 635–645.

——. 1971. "Rational Choice," in J. S. Chipman, et. al., eds., *Preference, Utility and Demand,* San Francisco: Harcourt Brace Jovanovich.

Riker, W. H., and Brams, S. 1973. "The Paradox of Vote Trading," *American Political Science Review,* 1973, vol. 67, pp. 1239–1247.

Riker, W. H., and Ordeshook, P. 1973. *An Introduction to Positive Political Theory,* Englewood Cliffs: Prentice-Hall.

Rosenthal, R. W. 1975. "Voting Majority Sizes," *Econometrica,* 1975, vol. 43, pp. 293–299.

Salles, M. 1975. "A General Possibility Theorem on Group Decision Rules with Pareto-Transitivity," *Journal of Economic Theory,* forthcoming.

Samuelson, P. A. 1967. "Arrow's Mathematical Politics," in S. Hook, ed., *Human Values and Economic Policy.* New York: New York University Press.

Saposnik, R. 1975. "Social Choice with Continuous Expression of Individual Preferences," *Econometrica,* 1975, vol. 43, pp. 683–690.

146   Charles R. Plott

Satterthwaite, M. A. 1975. "Strategy-Proofness and Arrow's Conditions," *Journal of Economic Theory*, 1975, vol. 10, pp. 187–217.
Schwartz, T. 1970. "On the Possibility of Rational Policy Evaluation," *Theory and Decision*, 1970, vol. 1, pp. 89–106.
———. 1972. "Rationality and the Myth of the Maximum," *Nous*, 1972, vol. 6, pp. 97–117.
———. 1975a. "Vote Trading and Pareto Efficiency," *Public Choice*, Winter 1975, vol. 24, pp. 101–110.
———. 1975b. "Notes on the Abstract Theory of Preference and Choice," mimeographed, Carnegie-Mellon University, Pittsburgh, 1975.
———. 1975c. "Choice Functions, 'Rationality' Conditions and Variations on the Weak Axiom of Revealed Preference," mimeographed, Carnegie-Mellon University, Pittsburgh, 1975.
Sen, A. K. 1970a. *Collective Choice and Social Welfare*. San Francisco: Holden-Day.
———. 1970b. "Interpersonal Aggregation and Partial Comparability," *Econometrica*, 1970, vol. 38, pp. 393–409.
———. 1970c. "The Impossibility of a Paretian Liberal," *Journal of Political Economy*, 1970, vol. 78, pp. 152–157.
———. 1971. "Choice Functions and Revealed Preference," *Review of Economic Studies*, 1971, vol. 38, pp. 307–317.
———. 1973. *On Economic Inequality*. Oxford: Clarendon Press.
———. 1976. "Social Choice Theory: A Re-Examination," a paper delivered to the Econometric Society, Toronto, 1975, mimeographed, London School of Economics, revised 1976.
Sengupta, M. 1974. "On a Concept of Representative Democracy," *Theory and Decision*, 1974, vol. 5, pp. 249–262.
Shepsle, K. A. 1970. "A Note on Zeckhauser's 'Majority Rule with Lotteries on Alternatives': the Case of the Paradox of Voting," *Quarterly Journal of Economics*, 1970, vol. 84, pp. 705–709.
———. 1972. "The Paradox of Voting and Uncertainty," in R. G. Niemi and H. F. Weisberg, eds., *Probability Models in Collective Decision Making*. Columbus: Merrill.
———. 1974. "The Theory of Collective Choice," in C. Cotter, ed., *Political Science Annual*, vol. 5, Indianapolis: Bobbs-Merrill, pp. 1–87.
Sloss, Judith. 1973. "Stable Outcomes in Majority Voting Games," *Public Choice*, Summer 1973, vol. 15, pp. 19–48.
Slutsky, S. 1975. "Abstentions and Majority Equilibrium," *Journal of Economic Theory*, 1975, vol. 11, pp. 292–304.
Smith, J. H. 1973. "Aggregation of Preferences and Variable Electorate," *Econometrica*, 1973, vol. 41, pp. 1027–1041.

Smith, T. E. 1974. "On the Existence of Most Preferred Alternatives," *International Economic Review,* 1974, vol. 15, pp. 184–194.

Sonnenschein, Hugo. 1974. "An Axiomatic Characterization of the Price Mechanism," *Econometrica,* May 1974, vol. 42, pp. 425–434.

Tversky, A. 1969. "Intransitivity of Preferences," *Psychological Review,* 1969, vol. 76, pp. 31–48.

Wilson, R. B. 1969. "An Axiomatic Model of Logrolling," *American Economic Review,* 1969, vol. 59, pp. 331–341.

——. 1970. "The Finer Structure of Revealed Preferences," *Journal of Economic Theory,* 1970, vol. 2, pp. 348–353.

——. 1971a. "A Game-Theoretic Analysis of Social Choice," in B. Lieberman, ed., *Social Choice.* New York: Gordon and Breach, Science Publishers.

——. 1971b. "Stable Coalition Proposals in Majority Rule Voting," *Journal of Economic Theory,* 1971, vol. 3, pp. 254–271.

——. 1972a. "Social Choice Theory without the Pareto Principle," *Journal of Economic Theory,* 1972, vol. 5, pp. 478–486.

——. 1972b. "The Game-Theoretic Structure of Arrow's General Possibility Theorem," *Journal of Economic Theory,* 1972, vol. 5, pp. 14–20.

——. 1975. "On the Theory of Aggregation," *Journal of Economic Theory,* 1975, vol. 10, pp. 89–99.

Young, H. P. 1974a. "An Axiomatization of Borda's Rule," *Journal of Economic Theory,* 1974, vol. 9, pp. 43–52.

——. 1974b. "A Note on Preference Aggregation," *Econometrica,* 1974, vol. 42, pp. 1129–1131.

——. 1975a. "Social Choice Scoring Functions," *SIAM Journal of Applied Mathematics,* June 1975, vol. 28.

——. 1975b. "Extending Condorcet's Rule," City University of New York, Graduate School, December 1975.

Part II

Data Analysis

HERBERT F. WEISBERG

The Fundamentals of Data Analysis

The key step in data analysis is not employing statistics but deciding which statistics to employ. Different statistics can be appropriate, depending on the researcher's objectives and on the level of measurement of the data. Unfortunately, there can be a tension between these considerations, with the researcher desiring to employ statistics which require data with different measurement properties than are available. This dilemma is discussed, with examples from the realm of the single-variable statistics of central tendency and dispersion. The major focus is on relationships between two variables, with particular attention to measures for nominal, ordinal, and dichotomous data. Finally, the notion of controlling a relationship is presented as a prelude to the analysis of relationships among multiple variables.

The next pair of readings focus on measures of relationship, but this chapter will begin with a more basic topic—an explanation of what data analysis is about. Statistical topics to be introduced in this chapter include levels of measurement, central tendency, dispersion, statistical inference, measures of relationship, and controls. Particular attention will be given to alternative measures of relationship based on different interpretations of the concept of statistical relationship.

It is useful to begin with a review of the definitions of a few terms. A "variable" is simply something that varies. If we were studying differences in nations' Gross National Products, the variable would be the Gross National Product. The "unit of analysis" is the unit over which the variable varies. For example, if we were studying individual voting in the latest presidential election, the unit of analysis would be the individual voter (and the variable would be the vote). In the GNP example above, the unit of analysis is the nation, since different nations have different GNPs. If we studied change in a nation's GNP over time, the variable would still be GNP, but the unit of analysis would be time, since the different observations would be for different time points. For convenience of exposition in this chapter, we will generally treat individual people as the unit of analysis—though the same statistical principles would hold with any other unit of analysis. Finally, a "case" is an observation. For example, if people are the units of analysis, then each person studied in a case and the "number of cases" is the number of people studied.

Statistical Objectives

While there are a large number of statistical procedures, the purposes behind the use of these statistics are really very few. The first broad purpose is
the *description* of a variable. Often we have a large amount of data, and we
want to summarize it in a single "descriptive statistic." Actually, there are
several types of descriptive statistics, corresponding to different aspects of
data that we might want to summarize. The most familiar is the "central
tendency," as measured by statistical indicators like the mean, median, and
mode. The central tendency indicates what the typical values are for a variable. Another is the "dispersion," often measured by the range, standard
deviation, and variance, which summarizes the extent of differences on the
variable. Descriptive statistics are also used to summarize the degree of "relationship" between a pair of variables. Several descriptive statistics will be
explained later in this chapter.

In addition to data description, statistics are sometimes used to focus on
significance of results along with *inference* beyond the cases studied. Often the
data being analyzed are based on a sample of a larger population of interest.
The researcher is then concerned with generalization to that larger population
on the basis of the results for the sample—a problem which is known as
"statistical inference." A related question is what findings for the sample are
striking enough to be likely to hold for the larger population—a problem which
is known as determining the "statistical significance" of a finding. Significance
and inference will be explained further in the middle of this chapter.

Another major objective has to do with the exploration of *causation*. Typically, we are interested in understanding the reasons different people exhibit
different values of the variable being measured, and we seek to account for
these differences in terms of differences of other explanatory variables ex-
hibited by those people. Conventionally, the variable being explained is
termed the "dependent variable," while the explanatory variables are termed
"independent variables." The regression and causal procedures discussed in
the "Regression Models" section of this book emphasize this goal of understanding causation.

A related objective in statistics is the analysis of *change*. We can study
change in one variable over time or examine how a dependent variable is
affected by independent variables in a time process. There are a variety of
procedures for dynamic analysis—including panel analysis, cohort analysis,
and time-series analysis—and most are based on the regression procedures
explained in the "Regression Analysis" chapter.

Another important objective in the use of statistics is the examination of the *structure* of data. In the typical application, the researcher is interested in whether several different variables all measure the same thing or what differences there are among them. For example, we might check whether public attitudes toward the political parties in a multiparty nation are compatible with the existence of a single left-right ideological dimension or whether there are multiple dimensions of party competition in that nation. The dimensional analysis procedures discussed in the "Scaling Techniques" section of this book focus on this goal of determining structure.

A related goal in statistics has to do with *measurement*. We can study the measurement properties of a single variable or focus on the measurement error that becomes evident when we compare different measures of what should be the same thing. The topic of measurement is related to dimensional analysis as well as to causal concerns. The interested reader might want to check further sources on such topics as reliability, validity, and multiple indicators.

Introductory statistics texts generally focus on descriptive statistics, particularly those for analysis of a single variable ("univariate statistics") or of the relationship between two variables ("bivariate statistics"). We will be giving needed background on those topics in this chapter, but it is important to realize that advanced statistics courses focus instead on the procedures described in later sections of this book for analyzing the relationships among a large number of variables ("multivariate statistics").

Levels of Measurement

The beginning point in statistics is to distinguish among four different types of data according to their "measurement properties." When we collect data, the data can be of these different types, and it turns out that different types of statistical analysis procedures are appropriate for the different types of data.

Four Measurement Levels

In the lowest level of measurement, known as "nominal," observations are placed into unordered categories. For example, if we asked people which television network news they watched most recently, the responses would divide people into separate categories: ABC, CBS, NBC, and perhaps one of the cable networks. These are different categories, but without any real order to them. If we were analyzing media usage with the aid of a computer, we would probably find it convenient to associate numbers with the categories, so that 1 might be ABC, 2 CBS, 3 NBC, and 4 a cable network. But it is important to remember that the variable is just nominal, so the numbers assigned are arbitrary. Very few statistical operations would be appropriate on such arbitrary numbers, mainly just counting the number of occurrences of a category.

The next level of measurement is "ordinal," with observations placed into ordered categories. For example, if we queried people about how accurate they considered the network news, they might be asked to use one of the ordinal response categories: "completely accurate," "very accurate," "somewhat accurate," "not very accurate," or "completely inaccurate." The categories are meant to have an order, which was not true for nominal data categories. Still, the categories lack numerical properties. We could assign numbers to the categories for computer analysis. The most common procedure for such number assignment is having 1 stand for the first category ("completely accurate"), 2 for the second ("very accurate"), and so on. The numbers would be in the proper order, but they could instead be any set of numbers with that same order, like 1 for the first category, 3 for the second, 4 for the third, 7 for the fourth, and 9 for the fifth. Since the interval steps between the numbers are arbitrary for ordinal data, many statistical operations would be invalid. The ordinal level is regarded as a "higher" level of information than the nominal level since there is information about the category order.

One level further up is "interval" measurement, in which the intervals between numbers are meaningful. This requires a unit of measurement, as in physical measurement of temperature. The difference between a temperature of 51° and 50° is 1°, the same difference as between a temperature of 71° and 70°.

The highest level of measurement is "ratio." Not only are there meaningful units of measurement at the ratio level, but there is a natural zero point. The usual temperature scales are not ratios, since 0° does not represent the absence of temperature in either the Fahrenheit or Celsius (Centigrade) scale. Since they are not ratio scales, we would not say that a temperature of 64° is twice as high as one of 32°. By way of contrast, how many minutes of television network news a person watched the previous day is a ratio variable. There is a natural zero point—watching no news—as well as a meaningful unit of measurement—one minute of news watching. Since this is a ratio scale, watching 30 minutes of news is watching twice as much as watching 15 minutes.

Nearly all statistical operations appropriate for interval variables are also appropriate for ratio variables, and vice versa, so we shall not have to treat these two levels separately in the remainder of this chapter. It is important to remember that the numbers employed in interval and ratio measurement are fully meaningful, while those employed for nominal and ordinal variables are arbitrary.

"The Dilemma of the Social Scientist"

As Clyde Coombs (1953) has suggested, the "dilemma of the social scientist" is that the standard statistical analysis techniques require ratio or interval data, whereas most social science variables are measured only at nominal or ordinal levels. The problem is that using ratio or interval procedures on nominal or ordinal data can lead to fallacious results. Since this dilemma is quite real in many fields, it has led to the proposal of several solutions over the years.

The simplest solution is to treat ordinal data as interval, usually adopting "integer scoring" for the ordinal variable—assigning the number 1 for its first category, 2 for its second, and so on. This procedure can still lead to fallacious results, but it actually does very well under most circumstances. There has been a lively debate on this approach in the pages of the *American Sociological Review* (Labovitz, 1970; Mayer, 1970; Vargo, 1971; Schweitzer and Schweitzer, 1971; Mayer, 1971; Labovitz, 1971; Grether, 1976). A related approach is to seek "proper" numerical assignments for the ordinal categories, through maximizing or minimizing some statistical criterion. Abelson and Tukey (1970) have presented one such technique. A Workshop article by Hensler and Stipak (1979) presents another technique and reviews this approach more generally.

Another solution is to improve the quality of our measurements, attempting to move up to interval level data instead of settling for ordinal measurements. Some of the scaling techniques discussed in the last three chapters of this book adopt this approach at the analysis stage, particularly the nonmetric multidimensional scaling described by Rabinowitz. Alternatively, this approach can be employed in the data collection. A Workshop article by Lodge and Tursky (1981) presents magnitude scaling techniques for public opinion research in surveys, a procedure designed to move beyond ordinal data, and criticizes common ordinal attitude scales.

A final solution is to develop more statistics for use with ordinal and nominal data. Indeed, in recent years there has been a proliferation of statistics for these lower levels. For example, many of the relationship measures described in the following two chapters were developed specifically to facilitate valid statistical analysis at the ordinal and nominal analysis. Similarly, the Aldrich and Cnudde chapter of this book presents procedures for regression-like analysis at the ordinal and nominal levels.

Each of these solutions can help to handle the "dilemma of the social scientist," but it is still important to emphasize the underlying rule: apply only those statistics that are appropriate for the measurement level of our data.

Unless the researcher is confident that fallacious conclusions would not result from violation of that rule, it is best to adhere closely to the measurement level of the data. We shall illustrate these considerations as we turn to the most elementary descriptive statistics—those used to summarize the "central tendency" and "dispersion" of a variable.

Central Tendency and Dispersion

In describing the values measured for a variable, the first obvious question is what the results are for the "typical" person (or case). We might just compute the arithmetic average of the different results, but that does not always work because of the level of measurement problem just discussed. The appropriate measure of central tendency depends on the measurement level.

Measures of Central Tendency

For nominal data, all we can do is determine which is the category which occurs with the greatest frequency. That is termed the "mode." If more people view CBS news than ABC, NBC, or cable, then the modal person watches CBS news. The mode answers the question: "Which is the most commonly occurring category?" The mode is fully appropriate at the nominal level, as it does not depend on the numbers assigned to the categories.

For ordinal data, we can compute a mode, but we can additionally make use of the order of the variable to determine the category corresponding to the middle person's response. This is termed the "median." If 25% of the people consider the network news completely accurate, 20% very accurate, 15% somewhat accurate, 22% not very accurate, and 18% completely inaccurate, then the middle person (at the 50% mark) is in the "somewhat accurate" category. The median answers the question: "What is the response of the middle case?" It is fully appropriate at the ordinal level, as it makes use only of the order of the categories.

For interval and ratio data, the mode and median can still be used, but the full power of the arithmetic average can also be employed. This is termed the "mean." As an example, if four people had watched 5, 10, 20, and 25 minutes of network news the previous day, their average amount of network news watching would be 15. The mean is computed by adding up the separate observations (5 + 10 + 20 + 25) and then dividing that sum (60) by the number of observations (4 people). The mean answers the question: "What is the average behavior?" It is fully appropriate at the interval and ratio levels, as it requires meaningful numbers and a unit of measurement but not a meaningful zero point.

Choosing an Appropriate Measure

As was stated in the previous section, it is important to apply only those statistics that are appropriate for the level of measurement of the data. Specifically, statistics designed for higher levels of measurement cannot be used when the data are collected at lower levels—unless the researcher is willing to take the chance of making an error. Thus, strictly speaking, means cannot be used to determine the average level of accuracy the public feels the network news has (at least if we used the ordinal response categories given above). Similarly, neither means nor medians can be used on nominal data. It would not make sense to say that the median person watched CBS news or that the average person watched network 1.325.

The statistics designed for the lower levels, however, are sometimes useful for the higher levels too. For example, it is appropriate to ask not only what is the average number of minutes people spend daily watching network news but also what is the middle value (the median) and what is the most common value (the mode). Indeed, the median is sometimes more appropriate than the mean as a measure of central tendency for interval data, particularly when there are a few cases which would deflect the mean. Thus, if the numbers of minutes that nine people spent watching network news were 0, 10, 15, 15, 20, 30, 30, 30, and 300 (the latter for someone addicted to an all-day news operation like Cable News Network), the median (20) would better reflect the behavior of most of the people than would the mean (50), which is so high only because of the one extreme outlier.

Finally, the case of dichotomous variables requires a special mention. Strictly speaking, a variable with just two categories can be treated as any level of measurement. Let us consider the variable of election turnout, whose two categories correspond to whether or not a person voted, and say 55% of the people voted and 45% did not. The variable can be treated as nominal, in which case the modal category is voting. Or it can be treated as ordinal, in which case the median category is again voting. Or it can be scored in a 1–0 version (1 for voting and 0 for not voting), in which case the mean is .55, corresponding to 55% of the people voting. The use of dichotomous variables sometimes leads to violations of the assumptions of common analysis procedures, so some caution is required in dealing with them. In later chapters of this book, Aldrich and Cnudde discuss this problem for regression analysis, while Weisberg mentions the effects on factor analysis. In addition, the next two chapters give special attention to the problem of measuring relationships among dichotomous variables.

Measures of Dispersion

If the first question in data analysis is what the results are for the typical person or case, the second question is how typical is typical. The central tendency measures are more descriptive if the same value of the variable is found for everyone studied than if there is wide dispersion of it. Yet what makes data analysis interesting is the existence of dispersion. If different values of the variable are found for different people, then the problem becomes one of explaining that dispersion. In any case, it becomes necessary to measure the dispersion, the extent of differences for the variable. Again, how we measure dispersion depends on the level of measurement of the data.

Because of the dilemma that Coombs pointed out, the best statistical measures of dispersion are for interval and ratio data. The basic measures used for such data are the "variance" and the "standard deviation." In a loose sense, they measure how much the average case's value deviates from the mean. Specifically, if we let the ith person's value for variable Y be denoted as Y_i, and if we represent the mean of Y as $\bar{Y}$ (so $\bar{Y} = \sum Y_i/n$ where n is the number of people or cases and $\sum$ denoted summation over the Y values for the different people), then the variance of Y is $\sum (Y_i - \bar{Y})^2/n$ the average squared deviation from the mean. The standard deviation (S) is the square root of the variance, returning to the original unit of measurement instead of the squared units employed by the variance statistic.[1] If there is no dispersion—if everyone has the same value of the variable—then the variance and the standard deviation equal zero. The larger the dispersion around the mean, the greater the variance and the standard deviation.

There are some comparable measures for nominal and ordinal data, but none so conventional as the variance and standard deviation. One approach based on "information theory" has been explained in a Workshop article by Darcy and Aigner (1980) on entropy analysis. Entropy is a measure of the uniformity of the distribution of cases in the categories of the variable, so entropy is maximal if there is an even distribution of cases along the categories of the variable, as if equal numbers of people watched ABC, CBS, NBC, and cable networks for

[1] The conventional statistical notation is to represent parameters for the entire population being studied by Greek letters, μ (mu) for the population mean and σ (sigma) for the population standard deviation. The Roman letters used here are for sample statistics, the sample estimates of the population parameters, such as Y for the sample mean and S for the sample standard deviation.

the news. This would be a case of maximal dispersion but at the nominal level. Entropy analysis can also be used on ordinal data. Full details on entropy analysis and its multivariate extensions are given in Darcy and Aigner.

In the same way that we speak of trying to "explain variance" for interval and ratio level variables, at other levels of measurement we are trying to explain the order of responses for ordinal data and to predict values for nominal data. At the nominal level, we can predict a person's value for a variable perfectly if there is no dispersion, so the level of prediction error indicates the amount of dispersion—and how typical the model value is. If the modal person watches CBS news, that mode is more descriptive if it is 95% of the public watching CBS news than if it is just a bare plurality (perhaps 26% watching CBS compared to 25% for ABC, 25% for NBC, and 24% for cable). We would be more accurate in predicting a person's news network in the first case than in the second.

At the ordinal level, we can seek to explain the order of responses. The order is fully meaningful, so it can be analyzed. We shall not present any summary measures of dispersion at the ordinal level, but we shall make use of this concept of explaining the order of differences as we move to measures of relationship.

Standardized Variables

A final notion should be introduced before leaving the case of single variable descriptive statistics—the "standardized variable." A standardized variable is an interval or ratio variable whose values have been transformed to have a mean of zero and a standard deviation (and variance) of one. This standardization is accomplished by first computing the mean ($\bar{Y}$) and the standard deviation (S_y) of the original variable (Y) and then applying for the ith case the linear rule:

$$Z_i = (Y_i - \bar{Y})/S_y.$$

Since standardized variables are useful because of their mathematical properties, they will be used in proofs and discussions in several later chapters.

Univariate Statistical Inference

To introduce the topic of statistical inference, we shall consider the single variable case. The central tendency and dispersion measures discussed so far have been merely descriptive measures. They would be appropriate for describing the central tendency or dispersion for the cases studied. However, we are often instead interested in discussing a broader population than the cases studied, particularly when the cases studied are a sample drawn from a larger population.

For interval data (the only type of data we shall treat in this section), we would want to make statements about the population mean on the basis of the sample mean and standard deviation. The best estimate of the population mean is the sample mean, but the sample variance turns out to be a "biased" estimate of the population variance—on the average it underestimates the population variance. This bias can be correction by multiplying the sample variance by the fraction $(n/(n - 1))$, where n is the sample size. We shall denote the unbiased estimate of the variance by s^2.

We can use the sample mean and the unbiased estimate of the variance to make more powerful statements about the population mean. If we were taking not just a single sample and recording its mean but several samples and the mean of each, this set of sample means is called a "sampling distribution of means." Regardless of the shape of the distribution of the variable, the sampling distribution of the mean can be shown to have a "normal distribution"—the bell-shaped distribution of Figure 1. The figure shows that most of these sample means will be fairly close to the mean for the population. Just as we computed a standard deviation for a variable, we can compute a standard deviation for this sampling distribution. This statistic is termed the "standard error of the mean." Its formula is:

$s_m = \sqrt{(s^2/n)}$, where s^2 is the unbiased estimate of the variance,

or

$s_m = \sqrt{(S^2/(n - 1))}$, where S^2 is the biased estimate of the variance.

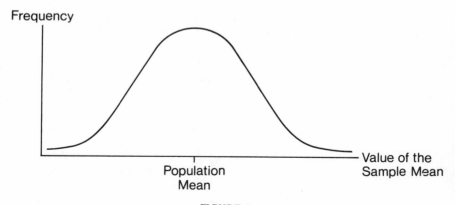

FIGURE 1

Sampling Distribution of the Mean

Because the shape of the normal distribution is well-known, we can determine the likelihood of sample means that are far from the true population mean. When the number of cases in the sample is large, the likelihood of a sample mean being more than 1.96 standard errors above or below the true population mean is only .05. Stated in another way, there is only a five percent chance of a sample mean being more than two (actually 1.96) standard error units from the population mean. Or to put it yet another way, in all but five samples out of every 100 the sample mean will be within two (1.96) standard errors from the population mean.

This fact can be used for "hypothesis testing." For example, say that we were interested in whether the mean for a variable differs "significantly" from zero. If the standard error were 3, a sample mean of 4 would not be considered significantly different from zero (since it is less than two standard errors above zero), but a sample mean of 7 would be termed significant (at the .05 level). This type of significance is sometimes labelled "statistical significance" to distinguish it from "substantive significance," because the fact that a result attains significance in this statistical sense does not guarantee that it has any substantive importance. In the end, substantive significance is at least as important as statistical significance, though there is no simple statistical rule that can be applied to guarantee substantive significance.

Other statistical inference procedures will be mentioned in later chapters, including the χ^2 (*chi*-square) test for checking the significance of a relationship in the following two chapters and tests of the significance of regression coefficients (see Asher's chapter on "Regression Analysis").

Relationships

Now that statistics for single variables have been described, we can turn to the more important case of two-variable relationships. If we want to explain the dispersion of a dependent variable (why some cases have different values for it than do other cases), we must compare their values for that variable with their values for some independent variables. For example, if we wanted to understand why some people watch more network news than others, we might examine their education to see whether the people with more education are those watching more news. Figure 2 illustrates what the relationship might look like: each dot is meant to represent a person, the horizontal axis indicates the amount of education the person has (in years of formal education), and the vertical axis indicates the amount of time the person watched network news (in minutes). The diagram of Figure 2 is often called a "scattergram" or "scatterplot."

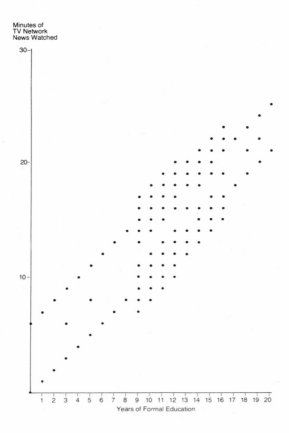

FIGURE 2

Relationship between Education and Television Network News Watching
(Hypothetical Data)

The scattergram approach becomes hard to read when several people have the same combination of values for the two variables, so often (and especially for nominal and ordinal variables) the relationship is displayed by means of a "crosstabulation" like Table 1. The columns in Table 1 correspond to the person's years of education, the rows correspond to the amount of network news watched (now collapsed into a small number of categories), and the cell entry shows how many people with that many years of education watched each amount of network news.

It is clear from Figure 2 and Table 1 that the factor of education helps

TABLE 1

Crosstabulation Based on Figure 2

1a. Four-Category Variables

Time Spent Watching TV Network News (In Minutes)	Years of Education				
	0-8	9-12	13-16	17-20	Totals
0	1	0	0	0	1
1-10	15	10	0	0	25
11-20	4	30	24	3	61
21-30	0	0	6	7	13
Totals	20	40	30	10	100

1b. Dichotomous Variables

Time Spent Watching TV Network News (In Minutes)	Years of Education		
	0-12	13-20	Totals
0-10	26	0	26
11-30	34	40	74
Totals	60	40	100

explain network news watching, but it is not a complete explanation in itself. In social science, we do not expect any single variable to explain any dependent variable perfectly—because there is inevitably a random component in human behavior, because there is inevitably some error in our measurements, and because there are generally multiple causes of human behavior. What we would find useful in examining a single predictor like education is to summarize the prediction that education is providing so that we can compare it to the contributions of other possible independent variables, such as age or interest in politics. We might be able to compare figures and tables, like those already shown, to determine the relative impact of different predictors, but it can be difficult to gauge the relative explanation of different variables by just glancing at figures and tables. Also, while the figure and table provide much precise information, this information would be easier to communicate to someone if it could be summarized in a more concise manner.

"Measures of relationship" are used because they provide a nice way of summarizing a relationship. The relationship in the figure or table might be summarized with a single number—easy to communicate—which could be compared to similar values for other explanatory variables to see which is the more important predictor of the dependent variable. Much attention is thus given to measures of relationships between variables. The complication is that there are different measures of relationship that can be used—because of the existence of different levels of measurement, because there are different notions of what a relationship is, and because of the susceptibility of some measures to various facets of the data. These factors affecting the choice of a measure of relationship will be discussed in detail in this section and in the next two chapters.

Measures for Interval and Ratio Data

In accord with "the dilemma of the social scientist," the classical statistics for measuring the relationship between a pair of variables are based on interval and ratio variables, even if much social science data are just nominal and ordinal. Measures of relationship have been developed for nominal and ordinal data, but these nominal and ordinal statistics can be understood better after familiarity with the classic measures for interval and ratio data. Since the interval and ratio statistics will be explained in detail in the "Regression Analysis" chapter, the description of them here will be relatively brief.

The standard approach for interval and ratio data is to adopt a "linear" model, which assumes a constant change in the dependent variable for a unit change in the independent variable. Figure 3 shows what a linear model

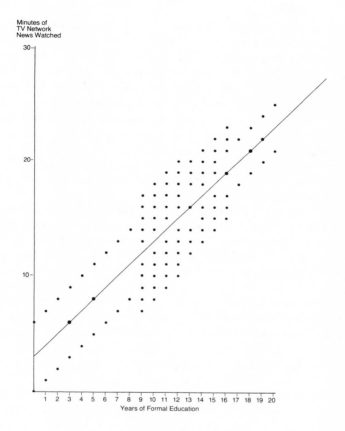

FIGURE 3

Linear Regression for Figure 2

might find for the data of Figure 2. An increase of one year of formal education is found to be associated with an increase of 1.0 minutes in watching network news. This statistic is termed a "regression slope," or b, and it represents the amount of change in the dependent variable associated with a one-unit change in the independent variable. Additionally, the regression line crosses the vertical axis at 3 minutes, indicating that 3 minutes of TV news watching is the level predicted for those with zero years of education—this is called the "intercept" of the regression equation, or a. The "Regression Analysis" chapter will explain how the regression line is placed and how the regression slope and intercept are computed.

The remaining statistical question is how well the regression equation fits the data. There would be a perfect fit only if all the points are exactly on the regression line, so it is obvious from Figure 3 that the fit is not perfect. The degree of fit is measured by comparing the person's actual value of the dependent variable with the value predicted for him or her on the basis of the regression equation. For example, the regression equation predicts that everyone with 6 years of education watches network news $3 + (1.0)6 = 9$ minutes, but the figure shows that some of the people with 6 years of education instead watch 12 and 6 minutes. The difference between 12 and the predicted 9 is the error in prediction for the first person—a regression "residual" of 3.0—while the difference between 6 and 9 gives a regression residual of -3.0 for the second person.

If all the points were exactly on the regression line, all the regression residuals would be zero. Thus the size of the residuals tells us the quality of the fit of the regression equation to the data. However, some standardization is required because the size of the residuals depends on the units in which the dependent variable is being measured. (For example, the residuals listed above would look much larger—180 and -180—if the television watching time were being measured in seconds rather than minutes.) One way of handling this is to standardize the variables before computing the residuals. An equivalent approach is to compare the variance of the residuals with the variance of the dependent variable. The smaller the variance of the residuals compared to the variance of the original dependent variable, the better the fit of the regression equation.

The actual statistic employed to measure the fit of the regression equation is known as r^2. It equals $1 -$ (the variance of the residuals)/(the variance of the dependent variable). This equals 1.0 if there is a perfect fit—if all the points are exactly on the regression line, so the residuals are all zero and their variance is zero. If r^2 equals zero, the linear regression equation is useless because the regression residuals have as much variance as the original dependent variable. The larger the r^2 value, the greater the proportion of "explained variance" and the better the fit of the regression equation. The statistic r^2 is interpreted as "the proportion of the variance in the dependent variable accounted for by a linear relationship with the independent variable."[2] The r^2 value for the regression equation of Figure 3 is .71, indicating that 71 percent of the variance in minutes of network news watched can be accounted for statistically by educa-

---

[2]Mathematically, the regression equation is determined by using calculus to determine the regression slope and intercept which maximize the value of r^2. The formula for r^2 is

$$r^2 = (\sum_i X_i Y_i/n - \overline{X}\ \overline{Y})^2/ (\text{var } X \text{ var } Y).$$

tion. How good a fit this is depends largely on the standards in a field—this would be considered a very impressive linear fit in most substantive fields, though it would be considered less impressive in a few fields where nearly perfect fits are routine.

The conventional statistic used to measure strength of relationship for interval and ratio variables is known as Pearson's r. This correlation coefficient is simply the square root of the r^2 value we have been discussing. The larger the Pearson's r value, the greater the degree of linear relationship between the variables. Pearson's r can also have negative values to show that an increase in the independent value is associated with a decrease in the dependent variable—in which case the more negative the correlation, the greater the relationship. A correlation of zero indicates no association between the variables. The Pearson's r correlation for Figure 2 is .84, indicating a very substantial linear correlation between education and time spent watching network news.

How useful is the linear regression and correlation approach described in this section? It is restrictive in that relationships are not always linear. For example, Figure 4 shows a case in which increased education leads to increased news watching up to a point, after which people with advanced degrees watch less television news (maybe because they watch less television). A curvilinear

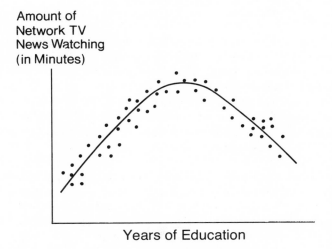

FIGURE 4
Curvilinear Relationship

regression would fit the data in Figure 4 perfectly, and there are procedures for curvilinear regression. It is useful to examine scatterplots to see if curvilinear regression is required. But the point of the current discussion is to realize that Pearson's r summarizes only the degree of linear relationship between the variables, even when more of the variance of the dependent variable can be explained by the independent variable through curvilinear regression.

The approach utilizing linear regression and correlation is limited to the case of nondichotomous dependent variables that are either at the interval or ratio levels of measurement. Dichotomous dependent variables result in violations of some of the assumptions underlying regression analysis. The variance concept does not apply to nominal and ordinal dependent variables, so the calculations underlying regression and correlation analysis are inappropriate.[3] The measures of relationship discussed in the rest of this section are attempts to emulate the logic of Pearson's r for nominal, ordinal, and dichotomous variables.

Measures for Nominal, Ordinal, and Dichotomous Data

Most measures of relationship for nominal, ordinal, and dichotomous variables follow the conventions developed for Pearson's r:

- a value of + 1.0 represents a perfect positive relationship,
- a value of 0.0 represents a null relationship, and
- a value of − 1.0 represents a perfect negative relationship.

However, different measures call for different interpretations of what is meant by a perfect or a null relationship. Weisberg (1974) describes several different "models of a relationship" based on various combinations of definitions of perfect and null relationships, but we shall present here only the four on which the measures discussed in the next two chapters are based.[4] Also, different measures employ different interpretations of values between zero and one, so some of these interpretations of intermediate values must also be introduced here.

The Pearson's r model of a relationship. It is useful to begin by specifying precisely the approaches taken by Pearson's r. It has the value of zero when the

---

[3] This problem does not affect the case of nominal or ordinal independent variables when used with interval or ratio dependent variables. There is a special application of the general linear model—known as "analysis of variance"—which is used for this case. "Analysis of covariance" is used for the case of an interval or ratio dependent variable along with a mixture of independent variable measurement levels.

[4] See also the presentation in Garson (1976, pp. 282–308).

variables are "statistically independent." Table 2a illustrates this situation by showing a case in which the proportions of people watching TV network news 0 minutes, 1–10 minutes, 11–20 minutes, and 21–30 minutes are the same for each education category (30% watching no news, 20% watching 1–10 minutes, 20% watching 11–20 minutes, and 30% watching 21–30 minutes). There is no relationship here, since the distribution of network news watching is identical for each independent variable category. Table 2b shows what this would look like for the "fourfold" table of dichotomous variables. As indicated below the tables, not only is Pearson's r zero here, but so are the other coefficients to be discussed in this chapter.

Pearson's r has the value of one under a condition known as "strong monotonicity." This is illustrated in Table 3, where increases in education are always matched by increases in amounts of news watching. All the cases are lined up along the main diagonal of the table.

Intermediate values of Pearson's r are interpreted by squaring their values, since r^2 indicates the proportion of the variance of the dependent variable accounted for by the independent variable. Because of this interpretation for its intermediate values, r^2 is known as a "proportional-reduction-in-error" (PRE) measure. That is, r^2 indicates how much knowledge of the independent variable category for a person helps diminish the error in predicting the person's dependent variable score—or, how small the residual variance is as compared to the variance of the original dependent variable.

Measures of association have been developed for ordinal and dichotomous variables that employ the exact model of a relationship used by Pearson's r. Kendall's τ_b (*tau*-b), probably the most used coefficient for ordinal data, adopts this approach. As can be seen in the tables in this chapter, its values tend to be roughly about the size of Pearson's r values calculated on the same data (with integer scoring of the ordinal values), so its intermediate values are generally interpreted roughly as we would interpret intermediate Pearson's r values.

For dichotomous variables, Pearson's r and Kendall's τ_b are equal, and they both equal a third statistic for nominal variables, known as ϕ(*phi*). As these are all equal, they employ the same model of a relationship among dichotomous variables, and they all can be interpreted by squaring their values roughly as we would square r values. The perfect relationship among dichotomous variables in Table 3b is termed a "two-way relationship" in that college education is both a necessary and sufficient condition for watching network news for more than 10 minutes. We can predict news watching perfectly from education, and vice versa.

Pearson's r, Kendall's τ_b, and ϕ for dichotomous variables are all part of the same family of relationship measures. The regression slope b is also part of this

TABLE 2

Statistical Independence as a Null Condition

2a. Four-Category Variables

Time Spent Watching TV Network News (In Minutes)	Years of Education				Totals
	0-8	9-12	13-16	17-20	
0	6	12	9	3	30
1-10	4	8	6	2	20
11-20	4	8	6	2	20
21-30	6	12	9	3	30
Totals	20	40	30	10	100

Symmetric Coefficients		Asymmetric Coefficients	
Goodman and Kruskal's λ	.00	Goodman and Kruskal's λ	.00
Pearson's r	.00	slope b	.00
Kendall's τ_b	.00	Somer's d	.00
Kendall's τ_c	.00	Goodman and Kruskal's τ	.00
Goodman and Kruskal's γ	.00		

2b. Dichotomous Variables

Time Spent Watching TV Network News (In Minutes)	Years of Education		Totals
	0-12	13-20	
0-10	30	20	50
11-30	30	20	50
Totals	60	40	100

Symmetric Coefficients		Asymmetric Coefficients	
Goodman and Kruskal's λ	.00	Goodman and Kruskal's λ	.00
φ statistic	.00	Percent difference	.00
Kendall's τ_c	.00	Goodman and Kruskal's τ	.00
Yule's Q	.00		

TABLE 3

Strong Monotonicity as a Perfect Relationship

3a. Four-Category Variables

Time Spent Watching TV Network News (In Minutes)	Years of Education				
	0-8	9-12	13-16	17-20	Totals
0	20	0	0	0	20
1-10	0	40	0	0	40
11-20	0	0	30	0	30
21-30	0	0	0	10	10
Totals	20	40	30	10	100

Symmetric Coefficients		Asymmetric Coefficients	
Goodman and Kruskal's λ	1.00	Goodman and Kruskal's λ	1.00
Pearson's r	1.00	slope b	1.00
Kendall's τ_b	1.00	Somer's d	1.00
Kendall's τ_c	.93	Goodman and Kruskal's τ	.93
Goodman and Kruskal's γ	1.00		

3b. Dichotomous Variables

Time Spent Watching TV Network News (In Minutes)	Years of Education		
	0-12	13-20	Totals
0-10	60	0	60
11-30	0	40	40
Totals	60	40	100

Symmetric Coefficients		Asymmetric Coefficients	
Goodman and Kruskal's λ	1.00	Goodman and Kruskal's λ	1.00
φ statistic	1.00	Percent difference	1.00
Kendall's τ_c	.96	Goodman and Kruskal's τ	1.00
Yule's Q	1.00		

family. It is an asymmetric measure of the change in the dependent variable induced by a unit change in the independent variable. Whereas the slope b is appropriate for only interval data, Somers' d statistic is an attempt to develop an analogue to the regression slope for ordinal variables. Its relationship to Kendall's τ_b is the same as the relationship of the regression slope to Pearson's r. For dichotomous variables, the regression slope and Somer's d are both equivalent to the simple percentage difference—the proportion of cases in one category of the independent variable that are high on the dependent variable minus the proportion of cases in the other category of the independent variable that are high on the dependent variable. All of these coefficients are discussed in more detail in the following two chapters. We now turn to some measures which adopt different models of a relationship.

Accord as a null model. Instead of treating statistical independence as a null model, it is sometimes appropriate to say there is a zero relationship between two variables when the mode of the dependent variable is the same for each category of the independent variable. Table 4a illustrates this possibility with an example in which the most frequent amount of news watching for each educational category is 0 minutes. If we were predicting a person's news watching on the basis of the person's education, the best prediction for each educational category would be the same—zero minutes. This has been termed an "accord" null model, because each independent variable category is in agreement in terms of modal behavior on the dependent variable.

Goodman and Kruskal's asymmetric λ (*lambda*) statistic is a measure of relationship for nominal variables which adopts this accord definition of a null relationship (and the strong monotonicity definition of a perfect relationship). As shown under Table 4, it is the only statistic with a value of zero for this situation.

The intermediate values of the asymmetric λ have a PRE interpretation. Specifically, λ assumes that the best prediction of the value of the dependent variable for a person (or case) is the modal value of the dependent variable for that person's independent variable category. For example, the best prediction of how much network news a person with college education watches is the modal amount for all people with college education. What λ then indicates is how much less prediction error in the dependent variable there is when the person's category for the independent variable is known than when it is not. Thus, it measures the proportional-reduction-in-error in prediction of the person's dependent variable category. The λ statistic is discussed further in the two following chapters.

TABLE 4
Accord as a Null Condition

4a. Four-Category Variables

Time Spent Watching TV Network News (In Minutes)	Years of Education				Totals
	0-8	9-12	13-16	17-20	
0	20	16	10	4	50
1-10	0	15	6	1	22
11-20	0	5	9	2	16
21-30	0	4	5	3	12
Totals	20	40	30	10	100

Symmetric Coefficients		Asymmetric Coefficients	
Goodman and Kruskal's λ	.08	Goodman and Kruskal's λ	.00
Pearson's r	.42	slope b	.49
Kendall's τ_b	.39	Somer's d	.38
Kendall's τ_c	.35	Goodman and Kruskal's τ	.16
Goodman and Kruskal's γ	.55		

4b. Dichotomous Variables

Time Spent Watching TV Network News (In Minutes)	Years of Education		Totals
	0-12	13-20	
0-10	51	21	72
11-30	9	19	28
Totals	60	40	100

Symmetric Coefficients		Asymmetric Coefficients	
Goodman and Kruskal's λ	.15	Goodman and Kruskal's λ	.00
φ statistic	.35	Percent difference	.32
Kendall's τ_c	.31	Goodman and Kruskal's τ	.13
Yule's Q	.67		

Weak monotonicity as a perfect relationship. There are also alternative definitions of a perfect relationship. Instead of requiring strong monotonicity, we could settle for "weak monotonicity", a condition in which (for a perfect positive relationship) an increase in the independent variable never results in a decrease in the dependent variable. Table 5 illustrates this situation. Greater amounts of education lead to the same or more network news watching but, never less. It should be noted that this is a case in which the independent variable categories are not perfectly united for the dependent variable (as they would have to be for strong monotonicity), but they are as united for it as possible, given the marginals of the variables. That last phrase is critical. Strong monotonicity can hold only if both variables have the same marginal distributions. But it is not clear whether the univariate distributions of the two variables should affect our assessment of the degree of their bivariate relationship.

The γ (*gamma*) statistic developed by Goodman and Kruskal embodies this notion of a perfect relationship (while treating statistical independence as its null condition). As shown under Table 5, it is the only statistic with a value of one for this situation. Although γ has a PRE interpretation, that interpretation is too complicated to describe here. In frequency of use for ordinal data γ is probably second only to Kendall's τ_b.

Yule's Q statistic is the equivalent of γ for dichotomous variables. The perfect relationship for dichotomous variables in Table 5b is termed a "one-way relationship" in that college education is a "sufficient" condition for watching more than 10 minutes of news but not a "necessary" condition. News watching can be predicted perfectly for the college educated but not for the rest, in contrast to the two-way relationship of Table 3b. Yule's Q and γ are discussed further in the next two chapters, and a special application of Yule's Q in scaling will be described in Weisberg's chapter on "Scaling Objectives and Procedures."

Moderate monotonicity as a perfect relationship. One further definition of a perfect relationship will be mentioned briefly here. "Moderate monotonicity" accepts as a perfect ordinal relationship a case in which the variables have unequal numbers of categories, the cases in the same category of the variable with more categories also are in the same category of the other variable, and an increase in the variable with more categories never results in a decrease in the other variable. This situation is best understood by referring to Table 6. More education leads to the same amount or more television watching, never less. The relationship is as close to strong monotonicity as possible, given the unequal numbers of categories for the two variables. Should the fact that two

TABLE 5

Weak Monotonicity as a Perfect Relationship

5a. Four-Category Variables

Time Spent Watching TV Network News (In Minutes)	Years of Education				
	0-8	9-12	13-16	17-20	Totals
0	10	0	0	0	10
1-10	10	30	0	0	40
11-20	0	10	20	0	30
21-30	0	0	10	10	20
Totals	20	40	30	10	100

Symmetric Coefficients		Asymmetric Coefficients	
Goodman and Kruskal's λ	.50	Goodman and Kruskal's λ	.50
Pearson's r	.87	slope b	.89
Kendall's τ_b	.83	Somer's d	.83
Kendall's τ_c	.77	Goodman and Kruskal's τ	.45
Goodman and Kruskal's γ	1.00		

5b. Dichotomous Variables

Time Spent Watching TV Network News (In Minutes)	Years of Education		
	0-12	13-20	Totals
0-10	50	0	50
11-30	10	40	50
Totals	60	40	100

Symmetric Coefficients		Asymmetric Coefficients	
Goodman and Kruskal's λ	.78	Goodman and Kruskal's λ	.80
φ statistic	.82	Percent difference	.83
Kendall's τ_c	.80	Goodman and Kruskal's τ	.67
Yule's Q	1.00		

TABLE 6

Moderate Monotonicity as a Perfect Relationship

Time Spent Watching TV Network News (In Minutes)	Years of Education				
	0-8	9-12	13-16	17-20	Total
0	20	0	0	0	20
1-10	0	40	0	0	40
11-30	0	0	30	10	40
Totals	20	40	30	10	100

Symmetric coefficients		Asymmetric coefficients	
Goodman & Kruskal's λ	.92	Goodman & Kruskal's λ	1.00
Pearson's r	.95	Slope b	.79
Kendall's τ_b	.96	Somer's d	.91
Kendall's τ_c	.96		
		Goodman & Kruskal's τ	1.00
Goodman & Kruskal's γ	1.00		

variables have different numbers of categories prevent a perfect relationship between them? In some substantive situations it should, and in some it should not. Particularly with collapsed ordinal variables (as in the Table 6), the analyst may feel that the number of categories of the variables is arbitrary and thus irrelevant to the degree of relationship. Then the moderate monotonicity model would be more appropriate than the strong monotonicity model.

At the same time, the moderate monotonicity model is more stringent than the weak monotonicity model. Some relationships (such as that of Table 5) will be deemed perfect by the weak monotonicity model but not according to the moderate monotonicity model, because the moderate monotonicity model imposes the extra requirement for a perfect relationship that the cases in the same category of the variable with more categories also be in the same category of the other variable—which is the case for Table 6 but not Table 5.

Two measures of relationship are loosely based on the moderate monotonicity model, but each attains the value of one only under very particular circumstances. Goodman and Kruskal's τ (tau) statistic is a measure for nominal variables which employs this model of a perfect relationship, but it can attain the value of one only if the dependent variable has no more categories than the independent variable.[5] It should be noted that Goodman and Kurskal's τ has a

[5] This corresponds to Garson's (1976: 285) model of "predictive monotonic association."

value of one in Table 6. (Here γ also has a value of one, since a relationship that satisfies moderate monotonicity also satisfies weak monotonicity, but the reverse is not true, so τ is less than one in Table 5.) Goodman and Kruskal's τ has a PRE interpretation that is explained in the final section of the Buchanan chapter.

Kendall's τ_c (tau-c) is a measure for ordinal variables which is based on moderate monotonicity, but it can attain the value of one only when each independent variable category has the same number of cases. As a result, it is less than one in Table 6 (and even for the strong monotonicity case in Table 3). Although τ_c is an adjustment of Kendall's τ_b for tables in which the two variables have different numbers of categories, it should be emphasized that it does not necessarily have the value of 1.0 even in situations like Table 6, in which the relationship is perfect except for the unequal numbers of categories. In the next two chapters τ_c is explained in more detail.

The emphasis given to relationship models in this section is designed to suggest a strategy for selecting a relationship measure for a particular substantive case. When studying a particular problem, we should think through what would be a null relationship in that instance and what would be a perfect relationship and then adopt the corresponding relationship model and a measure based on that model.

If more than one relationship model makes substantive sense for the problem being studied, then we should use more than one relationship measure. After all, since it is impossible to summarize a real relationship fully with just one number, it can be appropriate to summarize different aspects of that relationship with different numbers.

Sensitivities of measures. We have pointed out the relationship models on which many of the common measures of relationship are based, and we have shown that intermediate values of some of these coefficients have PRE interpretations. But it is also appropriate to indicate that there are other factors affecting the magnitude of some of the measures. Some of the measures are sensitive to certain aspects of the data, while other measures are not sensitive to those same features of the data. The values of a measure can be misleading if its sensitivites are not taken into account.

First is a sensitivity to which is the independent variable and which is the dependent variable. Some measures are "symmetric"—their value is the same regardless of which variable is seen as the dependent variable. But other measures are "asymmetric"—their value depends on which is seen as the dependent variable. Pearson's r is the interval level symmetric coefficient, while the regression slope b is asymmetric: it shows the change in the dependent variable for a unit change in the independent variable, and its value would change if the other variable were viewed as independent.

As has been shown below the tables in this chapter, the symmetric coefficients include Kendall's τ_b and τ_c and γ (and ϕ and Yule's Q for dichotomous variables), while the asymmetric statistics include Somer's d and Goodman and Kruskal's τ (and the percentage difference for dichotomous variables). There are both symmetric and asymmetric versions of λ, but the asymmetric version has the clear interpretation.

Sensitivity to the marginals of the independent variable is also important. Returning to the example used in this chapter, should the value of the measure of relationship between education and news watching time be affected by the educational level of the sample? On the whole, we might prefer a lack of sensitivity, but most common measures are sensitive to the independent variable marginals (especially for nondichotomous independent variables). In his chapter, Bruner gives special attention to this sensitivity and presents an equiweighting procedure designed to handle the problem.

Additionally, some measures turn out to have higher values than others, even when computed on the same data and after taking into account the other factors that have been considered in this chapter. When interpreting a correlation value, it is important to realize whether the measure employed has particularly low or high values. For example, the two most commonly used coefficients for ordinal data turn out to be noncomparable, since Goodman and Kruskal's γ is generally much larger than (and always at least as large as) Kendall's τ_b. A research report claiming very high correlations should be discounted somewhat if those correlations are γs, while a research report finding moderate correlations should be given extra credence if those correlations are τ_bs.

Summary. Table 7 summarizes the various sensitivities discussed in this section for many of the relationship measures as well as their underlying models of a relationship. Each of the measures in the table is discussed further in the two chapters which follow. The table also points out some of the equivalent coefficients for dichotomous variables.

As an example of the considerations underlying the choice and interpretation of a relationship measure, Table 8 shows the values for the coefficients for the statistics discussed in this chapter for the data originally displayed in Table 1. These data are based on Figure 3. The regression equation in Figure 3 was $Y = 3 + 1.0X$, with an associated Pearson's r value of .84. Collapsing the interval variables into four categories each affects the correlation value. The correlations for the tables are all lower than .84, except for the γ value, which is close to 1.0. The λ values are also of interest here: they show that the knowl-

TABLE 7

Properties of Measures of Association

Multiple Category Variables		Dichotomous Variables		Model of Relationship		Level of Measurement	Values
Symmetric Measures	*Asymmetric Measures*	*Symmetric Measures*	*Asymmetric Measures*	*Perfect Relationship*	*Null Condition*		
Goodman and Kruskal's λ	Goodman and Kruskal's λ	Goodman and Kruskal's λ	Goodman and Kruskal's λ	Strong Montonicity	Accord	Nominal	Moderate-to-Low
Pearson's r	Slope b	ϕ Statistic	Percent Difference	Strong Monotonicity	Statistical Independence	Interval	Moderate
Kendall's τ_b	Somer's d					Ordinal	Moderate
Kendall's τ_c		Kendall's τ_c		Moderate Monotonicity	Statistical Independence	Ordinal	Moderate
	Goodman and Kruskal's τ		Goodman and Kruskal's τ	Moderate Monotonicity	Statistical Independence	Nominal	Low
Goodman and Kruskal's γ		Yule's Q		Weak Monotonicity	Statistical Independence	Ordinal	High

TABLE 8

Measures of Association for Table 1

8a. Four-Category Variables				8b. Dichotomous Variables			
Symmetric Coefficients		Asymmetric Coefficients		Symmetric Coefficients		Asymmetric Coefficients	
Goodman and Kruskal's λ	.28	Goodman and Kruskal's λ	.38	Goodman and Kruskal's λ	.09	Goodman and Kruskal's λ	.00
Pearson's r	.72	Slope b	.51	ϕ statistic	.48	Percent Difference	.43
Kendall's τ_b	.67	Somer's d	.59				
Kendall's τ_c	.56			Kendall's τ_c	.42		
		Goodman and Kruskal's τ	.33			Goodman and Kruskal's τ	.23
Goodman and Kruskal's γ	.95			Yule's Q	1.00		

edge of the independent variable category helps predict the dependent variable category to a limited extent.

Table 8 also demonstrates that dichotomizing variables further affects correlation values, considerably in some instances. Measures of association are often very sensitive to combining categories of a variable. As a result, it is usually best to use the full version of a variable rather than collapse codes; unnecessary dichotomization should especially be avoided.

The discussion here has not focused on any single measure of relationship as the "proper" measure, because most statisticians would agree that there is no single proper measure. Instead, different measures have been developed in order to examine different conceptions of a relationship. Actually, Hunter (1973) has attempted to determine the most "valid" measures for crosstabulations of dichotomous data by seeing how different measures compare to experts' intuitive judgments of the amount of relationship in a table and by analyzing the factor measures. He finds that sociologists' intuitive judgments of the amount of relationship in a table correlate nearly perfectly ($r = .98$) with the percentage difference statistic. However, his overall interpretation of the intuitive judgment data and of the first rotated factor is that λ and Goodman and Kruskal's τ are the most valid measures.

Hunter's approach is considered very controversial (see the comments in the January 1975 issue of the *American Journal of Sociology* by Bagley, Erickson, Hornung, Schmitt, and especially Gordon, along with Hunter's rejoinder). In particular, Gordon does a nice job of explaining that, since there is no reason to prefer one rotated factor in a factor analysis more than another, Hunter should not have focused on his first rotated factor. Gordon also points out why sociologists' intuitive judgment of the amount of relationship correlates so strongly with the percent difference measure: the percent different is the easiest statistic to compute by simple inspection of a table. To repeat the basic point, most statisticians would agree that rather than seek one or two "valid" measures, it is better to understand the circumstances in which each measure should be employed. That is the approach taken here and in the following two chapters.

Controls

To understand a relationship between two variables, it is often necessary to take into account a third variable. This is done routinely in the natural sciences, where extraneous third variables are "experimentally controlled' so as to study the effect of one variable on a second. In the typical physical science laboratory, as many third variables as possible are held constant while the experimental variable is varied to determine its separate effects on the dependent variable. Unfortunately, experimental controls of this type are generally not feasible in the social sciences. Instead of introducing controls in the data collection, the social sciences typically introduce controls in the data analysis stage.

One common social science procedure is known as "physical controlling." In this procedure, the cases are physically divided into categories according to their values for a third variable, and then the two-variable relationship of interest is examined for each category of the third variable. For example, if we thought that the relationship between education and television news watching might be different for men and women, we could examine the education-news watching relationship separately for men and women, possibly by computing the correlation between the two variables first for men and then for women. If the relationship were the same for both men and women, then we would conclude that gender does not affect the relationship between education and news watching. It might instead happen that the correlation between education and news watching is greater for the total sample than for men and women taken separately. That would mean that part of the original apparent relationship between education and news watching was really a gender effect, due to the differences in education between the sexes. At the extreme, there could be a large relationship between education and news watching for the total sample, but no relationship for either men or women taken separately. In that case, we would speak of the original relationship between education and news watching as being spurious—that gender affects news watching, and that the only reason for the correlation of education with news watching is the educational differences between the sexes.

Physical controls get awkward when there are many categories of the control variable (which is especially likely if the control variable is interval), so a strategy of "statistical control" is sometimes employed. A single partial correlation coefficient is computed to gauge the relationship between the independent variable and the dependent variable when controlling for one (or more) control variable(s). For example, we could compute the partial correlation between education and news watching, statistically controlling for age. That would indicate the effect of education on news watching when age is "held constant." Let us denote the dependent variable as Y, the independent variable as X, and the control variable as Z. Then the partial correlation is:

$$r_{xy.z} = (r_{xy} - r_{xz} r_{yz}) / \sqrt{(1 - r^2_{xz})(1 - r^2_{yz})}.$$

If the partial correlation is the same as the original correlation between the independent and dependent variables, then the control variable does not affect that bivariate relationship. On the other hand, if the partial correlation is zero, then the original relationship was in fact due to the control variable being correlated with both the independent and dependent variables. A related statistical control procedure is used in regression analysis to determine the effect of one independent variable on the dependent variable, while controlling other independent variables. These partial regression coefficients will be explained further in Asher's chapter on "Regression Analysis."

The most common partial correlation is based on Pearson's r. An analogous formula is sometimes used to generate partials for Kendall's τ_b, though many analysts prefer to treat their ordinal variables as interval and use the partial r. (Generally, the r values are about the same as the τ values, and computer programs for partial r's are more readily available than for partial τs.) There is also a partial γ statistic, but it has a more complicated formula and is rarely used.

Conclusions

The two following chapters further present measures of relationship. Buchanan's chapter gives a nice introduction to the different measures and to the stakes involved in a choice among them. Buchanan presents measures for dichotomous variables, measures for ordinal variables, statistical significance testing, and then measures for nominal variables. The ∇_p (del-p) measure introduced at the end of his chapter has subsequently been elaborated on in Hildebrand, Laing, and Rosenthal (1976, 1977). Those works also present procedures for multivariate analysis of ordinal data based on the ∇_p logic.

Bruner's chapter returns to the standard measures of relationship, focusing on which questions the particular coefficients are designed to answer. Bruner devotes special attention to the dependence of the coefficients on the marginals of the independent variable, and he presents an equiweighting procedure designed to eliminate that dependence.

There is a further literature on the analysis of crosstabulations for nominal data, with an emphasis on multivariate nominal analysis. These procedures are discussed in such works as Fienberg (1980), Reynolds (1977), Lehnen and Koch (1974), and the Workshop article by Kritzer (1978). Additionally, the Workshop article by Darcy and Aigner (1980) on entropy analysis presents a procedure for multivariate nominal analysis based on concepts from information theory.

There has also been continuing concern about the development of better measures of relationship for ordinal data. Particularly useful are the discussions of ordinal dependent variables by Crittenden and Montgomery (1980), predictive measures for ordinal data by Kim (1971), and asymmetric monotonic relationships by Leik and Gove (1969, 1971), as well as the Hildebrand, Laing and Rosenthal (1976, 1977) treatment of ordinal prediction analysis.

Two final points should be stressed. First, there is no perfect measure of a relationship. Instead, many different measures have been devised because analysts may have different goals in summarizing relationships. The substantive analyst must decide which is most useful for his or her purposes. The ideas in this chapter and the next two are useful to bear in mind in selecting a measure of relationship, but the reader should not expect to be told which is the correct universal measure of relationship. Second, measuring the strength of a relationship should not be seen as the end point of data analysis. If we are seeking to understand the pattern of dispersion of a variable, then it is necessary to turn to procedures for the analysis of several variables. This topic has been introduced in the above section on controls, but the final two sections of this book consider the multivariate case more fully. All in all, measuring the strength of a relationship is the beginning of statistical analysis, not its end.

REFERENCES

Abelson, Robert P., and Tukey, John. 1970. "Efficient Conversion of Non-Metric Information into Metric Information," in Edward R. Tufte, ed., *The Quantitative Analysis of Social Problems*. Reading, Massachusetts: Addison-Wesley, pp. 407–417.

Bagley, Christopher. 1975. "Other Analyses Similar to Hunter's," *American Journal of Sociology*, January 1975, pp. 992–993.

Coombs, Clyde H. 1953. *A Theory of Data.* New York: Wiley.

Crittenden, Kathleen S., and Montgomery, Andrew C. 1980. "A System of Paired Asymmetric Measures of Association for Use with Ordinal Dependent Variables," *Social Forces,* June 1980, pp. 1178–94.

Darcy, R., and Aigner, Hans. 1980. "The Uses of Entropy in the Multivariate Analysis of Categorical Variables," *American Journal of Political Science,* February 1980, pp. 155–174.

Erickson, Bonnie. 1975. "Tautological Findings," *American Journal of Sociology,* January 1975, pp. 991–992.

Fienberg, Stephen E. 1980. *The Analysis of Cross-Classified Categorical Data,* 2nd ed. Cambridge, Massachusetts: MIT Press.

Garson, G. David. 1976. *Political Science Methods.* Boston: Holbrook.

Gordon, Robert A. 1975. "On 'Validity' as a Criterion," *American Journal of Sociology,* January 1975, pp. 980–987.

Grether, David M. 1976. "On the Use of Ordinal Data in Correlation Analysis," *American Sociological Review,* October 1976, pp. 908–912.

Hensler, Carl, and Stipak, Brian. 1979. "Estimating Interval Scale Values for Survey Item Response Categories," *American Journal of Political Science,* August 1979, pp. 627–649.

Hildebrand, David K.; Laing, James D.; and Rosenthal, Howard. 1976. "Prediction Analysis in Political Research," *American Political Science Review,* June 1976, pp. 509–535.

Hildebrand, David K.; Laing, James D.; and Rosenthal, Howard. 1977. *Analysis of Ordinal Data.* Beverly Hills, California: Sage Publications.

Hornung, Carlton A. 1975. "Errors of Omission and Commission in 'On the Validity of Measures of Association: The Nominal-Nominal Two-by-Two Case,' " *American Journal of Sociology,* January 1975, pp. 975–980.

Hunter, A. A. 1973. "On the Validity of Measures of Association: The Nominal-Nominal Two-by-Two Case," *American Journal of Sociology,* July 1973, pp. 99–109.

Hunter, A. A. 1975. "Reply and Further Elaboration," *American Journal of Sociology,* January 1975, pp. 993–1002.

Kim, Jae-on. 1971. "Predictive Measures of Ordinal Association," *American Journal of Sociology,* March 1971, pp. 891–907.

Kritzer, Herbert M. 1978. "An Introduction to Multivariate Contingency Table Analysis," *American Journal of Political Science,* February 1978, pp. 187–226.

Labovitz, Sanford. 1970. "The Assignment of Numbers to Rank Order Categories," *American Sociological Review,* June 1970, pp. 515–524.

Labovitz, Sanford. 1971. "In Defense of Assigning Numbers to Ranks," *American Sociological Review*, June 1971, pp. 521–522.

Lehnen, Robert G., and Koch, Gary G. 1974. "A General Linear Approach to the Analysis of Non-Metric Data," *American Journal of Political Science*, May 1974, pp. 283–313.

Leik, Robert, and Gove, Walter. 1969. "The Conception and Measurement of Asymmetric Monotonic Relationships in Sociology," *American Journal of Sociology*, May 1969, pp. 696–709.

Leik, Robert, and Gove, Walter. 1971. "An Integrated Approach to Measuring Association," in Herbert Costner, ed., *Sociological Methodology 1971*. San Francisco: Jossey, Bass, pp. 279–301.

Lodge, Milton, and Tursky, Bernard. 1981. "On the Magnitude Scaling of Political Opinion in Survey Research," *American Journal of Political Science*, May 1981, pp. 376–419.

Mayer, Lawrence S. 1970. "Comment on the Assignment of Numbers to Rank Order Categories," *American Sociological Review*, October 1970, pp. 916–917.

Mayer, Lawrence S. 1971. "A Note on Treating Ordinal Data as Interval Data," *American Sociological Review*, June 1971, pp. 519–520.

Reynolds, H. T. 1977. *Analysis of Nominal Data*. Beverly Hills, California: Sage Publications.

Schmitt, Raymond L. 1975. "Methodology and Operational Problems," *American Journal of Sociology*, January 1975, pp. 987–990.

Schweitzer, Sybil, and Schweitzer, Donald G. 1971. "Comment on the Pearson r in Random Number and Precise Functional Scale Transformation," *American Sociological Review*, June 1971, pp. 518–519.

Vargo, Louis G. 1971. "Comment on the Assignment of Numbers to Rank Order Categories," *American Sociological Review*, June 1971, pp. 517–518.

Weisberg, Herbert F. 1974. "Models of Statistical Relationship," *American Political Science Review*, December 1974, pp. 1638–55.

Measures of Association

WILLIAM BUCHANAN

Nominal and Ordinal Bivariate Statistics: The Practitioner's View

The menu of statistics used in the analysis of bivariate tables of nominal and ordinal data is substantial, including among others C, γ, D, d_{yx}, d_{xy}, ∇p, κ', λ_a, λ_b, ϕ, Q, T, two kinds of τ_a and τ_b, τ_c and V, not to mention χ^2 and other significance tests. This bewildering array is more satisfactory to those who invent statistics than to those who use them, either as analysts or as consumers of political analysis. In choosing a measure of relationship between two attributes, it is necessary to consider more than their mathematical or statistical qualities. The level of measurement of the variables, the number of categories, the substantive meaning of the data, the analyst's purpose, whether testing significance in a sample or measuring association in a population, the proposition being investigated (whether it implies necessary or sufficient consequences or both), and the usefulness of statistics as communication devices (particularly whether they are familiar and understandable to the readership), are among the criteria for selecting measures.

In choosing a measure to use in analyzing a table or a series of tables, three sets of criteria are brought to bear. The first are mathematical or statistical. The number of categories in each variable, the level of measurement, the effect of the marginals, assumptions about the distributions of the population being sampled, the equivalence of one measure to another, norming properties of correlation measures, and the power of statistical tests are examples. These are treated in statistics texts.

A second set of criteria, not always acknowledged, includes time, effort, and convenience. In this category we might also include the superiority of a statistic the researcher knows and has used before over one he hasn't, or one that is included in a package that is up and running at the computer center over one that isn't. The availability of rotary calculators in the 1930s, punch card equipment in the 1940s, and computers in the 1950s each had the effect of making complex measures and those requiring iterative processes more popular. The recent availability of minicomputers and a price break on desk and pocket calculators may presage another minor technological revolution. One can often calculate the simple nonparametric statistics to be presented

Reprinted from AMERICAN JOURNAL OF POLITICAL SCIENCE, Vol. XVIII, No. 3, August 1974, pp. 625-646, William Buchanan, "Nominal and Ordinal Bivariate Statistics: The Practitioner's View," by permission of the University of Texas Press.

here at one's desk in less time than he can persuade the computer center bureaucracy to do it for him.

A third set of criteria consists of the advantages and disadvantages of each measure as a communication device. Among these are: (1) The ability of a statistic to reduce an unwieldy mass of information to a single index that reveals its elusive essence and helps us to cope with the besetting curse of our age, information overload. (2) Intelligibility. The correlation coefficient r, for example, is a more complex measure than the regression slope, yet it is understood by many more people because it varies understandably from +1 for positive to −1 for negative correlation. (3) Familiarity to readers, though a perversely self-fulfilling standard, is a legitimate one. For example, kilometers per liter may be a superior measure to miles per gallon, but not for discussing fuel economy with Americans.

In the following discussion I shall apply all three sets of criteria—not always with the same weights, not always explicitly and not, for the sake of the reader, exhaustively—in recommending certain measures. Each user should take them into account in relation to his own resources, his own purposes, his own data and his own readership. Table 1 classifies the measures according to the more relevant mathematical criteria. The other criteria will be used to evaluate the measures in each box.

Levels of Measurement

We are here concerned only with nominal and ordinal levels. Nominal variables consist of the names of classes, qualities or attributes. A two-place nominal scale is a *dichotomy*. Examples are men or women, western or nonwestern nations, open or closed primaries. Thus they distinguish the presence or absence of an attribute: maleness, westernness, openness. Sometimes interval level variables are dichotomized, *e.g.,* less than 8 years of schooling *vs.* more than 8 years is dichotomized as no high school *vs.* some high school.

Another, more troublesome, kind of nominal variable is the *polytomy*, with three or more classes which fall into no intrinsic order. Examples are Protestants, Catholics, and Jews: city manager, mayor-council, and commission governments; Labour, Liberal, and Conservative parties. If one can reorder any pair of categories in a manifold variable without doing violence to logic, it is a polytomy.

Ordinal variables are those susceptible to ordering or ranking: 1st, 2nd, 3rd, *etc.* These numbers do not represent equal measurement intervals; for example upper, middle, working, and lower classes cannot be assumed to be of the same width. Likewise traditional, transitional, and modern societies, and Republican, Independent, and Democratic party identifiers form scales where the order of categories cannot be altered, although the width of the brackets remains vague and unsusceptible to precise measurement. All Guttmann scales measure at the ordinal level, as do scales of hardness of minerals and of loudness or brightness in psychological research. Thus ordinal measurement is a level "higher" in precision than nominal, but not as high as interval.[1]

The reason for making this distinction is that certain statistics are appropriate at each level. An ordinal scale contains information about the rank order of cases, but a polytomy does not. This information is incorporated into the calculation of the statistic, hence an ordinal measure used with a table containing a polytomy could be misleading. On the other hand, a measure meant for polytomies would be inefficient for an ordinal table, since it would not take advantage of all the information conveyed by the numbers. Any dichotomy may be considered a two-level ordinal scale, hence ordinal measures may be used with tables where one variable is ordinal and the other dichotomous. Table 1 is confined to measures used in bivariate analysis at the ordinal and interval level. Multivariate problems, involving control by a third variable, will not be considered here.

Dichotomies

The most basic form of analysis, on which a good proportion of formal knowledge and a larger proportion of intuitive understanding of human behavior is based, is the cross-tabulation of two dichotomies. It was originally called the 2 X 2 fold table, shortened somewhat erroneously to the term "fourfold table."

Let us retest, as of 1973, a familiar hypothesis: Southern senators tend to be committee chairmen. The proposition appears to be straightforward, largely because we know how the test will come out. So let's first construct another less obvious hypothesis in the same form: Women tend to die of fluentive diseases. What does the statement mean? I have tried it out on several groups of well-educated nonresearchers. Characteristically, about one-

---

[1] The interval scale, not treated here, derives its precision and other mathematical qualities from the fact that its units of measure, such as dollars, votes, or people, are of equal value. The ratio scale, in addition, has an absolute zero point. Interval and ratio scales are also called cardinal, as distinguished from ordinal, numbers. See Theodore R. Anderson and Morris Zelditch, Jr., *A Basic Course in Statistics,* 2nd ed., (New York: Holt, Rinehart & Winston, 1968) ch. 1.

TABLE 1

Selected Bivariate Statistics[*]

Level of Measurement	Nominal		Ordinal	Interval
Number of Categories	3 or more (polytomies)	2 (dichotomies)	3 or more	Any
Purpose: Association	ϕ, C, T, V, λ, Goodman & Kruskal's τ	Q, ϕ	γ, Kendall's τ_b and τ_c	Not treated here. Pearsonian correlation coefficient r, and regression serve the same purpose.
	∇_p	∇_p, d_{yx}, d_{xy}		
Significance test	χ^2			

[*]Comparable charts, much more complete with respect to tests of significance, appear in Sidney Siegel, *Nonparametric Statistics for the Behavioral Sciences* (New York: McGraw-Hill, 1956) and Hubert M. Blalock, Jr., *Social Statistics,* 2nd ed., (New York: McGraw-Hill, 1972).

third say it means that a majority of women die of fluentive diseases. Another third say it means that more women than men die of these diseases. The remainder either rephrase it without improving its clarity or give up trying. It seems that the English language does not contain any familiar verb that clearly states such a proposition. Its inadequacy is even more obvious when we examine such colloquial observations as "politicians are dishonest." Assuming the words can be defined, does this mean that all politicians are dishonest, that more politicians are dishonest than are honest, that politicians are more dishonest than nonpoliticians (a statement implying at least ordinal level measurement), or that there are more politicians who are dishonest than

TABLE 2

Committee Chairmanships, by Region

	Southern Senators	Nonsouthern Senators		
Committee chairmen	8	9	=	17
Nonchairmen	14	69	=	83
Total	22	78		100

there are nonpoliticians who are dishonest (even though only a small minority of each group may be dishonest)? No wonder people become confused in political arguments. It is this sort of ambiguity that quantification should alleviate.

The data on U. S. senators appears in a fourfold table, along with both row totals and column totals, called "marginals," in Table 2.

Obviously neither a majority of southerners are chairmen nor a majority of chairmen are southerners, so we must rely on proportions or percentages to demonstrate our hypothesis.

Percentage Tables

The percentage is the most useful statistic ever invented, ranking high on most of the criteria suggested above. The percentage table incorporates that soundest of analytical devices, the control group. But in this case, which is the control group: nonchairmen (reading across the rows) or nonsoutherners (reading down the columns)? We must decide this before we know whether to make the row or the column marginals equal to 100%.

The conventional answer in hypothesis testing is to percentage upon totals for the independent, antecedent or "causal" variable, as in Table 3.

How did we decide this? Logically, region must be the prior variable because senators do not move south after becoming committee chairmen. This decision stems from an understanding of the *data;* it is a substantive, not a statistical one. Though easy in this case, it is not always possible to assign one variable independent status. For example, analyzing 1972 trial heat poll results, one might be interested in the correlation between voters preferring Humphrey to Nixon and those preferring Muskie to Nixon. Neither Humphrey nor Muskie is logically prior to the other.

The crucial value in the table, of course, is the difference between 36.4%

TABLE 3

Committee Chairmanships (percentaged by
column), by Region

	Southern Senators	Nonsouthern Senators
Committee chairmen	36.4%	11.6%
Nonchairmen	63.6	88.4
	100%	100%
	(N = 22)	(N = 78)

and 11.6%, which is 24.8%. This single figure reduces the entire matrix to a statistic which sums up the relationship between the two variables. Its range is from 0, for no association between the variables, to 100% for maximum or perfect association. It has a number of names: D in percentage terms; or d_{yx} or κ' (kappa-prime) when reduced to a proportion, .248.[2]

As a summary measure, D has some drawbacks. Suppose we had percent-aged across the rows, an unlikely tactic with these data, but a perfectly reasonable one with the Humphrey-Muskie data mentioned. Going back to Table 2, we find that 8/17 = 47.1% and 14/83 = 16.9% for a D of 30.2%. This is not the same as our previous D of 24.8%, so D proves not to be a *unique* measure of the association between variables.

A second difficulty is that while D may theoretically range from 0 to 100, there are instances where it cannot reach its maximum, and this is one of them. It is possible for all 17 chairmen to be southerners or nonsoutherners, but it is not possible for all 22 southerners—or all 78 nonsoutherners—to be chairmen when there are only 17 committees. At most 17/22 = 77.3% southerners can be chairmen, and thus D is limited in its maximum value to 77.3% − 0 = 77.3%. We say the measure is not "margin-free," a limitation shared with most of its competitors. We might correct for this by dividing D by its maximum value or by some other adjustment, but we would then sacrifice the immediate understandability and universal familiarity of the percentage difference, which are the very qualities that recommend it to us in the first place.

[2] See Robert H. Somers, "A New Asymmetric Measure of Association for Ordinal Variables," *American Sociological Review,* 27 (1962) 799–811; Roy G. Francis, *The Rhetoric of Science: A Methodological Discussion of the Two-by-Two Table* (Minneapolis: U. of Minnesota Press, 1961) pp. 128–130.

Fourfold Measures of Association

There are several measures that give a unique value for the relationship or association between two dichotomies.[3] Before looking at them, let us ponder the logic underlying the questions we are asking of the data. For a simple example, consider a parliament of 100 members with 40 Socialists and 60 members from other parties. We shall think of them as voting on a resolution, although one might substitute incumbency, religion, or some other row variable. Three possible distributions of the votes appear in Table 4.

These three votes differ in their outcomes, but they differ even more drastically in their distributions. Despite the variety in the location of the empty cells and the consequent meaning of the table, any one of these could be offered to "prove" the statement: Socialists vote Aye. Tabular presentation is clearly more precise than English prose.

TABLE 4

Vote Distributions in a Hypothetical Parliament

	Socialists	Others	
Aye	40	30	Being a Socialist is a *sufficient* condition for
Nay/Abstain	0	30	voting Aye, since no Socialists voted otherwise.
Aye	20	0	Being a Socialist is a *necessary* condition for
Nay/Abstain	20	60	voting Aye (no Others so voted) but it is not a sufficient condition (some Socialists voted otherwise).
Aye	40	0	Being a Socialist is a *necessary and sufficient*
Nay/Abstain	0	60	condition for voting Aye, and by knowing his party one can perfectly predict each member's vote.

[3] "Correlation" is normally used to refer to a relationship between interval level variables, "association" to a comparable relationship between nominal variables, and either term with ordinal variables.

Now for the two most frequently used measures of association, Q and ϕ, expressed in terms of a square table whose cells are designated

a	b
c	d

The simplest and most popular measure is Yule's Q, devised at the turn of the century by a pioneer British statistician.[4] The formula is easy to remember and can be worked on the back of an envelope:

$$Q = \frac{ad - bc}{ad + bc}$$

For all three of the parliamentary examples, $Q = +1$, as it does whenever there are zeroes in the b cell, in the c cell or in both. Going back to Table 2 data on U. S. Senate chairmen:

$$Q = \frac{(8 \times 69) - (9 \times 14)}{(8 \times 69) + (9 \times 14)} = \frac{552 - 126}{552 + 126} = \frac{426}{678} = +.63$$

The plus before .63 tells us that the bulk of the cases lie on the *ad* diagonal. Here "positive" has reference only to the fact that one usually puts the categories he is interested in, or those whose coincidence supports his hypothesis, in the first column and the top row. If the data are evenly distributed among the cells, as when the variables are "independent" of one another, *i.e.,* uncorrelated, the value of Q is at or near zero. When they tend to cluster on the *bc* diagonal, Q is negative, reaching -1 when the a and/or d cells are empty.[5] Since Q can reach its maximum when the data "bend around" a single empty cell, it is referred to as a *curvilinear* measure, which is another way of saying that it measures tendencies toward necessary and/or sufficient conditional relationships. Thus, $Q = +1.0$ for all three cases in Table 4. The trouble is that one must look for the location of the near-empty cells to say which. Francis calls Q an "undisciplined" measure because it approaches unity whenever any logical relationship other than independence is achieved.[6]

[4] G. Udny Yule, *An Introduction to the Theory of Statistics* (London: Griffin, 1910) brought together the author's earlier papers and lectures into the classic text on social and biological statistics, particularly at the nominal level.

[5] An exasperating consequence of the independent historical development of nominal and interval statistics is that a downward sloping pattern (bulk of cases in a and d cells) is *positive* with nominal and ordinal measures, while a downward sloping line is *negative* with interval level correlation and regression.

[6] Francis, *The Rhetoric of Science,* p. 166.

If the inquiry poses more demanding standards of necessary *and* sufficient consequences (and not too many researches into this imperfect world are that sanguine) the appropriate measure is a *linear* one, *phi*. Some statisticians prefer ϕ^2 to ϕ, and the easiest formula for desk calculators gets that first:

$$\phi^2 = \frac{(ad - bc)^2}{(a+b)\,(c+d)\,(a+c)\,(b+d)}$$

Phi reaches a maximum of +1 only if *both* b and c cells are empty. While Q could reach its maximum of +1 if all 17 chairmanships were filled by southerners, hence cell b = 0; *phi* could not reach +1 with these marginals, and thus it is a less appropriate measure.[7] Nevertheless we shall calculate it, simply for contrast with Q for the same table.

$$\phi^2 = \frac{[(8 \times 69) - (9 \times 14)]^2}{(8+9)\,(14+69)\,(8+14)\,(9+69)} = \frac{426^2}{17 \times 83 \times 22 \times 78} = \frac{181,476}{2,421,276} = +.075$$

$$\phi = \sqrt{.075} = .27$$

Choice of Measures

With numbers as small and simple as these examples, one may communicate all he needs with the fourfold table of raw data, but percentages are advisable if the figures go to three digits. When one undertakes *comparative* analysis, seeking to say whether a relationship is stronger in one table than in another, he needs Q or ϕ. For example, in 1955 there were 96 senators and 16 standing committees, 9 of them chaired by southerners. This gives a Q of

---

[7] *Phi* reaches its maximum only in the event, improbable for political data, that the marginals for Row 1 = Col. 1 and for Row 2 = Col. 2. To free it from this constraint we may divide it by its effective limit, given the marginals, to get another measure, ϕ/ϕ_{max}. This formula, and discussion of the measures may be found in Anderson and Zelditch, *A Basic Course in Statistics;* Dennis J. Palumbo, *Statistics in Political and Behavioral Science* (New York: Appleton-Century-Crofts, 1969); Hubert M. Blalock, Jr., *Social Statistics,* 2nd ed. (New York: McGraw-Hill, 1972); and G. David Garson, *Handbook of Political Science Methods* (Boston: Holbrook Press, 1971).

When dichotomies are not "natural" (*e.g.,* Republican, Democratic) but are "forced" by dividing an interval measure (*e.g.,* age or income) at some cutting point, statisticians suggest the use of other measures such as the tetrachoric (r_t) or biserial (r_b) coefficient of correlation. This is explained in Garson, pp. 185–188. Political scientists usually ignore this distinction.

TABLE 5

Governor's Power in Tennessee
Assembly, 1957–1963

	Governor Favored	Governor Opposed	Total
Bills Passed	17	0	17
Bills Failed	1	10	11
Total	18	10	

Source: Lawrence D. Longley, "Interest
Group Interaction in a Legislative System,"
Journal of Politics, 29 (August 1967), 637–
658, Table VI.

.74, compared with the value of .63 we calculated for 1973. This indicates
that the southerners' hold on chairmanships has slightly relaxed, though it is
still far from a Q of 0, which would indicate no effect of region at all. In
comparisons over time or across nations it is, of course, necessary to use the
same measure for all tables. Another substantive criterion is the freedom of
the marginals to vary. To illustrate this, compare Table 5, showing the
influence of the Governor of Tennessee on the Legislature, with Table 2 on
Senate committees.

The number of southern senators was determined in 1789 by the Constitution; the number of committees has varied by only 2 since the Legislative
Reorganization Act of 1946. These long-standing arrangements determine
that *phi* in practice cannot reach its maximum. But the marginals in Table 5
are dependent on what bills the Governor chooses to support or oppose and
how members of the two chambers react to his positions. Therefore *phi* could
reach its maximum, and in this instance almost does ($\phi = .93$). That it, rather
than Q, is the appropriate measure for the Tennessee data but not for the U.
S. Senate data is a decision made not by the statistician but by the political
scientist who understands the institutions being studied.

(For the reader's convenience we now move on to the ordinal extensions
of Q and ϕ, returning later to the measures of the other kind of nominal
variables, polytomies.)

Ordinal Measures of Association

While Q and ϕ have been around since the turn of the century, their
ordinal extensions, *gamma* and Kendall's *tau,* have been in use only for the

last decade or two. Q and ϕ should be used in 2×2 tables, while γ and τ_b or τ_c may be used with tables of any reasonable size, so long as both variables are ordinal (or higher) or one is ordinal and the other is a dichotomy. A third measure, d_{yx}, is now appearing more frequently.[8]

All three measures have the same term in their numerator, and we start with explaining how to calculate this, which also reveals the logic of the measures. Remember that the numerator of both Q and ϕ contain the term *ad-bc* which expresses the tendency of the cases to fall in the two cells along the descending diagonal, from upper left to lower right. Now we simply extend this to the case where both variables have more than two values, ordered from left to right and from top to bottom. For an example, we take two variables from the *Cross-Polity Survey*. The independent variable is literacy, with four value categories: high (90% or more literate), medium (50–89%), low (10–49%), and very low (under 10%). Note that literacy in percentages would be an interval level scale, but since the first and last brackets are only 10 percentage points wide, while the second and third are 40 points wide, the reduced measure is only of ordinal quality. The dependent variable is electoral competition, with three ordered categories. Table 6 presents the distribution, from which we are to calculate measures which answer the question: How strong an association is there between literacy and electoral competition?

TABLE 6

Effect of Literacy on Party Competition

	Literacy				
Party Competition	High	Medium	Low	Very Low	Total
Competitive	19	15	7	2	43
Partly Competitive	0	1	1	7	9
Noncompetitive	6	6	6	5	23
Total	25	22	14	14	75

Source: Data from Arthur Banks and Robert Textor, *A Cross-Polity Survey* (Cambridge, MIT Press, 1963) supplied by the Inter-University Consortium for Political Research. I have omitted unascertained or ambiguous categories, leaving an N of 75 nations classified on both variables.

[8] The original sources are Leo Goodman and William Kruskal, "Measures of Association for Cross Classifications," *Journal of the American Statistical Association,* 49 (1954) 732–64; Maurice G. Kendall, *Rank Correlation Methods,* 2nd ed. (London: Griffin, 1959); and Somers, "A New Asymmetric Measure."

The first step is to measure the cases clustering about the descending diagonal. This is done by an iterative process which computers enjoy but humans find slightly tedious. Just as in calculating Q we multiplied the upper left cell by the lower right, so we now multiply the upper left cell by the sum of all the cell values below and to the right of it. Then we do the same for every other cell for which this is possible, summing the results.

$$
\begin{array}{lcr}
19\ (1+1+7+6+6+5) & = & 494 \\
15\ (1+7+6+5) & = & 285 \\
7\ (7+5) & = & 84 \\
0\ (6+6+5) & = & 0 \\
1\ (6+5) & = & 11 \\
1\ (5) & = & 5 \\
& S\ = & 879
\end{array}
$$

What we have done is compile a measure of the extent to which the rank order on the independent variable is the *same* as the rank order on the dependent variable. (For instance, the first multiplication—19 X 1—is the pair consisting of one of the 19 cases high on literacy and competitive on elections and the one case that was medium on literacy and partly competitive on elections.)

Now we calculate the extent to which the rank is *different; e.g.*, where pairs that are low on literacy are higher on competition. Here we multiply each cell starting in the upper right by all the values below and to the left of it. The total, D = 365.

Now *gamma* is calculated the same way as Q:

$$
\gamma = \frac{S-D}{S+D} = \frac{879 - 365}{879 + 365} = \frac{514}{1244} = .41
$$

It is apparent that *gamma* will reach +1 only if there are no cells in the table with values below and to the left of them. It can do this in a variety of ways, each of them consisting of "blocks" or "strings" of adjacent cells starting at the upper left and ending in the lower right corner. The strings may hump or sag, so γ retains the curvilinear character we noted with Q. One should look at the meaning of the data in his table and ask himself whether a "perfect" relationship of this sort is the standard by which he wishes to judge the association of the particular pair of variables he is studying. Two of the many strings which would give a perfect *gamma* with a table like the one above are:

19	15	7	2		19	15	0	0
0	0	0	9		0	9	0	0
0	0	0	23		0	12	13	7

Tau-b and *tau-c,* like *phi,* reach +1 when all the cases are on the descending diagonal and −1 when they are all on the ascending diagonal. For square tables, where the number of rows is the same as the number of columns, τ_b is the right measure; τ_c is for rectangular ones like Table 6, where it works out to +.27. Somer's d_{yx}, which is this case is +.24, may be used with either. All of these measures have the same numerator as *gamma,* but each has a different denominator.[9]

At this point those interested in practice rather than theory ask such questions as: Why should there be three measures giving different results from the same table (in this instance .41, .27, and .24)? Which should one use? What is a meaningful level of association?

Statistics texts seldom give satisfactory answers to these very sensible questions, and I can advance only rather tentative ones. *Gamma* appears most frequently in the literature, probably because the imprecise but monotonic standard it sets corresponds with our fuzzy thinking in English prose about relationships between social and political variables. *Gamma* is an extension of Q, and among the patterns where Q = +1 is the "sufficient condition" treated above, with 0 in the lower left cell. The rough equivalent for ordinal tables is a block of empty cells below the diagonal, thus:

	High	Low
High	x x	x x
	0 0	x x
Low	0 0	0 x

This is among the patterns that would give a high positive value for *gamma,* though not quite +1, but a rather low value for *tau-c.* High values on

---

[9] The denominators are given in Blalock, *Social Statistics,* pp. 416–426, as well as the sources just cited. Kendall's *tau-a* and Spearman's R_s or *rho* (ρ), ordinal measures used with a small number of individual cases rather than cross-tabulations, are also treated by Blalock. Terminology is confused by the fact that there is another set of *tau-a* and *tau-b* statistics invented by Goodman and Kruskal for association with polytomies. Added to the terminological obscurity is the cognitive dissonance resulting from Greek letters followed by Roman subscripts, which researchers try to eliminate by calling *tau-b* "tau-beta." I have never seen *tau-c* referred to as "tau-gamma" although political scientists wobbly on their Greek have called it "tau-chi." There is no known remedy for this confusion.

the independent (column) variable associate with high values on the dependent variable, but low values on the independent variable lead to high *or* low values on the dependent. This pattern of limited, curvilinear or triangular association is a familiar one to researchers. It may reflect reality in the distributions of the phenomena we are examining, or it may be that we can observe only a limited range of values, or that our ordinal measuring instrument is imprecise at the low range of the scale. Whatever the case, *gamma* is more sensitive to this sort of association than is *tau-c.*

Other advantages of *gamma* are its ease of calculation and its versatility, being applicable to any size or shape of table. Because it is "undisciplined," and takes on high values for a wide variety of monotonic "strings," it generally runs .1 to .5 above *tau* or Pearson's *r* for the same table. Experienced researchers dislike "rules of thumb" because of the wide variety of factors that affect the size of a coefficient, but it can be said, very roughly, that a *gamma* of .6 or above is high, and one below .2 is not worth attention unless the data fall into some particularly meaningful pattern.

Tau-b and *tau-c* make it possible to adjust for table shape, improving accuracy. Being linear measures, they correspond more closely to the idea of linear regression and correlation at the interval level, although it is not proper to carry over to them the "explained variance" meaning of r^2. Somers' d_{yx} is an extension of the easily understood percentage difference, but has the disadvantage of requiring a decision as to which is the independent variable. That is why it is called an "asymmetric" measure. (When the row variable is independent, another measure, d_{xy} is computed.) *Gamma* and d_{yx} have meanings in terms of the reduction of error in guessing the order of pairs on one variable from the order on the other.[10]

Tau is always lower than *gamma* and for Table 6 it is a good bit lower because the cells along the descending diagonal are rather thin in the center of the table. The rule of thumb for *tau* is to pay little attention to values below .15 and to be impressed with values over .4. However, the nature of the data should be considered, including the possibility of random measurement errors, which would reduce our expectations. With our senatorial example, there is no doubt who is a southerner and who is a chairman, whereas such variables as social class or intelligence cannot be measured so precisely, and we should accept lower values as meaningful. Another solution to the problem is statistical significance, which will be considered next.

---

[10] See R. H. Somers, "Statistics, Descriptive: Association," *International Encyclopedia of the Social Sciences,* (New York: Macmillan, 1968) vol. 15, pp. 240–245.

Statistical Significance: Chi Square

The foregoing discussion of association and the examples illustrating it have been confined to legislative bodies and the nations of the world; that is, to universes or populations rather than samples. However weak an association we find, it may properly be said to describe that population. With large universes which cannot be enumerated due to limits of time, distance, cost, or other resources, we have to rely on *samples* we hope are representative of the larger population. With samples, there is a possibility that we may find an association in our table which does *not* occur in the population, but instead is due to random variation in the selection of cases. Tests of significance indicate how likely it is that the observed association could appear in the sample when there is in fact none in the universe. This probability is greater, of course, when the sample is small than when it is large.

Many of the measures discussed have their individual tests of significance, but these are not often used, because *chi square,* a venerable, familiar test, is applicable to all nominal and ordinal tables. The formula is:

$$\chi^2 = \Sigma \frac{(0 - E)^2}{E}$$

For it to be meaningful, the χ^2 value found must be looked up in a table which gives the probability of such a value occurring by chance in the sample if there is no relationship between the variables in the population being sampled. We shall work through one calculation here to show what goes into *chi square* and to call attention to some considerations that may escape those who habitually have their statistics ground out by computer, untouched by human minds. The data are recomputed from a national survey of attitudes about population growth.

Table 7 contains an example of the calculation of *chi square.* Ignoring for the moment the observed frequencies O which appear in the top line in each cell, we multiply row and column marginals and divide by the total number of cases to get the expected frequencies E which appear in the second line of each cell. (For example, the upper left-hand cell is the product of the top row marginal, 1458, and the first column marginal, 511, divided by 2247, giving 331.57.) Naturally these E values add up to the respective row and column totals. They are the cell values that would be expected if the variables were totally independent of one another, *i.e.,* were not related. If we calculated column percentages, based upon the totals at the bottom, they would be the

TABLE 7

Regional Attitudes toward Population Growth:
An Example of the Calculation of Chi Square

Population growth is:	Region				
	Northeast	South	North Central	West	Total
A serious problem	337	494	368	259	1458
	331.57	485.35	404.24	236.84	
	5.4	8.6	−36.2	22.2	
	.09	.15	3.24	2.08	
Not so serious	123	194	193	77	587
	133.49	195.41	162.75	95.35	
	−10.5	−1.4	30.2	−18.4	
	.83	.01	5.60	3.55	
Not a problem	46	30	56	22	154
	35.02	51.26	42.70	25.01	
	11.0	−21.3	13.3	−3.0	
	3.46	8.84	4.14	.36	
No opinion	5	30	6	7	48
	10.92	15.98	13.31	7.80	
	−5.9	14.0	−7.3	−.8	
	3.19	12.25	4.01	.08	
Total	511	748	623	365	· 2247

Key: In each cell, the top line is the Observed Frequency, the second line is the Expected Frequency, the third line is the Difference between the Observed and Expected Frequencies, and the bottom line is the contribution of that cell to the total Chi Square for this relationship.

For example, for the top left-hand cell:

$$O = 337$$
$$E = 331.57$$
$$(O–E) = 5.4$$
$$(O–E)^2/E = .09$$

For the entire table:
$$\Sigma (O–E)^2/E = \chi^2 = 51.88$$

Source: A. E. Keir Nash, ed., *Governance and Population: The Governmental Implications of Population Change, IV,* U.S. Commission on Population Growth and the American Future (Washington: Government Printing Office, 1972), p. 305.

same all across the row, *e.g.,* 65% would say "serious" in the Northeast, the South, the North Central States, the West, and the nation as a whole.

The calculation of *chi square* involves taking the difference between the Observed and Expected frequencies (which appear in the third line in each cell in Table 7), and then taking the square of this difference and dividing that value by the Expected frequency (which gives the figures in the bottom line in each cell in Table 7). These calculations result in a value that tells how much each cell contributes to χ^2, and summing these gives the χ^2 value, 51.9, which we look up in a table given in every statistics book. The table tells us in this instance that with a sample of this size a value this large could occur by chance fewer than one time in 1,000 (*i.e., $p < .001$*) if there were in fact no departure from independence in the population as a whole. Therefore we may say that the relationship between our variables is "highly significant" statistically. But Table 7 deserves a closer look. Note that all the *chi square* contributions for the top row, the critical response, added together yield only 5.56, barely more than a tenth of the total value of *chi square.* However, Row 4, Column 2 contributes 12.25, nearly a fourth of the total; but this results from southern respondents having no opinion on the issue. *Chi square* measures the departure of the table as a whole from expectation, and this may depend largely on differences that are trivial in their substantive meaning. If one relies on a computer to calculate his statistics he should look very closely at the percentage table to make sure that the *chi square* value is not inflated by some irrelevant departure from independence in one of the missing data cells. With ordinal tables it is quite possible to get a high *chi square* but a *gamma* or *tau* close to zero, meaning that the observed frequencies differ from expectation, but not in a monotonic or linear pattern.

It is tempting to use *chi square* as a measure of association, but this cannot be done, for this statistic is affected by two components, the strength of the association and the size of the sample. There are other measures, such as ϕ, *C, T* and *V,* which remove the contribution of sample size and measure the remaining association. But there is more to it than this. If all the *(O−E)* values in Table 7 were divided by 10—as might be the case if a researcher who could afford a sample of only 225 cases were to conduct the same survey—then *chi square* would be only 5.19, and the table lookup would indicate that these results could be obtained by chance 4 times out of 5, not very impressive evidence. The accepted way of going about research is to set in advance one's standard of significance (usually $p < .05$) and then to believe, and report, whatever findings reach that level, rejecting the rest. This means that the political world as seen by a well-endowed researcher who can afford an expensive survey is not the same world perceived by an impecunious student who can afford only a few cases. Recently there appears to be a tendency to rely less on significance tests and more on the meaning of the data in context, especially when one is working with a large sample that will turn up many trivial but statistically significant differences. As concepts and their operational definitions are refined and standardized, this should produce a social science which takes for granted evidence from earlier studies that certain relationships do exist, and concentrates instead on discovering how strong the relationships are under varying circumstances. This involves more emphasis on association and correlation and less on statistical significance.[11]

Association with Polytomies

Measures of association for polytomies should properly have been treated earlier under nominal variables, but were deferred until after *chi square.* Polytomies have three or more categories, so they look like ordinal variables, but they may be distinguished by asking whether the categories can be transposed. In the preceding example the South and North Central columns could have changed place without logical difficulty, so we know the independent variable is a polytomy. The dependent variable could have been made ordinal by omitting the No Opinion category, since the first three responses indicate a decreasing concern with population growth, but we did not do this. If *either* variable in a table is polytomous, the table must be analyzed with one of the measures discussed below.

Since there is no high or low end to a polytomy, there can be no such thing as negative association, so the measures should vary from 0 to 1. There is indeed some question as to whether these measures really tell us anything that could not just as well be discovered from a percentage table. Their principal utility is in comparing tables, for example to find whether region or religion has more effect on votes, or whether one of these has more effect in one state or at one time than another. These are two kinds of measures of association with polytomies.

Measures Based on Chi Square

These work on the principle of removing from χ^2 the contribution made by size of sample, leaving only the contribution due to association. They are

---

[11] Lack of space precludes attention here to some problems in the calculation of *chi square,* notably the concept of degrees of freedom and the corrections necessary when cells have expected values less than 5. All the texts cited explain these.

ϕ (note that for polytomies $\phi^2 = \chi^2/N$), Cramer's V Tschuprow's T and the coefficient of contingency, C. All give a value of zero when all Observed frequencies are equal to their Expected frequencies, hence $\chi^2 = 0$, there being no departure from complete independence between the two variables. Perfect association presumably is the condition in which the largest possible number of cells contain zeros and the remaining values are concentrated in the other cells. There are several ways this can occur. All the measures have χ^2 as their numerator, and N, adjusted for some factor to take account of table size and shape, as their denominator. For certain table formats each of the measures either exceeds +1 or cannot reach it. The ideal measure therefore has not been developed, but the current consensus is that V is the best of the lot. [12]

$$V = \sqrt{\frac{\chi^2}{mN}}$$

where m is the number of rows minus 1, or the number of columns minus 1, whichever is smaller. Calculating V for the data in Table 7 we find:

$$V = \sqrt{\frac{51.88}{3 \times 2247}} = \sqrt{\frac{51.88}{6741}} = \sqrt{.008} = .09$$

For this table $T = .09$, $\phi = .15$ and $C = .15$. Thus we have only a moderate association (and, as we have seen, one based on a substantively trivial relationship) but a very impressive level of statistical significance as measured by *chi square*. This confirms the earlier *caveat* against depending too heavily on significance in the analysis of survey findings based on large samples.

Measures of Reduction of Errors in Prediction

This second type of statistic for association with polytomies calculates the proportionate reduction in the error in predicting the category of cases on the dependent variable if one knows their category on the independent variable

---

[12] The formulas for the denominators, and discussion of the measures, appear in Garson, *Handbook,* and Blalock, *Social Statistics.* Most of these, and the measures of association treated earlier, are calculated in the program packages for the social sciences such as OSIRIS and SPSS for large computers. The software for smaller computers is more troublesome, since they vary in size of storage and not all packages will fit. For minicomputers that accept BASIC language, programs for χ^2, V, *gamma, tau-b* and *tau-c* appear in William Buchanan, *Understanding Political Variables,* 2nd ed., (New York: Charles Scribner's Sons, 1974).

and has at hand the table showing how they are associated. The measures are *lambda* and Goodman and Kruskal's *tau*, and both are asymmetric, involving adding the subscript *a* or *b* (sometimes *c* or *r*) to indicate whether the column or the row variable is independent.[13] *Lambda* has the defect of occasionally giving a value of 0 when the variables are not entirely independent, and indeed does so with Table 7. *Tau* is better in this respect, and gives a value of .01 for these data. Calculating it for Table 7 would be space consuming, but we can get an idea of its meaning by doing it for Table 2. If we knew only the right-hand marginals in that table and were to guess whether a senator chosen at random was a committee chairman, we would guess 17 times that he was and 83 times that he was not. On the average we would get 17/100 of the 17 chairmen right, or 2.89, and 83/100 of the nonchairmen right, or 68.89. Thus we would have a total of 2.89 + 68.89 = 71.78% of our guesses right, and 100 − 71.78 = 28.22% errors. But if we had the table before us, and knew whether each senator was a southerner, we could do better. We would expect to get 8/22 of the 8 southern chairmen right, 14/22 of the 14 southern nonchairmen right, 9/78 of the 9 nonsouthern chairmen and 69/78 of the 69 nonsouthern nonchairmen right. This all works out to 26.10 errors out of 100, a prediction that is more accurate than the first by 2.12. The improvement in prediction, 2.12, as a proportion of the original prediction with 28.22 errors, is .08, which is *tau-a* for Table 2. Reduction in error then gives a definite meaning to these statistics, which χ^2-based measures do not have. Whether it is a useful meaning the researcher must decide.

A recently developed reduction in error measure ∇_p (del-p) promises to alleviate some of the difficulties of measuring association in a table with one or more polytomies.[14] First one decides which cell or cells should show a higher observed than expected frequency, given his hypothesis, which may be stated in terms of necessary and/or sufficient conditions, association or correlation, or predicted effect of the independent upon the dependent variable. One cell, or several, or a triangular portion of the matrix, may be selected. The choice is based upon the kind of information conveyed by each

[13] These measures are described in Blalock, *Social Statistics,* pp. 300–302 and John H. Mueller, Karl F. Schuessler and Herbert L. Costner, *Statistical Reasoning in Sociology,* 2nd ed., (Boston: Houghton Mifflin Co., 1970), pp. 244–248, which gives a detailed description of how they are calculated.

[14] David K. Hildebrand, James D. Laing, and Howard Rosenthal, "Prediction Logic: A Framework for Theory Statement and Data Analysis in Political Science," paper presented to the American Political Science Association, New Orleans, Louisiana, September 1973. Their measure may be used with ordinal or interval variables as well.

variable and the theoretical relationship between them. The opposing cells, the ones where the observed frequencies would reach zero if the proposition being tested were absolutely true, are designated as "error cells." The variation of the observed frequency in these cells from zero up to the point where they are equal to their expected frequency indicates an increasing weakness of the proposition being tested. If $O = E$ there is no evidence for the proposition; if $O > E$, there is evidence that it runs contrary to reality.

For the Senate example (Table 2) the "error cell" would be b, since it would reach O if all committee chairmen were southerners. The formula presented by the authors is a more general one, but it reduces in the situations that concern us to $V_p = 1 - \frac{\Sigma O}{\Sigma E}$ where O and E refer to the error cell(s) only. For this example

$$V_p = 1 - \frac{9}{(17 \times 78)/100} = 1 - \frac{9}{13.26} = 1 - .68 = .32$$

With a polytomy we select only those cells which are theoretically relevant to the hypothesis. To test the proposition that the Northeast and North Central regions, being most crowded, are most concerned about population growth, we would choose the South and West cells from the first row of Table 7 as error cells. Hence

$$V_p = 1 - \frac{494 \times 259}{485.4 + 236.8} = -.04.$$

The negative value shows that the data tend to refute rather than support the proposition. The most striking difference in Table 7 is the high No Opinion response in the South. Designating the other three responses in the bottom row error cells, V_p may be calculated as .44, supporting the proposition that southerners tend to be opinionless, if that should be a theoretically intriguing proposition. This measure has not had the chance to gain familiarity or to be employed in the variety of studies that would demonstrate how useful it may be. Its advantage over the other measures is that it focuses on a particular theoretically relevant departure from expectation rather than the sum of all departures, as do the other measures.

Whether one wishes to use his data merely to report the degree of departure from independence, or to make a predictive statement, or to test a clearly structured hypothesis will determine which of these measures he uses.

* * * * *

As noted at the beginning of this review, there are three sets of criteria that govern the choice of a statistic to use: mathematical or statistical; time, effort and convenience; the utility of the measure as a communication device. All of these criteria imply some things that lie beyond the analyst's control, but each also suggests some ways that a modicum of knowledge can vastly expand the power of the analysis. By the time one reaches the stage of data analysis, there is little that can be done about such considerations as the level of measurement. If, however, one knows the statistical properties we have reviewed and which are summarized in Table 1, he can assure himself that he is choosing a statistic that is appropriate in view of these formal properties. One is often dependent on the statistics that happen to be available in existing computer software, or which can be easily computed, but if one is aware of the range of available statistics, the number of those he can calculate easily is also going to be larger. In choosing a statistic as a communication device, there is little the individual investigator can do to alter his readers' familiarity with various measures, but if one is aware of the logical properties that have been discussed, then one can choose the measure that best accents the substantive relationships he wants to draw to his readers' attention. And of all skills, this ability to focus readers' attention where it needs to be is *the* critical attribute, whether one believes numbers are a curse devised by an angry God or is only happy when exploring the labyrinths of multivariate analysis.

Manuscript submitted January 4, 1974.
Final manuscript received March 21, 1974.

JERE BRUNER

What's the Question to That Answer? Measures and Marginals in Crosstabulation*

In the context of a practitioner's view of statistics, this paper attempts to revive and clarify G. Udny Yule's concern with the effects of marginal distributions upon summary measures of association. Ignoring these effects may give you the right answer to the wrong question. In particular, when the hypothesis is causal, varying independent-variable distributions can artifactually distort association measures. The distortions of some common measures are shown in three kinds of tables. A cure, equiweighting, is explained. Reasons are given for not also equiweighting the dependent variable. A socialization example illustrates the use of equiweighting in a complex problem.

The use of crosstabulations and percentages in analyzing data shows no sign of fading away, even though more powerful parametric multivariate methods are increasingly applied where once angels feared to tread on measurement-level and distribution assumptions.[1] One reason for the durability of crosstabulations may be that they keep the researcher and the reader close to the data in the sense that percentages seem simple, natural, and immediately understood. But as soon as comparisons have to be made from one table to another, or to a whole series of tables—and virtually all research involves such comparisons—the need becomes apparent for summary statistics as measures for the amount of association or relationship in a table.[2]

As Goodman and Kruskal's classic papers (1954, 1959) showed, the invention of summary measures of association for crosstabulations dates from

*Thanks to Paul A. Dawson, my colleague at Oberlin, who urged me to write this in the first place, to two anonymous referees, and Robert C. Luskin for helpful comments and criticisms. Thanks also to Germaine Jackson, who wrote the original version of the program I used to do the computations for the tables and figures.

[1] For the newer position, see Labovitz (1970) and the subsequent discussion the following year in the *American Sociological Review*, also Tufte (1969) and Abelson and Tukey (1970). For instances of practitioners' applications and their justification, see Jennings and Niemi (1974, pp. 32–33) and Verba and Nie (1972, Appendix G). A recent effort to point the way from lower-level measurement into parametric procedures is Aldrich and Cnudde (1975).

[2] Hyman (1955) and even more so, Rosenberg (1968) are tours de force in the use of percentages alone.

Reprinted from AMERICAN JOURNAL OF POLITICAL SCIENCE, Vol. XX, No. 4, November 1976, pp. 781-804, Jere Bruner, "What's the Question to that Answer? Measures and Marginals in Crosstabulation," by permission of the University of Texas Press.

the closing years of the nineteenth century, although the departure from chi-square-based measures and the elaboration of rank-order coefficients for tables larger than 2 × 2 is a somewhat more recent development (Kendall, 1948; Goodman and Kruskal, 1954; Kruskal, 1958; Somers, 1962). Instead of a single measure, we have many. It has become customary to express either impatience or dismay at the embarrassment of riches represented by the large variety of available nominal and ordinal association measures. Goodman and Kruskal's work was influential in cataloging the variety, and in establishing as a prime standard of choice among measures the extent to which they could be interpreted probabilistically, or in terms of proportional reduction in error. But the "operationality" of these criteria of choice has been more pleasing to statisticians than to data analysts.

Two recent papers may be seen as signs of a turn to a new direction in interpretation of the measures, and hence in criteria of choice. Buchanan (1974) subtitles his article "The Practitioner's View," not the statistician's, and devotes his efforts to an interpretation of various measures in terms of substantive questions the researcher has to deal with. He remarks: "Why should there be three measures [gamma, tau-c, and Somers' d_{yx}] giving different results from the same table? Which one should one use? What is a meaningful level of association? Statistics texts seldom give satisfactory answers to these very sensible questions . . ." (p. 637). Weisberg (1974) made a point of having his article appear on the twentieth anniversary of the publication of Goodman and Kruskal's first paper, and implies that his work aims to change the direction they set, by moving toward an emphasis on the substantive import of various relationship models, models defined by the conditions under which the measures reach minimum and maximum.

This article is intended to cast some light on the interpretation problems involved in a feature of crosstabulations which both Buchanan and Weisberg refer to incidentally: the effect of the distribution of marginals on summary statistics, and the bearing of that effect on the substantive meaning of the statistics. I will show at what point of marginal imbalance the distortion of certain summary statistics becomes serious, and suggest which kinds of inquiries are particularly likely to be in danger of distorted results. I will point out conditions under which some frequently used measures will be distorted with respect to the substantive question at hand, while others are not; and conditions under which they will all be distorted. Finally, I will suggest a cure, and show how to make it computationally practical.[3]

---

[3] Econometricians and other users of regression analysis are aware of the equivalent interval-level problems, such as outliers and skewed distributions, and the common cures

Percentages and Summary Measures in the 2 × 2 Table

As an example of the differing questions for which differing association measures provide answers, let us begin with a crosstabulation of voting participation by race of respondent, taken from a 1956 presidential election survey.[4] The raw frequencies for the table cells and for the marginals are as shown in Table 1a. It would be customary to consider race the independent and voting participation the dependent variable, and to percentage down the columns, as in Table 1b. Comparing column percentages in the "voted" row, we find that 41.6 percent more whites than blacks voted. In a 2× 2 table, this percentage difference is numerically equal to Somers' d_{yx} (row variable dependent), which is .415 (Somers, 1962). Somers' d_{yx} then, measures the column percent difference. (Its usefulness is more obvious in tables larger than 2 × 2, where it still provides an *average* percentage difference.) It is the answer to the question: How large is the difference between white and black turnout rates? Or: How big is the effect of race on whether a person will vote or not? This is a question about causality in one sense, the sense of conditional probabilities.

We might also take percentages across the rows, as in Table 1c, and find that 96 percent of the voters are white, and only 4 percent black—compared to 20 percent black among nonvoters. In this case, we compare row percentage p_{11} (top row, left column) to row percentage p_{21} (second row, left column) and find a percentage difference of 96−80=16. The corresponding measure is Somers' d_{xy} (column variable dependent), here .160. This d_{xy} is the answer to the question: How large is the difference in race composition between voters and nonvoters? That is a useful question in some contexts. It is not a question about causality.

Thus the two asymmetric Somers' d's provide measures corresponding to two kinds of questions for which we would seek answers in two corresponding kinds of percentage differences, which is to say, in differences between conditional probabilities. The symmetric statistic Kendall's tau-b is always imtermediate in value between d_{yx} and d_{xy}; it is equal to their geometric

---

(Windsorizing, log and other transformations). See Tufte (1974, pp. 101−132 and references there); also Kruskal (1968).

[4] The data were originally collected by the Survey Research Center, University of Michigan, and were made available through the Inter-University Consortium for Political Research, neither of whom is responsible for the computations nor for the interpretations expressed here.

TABLE 1

Illustration: Turnout by Race, 1956

1a: Raw Frequencies

	White	Black	Totals
Voted	1231	51	1282
Did not	379	95	474
Totals	1610	146	1756

1b: Column Percentages

	White	Black	Marginals
Voted	76.5	34.9	73.0
Did not	23.5	65.1	27.0
Totals	1610	146	1756

Column percent difference = 76.5 − 34.9 = 41.6

Somers' d_{yx} = .415

1c: Row Percentages

	White	Black	Totals
Voted	96.0	4.0	1281
Did not	80.0	20.0	474
Marginals	91.7	8.3	1756

Row percent difference = 96.0 − 80.0 = 16.0

Somers' d_{xy} = .160

Kendall's tau-b = $\sqrt{(.415)(.160)}$ = .258

Source: University of Michigan Survey Research Center and Inter-University Consortium for Political Research

mean, the square root of $d_{yx}d_{xy}$.[5] Now, if the question we are actually asking is about the turnout gap between blacks and whites, or the effect of race on one's probability of voting, then the Kendall's tau-b of .26 is the wrong measure. It is too low. It is held down, in effect, by the small proportion of blacks in the total sample. Given the same column percentages, if blacks formed only 1 percent of the sample, then the Kendall's tau-b would fall still further to .10.

[5] For an explanation of the calculation of Kendall's tau, Goodman and Kruskal's gamma, and Somers' d, see Blalock (1972, pp. 421–426) or, in spite of an idiosyncratic table format, Kohout (1974, pp. 224–236).

What sort of question, then, *does* Kendall's tau-b answer? In this illustration, the question it answers is: How big is the effect of race on the voting participation of the sample altogether?—or, more exactly, how big is the effect of race differences on turnout differences? This effect will be smaller, for any given *rate* difference between blacks and whites, the smaller the ratio of black to whites in the sample, as the ratio declines from 1.0. If blacks are a very small proportion of the sample, then whatever they do will not affect the turnout of the whole sample very much. Here the question is about causality again, but in a different sense from that associated with the column-percentage difference, which has to do with the conditional probability of voting.

The question here, about the effect of race differences on turnout differences, would be the right one to ask in comparing the relative impact of a number of different turnout determinants on the turnout of the whole sample. But for a large class of problems, Kendall's tau-b is the wrong answer, since the question actually being asked is answered by inspecting subgroup differences in rates. If percentages on categories of the independent variable give the desired answer in detail, then the proper summary measure is not Kendall's tau-b or Pearson's r. If it makes no difference to the question what proportion of the sample falls in each category of the independent variable (and when we are talking about rate comparisons, it does not), then we would want a summary statistic which is not affected by variations in those proportions. In this case, we would want a measure of the difference between black and white turnout rates which is indifferent to the proportion of blacks in the sample. Let us see if there is a such a measure.

Column-Marginal Disparity and Shrinking Coefficients

Figures 1, 2, and 3 graph the response of various association measures (most of those computed by SPSS, Nie, et al., 1975) under two conditions: the column percentages are kept constant; but the percentage of the sample falling in the left column total is steadily increased. The vertical axis measures coefficient size; the horizontal axis is the percentage of the sample in the left column total. Figure 1 is an example of the 2 X 2 case. The data used are those for race and turnout in Table 1.

We can make several observations. (1) d_{yx} remains constant as the column-marginals ratio changes, and is always equivalent to the column-percentage difference. Goodman and Kruskal's gamma also stays constant, but is characteristically higher than the other statistics. (2) All the other measures decline as column-marginal disparity increases. These others include

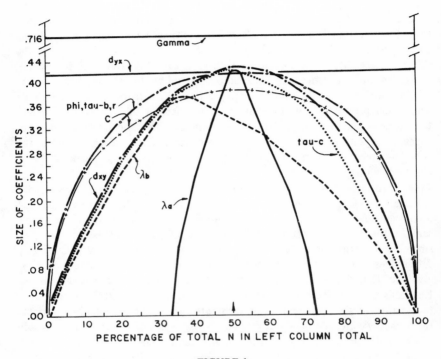

FIGURE 1

Measures and Column Marginals, 2 × 2 Table

Goodman and Kruskal's lambdas, and the asymmetric d_{xy} as well as the symmetric statistics, such as Kendall's tau-b and tau-c, the contingency coefficient C, and phi (equal to Pearson's r for the 2 × 2 case). (3) When the column marginals are equal (above the arrow, at 50 percent on the x-axis), the values of Kendall's tau-b and tau-c, Somers' d_{yx} and d_{xy} and phi are about the same, and closely equivalent to the mean of both percentage differences. (4) The problem of coefficient shrinkage accelerates rapidly as more than 70 percent of the cases accumulate in one column-total.

Figure 1 is, of course, only one instance of a *family* of curves for each coefficient; each strength of relationship as measured, say, by the column-percentage difference; and each configuration of column-marginal disparity and (except for gamma and d_{xy}) row-marginal disparity as well. For tables larger than 2 × 2, the variations in the curves become more elaborate still as the rising number of degrees of freedom allows more variations in cell-frequency patterns.[6] But the tendency to peak when the column totals are equal, that remains. In the instance given, we have a fairly strong relationship, as survey relationships go, with a column-percentage difference of 42. It can be seen that individual coefficients vary as much as .15 to .20 while column percentages remain fixed, and column-marginal disparity ranges to the extent one might normally find, say, from 10 to 90 on the x-axis. However, for a weaker relationship the impact of marginals on measures would be less; for a stronger relationship, much more.

Figure 2 shows corresponding results for the hypothetical data given in Table 2a, a table of 4 rows and 2 columns. The results are similar to those in Figure 1. In particular, Somers' d_{yx} and gamma remain constant. But in this case, we see that the close similarity of Kendall's tau-c, d_{yx} and d_{xy} at the point of equal column marginals, is broken, However, tau-c and d_{yx} are equal when the column marginals are equal.

Figure 3 employs the data shown in Table 2b, also artificial. The percentage of cases in the left column is varied, while the other two columns share equally in what is left. Again, the ordinal-level coefficients (except gamma) are closely similar when the column totals are equal (at 33.3 percent). Their values do not peak at this point, however, but rather in the vicinity where the left-column share is 50 percent. And this time, Somers' d_{yx} and gamma do not remain constant; they increase slightly as the left-column total grows. (Gamma, off the scale of Figure 3, rises in a decelerating curve like that of d_{yx} from .53 to .69.) This tendency is not general, in the sense that if the *middle* column is augmented, the other coefficients fall in the same sort of curve as usual, while d_{yx} and gamma decline slightly.

Thus the sensitivity of the common summary measures to column-marginal disparity, with the exception of gamma and d_{yx} in two-column tables, is quite general. The larger the relationship, the more it is affected by marginal disparity.

[6] For the data in our 2×2 table, when the column totals are expressed as proportions of the total N, and P is the product of these two proportions, several coefficients are well "explained" (r^2 more than .98) in regression equations where P figures as the only predictor. I find, for the 21 points plotted in Figure 1:

Coefficient		Prediction equation	r^2
C^2	=	.01083 + .56907P	.98320
Tau-b^2	=	.00696 + .68287P	.98850
Tau-c	=	1.66019P	1.00000
d_{xy}	=	.01677 + 1.64523P	.98850

Of the other coefficients, phi and r are equal to tau-b; gamma and d_{yx} constant; and the lambdas are irregular.

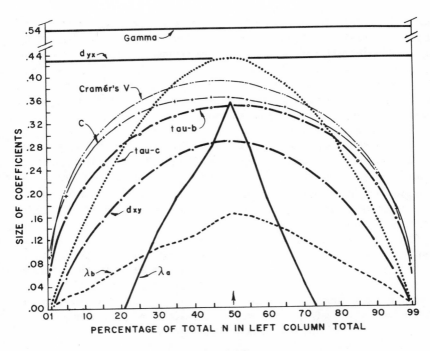

FIGURE 2

Measures and Column Marginals, 4 × 2 Table

When Are You in Trouble?

When is column-marginal disparity likely to become a serious problem?

If your hypothesis distinguishes between an independent and a dependent variable; and is about causality in the conditional-probability sense; and it would therefore be natural for you to seek your answer in a table of percentages on the independent (conventionally, the column) variable: then you want an association measure that is not vulnerable to artifactual distortion by variations in the proportions of the sample that happen to fall into the respective categories of the independent variable.

More hypotheses are causal than will admit it. As Tufte (1974, p. 3) has contended, it is often an evasive scruple to evoke the precaution that "correlation does not prove causality," and therefore to fall back on "mere association" in the statement of the hypothesis. We should work with causal hypotheses, he says, and offer the association in evidence, even though additional evidence is required. There are, of course, instances in which the hypothesis is clearly one of association only, e.g., that between elements of a syndrome, whose joint appearance is the result of some underlying cause; or between items in a belief system, such as issue stands, all of them at the same level of causal priority.

Given a directional hypothesis of the conditional-probabilities sort, you are in trouble when the imbalance of the independent variable distribution reaches large proportions, for instance, in the 2 X 2 case, ratios of 2:1 or more. As the example we have used suggests, researchers working with the race variable in United States national samples need to be aware of the imbalanced-marginals problem. Rare experiences, as independent variables in

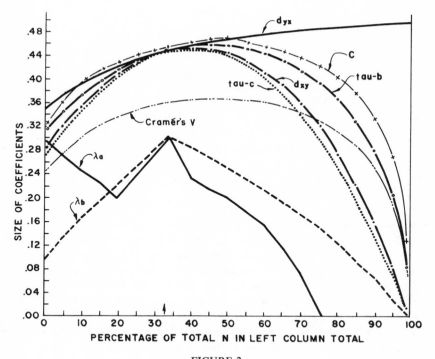

FIGURE 3

Measures and Column Marginals, 3 X 3 Table

TABLE 2

2a: Artificial Data Used in Figure 2

Totals

		Totals
160	40	200
38.1	*10.5*	*25.0*
120	80	200
28.6	*21.1*	*25.0*
80	120	200
19.0	*31.6*	*25.0*
60	140	200
14.3	*36.8*	*25.0*
Totals 420	380	800
52.5	*47.5*	*100.0*

2b: Artificial Data Used in Figure 3

Totals

			Totals
60	30	10	100
60.0	*30.0*	*10.0*	*33.3*
30	40	30	100
30.0	*40.0*	*30.0*	*33.3*
10	30	60	100
10.0	*30.0*	*60.0*	*33.3*
Totals 100	100	100	300
33.3	*33.3*	*33.3*	*100.0*

Raw frequencies and column percentages in the cells; grand
total percentages on marginals

political socialization, are another instance. Some kinds of data, however, exclude unbalanced distributions either naturally or by purging. Thus in Weisberg's (1974) congressional roll-call data, the party variable is naturally not very lopsided; and the votes have been purged of lopsided outcomes, with the comment that "variables lacking variance are of limited interest (p. 1644)." That may be true for the impact-of-differences-on-differences type of causal hypothesis, but not for the conditional-probabilities type. And it may be true for the congressional roll-call subject matter, but surely not, for instance, when the subject matter involves rare categories, such as murderers, members of small minorities, or adherents of uncommon political movements.

In comparing coefficients in subtables generated by holding constant some third or fourth variable—one of the important uses of association coefficients—the comparison may be interfered with by distortions due to marginal disparity. This is likely to happen precisely in those cases which are of the most theoretical interest: ones in which the independent variable is strongly related to the control variable, and therefore the distribution of the independent variable shifts strongly from one subtable to the next.[7]

A relationship that is large when column marginals are equal may shrink when they are not. And a relationship that looks small when marginals are grossly unequal, may be large when they are equalized.

Is There an Invulnerable Coefficient?

We could safeguard against marginal-imbalance distortion if we could find a summary coefficient which remained constant under conditions of fixed column percentages but changing column total ratios. The graphs in Figures 1 and 2 show that gamma and d_{yx} have the requisite constancy in 2 X 2 and r X 2 tables. With the aid of Table 3, we can see why they will have this constancy in any table limited to two columns, but not, in general, in tables of more than two columns.

Looking at Table 3, consider a table with raw frequencies a, b, . . . f in the cells, as shown upper left, and with equal column totals. Now we will create a second table in which the column percentages remain the same, but the left column total becomes larger by a factor k. Therefore the raw frequencies in the left column of the second table (Table 3, upper right) are equal to those in the first table, multiplied by k. In computing gamma and d_{yx} (see Somers, 1962) one collects as P the sum of the products of each cell times any cell below and to the right, as shown. The sum Q is the sum of all cell-pair products in which the second cell of the pair lies below and to the left. Finally, the tie-sum T_y is the sum of cell-pair products in which the second cell lies to the right in the same row, i.e., where there is a tie on the dependent variable. As Table 3 shows, every term involved in the computation of gamma or d_{yx} contains the factor k, whether that term is located in

---

[7] The Lazarsfeld tradition of table analysis treats this situation as the point where real understanding can begin, in "elaboration" (Hyman, 1955, ch. VII, and perhaps more clearly in Kohout, 1974, pp. 84–117), but the econometric tradition deals with it in terms of the danger of multicollinearity (Tufte, 1974, pp. 148–155; Tufte, 1969, section VIII), for which there is no cure.

TABLE 3

Calculation of Coefficients of Association in Two-Column
Tables

a	b
c	d
e	f

ka	b
kc	d
ke	f

Cell entries are raw frequencies.
Product sums for second table:

Concordant pairs P = kad+kaf+kcf = k(ad+af+cf)
Discordant pairs Q = kcb+keb+ked = k(cb+eb+ed)
Row Tie pairs T_y = kab+kcd+kcf = k(ab+cd+ef)
Col Tie pairs $T_x = k^2 ac + k^2 ae + k^2 ce + bd + bf + df$

Coefficient formulas second table:

$$\text{gamma} = \frac{P-Q}{P+Q} = \frac{k(ad+af+cf)-k(cb+eb+ed)}{k(ad+af+cf)+k(cb+eb+ed)}$$

$$d_{yx} = \frac{P-Q}{P+Q+T_y} = \frac{k(ad+af+cf)-k(cb+eb+ed)}{k(ad+af+cf)+k(cb+eb+ed)+k(ab+cd+ef)}$$

$$d_{xy} = \frac{P-Q}{P+Q+T_x} = \frac{k(ad+af+cf)-k(cb+eb+ed)}{k(ad+af+cf)+k(cb+eb+ed)+k^2(ac+ae+ce)+bd+bf+df}$$

$$\text{tau-b} = \frac{P-Q}{\sqrt{(P+Q+T_y)(P+Q+T_x)}}$$

the numerator or the denominator of the coefficient's formula, with the result that k cancels out, leaving the same formula as that for the table upper left. Consequently gamma and d_{yx} will always be the same under fixed column percentages, as column-total ratios change. It can also easily be seen that a third column would produce, as cell-pair products, terms without the factor k. Also, even in the r × 2 case, the computation of other coefficients, such as d_{xy} or tau-b, does not attach exactly k to each term, so the constancy does not obtain.

For the constancy we seek, either d_{yx} or gamma will do for any r × 2 table. d_{yx} has the virtue of being asymmetric: that is, it is interpretable as the ordinal analogue of a regression coefficient (Somers, 1962). More usefully, it is equivalent to the column-percentage difference in a 2 × 2 table, and to an average percentage difference, in the sense explained by Somers (1962) in r × 2 tables. It reflects an "if and only if . . . then" implication, while gamma is analogous to the weaker "if . . . then" implication (McGinnis, 1958). d_{yx} reaches maximum only when there is strong monotonicity in the relationship;

gamma whenever there is weak, moderate, or strong monotonicity (Weisberg, 1974, p. 1643). For instance, since in recent times almost all blacks are Democrats, but it is not so that almost all Democrats are blacks, the party-by-race relationship will show a moderate d_{yx}, but a very strong gamma.

We might be tempted to suppose that the column-percentage difference, or a summary measure tied to such differences, such as d_{yx}, is the operational equivalent of a Platonic or intuitive One True Measure of association. The search for the One True Measure has been as long as the search for the Holy Grail; but it can now be decently abandoned. Thus in early controversies Karl Pearson (see Pearson and Heron, 1915) vehemently insisted that Pearson's r was *the* measure of correlation against which the performance of all other measures was to be tested. Disagreeing, Yule (1912, and Major and Yule, 1915) was equally monistic in his insistence on coefficients unresponsive to changing marginals. Later, even Goodman and Kruskal, in the midst of their encyclopedic inventory of measures, refer as to a standard to the concept of "intuitive association (1959, p. 141)." Recently Hunter (1973) asked 19 fellow sociologists to rank a series of 2 X 2 tables "intuitively" by strength of association. Correlating the intuitive ranks to the ranks produced by a number of measures, Hunter found that his colleagues' intuition corresponded most closely to the percentage difference. But clearly, if the sociologists' intuitive measure amounted to "group differences," in Hunter's phrase, it was because that is largely what sociology is about.

One would hope that after Weisberg (1974) it will become common practice to treat various measures as corresponding to various models of relationship, not all equally familiar, and not all as yet accessibly named for talking about. Directional causal hypotheses in terms of conditional probabilities, which do imply "group differences" as a measure, and should employ association statistics insensitive to independent variable marginal disparity, are very common. But other forms of relationship abound in other special contexts, such as those of attitude measurement (see Carroll, 1961) or legislative voting (Weisberg, 1974; MacRae, 1970, pp. 41–51).

The General Cure: Equiweighting

Gamma and d_{yx} are, insensitive to column-marginal disparity in two-column tables. The more general cure, however, is to compute the summary statistics from transformed cell frequencies. This works for any table and any association measure. Expressed as a verbal algorithm, the procedure is: (1) from the naturally occurring data, compute the column percentages;

(2) provide new column-total raw frequencies by dividing the total N by the number of categories in the independent variable, and substituting this figure for the original column totals; (3) using the new equalized column totals and the original column percentages, recompute the raw cell frequencies; (4) from these new cell frequencies, compute the summary statistics.

The procedure can also be expressed as a formula:[8]

$$a'_{ij} = a_{ij} \frac{1}{c} \frac{N}{n_j}$$

where

a_{ij} = the cell frequency before equiweighting
a'_{ij} = the new cell frequency after equiweighting
c = the number of categories in the independent variable
n_i = the column total before equiweighting of the column in which a cell is
    located
N = the total number of cases in the table

It is relatively simple for a programmer to add the equiweighting option to a crosstabulation program.[9]

Equiweighting eliminates variations in measures due to column-marginal disparity, which are artifactual distortions when the hypothesis is directional-causal, in terms of group differences or conditional probabilities. The choice and use of association statistic can then draw on other considerations involved in fitting the relationship model implicit in the statistics, to the form of relationship useful in the theoretical context. Weisberg's (1974) treatment of seven relationship models (classifying some 18 measures) is so terse and clear, but also so densely interconnected, that I will not try to pack it into a nutshell here. It is also helpfully illustrated and very

---

[8] With notational differences, this is the formula given in Goodman and Kruskal (1954, p. 746).

[9] If the matrix of percentages is computed entire before printing, and thus is held intact, then the simplest method is to follow the verbal algorithm. If the percentage matrix is retained only a row vector at a time, or even only a cell at a time, to save storage, it will still be possible to use the formula, the elements of which are invariably kept in storage by any crosstabulation program. If you are not interested in seeing the transformed table, but only the association measures under equiweighting, then a simple expedient is to substitute the column percentages for the raw frequencies, and proceed as usual to compute new marginals as needed, and new association measures.

widely available. Especially instructive are his demonstrations of how to use *several* statistics to illuminate the same data.

Of course, equiweighting changes the conditions for determining statistical significance levels. These must be computed from the untransformed tables. Given that caution, it would seem that equiweighting ought to be used whenever the proper conditions are met: a causal hypothesis in terms of conditional probabilities, and a need to use association measures. Whenever column percentages are appropriate, equiweighting is appropriate.

Why Not Equiweight Both Ways?

With certain exceptions (gamma and d_{xy} in $2 \times c$ tables) the summary statistics also respond to imbalance in *row* marginals. Should we not, then, also equiweight the rows?

Some sixty years ago G. Udny Yule, who might well be called the father of equiweighting, pursued this question to an inconclusive finish. It seemed to him absurd (and it is) that Pearson's r, applied as a measure of vaccination effectiveness, should show maximum effectiveness when exactly half the population was vaccinated, diminishing as almost all, or almost none were treated—even when the recovery rates of vaccinated and nonvaccinated were constant throughout. He sought a solution in table transformations which equalized both row and column marginals simultaneously (Yule 1912; Greenwood and Yule, 1915).[10] The esthetic elegance of the bilaterally equiweighted table (Yule called it "symmetric") is hard to resist: in the 2×2 table, Pearson's r, Yule's Y (Yule and Kendall, 1950, pp. 25–31), phi, both percentage differences, Goodman and Kruskal's lambdas a and b, Somers' d_{yx} and d_{xy}, and the correlation ratio eta all become equal. The equivalence breaks down, to be sure, in the general $r \times c$ table.

But as Yule later saw (Greenwood and Yule, 1915), bilateral equiweighting is logically flawed. When we are dealing with a conditional-probabilities causal hypothesis, the distribution of the independent variable is arbitrary, and thus should not be allowed to influence the summary measures. But the distribution of the dependent variable within categories of the independent variable is precisely what is not arbitrary; and equiweighting the rows disturbs it. For

---

[10] Yule used a system of simultaneous equations. An easily programmable alternative is first to equiweight on the columns; then, using the new frequencies, on the rows; then on the columns, etc. After about three such cycles, equilibrium extends to the third digit of all frequencies and coefficients. If I understand the sources correctly, this is the method of Gini's recursive index (see Pompilj, 1950).

such problems, measures *implying* bilateral equiweighting, such as phi/phi-max (there is even an r/r-max) ought to be avoided.[11]

Intermediate Equiweighting: A Socialization Example

Suppose we are investigating personal or intergenerational attitude change. We have "before" and "after" measures of the same attitude, either on the same people at two times (personal change) or on parents and their children (intergenerational change). We also have variables that tap intervening experience, analogous to treatment groups in an experiment, and we are using them to try to explain the attitude change.

Our analysis might form tables and compute association measures from them in two distinct ways, to answer two different questions. In the first way, the association measure will express *how much* change there is, but not its direction. In the second, the measure will express the *direction* of change. Each method, particularly the second, can hold inferential traps from which equiweighting can provide a rescue.

Tables 4 and 5 are hypothetical-data illustrations of the problems involved. Here the "before-after" variable is party identification. The "treatment groups" making up the experience variable are called Democratic school and Republican school to suggest the direction of the influence tendencies within them. Reading the column percentages in Table 4a, we can see what "influence tendencies" means. In the Democratic school, 60 percent of the original Democrats stay Democrats, and 15 percent turn Republican; the Republicans keep only 53 percent, and lose 20 percent to the Democrats; and twice as many Independents go Democratic as go Republican. In the Republican school, the conversion tendencies are reversed, somewhat more emphatically. All that is expectable.

Yet in terms of their output, each school seems to be counterproductive! The entering class at Democratic school is 70 percent Democratic and 15 percent Republican, but it emerges only 53 percent Democratic and 20 percent Republican. The small percentage loss from the large group of entering Democrats outweighs the larger percentage loss from the small group of entering Republicans. The converse is true at the Republican school.

---

[11] On phi/phi-max, see Cureton (1959). For a warning against phi/phi-max or r/r-max, and a superb treatment of distribution problems, see Carroll (1961). Costner (1965) raises the right questions about when marginals can be said to be "given," and the bearing of the answer upon the use of phi/phi-max.

Situations like this are far from being confined to logic-popping artificial stunts. In fact, they are likely to appear wherever there is some tendency for the "treatments" to recruit under selective influence of the "before" variable. And socialization experiences, especially later ones, have at least some tendency to be chosen, not randomly assigned: people enlist in experiences calculated to make them more like what they already are.[12]

Whether or not we want to apply equiweighting to such tables depends on the question we are asking. Or rather: the "raw" 4a tables answer certain questions, the "equiweighted" 4b tables certain other questions. We must just avoid applying answers to the wrong question. The raw tables can be read for the input and output distributions in the "real world," and thus for the actual net change in the sample. They can also be read for the column percentages (which are of course the same in the equiweighted 4b tables); these form, allowing for notational differences, a Markov transition matrix. But a tau-b applied to the "raw" tables would not measure what is probably being asked about: namely, the amount of stability vs. change inherent in the transition matrix, which stands for the influence tendencies inside the "school." For the tau-b, like the distribution of the "after" variable, is the product of two things: the transition matrix, *and* the distribution of the "before" variable.

So the equiweighted version in 4b is preferred if we want to look at the effects of treatments apart from differences in "before" variable distribution, as in a quasi-experiment. Tau-b applied to such tables will summarize the amount of stability vs. change implicit in the column percentages, and allow standardized comparisons of tables with varying "before" variable distributions. We can also then compare "after" variable distributions to see output "from a fair start."

We have to turn to the second method to get summary measures of *direction* of change associated with the treatment variable. We compute a new variable, a change index which is the "before" variable minus the "after" variable (plus possibly a constant, here 3, to avoid zero and negative codes).

[12] The paradox can even occur when the "school" variable is demographic, as Jennings and Niemi (1974, p. 42) report, with exclamation point, about intergenerational change in the South: "The Democratic party clearly has greater holding and pulling power [than the Republican] among Southern youth. Yet the pool of Democratic parents is so much larger than the number of Republican parents, that the student distribution shifts in a Republican direction!" They give a good explanation of the phenomenon. For an even more explicit treatment of three kinds of relationship measurement that could be applied to the question of intergenerational value transmission, see Tedin (1974).

TABLE 4

Comparison of Raw and Equiweighted Transition Matrices

4a: Transition Matrices with Raw Data

		Democratic School						Republican School			
		Before						Before			
		D	I	R				D	I	R	
	Dem	420	60	45	525		Dem	52	15	70	137
		60.0	*40.0*	*30.0*	*52.5*			*35.0*	*10.0*	*10.0*	*13.8*
After	Ind	175	60	45	280	After	Ind	22	60	140	222
		25.0	*40.0*	*30.0*	*28.0*			*15.0*	*40.0*	*20.0*	*22.3*
	Rep	105	30	60	195		Rep	75	75	490	640
		15.0	*20.0*	*40.0*	*19.5*			*50.0*	*50.0*	*70.0*	*64.0*
		700	150	150	1000			150	150	700	1000
		70.0	*15.0*	*15.0*	*100.0*			*15.0*	*15.0*	*70.0*	*100.0*

4b: Transition Matrices with Equiweighted Data

		Democratic School						Republican School			
		Before						Before			
		D	I	R				D	I	R	
	Dem	200	133	100	433		Dem	117	33	33	183
		60.0	*40.0*	*30.0*	*43.3*			*35.0*	*10.0*	*10.0*	*18.3*
After	Ind	83	133	100	316	After	Ind	50	133	67	250
		25.0	*40.0*	*30.0*	*31.7*			*15.0*	*40.0*	*20.0*	*25.0*
	Rep	50	67	133	250		Rep	167	167	233	567
		15.0	*20.0*	*40.0*	*25.0*			*50.0*	*50.0*	*70.0*	*56.7*
		333	333	333	1000			333	333	333	1000
		33.3	*33.3*	*33.3*	*100.0*			*33.3*	*33.3*	*33.3*	*100.0*

Note: Table conventions as in SPSS: integers are raw frequencies; decimal numbers in cells are column percentages; those in margins are the marginal frequencies as percentages of grand total N.

The change index has five categories, labelled in Table 5 to show which before-after combinations of party identification fall into each. The middle category is made up of the three "no-change" cells in the main diagonal of Table 4a; the first (top) category represents maximum change in the Republican direction, the bottom category, maximum change in the Democratic direction. We can now run tables in which the change index is the dependent variable, and the treatment categories make up the independent variable.

But then we are once again brought up short as we see that the association measures computed on this table (5a, "raw") are *positive*—which means that going to Republican school, as opposed to Democratic school, is associated with change in a *Democratic* direction. Once again, although this time it is far harder to see, this result reflects two things: the internal influences of the schools, *and* the makeup of the entering class. It would be all too easy to think the association measures reflect the influence tendencies alone. And in actual practice, the usual result is not that anomaly which is the beginning of wisdom, but just muddle.

To get measures for the internal influences of the schools alone, we construct a new table (5b, "equiweighted") by entering raw frequencies which are the sums of the frequencies in those cells of tables 4b which are indicated by the school categories, and by the "before-after" combinations in

TABLE 5

Comparison of Raw and Equiweighted Transition Matrices

	5a: *Conversion Index with Raw Data*				5b: *Conversion Index with Equiweighted Data*		
Change	D Schl	R Schl		Change	D Schl	R Schl	
DR	105	75	180	DR	50	167	217
	10.5	*7.5*	*9.0*		*5.0*	*16.7*	*10.9*
DI,IR	205	98	303	DI,IR	150	217	367
	20.5	*9.8*	*15.1*		*15.0*	*21.7*	*18.4*
DD,II,RR	540	603	1143	DD,II,RR	466	483	949
	54.0	*60.2*	*57.1*		*46.6*	*48.3*	*47.5*
ID,RI	105	155	260	ID,RI	233	100	333
	10.5	*15.5*	*13.0*		*23.3*	*10.0*	*16.7*
RD	45	70	115	RD	100	33	133
	4.5	*7.0*	*5.7*		*10.0*	*3.3*	*6.7*
	1000	1000	2000		1000	1000	2000
	50.0	*50.0*	*100.0*		*50.0*	*50.0*	*100.0*

Tau-c = .16, gamma = .26
d_{yx} = .16, d_{xy} = .15

Tau-c = −.30, gamma = −.42
d_{yx} = −.30, d_{xy} = −.25

Note: Table conventions as in SPSS: integers are raw frequencies; decimal numbers in cells are column percentages; those in margins are the marginal frequencies as percentages of grand total N.

the change-variable categories.[13] Now when we compute the association measures, they reflect the schools' influence tendencies alone, and thus are negative in sign.

Summary

Everyone is familiar with the textbook research-design procedure in which we state a theoretical proposition, give *conceptual* definitions to the variables in it, work out the rule for attaching numbers to observations that we call the *operational* definition of the same variables, and then go to work statistically to test the proposition, which is invariably that "there is a relationship" between the variables. Common practice, especially in psychology, has lavished attention on the conceptual-operational translation of variables, with its concern for reliability, validity, surplus meaning, dimensionality, etc. Compared to this preoccupation with the "nouns" of the language of social research, little attention has been paid to the link between conceptual and operational forms of the "predicate," or the relationship type. As Weisberg has shown (1974), specifying seven such types, we have a richer variety than is implied by the single word "association." More work remains to be done in

[13] An alternative method, especially if you do not have an interactive program which takes cell frquencies as input and produces association coefficients, employs the kind of weighting that is provided for in most statistical packages, such as SPSS or OSIRIS. Following the hypothetical example, first run the tables analogous to Table 4a. Then create a weight variable with, in this illustration, six categories. The formula for each weight is:

$$W_{jk} = \frac{N_k}{cn_{jk}}$$

where

W_{jk} = the weight associated with observations (here, before-after pairs) scored j on the "before" variable, and k on the "influence" variable
N_k = raw frequency grand total in the subtable for the kth category of the influence (functionally: control) variable
c = number of categories of the "before" variable
n_{jk} = raw column total for "before" variable, category j in the subtable for category k of the influence variable

There will be a weight variable corresponding to each "influence" variable to be used. Then the procedure involves construction of change indexes, and running them against the "influence" variables. Each such table must be run with the temporary weight corresponding to that particular combination of "before," "after," and "influence" variables.

this area, particularly for interval-level statistics, as Weisberg (1974, p. 1653) suggests, and for tables larger than 2 × 2. It is the analogic link between conceptual and operational versions of relationship forms that I have in mind with the "what's the question to that answer" in the title. This article itself bears only on the influence of marginal disparity on the questions that association measures answer.

To review the main points:

1. In a bivariate table in which we distinguish between the independent variable and the dependent variable, and thus are working with an implied causal hypothesis, we would naturally compute percentages on the categories of the independent (conventionally, column) variable.

2. If we keep the column percentages fixed, but vary the column totals (frequencies), the almost invariable tendency is for measures of association to shrink in proportion as column totals become more unequal. This shrinkage is either appropriate, or it is an artifactual distortion, depending on just what question we are asking. If we are asking about the causal impact of differences in the independent variable upon the dependent outcome for the whole sample, then we want the association measures to shrink as the independent variable becomes more lopsided while the column percentages stay the same. But if we are asking a quasi-experimental question, one about the conditional probability of the various dependent outcomes for each category of the independent variable, then we ought to remove the influence of marginal disparity on the association measures.

3. The procedure called "equiweighting"—keeping column percentages fixed, but equalizing column-total frequencies, produces a table of transformed frequencies from which association measures can be computed to answer the second, conditional-probability, group-differences-in-rate sort of causality question.

4. When the independent variable is a dichotomy, then even without equiweighting, Somers' d_{yx} and Goodman and Kruskal's gamma do not vary when column percentages are fixed, but column-marginal disparity varies.

5. A recursive "bilateral equiweighting" procedure converges to a table with equal column *and* row totals. The result does not appear to correspond to either kind of causal relationship, and seems to lack a conceptual equivalent.

6. In change problems such as those in the socialization example, the distribution of the "after" variable is a product of *two* things: the influence tendencies implicit in the column percentages, *and* the distribution of the "before" variable. This is very hard to see in change indexes used as dependent variables. If the question is about the influence tendencies alone, then

equiweighting ought to be used to remove the artifactual influence of the "before" variable distribution.

Manuscript submitted January 21, 1976.
Final manuscript received April 22, 1976.

REFERENCES

Abelson, Robert P., and Tukey, John W. 1970. "Efficient Conversion of Non-Metric Information into Metric Information," in Edward R. Tufte, ed., *The Quantitative Analysis of Social Problems.* Reading, Mass.: Addison-Wesley.

Aldrich, John, and Cnudde, Charles F. 1975. "Probing the Bounds of Conventional Wisdom: A Comparison of Regression, Probit, and Discriminant Analysis," *American Journal of Political Science*, August 1975, pp. 571–608.

Blalock, Hubert M., Jr. 1972. *Social Statistics*, 2d ed. New York: McGraw-Hill.

Buchanan, William. 1974. "Nominal and Ordinal Bivariate Statistics: The Practitioner's View," *American Journal of Political Science*, August 1974, pp. 625–646.

Carroll, John B. 1961. "The Nature of the Data, or How to Choose a Correlation Coefficient," *Psychometrika*, December 1961, pp. 347–372.

Costner, Herbert L. 1965. "Criteria for Measures of Association," *American Sociological Review*, June 1965, pp. 341–353.

Cureton, Edward F. 1959. "Note on phi/phi-max," *Psychometrika*, March 1959, pp. 89–91.

Goodman, Leo A., and Kruskal, William H. 1954. "Measures of Association for Cross-Classifications," *Journal of the American Statistical Association*, December 1954, pp. 732–764.

___. 1959. "Measures of Association for Cross-Classifications. II: Further Discussion and References," *Journal of the American Statistical Association*, March 1959, pp. 123–163.

Greenwood, Major, Jr., and Yule, G. Udny. 1915. "The Statistics of Anti-Typhoid and Anti-Cholera Inoculations, and the Interpretation of Such Statistics in General," *Proceedings of the Royal Society of Medicine*, vol. 8, part 2, 1915, pp. 113–194.

Hunter, A. A. 1973, "On the Validity of Measures of Association," *American Journal of Sociology*, July 1973, pp. 99–109.

Hyman, Herbert H. 1955. *Survey Design and Analysis*. New York: Free Press.

Jennings, M. Kent, and Niemi, Richard G. 1974. *The Political Character of Adolescence*. Princeton: Princeton University Press.

Kendall, Maurice G. 1962 (first edition, 1948). *Rank Correlation Methods*, 3d ed. London: Charles Griffin and Co.

Kohout, Frank J. 1974. *Statistics for Social Scientists: A Coordinated Learning System*. New York: Wiley.

Kruskal, Joseph B. 1968. "Special Problems of Statistical Analysis: Transformations of Data," in David L. Sills, ed., *International Encyclopedia of the Social Sciences*, vol. 15, pp. 182–193.

Kruskal, William. 1958. "Ordinal Measures of Association," *Journal of the American Statistical Association*, December 1958, pp. 814–861.

Labovitz, Sanford. 1970. "The Assignment of Numbers to Rank Order Categories," *American Sociological Review*, June 1970, pp. 515–525.

MacRae, Duncan, Jr. 1970. *Issues and Parties in Legislative Voting: Methods of Statistical Analysis*. New York: Harper and Row.

McGinnis, Robert. "Logical Status of the Concept of Association," *The Midwest Sociologist*, May 1958, pp. 72–77.

Nie, Norman H.; Hull, C. Hadlai; Jenkins, Jean G.; Steinbrenner, Karen; and Bent, Dale H. 1975. *SPSS: Statistical Package for the Social Sciences*, 2d ed. New York: McGraw-Hill.

Pearson, Karl, and Heron, David. 1913. "On Theories of Association," *Biometrika*, 1913, pp. 159–315.

Pompilj, G. 1950. "Osservazioni sull'omogamia: La trasformazione di Yule e il limite della trasformazione ricorrente di Gini," *Rendiconti de Matematica e delle sue Applicazioni*, Università di Roma, Istituto Nazionale di Alta Matematica, Ser. V, vol. 9, 1950, pp. 367–388.

Rosenberg, Morris. 1968. *The Logic of Survey Analysis*. New York: Basic Books.

Somers, Robert H. 1962. "A New Asymmetric Measure of Association for Ordinal Variables," *American Sociological Review*, December 1962, pp. 799–811.

Stuart, Alan, and Kendall, Maurice G., eds., 1971. *Statistical Papers of George Udny Yule*. New York: Hafner. (An alternative location for Yule 1912 and Major and Yule 1915.)

Tedin, Kent L. 1974. "The Influence of Parents on the Political Attitudes of Adolescents," *American Political Science Review*, December 1974, pp. 1579–1592.

Tufte, Edward R. 1969. "Improving Data Analysis in Political Science," *World Politics*, July 1969, pp. 641–654.

_____. 1974. *Data Analysis for Politics and Policy*. Englewood Cliffs, New Jersey: Prentice-Hall.

Verba, Sidney, and Nie, Norman H. 1972. *Participation in America: Political Democracy and Social Equality*. New York: Harper and Row.

Weisberg, Herbert F. 1974. "Models of Statistical Relationship," *American Political Science Review*, December 1974, pp. 1638–1655.

Yule, G. Udny. 1912. "On the Methods of Measuring Association Between Two Attributes," *Journal of the Royal Statistical Society*, 1912, pp. 579–642.

Yule, G. Udny, and Kendall, Maurice G. 1950. *An Introduction to the Theory of Statistics*, 14th edition. London: Charles Griffin and Co.

Regression Models

HERBERT B. ASHER

Regression Analysis

Regression analysis is a powerful tool for data analysis in the social sciences. The fundamentals of regression analysis are reviewed in this chapter beginning with an explication of the general linear model, the method of least squares, and the properties of least squares estimates. Attention then turns to the factors that can affect regression estimates such as collinearity, specification error and measurement error. The chapter concludes with a discussion of the linkages between regression analysis and causal modeling techniques.

Often in social research the investigator wishes to assess the effect of an independent variable or a set of independent variables on a dependent variable. Regression analysis is a technique for generating a numerical estimate of the effect of an independent variable while statistically controlling for the effects of the other independent variables. Regression analysis has many uses, one being to test explanatory models of some dependent phenomenon. For example, let us suppose that our research question is the determinants of citizens' votes in the presidential election. Voting behavior research suggests that citizens' party identification, their stands on the issues, and their assessments of the candidates might all affect their vote choices. We can represent this by the equation:

$$Y = b_0 + b_1 X_1 + b_2 X_2 + b_3 X_3 \quad ,$$

where

Y is the vote choice of a person ,
X_1 is the person's party identification ,
X_2 is the person's issue preferences ,
X_3 is the person's candidate evaluations ,
b_1, b_2, b_3 are unknown weights representing the effects of the independent variables on the dependent variable.

A more complete way of writing the equation would be:

$$Y = b_0 + b_{y1.23} X_1 + b_{y2.13} X_2 + b_{y3.12} X_3$$

The coefficient $b_{y1.23}$ stands for the effect of X_1 on Y while the effects of X_2 and X_3 are controlled. Likewise, $b_{y2.13}$ is the effect of X_2 on Y while the effects of X_1 and X_3 are controlled. If we have done a survey of voters and measured Y,

237

X_1, X_2, and X_3 appropriately, then we could regress Y on X_1, X_2, and X_3 to obtain the estimates of the coefficients. (If vote is a dichotomous variable, e.g., Democrat vs. Republican, then the use of ordinary least squares procedures to estimate the coefficients will be inappropriate and other estimation techniques will have to be employed; this problem will be discussed later.) Because we have multiple independent variables in the above equation, we call it a multiple regression equation.

In the above example, we are trying to explain a person's vote on the basis of some theoretically justified explanatory variable. Regression analysis may be used in a more predictive mode, although the distinction between prediction and explanation often breaks down. Let us consider the following example: a college admissions office is trying to make admissions decisions on applicants on the basis of their likely freshman year performance. Obviously, since their freshman grade-point average is an unknown quantity, some method must be used to generate a predicted performance. One way to proceed is to construct a regression equation of the form:

$$Y = b_0 + b_1X_1 + b_2X_2 + b_3X_3 \quad ,$$

where

  Y is grade-point average   ,
  X_1 is SAT math score   ,
  X_2 is SAT verbal score   ,
  X_3 is rank in high school class.

The values for b_0, b_1, b_2, and b_3 in this equation could be estimated by regressing the grade points of college sophomores on *their* SAT scores and high school rank. These numerical estimates might then be used to weight a prospective applicant's test scores and high school rank to generate a predicted performance in college. Let us suppose the sophomore class equation turned out to be

$$Y = 2.3 + .0006X_1 + .0008X_2 - 1.5X_3$$

and that an applicant had the following credentials: SAT math score, 700; SAT verbal score, 750; Rank, first in a class of 100 or 1/100 or .01. Then the applicant's predicted performance (ŷ) in college would be

$$\hat{y} = 2.3 + .0006(700) + .0008(750) - 1.5(.01) = 3.305 \quad ,$$

which (assuming a 4.0 grading system) might result in a decision to admit.

Regression analysis may also be used in a curve fitting mode where the major goal is to fit a set of observations to some functional form. Let us consider, for example, the relationship between the percentage of the popular vote a party wins in congressional elections and the percentage of seats that the party obtains in the U.S. House. The question we are asking is how well votes translate into seats. What is the functional relationship between the two? What biases, if any, are built into the electoral system and its allocation of seats? On the assumption that the number of seats won is a function of how well the party does in the popular vote, we might express the seats-vote relationship by the following equation:

$$Y = b_0 + b_l X \quad ,$$

where

Y is the percentage of seats won by the majority party,

X is the percentage of the popular vote won by that party,

b_0 is a constant or intercept term,

b_l is the slope which measures the effect of X on Y.

If the United States had a perfect proportional representation system, then b_0 would equal 0, b_l would equal one, and the relationship between Y and X might be represented simply by the equation $Y = X$. A plot of this equation would look like Figure 1.

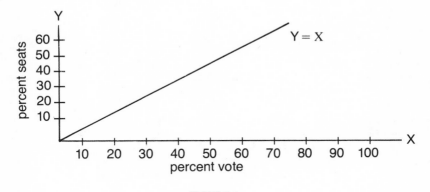

FIGURE 1

A Linear Relationship between Votes and Seats in a Legislature

The line intercepts the Y axis at 0; hence the intercept or constant term b_0 is 0. And for each unit change in X, Y changes by one unit; hence $b_l = 1$.

There is no reason why the relationship between X and Y need look like the above. For example, in a two-party system such as the one in the United States which is characterized by a single-member district electoral system, there is a tendency for the party winning a majority of the votes to receive an even larger majority of the seats. This might be represented by the various hypothetical lines in Figure 2.

For the lower line plotted in Figure 2, b_l, the coefficient of X, is 1.0, which indicates that a 1% increase in the popular vote results in a 1% gain in congressional seats. The constant or intercept term of 2 indicates that whatever vote percentage a party receives, its seat allotment will be that percentage plus two; hence, if a party received 55% of the vote, it would receive 57% of the seats. The top line in the figure is similar except here $b_l = 1.1$, which indicates that a unit change in the vote percentage results in a 1.1% change in the seats won. Hence, the slope of the upper line is somewhat steeper than that of the lower.

The seats-vote example has thus far assumed a simple straight-line, bivariate relationship between the independent and dependent variable. However, it is possible that the relationship between seats and votes might be curvilinear,

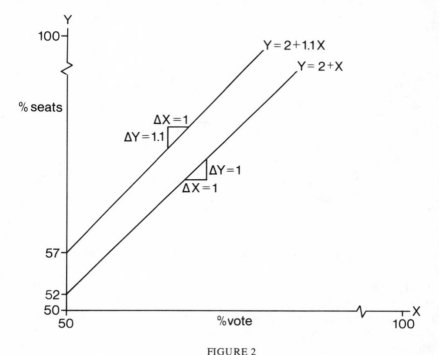

FIGURE 2
Two Hypothetical Seats-Vote Relationships.

perhaps represented by the quadratic expression $Y = b_0 + b_1 X + b_2 X^2$ and pictorially displayed in Figure 3.

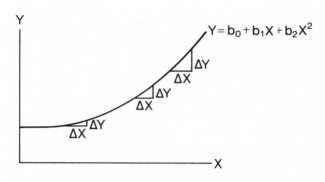

FIGURE 3

A Curvilinear Relationship between Votes and Seats

Since there are really two independent variables, X and X^2 in the quadratic expression, we have moved from a bivariate to a multivariate situation. The diagram clearly indicates that as a party's percentage of the vote increases, its percentage of the seats increases at an increasing rate (in contrast to the constant rates in the straight-line examples). We will return to this example when we talk about the method of least squares.

The General Linear Model

All of the equations we have considered thus far are specific instances of the general linear model, a statistical model widely used in social research. The general linear model relates a set of independent variables $X_1, X_2, \ldots X_k$ to a dependent variable Y in the following fashion:

$$Y = b_0 + b_1 X_1 + b_2 X_2 + \ldots + b_k X_k + e \quad,$$

where

Y is the dependent variable,

$X_1, X_2, \ldots X_k$ are the independent variables,

$b_1, b_2, \ldots b_k$ are unknown parameters which measure the respective weights assigned to the independent variables in the prediction of Y,

e is an error or residual term which incorporates random disturbances and variables omitted from the model.

A number of assumptions are made in the general linear model:

1. The variables are measured without error. This is an untenable asumption in most instances, and later we will briefly consider the effects of measurement error.

2. The model has been specified correctly. This means that the major variables which affect Y have been included in the equation and that irrelevant variables have not been included. How well this assumption is met is a function of the state of the theory guiding research. A well-developed theory implies that the major variables and relationships have been identified. We need not include all variables that affect Y, but we should make sure that the omitted variable(s) are not confounding ones, that is, variables that affect the dependent and independent variable(s) simultaneously. The presence of confounding variables will upset the inferences we wish to draw on the basis of the b coefficients.

3. There are a number of assumptions made about the error term. If we write,

$$Y_i = b_0 + b_1 X_{1i} + b_2 X_{2i} + \cdots + b_k X_{ki} + e_i, \text{ we assume}$$

a. The mean of the errors equals 0 or $E(e_i) = 0$. This is not a very critical assumption.

b. The variance of the e_i is constant, say σ^2. This is the assumption of homoscedasticity; it says that the variance of the error is constant for all values of X_{ki}. Violation of this assumption creates problems in using ordinary least squares procedures, a point returned to later.

c. The error terms are independent, that is, any e_i and e_j are independent and hence uncorrelated: $E(e_i e_j) = 0$. Also we assume that the error term and the independent variable(s) are uncorrelated: $E(e_1 X_j) = 0$. Assumptions a–c represent the weak set of assumptions about the error terms. When a fourth assumption is added about the normality of the distribution of the error term, we then have the strong set of assumptions. (We have glossed over the consequences of fixed vs. random independent variables.)

Fitting the General Linear Model: The Method of Least Squares

The key point is to fit the general linear model, that is, to obtain estimates of the unknown b coefficients and thereby draw conclusions about the effects of the independent variables on the dependent variable. In our votes-seats example, where $Y = b_0 + b_1 X$, we would like to obtain estimates of the b_0 and b_1 coefficients. One way to proceed is by the method of least squares. If we were to collect observations of X and Y, it would be highly unlikely that they would all fall along a straight line. The scatterplot of the X and Y values would more likely look like Figure 4.

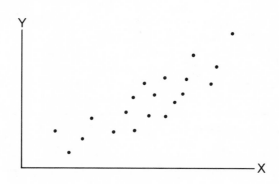

FIGURE 4

A Possible Scatterplot of the Votes-Seats Relationship

Although a straight line would appear to fit these observations reasonably well, it is obvious that there is no single line that can possibly go through all of the observations at once. Hence, the task is to find the best-fitting straight line, and here the criterion of least square enters.

Consider Figure 5.

Let $Y = b_0 + b_1 X$ represent the unknown, best-fitting straight line. As we can see, most of the observations do not fall on the line. Let us consider the observation (X_i, Y_i). When $X = X_i$, the predicted value of Y ($\hat{Y}$) according to the best-fitting line is $\hat{Y}_i$. Yet the actual value of Y when $X = X_i$ is Y_i. Hence, we have a departure or deviation from the best-fitting line of $Y_i - \hat{Y}_i$. We call this quantity a residual or error. For each Y observation, we will have a deviation, e.g., $Y_j - \hat{Y}_j$, $Y_k - \hat{Y}_k$.

Intuitively, we would like these deviations to be as small as possible, for that would mean that the best-fitting line was coming as close as possible to all the data points simultaneously. Hence, we would like the sum of these deviations $\sum_{i=1}^{n} (Y_i - \hat{Y}_i)^2$ to be as small as possible.

$$\text{Since } \hat{Y}_i = \hat{b}_0 + \hat{b}_1 X_i \quad ,$$

then the quantity we wish to minimize is

$$\sum_{i=1}^{n} (Y_i - [\hat{b}_0 + \hat{b}_1 X_i])^2.$$

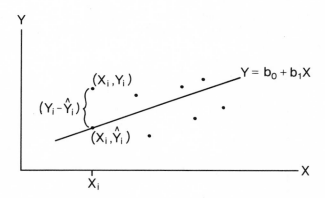

FIGURE 5

The Scatterplot of X and Y and the Best-Fitting Straight Line

This quantity is the sum of the squares of the errors (SSE) or the residual sum of squares (RSS). To minimize SSE we can take the derivative of the expression with respect to b_0 and b_1 and solve. (Any regression text will show the actual steps.) In this straight line example,

$$\hat{b}_1 = \frac{n \sum_{i=1}^{n} X_i Y_i - \sum_{i=1}^{n} X_i \sum_{i=1}^{n} Y_i}{n \sum_{i=1}^{n} X_i^2 - \left(\sum_{i=1}^{n} X_i \right)^2}$$

and

$$\hat{b}_0 = Y - \hat{b}_1 \bar{X}$$

The solution for $\hat{b}_1$ is expressed entirely in terms of known observations for the X and Y variables, where n is the number of observations. After solving for $\hat{b}_1$, we can readily obtain the solution for $\hat{b}_0$. In general, the least squares procedure is a very mechanical one. The investigator can choose to fit any curve to a set of observations, although it is best to examine the scatterplots to see which curves are reasonable to fit to the data. The residual sum of squares (RSS) gives a measure of the goodness of fit and allows a choice among competing curves.

An example may help clarify ordinary least squares. Table 1 presents the vote and seats percentages received by the majority party in elections for the U.S. House of Representatives from 1946 to 1978. A scatterplot of the data

TABLE 1

The Relationship between the Percentage of the Vote and the Percentage of the Seats Received by the Majority Party in U.S. House Elections from 1948 to 1978

Year	Percent of Vote (X)	Percent of Seats (Y)	Predicted Y for Straight $\hat{Y} = -37.1 + 1.82X$	Residual $(Y_i - \hat{Y}_i)$	Residual² $(Y_i - \hat{Y}_i)^2$	Predicted Y for Incomplete Quadratic $\hat{Y} = 11.2 + .0172X^2$	Residual $(Y_i - \hat{Y}_i)$	Residual² $(Y_i - \hat{Y}_i)^2$
1946	53.5	56.7	60.3	-3.6	13.0	60.4	-3.7	13.7
1948	51.6	60.6	56.8	3.8	14.4	57.0	3.6	13.0
1950	48.9	54.0	51.9	2.1	4.4	52.3	1.7	2.9
1952	49.3	50.9	52.6	-1.7	2.9	53.0	-2.1	4.4
1954	52.1	53.3	57.7	-4.4	19.4	57.9	-4.6	21.2
1956	50.7	53.8	55.2	-1.4	2.0	55.4	-1.6	2.6
1958	55.5	64.9	63.9	1.0	1.0	64.2	.7	.5
1960	54.4	60.0	61.9	-1.9	3.6	62.1	-2.1	4.4
1962	52.1	59.4	57.7	1.7	2.9	57.9	1.5	2.3
1964	56.9	67.8	66.5	1.3	1.7	66.9	.9	.8
1966	50.5	57.0	54.8	2.2	4.8	55.1	1.9	3.6
1968	50.0	55.9	53.9	2.0	4.0	54.2	1.7	2.9
1970	53.0	58.6	59.4	-.8	.6	59.5	-.9	.8
1972	51.7	55.8	57.0	-1.2	1.4	57.2	-1.4	2.0
1974	57.1	66.9	66.8	.1	.0	67.3	-.4	.2
1976	56.2	67.1	65.2	1.9	3.6	65.5	1.6	2.6
1978	53.4	63.7	60.1	3.6	13.0	60.2	3.5	12.3
					RSS$_{straight}$ = 92.7			RSS$_{quadratic}$ = 90.2

indicates that a straight line seems to be a reasonable approximation of the data. Hence, the curve to be fitted is $Y = b_0 + b_1 X$.

With the solutions for $\hat{b}_0$ and $\hat{b}_1$ presented earlier, the estimated equation is $Y = -37.1 + 1.82X$. This means that a party which gets 51% of the vote is predicted to receive about 55.7% of the seats, an indication that the majority party wins a greater share of the seats than it does of the vote.

An attempt was made to fit the complete quadratic expression $Y = b_0 + b_1 X + b_2 X^2$ to these data, but this turned out to be an impossible task since X and X^2 were almost perfectly collinear. (The topic of collinearity and its effects on estimates will be discussed later.) The incomplete quadratic expression $Y = b_0 + b_1 X^2$ was fit to the data resulting in the estimated equation $Y = 11.2 + .0172X^2$. The straight line and the incomplete quadratic fit the data nearly identically as evidenced by the residual sum of squares of about 92.7 and 90.2 for each equation.

Properties of the Least Squares Estimates

Although the method of least squares is a mechanical, curve-fitting procedure, there is a compelling reason for its use when the weak set of assumptions about the error terms (described previously) is met. According to the Gauss-Markov Theorem, within the class of linear, unbiased estimates of the unknown coefficients, $b_0, b_1, \ldots b_k$, the least squares estimates have minimum variance. Alternatively, the least squares estimates are said to be BLUE—best (minimum variance), linear, unbiased estimator.

In many situations in social research, we are dealing with a sample of observations drawn from a population. Our goal is to make inferences about the population on the basis of the sample estimates. Hence, if we are to avoid faulty inferences, it is critical that our sample estimates have desirable properties, such as being BLUE. Yet even when our sample estimates do have desirable properties, we must keep in mind that we often have selected only one sample from the population and that were we to select another sample our estimates might differ. For example, we might scientifically select a sample of 1500 Americans to query on their view of the President's job performance. Let us suppose the sample results indicated 65% approval of the President. Another sample of 1500 selected by similar methods and interviewed at the same time might show 61% approval. Which figure is correct, the 61% or 65%? Obviously, either is; both are sample estimates, and to make sense of sample estimates we need to take into account sampling error and confidence intervals. As we review below the properties of least squares estimators, the reader should keep in mind that investigators are likely because of time and resource constraints to have picked only one or a few samples from a potentially infinite number of samples.

The property of being unbiased is very straightforward. Let $\hat{\Theta}$ be a sample estimate of some population parameter Θ. $\hat{\Theta}$ is said to be an unbiased estimator of Θ if $E(\hat{\Theta}) = \Theta$. This means that *on the average,* the value of $\hat{\Theta}$ is Θ. If we pick a sample from a population to estimate Θ, the single sample estimate $\hat{\Theta}$ may not be equal to Θ. However, if we pick multiple samples and estimate Θ in each, the average of the various sample $\hat{\Theta}$s should approximately be equal to Θ.

Unbiasedness is an important property of an estimator, particularly when that estimator also has minimum variance. The combination of unbiasedness and minimum variance is referred to as efficiency. Let us consider the sampling distributions (variances) of two estimators $\hat{\Theta}$ and $\hat{\hat{\Theta}}$ of some population parameter Θ in Figure 6 obtained by estimating $\hat{\Theta}$ and $\hat{\hat{\Theta}}$ in multiple samples. Although both $\hat{\Theta}$ and $\hat{\hat{\Theta}}$ are unbiased (their average value is Θ), $\hat{\Theta}$ is the preferred estimate since its sampling variance is smaller. Let us now imagine that we have picked only one sample. According to the distribution of $\hat{\Theta}$ shown above, most of the sample estimates will be reasonably close to the population value, and sound inferences will be drawn. With respect to $\hat{\hat{\Theta}}$ and its wide sampling distribution, it is possible that any single sample estimate of Θ might be far off the mark.

A property of estimators appropriate for large samples is consistency. $\hat{\Theta}$ is a consistent estimator of Θ if:

$$E(\hat{\Theta}) \to \ddot{\Theta} \quad \text{as } n \to \infty.$$

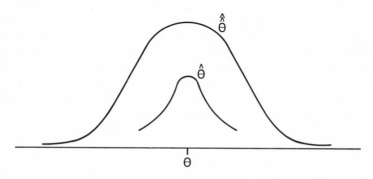

FIGURE 6

Sampling Distributions with Different Variances

In this case consistency means that as the sample size approaches infinity the sample estimate should approach the true population value. This would seem to be a very weak property in the sense that we would naturally expect the sample estimate to get very close to the true value as the sample got increasingly large. However, this is not the case for ordinary least squares (OLS) estimates when the assumptions about the error terms being uncorrelated with the independent variables are violated. In such a case, OLS procedures fail, and we must turn to other estimating techniques, such as two-stage least squares (2SLS), which yield biased but consistent estimates. We will discuss other regression estimation procedures shortly.

When the strong set of assumptions about the error term holds, then tests of significance of the overall regression equation as well as tests of the significance of specific coefficients are available to the investigator. Technically, these tests are appropriate only when we are dealing with a sample of observations selected from some population, although some analysts often informally apply tests of significance to population data.

Factors that Affect Regression Estimates

The central thrust of regression analysis is to estimate the unknown coefficients of the regression model and, on the basis of these estimates, draw substantive conclusions about the importance of the independent variables and their effects on the dependent variables. Unfortunately, there are a number of factors that can result in misleading estimates, which in turn could cause the investigator to arrive at incorrect substantive conclusions. Some of these factors deal with properties of the data, such as the pattern of correlations among the independent variables and the presence of measurement error. Others deal with errors in the structure of the model being tested; certain variables may improperly be included or excluded in the model. Finally, violations of the assumptions of regression analyses discussed earlier may also create problems in the interpretation of the obtained coefficients; of particular note here are the assumptions made about the error or residual terms being uncorrelated with each other and with the explanatory variables and the assumption of homoscedasticity or constant variance of the error term.

Collinearity

Although the explanatory variables in a regression equation are called independent variables, they are normally not independent in a statistical sense. Statistical independence implies that the independent variables are mutually uncorrelated, but if that is the case, then regression analysis would be superfluous, as the standardized regression coefficients would reduce to zero-order correlation coefficients and the unstandardized coefficients to covariance expressions. Hence, regression analysis and the notion of statistical control it entails become useful only when the independent variables are moderately intercorrelated. However, when the correlations among the independent variables are too high—the situation of multicollinearity—then problems occur in making inferences on the basis of the regression estimates.

High correlations among the independent variables result in larger standard errors of the estimated regression coefficients. This means that if two samples were drawn from the same population and the same regression equation estimated in each of the samples, it is entirely possible that the results of the two estimations would differ substantially even though both sets of estimates had the desirable properties of estimators discussed earlier. In short, multicollinearity makes it difficult to draw sound substantive conclusions since the regression estimates will be highly unstable; the investigator who selects a single sample may be unfortunate if that sample yields results highly divergent from the true population parameters.

This point can be demonstrated by examination of some simulated data with known properties. In the following example, multiple sets of observations on X_1, X_2 and Y were generated according to the function

$$Y = .3X_1 + .4X_2 + e \quad ,$$

where .3 and .4 are in effect the true regression parameters. Four samples of observations were generated for Y, X_1 and X_2 using Monte Carlo data simulation techniques with X_1 and X_2 being correlated at .8. Another four samples were generated according to the same functional form with the correlation between X_1 and X_2 now set at .95. Then for each of these eight samples, Y was regressed on X_1 and X_2 to see how close the estimated coefficients would come to the known parameter values of .3 and .4. The results are shown in Table 2.

Note that the effects of collinearity in this particular example are especially strong when $r_{x_1x_2} = .95$; here the standard error is larger and the sample estimates fluctuate widely. For example, sample 1 yields results close to the known true values, while sample 4 yields very disparate results. Obviously, the substantive interpretations that would emerge from the various samples would differ greatly.

When we have highly correlated independent variables, we might decide to eliminate one or more of such variables from the regression equation. Or we might combine the collinear variables into an index or scale. In some cases, data reduction techniques such as factor analysis may be used to reduce a large

TABLE 2

The Effects of Collinearity[a]

	$r_{x_1 x_2} = .8$		Standard Error	$r_{x_1 x_2} = .95$		Standard Error
	b_{y1}	b_{y2}		b_{y1}	b_{y2}	
Sample 1	.23	.44	.07	.33	.34	.12
Sample 2	.34	.42	.07	.38	.31	.12
Sample 3	.33	.34	.07	.12	.54	.12
Sample 4	.39	.31	.07	.06	.67	.12
True Value	.3	.4		.3	.4	

[a] These data were generated by Stuart Rabinowitz.

number of indicators, many of which might be highly intercorrelated, to a smaller number of underlying factors that may be uncorrelated. Of course, the composite variables resulting from such procedures as factor analysis may be more difficult to interpret than the original variables. Moreover, combining collinear variables (or simply removing one or more collinear variables from the equation) may violate the true specification linking the independent and dependent variables.

There is no automatic level at which collinearity becomes a problem, although some analysts arbitrarily set .7 as the correlational level at which to be concerned about collinearity. In general, the higher the correlations among the independent variables, the more serious the problem. Likewise, the higher the unexplained variance in the dependent variable, the greater the problem. Finally, collinearity is more likely to be a problem with aggregate data than with individual level (e.g., survey) data because the latter are likely to contain a random measurement error component. However, when data are aggregated, the random error component is likely to be cancelled. And as will be discussed in the next section, random measurement error attenuates (lowers) correlation coefficients, thereby lessening the problem of collinearity.

Measurement Error

The general linear model assumes that the independent variables are measured without error, a patently false assumption. The very process of measurement in the social sciences will result in measurement errors—deviations from the true value of a variable which arise from the process of measurement. Symbolically we can write

$$X' = T + e$$

where X' is the measured value of a variable, T is the true value (without measurement error), and e is the measurement error component.

Measurement errors may be either random or nonrandom (systematic). The key property of random error is that the measurement errors are uncorrelated with the true scores. Also, since the error is just as likely to be above the true value as below, the implication is that the sum of all errors for any single variable will be zero. Nonrandom error refers to systematic upward and/or downward biases in the observations. Here the errors and the true values are correlated, as in the case of having floor and ceiling effects in the measurement of certain variables.

Random measurement error is less worrisome than nonrandom for a number of reasons. Techniques for estimating the effects of random error are better developed, and hence the consequences of random error can be estimated more confidently (Asher, 1974). For example, random error attenuates *bivariate* correlation and regression coefficients and, unless corrected, can result in misleading, overly cautious interpretations based on these coefficients. In the multivariate case, the effects of random error are more complex, resulting in upward or downward biases in the regression coefficients, thereby making it difficult to sort out the separate effects of the independent variables. Nonrandom error is even more problematic since it can bias coefficients upward or downward in both the bivariate and multivariate cases. In summary, measurement error will result in regression estimates different from those that would be obtained had the independent variables been measured without error. This in turn means that the presence of measurement error makes it more difficult to draw sound substantive conclusions on the basis of the regression estimates.

Specification Error

If, in constructing the equation for some dependent variable Y, we have either included independent variables that should not be included or excluded ones that merit inclusion, then we have made a specification error. And if we then estimate the coefficients in the improperly specified equation, we run the risk of obtaining misleading estimates, which may result in inappropriate substantive interpretations.

Often in social science research we are unsure of the true causal specification linking a set of independent variables with some dependent variable; here the likelihood of making a specification error is high. However, this should not overly dismay the analyst, for the correctness of a model is not an either/or matter. It is much more serious to omit a variable with a major impact than one with a minor impact. Likewise, it is not very consequential if we mistakenly include a variable with little effect on the other variables in the model. To the extent that research is guided by solid prior theorizing, the construction of a reasonably well specified model is highly probable and the consequences of whatever specification error is made are likely to be relatively minor.

Another kind of specification error is made when the functional form chosen to represent the relationship among the variables is incorrect. It is all too common to view the world and the relationships among our dependent and independent variables as if they were linear and additive. But what if the relationships were non-additive (e.g., multiplicative)? Here we start talking about interaction effects. One way of defining interaction is to say that the relationship among variables differs for different categories of some other variables.

It is possible to express non-additive, interactive terms in a multiple regression equation by using multiplicative terms. For example, in the equation

$$Y = b_0 + b_1X_1 + b_2X_2 + b_3X_3 + b_4X_1X_2 + b_5X_1X_3 + b_6X_2X_3 + b_7X_1X_2X_3$$

the direct effects of X_1, X_2, and X_3 on Y are represented by b_1, b_2, and b_3; the joint effects of two independent variables by b_4, b_5, and b_6; and a three-way interaction term by b_7. We could regress Y on X_1, X_2, X_3, X_1X_2, X_1X_3, X_2X_3, and $X_1X_2X_3$ and obtain estimates for each of the coefficients b_0, b_1, . . . ,b_7.

This use of multiplicative terms has been criticized by various practitioners (including Gerald Wright in his article in this volume) on a number of grounds:
1. The interpretation of the coefficients is difficult.
2. The coefficient estimates themselves may be unreliable because of the likelihood of multicollinearity between the original variables and their products. For example, in the above equation, there is a strong likelihood that the correlations among X_1, X_2 and X_1X_2 might be very high, calling into question the stability of the coefficient estimates.
3. Such a procedure is meaningful only when we have ratio data; then and only then does multiplying terms together make sense.

Although Friedrich (1982) has effectively refuted these criticisms by proposing an interpretation of the coefficients of a multiplicative equation in terms of conditional rather than general relationships, nevertheless, Wright has proposed an imaginative way of handling interaction. His linear model approach is offered as an improvement over the multiplicative terms approach described above and also over the widespread use of standardized measures of association (i.e., correlation coefficients) in assessing interaction.

Wright's procedure enables us to assess interaction effects by the formal construction and estimation of regression equations. Modifying Wright's notation somewhat, let us assume that we have a dependent variable Y, an independent variable X, and a third variable Z, a dummy variable that takes on values of 0 and 1. For example, Z might be region where 0 represents the non-South and 1 the South. Let us further suppose that we are concerned with whether the relationship between Y and X differs for the two categories of Z, that is, whether Z and X interact in their effects on Y. One way to proceed is to regress Y on X for those cases where $Z = 1$ (South) and then regress Y on X for all those cases where $Z = 0$ (non-South). We could then compare the slopes across the separate equations to test for the presence of interaction.

Wright proposes a somewhat different strategy, which entails estimating a single equation of the form

$$Y = c_0 + c_1 X_S + c_2 X_N + c_3 Z + e \quad ,$$

where
  c_0 is the intercept for the base category, group N (non-South),
  c_1 is the slope of X for group S (south),
  c_2 is the slope of X for group N (non-South),
  c_3 is the difference between the intercept of group S and the intercept of group N (c_0),
  X_S equals X for cases in category S and equals 0 otherwise,
  X_N equals X for cases in category N and equals 0 otherwise.

This equation can be viewed as two separate regressions within a single equation—the regression of Y on X among group N and the regression of Y on X among group S. In mathematical notation, the single equation could be broken down into two equations of the form:

$$Y_N = a_N + c_2 X_N + e \quad \text{(regression of } Y \text{ on } X \text{ in group N)} \quad ,$$
$$Y_S = a_S + c_1 X_S + e \quad \text{(regression of } Y \text{ on } X \text{ in group S)} \quad ,$$

where
  $a_N = c_0$
  $a_S = c_0 + c_3$.

Although identical results are obtained by estimating a single equation or two separate equations, Wright argues that his single-equation method is superior when it comes to using R^2s and tests of significance to assess the effect of allowing unequal slopes (c_1 and c_2) in the same equation. The examination of the R^2 and tests of significance would be done by comparing the single equation estimation described above with the results of the estimation of

$$Y = b_0 + b_1 X + b_2 Z + e \quad ,$$

where
  b_0 is the intercept,
  b_1 is the slope of the independent variable X,
  b_2 is the slope of the group membership variable (e.g., region).

The difference between the R^2 values for the two equations is a direct measure of how much allowing unequal slopes affects our ability to explain the dependent variable. (See the Wright article for a discussion of how the two equations might be used to generate tests of significance for the equality of slopes.)

The general purpose of the Wright article is to provide a procedure for handling non-additive relationships. The automatic assumption of many analysts that relationships are linear and additive may do a serious injustice to the underlying structure of the processes we are trying to estimate. The Wright procedure is helpful and straightforward, though its avoidance of multiplicative terms is less of an advantage since Friedrich's recent (1982) explication of an interpretive scheme for such terms.

Robert Gordon (1968) presents another specification-related problem that can upset the substantive inferences that analysts would like to draw on the basis of the regression estimates. Let us consider the following regression equation

$$Y = b_0 + b_1 X_1 + b_2 X_2 + b_3 X_3 + b_4 V_1 + b_5 V_2$$

and assume that this equation has two clusters of independent variables—three X variables and two V variables. Gordon generates simulated data with known properties on these variables and then estimates the regression coefficients. Among the properties built into the simulated data are the following:

1. $r_{X_i y} = r_{V_i y} = .6$. That is, the correlation between any independent variable and the dependent variable is .6.
2. $r_{X_1 X_2} = r_{X_2 X_3} = r_{X_1 X_3} = r_{V_1 V_2} = .8$. That is, the correlation between any pair of independent variables within the same cluster is .8.
3. $r_{X_i V_j} = .2$. That is, the correlation between any independent variable in one cluster and any independent variable in the other cluster is .2.

In regressing Y on all five of the independent variables, we might intuitively expect that all the estimated coefficients should be approximately equal since each of the independent variables has the same pattern of relationships with the dependent variable and with the other independent variables. However, that is not the case; it turns out the coefficients for V_1 and V_2 are larger and statistically significant and those for X_1, X_2, and X_3 are smaller and not statistically significant. In such a situation, the analyst would be tempted to conclude that V_1 and V_2 were important in the prediction of Y and X_1, X_2, and X_3 were not.

The question becomes whether this would be a correct conclusion, and the answer is not necessarily. The significance of the Vs and the insignificance of the Xs may be wholly a function of the fact that there were three Xs and only two Vs in the equation. That is, the sheer number of different classes of predictors can very much affect the magnitudes and significance of the various independent variables. A substantive example may help illustrate the seriousness of the problem. Let us assume that we are interested in the importance of political and economic variables on state welfare expenditures and further suppose that we enter into the regression equation two economic predictors and four political predictors. *Ceteris paribus,* it is likely that the political variables will be less important than the economic variables, leading the investigator to proclaim the importance of economic variables. However, if the number of each class of variables were reversed, the substantive conclusion would also be changed, an obviously unsatisfactory state of affairs.

The obvious lesson here is that the analyst must be careful about entering variables into a regression equation. If the true specification is unknown (as it often is) or if certain classes of variables are more readily measured than others, then the very choice of the kinds and numbers of variables introduced as predictors may generate artifactual results which may mislead the analyst in important ways.

The preceding discussion should make it clear that specification errors can seriously distort interpretations based on regression estimates. However, as we mentioned at the outset of this section, specification error is not an either-or situation; regression analysis is reasonably robust in the presence of minor specification errors. If the theory and reasoning underlying the regression model that is to be estimated is sound, then specification problems will likely be less worrisome. And if we are primarily interested in prediction and the size of the R^2 (as opposed to explanation and the actual magnitude of the regression estimates), then specification concerns will be of lesser import.

Violations of Regression Assumptions

Earlier in this chapter the assumptions of the general linear model were discussed. The violation of some of these assumptions makes the use of ordinary least squares inappropriate, thereby requiring the use of other statistical techniques. Two key assumptions concern properties of the error terms. It was assumed that the variance of the error term was constant for all values of the independent variable (homoscedasticity) and that the covariance (correlation) among the error terms was zero. Without these assumptions, the use of ordinary least squares will generate estimates with undesirable properties. For example, although the obtained least squares estimates will be unbiased, they will no longer be the best (minimum variance) estimate, and thus in repeated sampling the obtained estimates could differ dramatically. Moreover, the usual tests of significance may yield misleading results because the estimated variance of the coefficients will be biased. Hence, the use of ordinary least squares when the assumptions about the error variances and covariances are untenable may result in misleading statistical estimates and faulty substantive conclusions.

One situation in which the errors assumptions are untenable occurs when the dependent variable is measured at a nominal or ordinal level rather than at an interval level. Since ordinary least squares will technically be inappropriate in such a case, other statistical procedures will have to be employed. This is the main point of the Aldrich and Cnudde article in this volume; the authors discuss estimation procedures appropriate for nominal vs. ordinal vs. interval data: namely, discriminant analysis, probit analysis, and linear regression, respectively.

Probit analysis, originally developed for dichotomous dependent variables and later extended to n-chotomous ones, yields estimates with the desirable (large sample) properties of being unbiased and consistent, having a normal sampling distribution, and being a minimum variance estimator. The probit estimates resemble ordinary least squares results, although, as Aldrich and Cnudde note, the ordinal nature of the dependent variable makes it impossible to talk in terms of a unit change in the independent variable producing a certain change in the dependent variable as we do with ordinary regression. The probit model has a probabilistic interpretation, yielding probabilities within the range of zero to one, unlike ordinary least squares, which often yields predicted values outside of the possible range of values of the dependent variable. Although the application of probit and ordinary least squares to the same set of data often yields similar results, this need not be the case, as demonstrated by Aldrich and Cnudde. Hence the use of ordinary least squares with ordinal dependent variables may produce estimates that result in substantively misleading interpretations. Likewise, the use of ordinary least squares or probit analysis with nominal dependent variables may generate nonsensical results. Hence, Aldrich and Cnudde discuss discriminant analysis, a multivariate classification scheme appropriate for categorical (nominal) data.

Aldrich and Cnudde note that the choice among ordinary least squares, probit, and discriminant analysis is only partly a function of the level of measurement of the dependent variable. We must also consider how well the assumptions required by each technique are met by our data and substantive model. Although regression analysis is much more developed and widely used than the other techniques, this does not provide an automatic reason to employ regression analysis in all situations.

Regression and Causal Analysis

A solid foundation in regression analysis will allow us to use many of the techniques that fall under the rubric of causal modeling, such as recursive and noncursive path estimation. In a Workshop article not in this volume, Stokes (1974) presents a basic introduction to recursive (one-way causation) path estimation and demonstrates that when the usual assumptions are made about the error terms, the path coefficients are regression coefficients. Hence, ordinary regression analysis will enable us to estimate the coefficients in a recursive path model, calculate the direct and indirect effects of one variable on another, and test the overall structure of the model. Let us consider, for example, the simplified model in Figure 7 of the intergenerational transmission of political attitudes (e.g., party identification)

X_1 is paternal grandfather's political attitudes
X_2 is maternal grandfather's political attitudes
X_3 is father's political attitudes
X_4 is mother's political attitudes
X_5 is child's political attitudes

In Figure 7 X_1 and X_2 are exogenous variables, that is, variables which are not determined within the model, while X_3, X_4, and X_5 are endogenous variables that are determined by other variables in the model. The error or residual variables, e_3, e_4, and e_5, represent those factors which affect X_3, X_4, and X_5 respectively, but which have not been formally measured in the model. The e_is are assumed to be uncorrelated with each other and with any explanatory variables in the equation in which they appear. The above path diagram can be

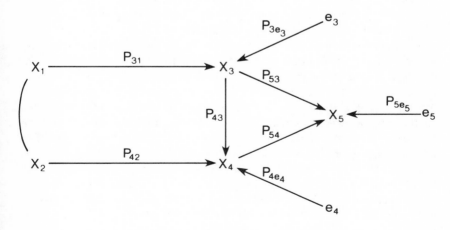

FIGURE 7
A Causal Model of Intergenerational Transmission of Political Attitudes

represented by a system of three equations, one for each of the endogenous variables:

$$X_3 = p_{31} X_1 + p_{3e_3} e_3 \quad ,$$
$$X_4 = p_{42} X_2 + p_{43} X_3 + p_{4e_4} e_4 \quad ,$$
$$X_5 = p_{53} X_3 + p_{54} X_4 + p_{5e_5} e_5 .$$

Hence, in the above equations, e_3 is assumed uncorrelated with X_1, e_4 uncorrelated with X_2 and X_3, and e_5 uncorrelated with X_3 and X_4.

In these equations p_{31}, p_{42}, p_{43}, p_{53} and p_{54} are called path coefficients and represent the impact of the independent variable on the dependent variable, while p_{3e_3}, p_{4e_4} and p_{5e_5} are residual path coefficients which represent the impact of the unmeasured variables on the endogenous variables. Stokes (1974) demonstrates that estimates of all of these coefficients can be obtained by use of ordinary regression procedures. By regressing X_3 on X_1, p_{31} would be obtained; p_{42} and p_{43} by regressing X_4 on X_2 and X_3, and p_{53} and p_{54} by regressing X_5 on X_3 and X_4. Hence,

$$p_{31} = b_{31} \quad ,$$
$$p_{42} = b_{42\cdot3} \quad ,$$
$$p_{43} = b_{43\cdot2} \quad ,$$
$$p_{53} = b_{53\cdot4} \quad ,$$
$$p_{54} = b_{54\cdot3} \quad .$$

The residual path coefficients also have a direct regression interpretation; in general, they are equal to $\sqrt{1 - R^2}$ where R^2 is the fraction of explained variance. For example, p_{5e_5} equals $\sqrt{1 - R_{5.34}^2}$ where $R_{5.34}^2$ is the fraction of the variance in X_5 accounted for by X_3 and X_4.

The path coefficients indicate the direct effect of one variable on another. Indirect effects can also be determined by using the regression estimates. For example, X_2 has an indirect effect on X_5 via its impact on X_4. This two-step indirect effect would be represented by the product of the simple paths comprising it: $p_{42} p_{54}$. Finally, we can test the structure of the model using regression coefficients. Wherever a linkage has been omitted from the model, we have implicitly said that the coefficient associated with that linkage is zero. For example, saying that there is no link from X_1 to X_5 and from X_2 to X_5 is equivalent to saying that p_{51} and p_{52} are zero.

This brief description of recursive path analysis has demonstrated how central an understanding of regression analysis is to the procedure. Even when we have a nonrecursive (two-way or reciprocal causation) model, ordinary least squares and variants of it can be very helpful in estimating the model. Let us consider the revised (and more realistic) attitude transmission model in Figure 8 in which mothers' and fathers' attitudes mutually influence each other.

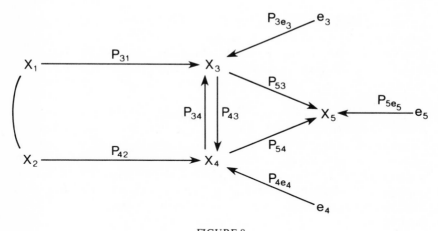

FIGURE 8
A Revised Model of Attitude Transmission

The equations for the path diagram in Figure 8 are:

$$X_3 = p_{31}X_1 + p_{34}X_4 + p_{3e_3}e_3$$
$$X_4 = p_{42}X_2 + p_{43}X_3 + p_{4e_4}e_4$$
$$X_5 = p_{53}X_3 + p_{54}X_4 + p_{5e_5}e_5$$

Ordinary least squares can no longer be used to estimate the coefficients in the equations for X_3 and X_4 because the error terms are now correlated with one of the explanatory variables in the equations in which they appear. For example, e_3 is now correlated with X_4. To confirm this, we can simply examine the path diagram, which shows that e_3 influences X_3 and X_3 influences X_4; hence, e_3 and X_4 are very likely to be correlated. A similar argument can be made for the correlation between e_4 and X_3. Because of the violation of the assumption that the independent variables and the error terms are uncorrelated, the use of ordinary least squares would yield inconsistent estimates.

Fortunately, there is a variant of ordinary least squares called two-stage least squares which can be used to generate consistent estimates in this situation. As the name suggests, two-stage least squares is the successive application of ordinary least squares. To explicate the technique briefly, we shall consider the equation for X_3:

$$X_3 = p_{31}X_1 + p_{34}X_4 + p_{3e_3}e_3$$

Ordinary least squares cannot be used since e_3 and X_4 are correlated. However, if we had a modified X_4 variable which was uncorrelated with e_3, then ordinary least squares could be used. The way to obtain this modified X_4 variable is to regress X_4 on all of the exogenous variables (the first stage) and generate a predicted set of X_4 values ($\hat{X}_4$). Because $\hat{X}_4$ is a linear combination of exogenous variables which are uncorrelated with the error term, then $\hat{X}_4$ is also uncorrelated with e_3. Hence, we can substitute $\hat{X}_4$ (the second stage) to obtain p_{31} and p_{34}.

This brief discussion of regression and causal analysis should suffice to demonstrate how central a solid understanding of regression procedures is to the causal analysis of data. Data analysis strategies in the social sciences are increasingly moving beyond simple regression models of direct effects to more complex, interdependent, often nonrecursive systems of equations. In order to employ some of these new techniques and approaches correctly, a full understanding of the properties and assumptions of the basic regression model is required.

Conclusion

In this chapter we have looked at some of the problems and issues in regression analyses. The preceding section provides a very cursory statement of the linkages between regression and causal analysis; for a fuller explication, see Asher (1983). More generally, certain topics have been touched upon only lightly, while others have been ignored in their entirety. For example, there are variants of ordinary least squares appropriate when certain core assumptions are violated. Weighted least squares is appropriate when the error term fails to satisfy the homoscedasticity assumption. Likewise, in the presence of heteroscedasticity (unequal error variances) and autocorrelation (correlated error terms), generalized least squares yields minimum variance estimates. The reader interested in a more elaborate treatment of regression analysis might consult a regression text, such as *Applied Regression Analysis* by Draper and Smith. For a more sophisticated and detailed presentation of various elaborations of the basic regression model, the reader should consult an econometrics text, such as Kmenta's *Elements of Econometrics*. A particularly helpful and understandable text with a more general social science orientation is *Statistical Methods for Social Scientists* by Hanushek and Jackson.

Regression analysis is a powerful tool for prediction and explanation in social science data analysis. However, as this chapter has suggested, there are many factors that affect the regression estimates, and a failure by the researcher to recognize these may result in improper substantive conclusions. Given that our ultimate goal is to employ statistical techniques as an aid in addressing our substantive concerns, the investigator must exercise sensitivity in the application of these techniques lest the results of data analysis mislead rather than inform the scholarly community. Careful attention to the problems discussed in this chapter will enable the analyst to avoid the pitfalls of misleading inferences and faulty conclusions.

REFERENCES

Asher, Herbert B. 1983. *Causal Modeling,* rev. ed. Beverly Hills, California: Sage Publication.

Asher, Herbert B. 1974. "Some Consequences of Measurement Error in Survey Data," *American Journal of Political Science,* May 1974, pp. 469–485.

Draper, Norman R., and Smith, Harry. 1981. *Applied Regression Analysis,* 2nd ed. New York: John Wiley.

Friedrich, Robert J. 1982. "In Defense of Multiplicative Terms in Multiple Regression Equations," *American Journal of Political Science,* November 1982, pp. 797–833.

Gordon, Robert A. 1968. "Issues in Multiple Regression," *The American Journal of Sociology,* March 1968, pp. 592–616.

Hanushek, Eric A., and Jackson, John E. 1977. *Statistical Methods for Social Scientists.* New York: Academic Press.

Kmenta, Jan. 1971. *Elements of Econometrics.* New York: Macmillan.

Stokes, Donald E. 1974. "Compound Paths: An Expository Note," *American Journal of Political Science,* February 1974, pp. 191–214.

JOHN ALDRICH
CHARLES F. CNUDDE

Probing the Bounds of Conventional Wisdom: A Comparison of Regression, Probit, and Discriminant Analysis*

The level of measurement of the dependent variable (nominal, ordinal, interval) crucially affects the selection of statistical techniques. Conventional wisdom further restricts the choice of an appropriate technique. In this Workshop paper, we compare three powerful statistical techniques appropriate for each of the levels of measurement and sharing, insofar as possible, a similar set of assumptions. The three techniques are ordinary least squares regression for intervally measured, probit for ordinally measured, and discriminant analysis for nominally measured dependent variables. The assumptions and uses of each technique are reviewed, and an example of the use of each in political research is presented.

Discussions of the levels of measurement problem in political science frequently lead to one of two conclusions. On the one hand, "radicals" argue that the increased leverage obtained from using statistical procedures which assume that the dependent variable is measured on an interval scale outweighs the consequences of their application to nonintervally measured variables. On

*These statistical evaluation procedures were initially explored in order to solve substantive problems that are only partly referred to in this paper. Further applications will be developed in subsequent reports. Part of the research reported herein was performed pursuant to a grant contract with the National Institute of Education, U.S. Department of Health, Education, and Welfare. Contractors undertaking such projects under Government sponsorship are encouraged to express freely their professional judgment in the conduct of the project. Points of view or opinions stated do not, therefore, necessarily represent official National Institute of Education position or policy.

Reprinted from AMERICAN JOURNAL OF POLITICAL SCIENCE, Vol. XIX, No. 3, August 1975, pp. 571-608, John Aldrich and Charles F. Cnudde, "Probing the Bounds of Conventional Wisdom: A Comparison of Regression, Probit, and Discriminant Analysis," by permission of the University of Texas Press.

the other hand, "purists" argue that the consequences of such a misuse are too serious to ignore, and that nominal or even ordinal dependent variables can only be analyzed through the use of the relatively less powerful techniques, such as cross-tabulation or ordinal measures of association and correlation. In this paper we discuss three techniques, all of which are useful for testing multivariate and quite sophisticated hypotheses. These three alternative statistical procedures—linear regression, probit analysis, and discriminant analysis—are suitable for the analysis of interval, ordinal and nominal dependent variables, respectively. Underlying our presentation is our belief that decisions concerning the choice of an appropriate statistical technique must consider not only the nature of the measurement of the dependent variable, but also the assumptions contained in the model underlying each procedure. Further, we would argue that it is of equal importance to ensure that these assumptions are compatible with the substantive assumptions of the theory/hypotheses under investigation.

Linear Regression

To begin this explication, let us first consider the linear regression model in a context of an application to political data.

One way to think of a linear function is to consider the identity between the predictions of a "true" theoretical model and the actual observations that the model addresses.[1] If the model were "true," then when we plot its predictions and the actual scores the intersections between these two sets of points would all fall on the main diagonal; i.e., they would form a particular type of a linear function. If there were some error in the predictions, then the validity of the model would depend upon whether the scatter plot of intersections fell about the main diagonal in a "random" way. This example is a special case of the general linear model,

$$y = a + bx + e,$$

which would apply whenever we can so account for actual observations with values predicted from a theoretical model. In this model, a "true" identity would mean that the data would all fall on the main diagonal, and the slope would intersect at the origin. These considerations would mean a slope coefficient (or b value) of 1.0, and an intercept of 0, respectively.

---

[1] The term "theoretical model" here means some theory which leads to predictions independent of the "statistical theory" (i.e., linear regression) which can be used to *test* the relationship between the theoretical predictions and reality.

A linear model of this type may be developed to predict U.S. House of Representatives seat gains and losses in "off-year" elections. The model's basic assumption is of stability in partisan preferences. Losses in the mid-term elections, then, are simply due to fluctuations back to a normal or expected level after a party gained more than that amount in the preceding presidential election. Therefore we calculate how many seats were gained due to the swing away from the expected partisan split in the presidential year by any party. That gain is what it should lose in the following midterm election, assuming a stable two party system and no systematic "short run forces," such as recessions or Watergate in the off year.

With this logic we obtain a set of predicted losses. If the model is correct, the actual losses should line up with these predictions in a roughly linear way, and in fact should approximate the special case of an identity.

The scatter plot of Democratic losses for the elections from 1938 to 1970 is shown in Figure 1. There are two major deviant cases, 1946 and 1958. In both years, the assumption of no systematic "short run forces" probably is invalid, and those cases are dropped.

To illustrate the theoretical model, we can briefly consider one particular case. In the Roosevelt landslide of 1936 the Democrats made considerable gains in House seats. Some portion of the total Democratic majority that year undoubtedly came from districts Democrats would "normally" win because of the differential affiliation of the electorate to the major parties. This normal or expected proportion of seats for a given party is assumed constant in the model. Our best evidence leads to the inference of relative stability in this proportion since the Great Depression, and so as a means of making a first approximation we may assume it to be a constant. However, refinements could and should be attempted by relaxing this assumption.[2] If this proportion is set as a constant, then the difference between such a value and the percent of the seats the Democrats received in 1936 would be due to factors other than that normal expectation due to party affiliation.[3] In general, we can conceptualize this difference as due to the peculiarities of the particular

[2] The assumed constant expected number of seats for a party would change markedly over time if the partisan split of the electorate markedly changed, or if apportionment rules changed in ways greatly uncorrelated with the partisan division in affiliation, or if electoral outcomes fell into extreme ranges where the "cube rule" curve is not well approximated by a linear function.

[3] The value adopted for the analysis is 55% of the seats in the House of Representatives to the Democratic Party. The value is approximately the same as the "normal vote" for the Democrats in the electorate, as estimated for the period 1952 to 1960 from survey data (Converse, 1966).

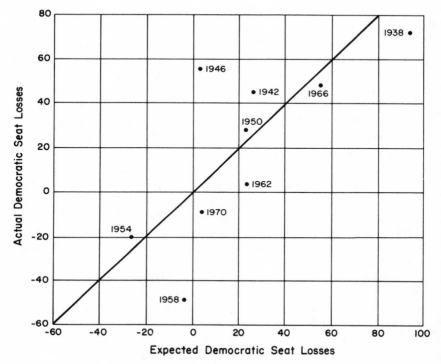

FIGURE 1
Expected and Actual Seat Losses

election of 1936; i.e., all those factors that combined to make up the Roosevelt landslide. Our calculations indicate that, given the number of seats in the House at that time, the number due to the "short run" effects of 1936 was about an 86-seat gain to the Democrats over and above what they would have normally received in the current partisan era.

In the long run, a gain of this sort would be lost in another election where the peculiar factors are apt to be different. As a second approximating assumption, we could hold that it would be entirely coincidental for two elections in a row to have short run factors that would operate to give the same outcome. Considering the gains in a given election, we can make a prediction about the losses in the next under this assumption: our best prediction, knowing nothing else about the next election, is that the outcome will return to the normal expectation. Thus in the long run the normal expectation is our best predictor of outcomes. The difference between the normal expectation and the actual outcome in a given election is therefore our best prediction of what would be lost or gained in the next election.

In 1936, if the Democrats gained 86 more seats than they should have, given the normal expectation, and if the normal expectation is our best prediction of the 1938 election, then they would tend to lose those 86 seats in 1938. In fact they lost only 62 seats in 1938. However, to examine the utility of this approach to predicting off-year elections, we would have to compare the losses given by the model with the actual losses for a whole series of elections. If we consider the actual losses as the values to be predicted, and the values given by the model as the predictor variable, we can use the linear regression model as a device for making this examination.

The linear regression model would link the actual losses (Y) to the losses given by the model of election outcomes (X), some linear coefficients (α and β), and an error term (e) which stands for all other influences on the actual outcomes. Thus, we have a version of the standard linear equation:

$$Y = \alpha + \beta X + e \tag{1}$$

If in the long run our normal expectation is the best predictor of actual outcomes, then the sum of all other influences across a large number of elections would equal zero. Formally,

$$\Sigma e = 0 \tag{2}$$

If in the long run the deviation from the normal expectation for a given election would only coincidentally be related to that deviation in the next election, then the covariation between e and X would sum to zero in a large number of elections. Formally,

$$\Sigma Xe = 0 \tag{3}$$

Denoting estimated values by hats, writing the linear equation in terms of estimates and rewriting it to set all values equal to the estimated residuals gives

$$e = Y - \hat{\alpha} - \hat{\beta} X \tag{4}$$

Substituting (4) into the versions of (2) and (3) which correspond to estimated values gives

$$n\hat{\alpha} + \hat{\beta} \Sigma X = \Sigma Y \tag{5}$$

$$\hat{\alpha}\Sigma X + \hat{\beta} \Sigma X^2 = \Sigma XY \tag{6}$$

Except for the estimated values of the regression coefficients, all values in the equations can be calculated from the data obtained for the election years in the scatter plot. Since we have two equations and two unknowns, solving for the two unknowns gives the values of the two linear regression coefficients:

$$\hat{\alpha} = 0.9$$

$$\hat{\beta} = 0.8$$

These values come reasonably close to our theoretically derived values; a value of 0.9 for $\hat{\alpha}$ is reasonably close to 0.0 (given a range of -20.0 to $+62.0$ for actual seat losses), and a value of $\hat{\beta}$ of 0.8 is reasonably close to 1.0. We can tentatively conclude that the linear regression model corresponds to the model of off-year congressional seat losses.[4]

The success of a regression such as this example can be judged by examining the error in fit. We expect some error, of course, in fitting predicted dependent variable values to the actual observations. If we square such error and sum the squared errors, we can examine this "residual variance" as a proportion of the total original variance in Y. That is, we have divided the original variance into "explained" variance and "unexplained" or error variance. The proportion of variance explained is the familiar R^2. This can be used as a measure of "goodness of fit" of the theoretical model to the data. In this case, the R^2 is a very high .830, giving us greater confidence in the adequacy of the estimation.[5]

The procedure used to obtain estimates of the coefficients in regression problems such as this is "ordinary least squares" (hereafter OLS). One crucial assumption of OLS is that the "error terms" have properties that result in zero outcomes under certain conditions. Without these conditions we cannot make the substitution of equations to derive the coefficient values. Another way of saying the same thing is that without this assumption we do not have enough information to solve for the unknown coefficients.

What are the conditions necessary to specify that the sum of the left-out factors and the covariation between the left-out factors and the measured independent variable are both zero? In order to obtain proper OLS estimates, the unknown causes must have values which are randomly selected from a

---

[4] For example, the estimated coefficients are well within the expected values of $\hat{\alpha} = 0$ and $\hat{\beta} = 1$ at any level of significance desired.

[5] In this case, we have a small number of observations (7). Therefore, it is appropriate to "correct" the R^2 for the relatively few degrees of freedom in the data set. This "corrected R^2" (also denoted as $\overline{R}^2$) is .796, thus not changing our basic conclusion. For the derivation of $\overline{R}^2$ see Johnston (1972, pp. 129–130).

population of such errors which is normally distributed and has a constant variance and a mean of zero.[6] Often in political science we do not have direct observations at the interval level for the dependent variable. When we observe some transformation of the interval level variable, we cannot insure that we have a population of errors that are normally distributed and that meet the other assumptions. In fact, we frequently measure dependent variables in ways that lead us to *suspect* these assumptions.

If our measure of the dependent variable is such that it may take only a limited range of values, we might question the possibility of normally distributed errors. For example, if our dependent variable is dichotomous, as when the vote is measured as "Democratic/Republican" (or as when participation is measured as "Vote/Didn't Vote"), we have the extreme case in which the range is limited to only two values. These dependent variables are linked, for our sample, to an equation which adds the weighted independent variable scores to a constant and the error term, to give these two values. Only under very peculiar circumstances could we have the kind of continuous error term values necessary for even an approximately normal distribution, and yet have such a limited range of variation in the dependent variable. As we move to trichotomous dependent variables, we can easily see that the problem is almost as severe. In general, as our dependent variable takes on a greater range in scores—approaches a continuous variable—OLS becomes more appropriate.

Put another way, a normally distributed error term implies an unrestricted range of variation in the dependent variable. A severely restricted range of variation in the dependent variable tends to undermine the assumption of normally distributed error.

If the assumptions concerning the distribution of unmeasured influences such as normality are called into question, then OLS is an inappropriate estimation procedure. For dichotomous and other categorically measured dependent variables, alternative procedures should be employed.

To illustrate the implication of limited variability in the dependent variable for the other assumptions, we can examine Figure 2. In Figure 2 the scores on the dependent variable are limited to 0.0 and 1.0. Therefore, when

[6] The assumption that the error is normally distributed is important when dealing with small samples such as our example. In large samples, many of the properties of OLS regression estimates, statistical tests, and the like do not require the normality assumption. This follows since in large samples, the sampling distributions of the estimates will be approximately normal regardless of the form of the distribution of the error term. There are many good sources which deal with the regression model and its assumptions (e.g., Johnston, 1972).

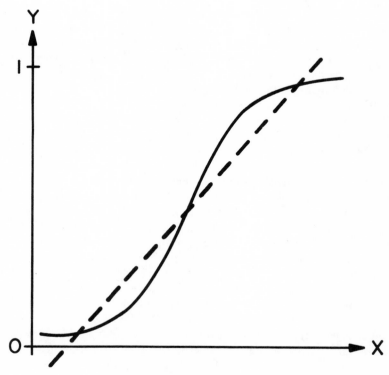

FIGURE 2
Comparison of OLS Estimate and "Typical" S-Shaped Relationship
with a Dichotomous Dependent Variable

an independent variable is plotted against a dichotomous dependent variable, the underlying relationship would appear better approximated by an "S" shape than a straight line. If we were to attempt to analyze these data with OLS procedures, we would obtain an estimate of a straight line such as the dotted line in the figure. The estimated slope would appear much like that drawn, because OLS will attempt to "average out" the vertical distances o the actual scores from the estimate, resulting in as many observations below the estimate as above.

Given this typical shape of the actual observations and the characteristic departure from it by the OLS estimate, we can draw conclusions about two assumptions:

1) The residuals (the estimated error) obtained from the OLS estimate will be correlated with the independent variable.

This conclusion can be easily seen from the illustration. The departures from the OLS estimate (the gap between the S-shaped curve and the straight line) are primarily above the line when the values of X are large. The departures from the estimate are primarily below the line when the values of X are small. Thus (assuming a positive X-Y relation) the residuals will be positively correlated with X.

2) The variance of the residuals will vary systematically with the independent variable.

The illustration shows that the variance of the residuals will tend to decrease as we move away from moderate values of X and toward the extreme values. The reason for this conclusion is that the positive and negative residuals—as has been pointed out above—are correlated with X.

In general, dependent variables with restricted variability—such as we find with ordinal and certainly categorical variables—will tend to produce "clumpiness" in actual relationships with independent variables. As OLS attempts to fit a straight line through these patterns, the result will be sets of residuals which are inconsistent with the assumptions of uncorrelated error and constant variance.

Probit Analysis

Thus, we have seen that the failure of the assumption that the dependent variable is intervally measured leads to the violation of several of the OLS assumptions about the error term. Consequently, nonintervally measured dependent variables imply that the OLS regression estimating procedure breaks down. The inapplicability of OLS in this situation is of serious consequence for political science, since we are so often faced with variables that are no more than ordinally measured. There is, however, an alternative model and associated estimating technique that is designed for just this situation, one that retains much of the power of OLS.

One interpretation of the *probit model* emphasizes the similarity of probit and OLS regression. Suppose that we assume a theoretical—but unmeasured—dependent variable which is related to a set of independent variables as in the OLS model. Similarly, the theoretical dependent variable has associated with it a stochastic term meeting the same assumptions as before. In this case, we further assume that the observations of the dependent variable are measured on only an ordinal scale, a collapsing of the "true" interval scale. In the extreme, only a dichotomy may be observed. Indeed, the most extreme dichotomous case was that for which probit was originally developed (Finney, 1971). Probit has, however, been extended to the n-chotomous case by Aitchison and Silvey (1957), and by McKelvey and Zavoina (1969). The latter citation provides the first application of the technique in political science, so far as we know.[7] They, therefore, discuss probit at some length, exemplifying its uses for our purposes and in our terms, as well as providing an important extension of the theory of probit with numerous useful refinements.

Estimates for the probit model are developed by the method of maximum likelihood. This method capitalizes on the assumed normality of the error term. With this assumption it is possible to determine the probability (or likelihood) of having observed the particular sample data for any given set of values that the parameters might assume. The maximum likelihood criterion is invoked by selecting, as estimates of the true parameters, those values which have associated with them the highest probability of having obtained the observed sample data. Even having imposed the normality assumption, the equations that must be solved are very complex and can only be approximated. However, the estimates thus obtained have a wide variety of important and useful properties, not the least of which include unbiasedness (in the limit or "consistency"), normal sampling distributions (again in the limit), and in this class of estimates, minimum variance ("best" or most "efficient"). A very similar set of properties hold for the OLS estimates if the assumptions of regression hold.

Estimated parameters appear much like those obtained from OLS regression, since the models are very similar. However, the fact that only an ordinal dependent variable is observed limits and weakens the straightforward interpretation of the coefficients. For example, since the scale or "unit of measurement" of the dependent variable is unknown, "slope" or "b" coefficients cannot be interpreted (as in OLS regression) as the amount of change in the dependent variable for a one-unit change in an independent variable. Or, since the concept of variance is undefined for an ordinally measured variable such as our dependent variable, there is no analogue to the "standardized beta" of OLS regression. In fact, since the dependent variable is only

---

[7] The basic presentation of n-chotomous probit can be found in McKelvey and Zavoina (1969). Also see Cnudde (1971, p. 104). The initial extension of probit for the case of a single independent variable is in Aitchison and Silvey (1957).

ordinally measured, estimates are only unique up to positive linear transformations. (Technically, all of these comments can be summarized by noting that the model is "underidentified.") Nonetheless one obtains an estimate of the best, weighted linear combination of the independent variables. In this case, the predicted $\hat{Y}$ variable may also be taken as an estimate of the unmeasured, theoretical Y that underlies the probit model.

The probit model has a second standard interpretation, in fact the initial sort of situation for which probit was developed. Suppose, for example, that the dependent variable is strictly dichotomous, say 0 or 1. In this case, one obtains estimates of the "weights" to attach to independent variable dimensions (plus an intercept term) which, by employing once again the assumed normality properties, allow us to predict the probability of any given observation being a 0 or 1. Finney (1971), in his classic study of (dichotomous) probit, used biological examples such as seed germination. A researcher might be interested in estimating the probability of germination of seeds, conditional upon such properties as rainfall, temperature, amount of fertilizer used, and other such independent variables. However, he can only observe whether or not the seeds actually germinated. The probit estimates and normality assumption allow for the estimation of such probabilities, conditional upon the values the case takes on the independent variables. Notice that the (erroneous) use of OLS regression may result in predictions that might be interpreted as "probabilities." However, these "probabilities" may be negative or exceed one, since the linear model is not restricted to the range of probability. (See, e.g., the OLS linear estimate of Figure 2.) Probit, on the other hand, yields probability estimates that are true probabilities, and therefore lie in the required ranges. The extension of probit to n-chotomous, ordinal, dependent variables has associated with it a parallel extension of the probabilistic predictions (e.g., a trichotomous dependent variable leads to the prediction of probabilities of being a 1, 2, or 3, if that is the coding of the variable, and of course one may obtain predictions of the probabilities of any combination as well). It is this probabilistic nature of the predictions of observed categories that led to the naming of the technique; probit is short for a "probability unit."[8]

[8] The reader should note that the assumed transformation of the linear model to the probabilistic one, viz. the cumulative normal, is only one possible "probability unit" yard stick which could be employed. E.g., Finney (1971, Section 3.8) discusses several alternatives including "logit," the most well known alternative, as well as the highly idiosyncratic assumptions that must be made about the error term to "legitimately" apply OLS regression to probabilistic questions.

To exemplify the use of probit and compare it to the estimates obtained through the use of OLS, we have chosen voting in 1972. Consider the attempt to predict the probability of a citizen voting for, say, McGovern, in that election (coded a 1) versus the probability of either abstaining or voting for Nixon (0). We might want to make the prediction of the citizen's probability of voting for McGovern, given the citizen's positions on issues. Thus, we obtain the following expression for the theoretical, linear, model underlying probit:

$$Y^* = a + b_1 X_1 + b_2 X_2 + \ldots + b_n X_n \tag{7}$$

where $X_1, \ldots, X_n$ are the positions (of a given citizen) on the n issues; $a, b_1, \ldots, b_n$ are the parameters which are to be estimated; and Y^* is the "theoretical, underlying" linear dependent variable. In this case, Y^* might be interpreted as measuring the "propensity" of a citizen to vote for McGovern. We observe Y (= 0 or 1), so we want to transform the linear "proneness" variable to a probabilistic prediction. In the dichotomous case, it can be shown (see McKelvey and Zavoina, 1969) that the probability of voting for McGovern [or Pr (Y = 1)] and the probability of not voting for McGovern [Pr (Y = 0)], given the independent variables and estimated coefficients (denoted $\hat{a}, \hat{b}_i$), are:

$$\Pr(Y = 1/\hat{a} + \hat{b}_1 X_1 + \ldots + \hat{b}_n X_n) = \Phi(\hat{Y}^*) = \Phi(\hat{a} + \hat{b}_1 X_1 + \ldots + \hat{b}_n X_n) \tag{8}$$

$$\Pr(Y = 0/\hat{a} + \hat{b}_1 X_1 + \ldots + \hat{b}_n X_n) = 1 - \Phi(\hat{Y}^*) = 1 - \Phi(\hat{a} + \hat{b}_1 X_1 + \ldots + \hat{b}_n X_n) \tag{9}$$

where "Φ" denotes the cumulative normal distribution function. In this manner a unique probability of voting for McGovern can be determined for each citizen, with his own particular configuration of positions on the issue dimensions.

We have reported the results of such an estimation of the probability of voting for McGovern in 1972 in Table 1, using data drawn from the 1972 CPS election survey.[9] In particular, we employed the 7-point issue scales upon which the respondent is asked to locate himself.[10] The actual positions of the

[9] This study was sponsored by the National Science Foundation under Grant GS-33956, and the results were made available through the Inter-University Consortium for Political Research. The authors are grateful for the aid of the Foundation and the Consortium, but neither, of course, bears any responsibility for the analysis reported here.

[10] The formats of the 7-point issue scales are discussed at length in Page and Brody (1972) and Aldrich (1975). The latter citation also includes this example, the basis for

TABLE 1

Comparison of OLS and Probit Predictions:
Probability of Voting for McGovern, 1972

7-Point Issue	Probit ($\hat{Y}*$)			OLS Regression		
	MLE	SE	MLE/SE	$\hat{\beta}$	SE	$F_{1,120}$
Federal Jobs	−.375	.082	−4.55*	−.087	.018	24.77*
Taxation	−.257	.066	−3.88*	−.050	.014	11.60*
Vietnam	−.593	.092	−6.46*	−.145	.020	50.71*
Marijuana	−.075	.058	−1.30	−.019	.014	1.98
Busing	−.205	.083	−2.47*	−.067	.019	12.76*
Women's Rights	−.038	.046	−0.83	−.010	.011	0.80
Rights of Accused	−.046	.068	−0.68	−.011	.015	0.50
Aid to Minorities	−.136	.072	−1.90	−.030	.017	3.13
Liberal/Conservative	−.639	.113	−5.64*	−.168	.025	43.93*
Constant	−.713			.303		
Est. R^2 =	.530			R^2 = .347		
Est. R =	.728			R = .589		
−2 x LLR =	441.64			$F_{11,120}^9$ = 66.06		
(chi square, 9 degrees of freedom)						
N = 1130						

*Indicates significance at .05 level (critical values, Z = 1.96, $F_{1,120} \sim 3.84$)

citizens in this analysis were determined by the employment of a scaling technique reported elsewhere.[11] In Table 1 we report the probit estimates of the linear Y* variable estimate, as well as the comparable OLS regression estimates done on the same dichotomous dependent variable.

The relevant comparisons between the two techniques are best summarized by looking at the OLS regression R^2 and the estimated R^2 of the probit estimators. In the probit case, the R^2 is a full 18% higher, indicating that approximately 53% of the variance is "explained." In the regression version of the estimates, only 35% of the variance is "explained" by the issue positions of the citizens, a reduction in explanatory power of slightly more than one-third. In this particular case, the two techniques do not differ in

the determination of this model, and how it corresponds with deductions from the spatial model of electoral competition.

[11] See McKelvey and Aldrich (1974), and Aldrich and McKelvey (1975).

tests of significance. All variables that are significant at the .05 level in OLS are so as well in the probit, and vice versa. However, in other reported comparisons of probit and OLS, there were differences in statistical significance (McKelvey and Zavoina, 1969).

The second major difference concerns individual predictions of the probability of voting for McGovern. In Figure 3, we have plotted the transformed Y^* variable, which is the linear predicted "propensity to vote for McGovern" (summarized in Table 1), obtained by the transformation outlined above (i.e., solving Equation 8). The S-shape of the predicted probability of voting variable is dramatically clear. In comparison with the OLS predictions, we note that OLS predictions are strictly linear, and that they exceed both the upper and lower bounds of probability at the extremes. Thus, if our interest is in predicting the probability of voting for McGovern, we would be led to some inexplicable predictions. For example, the smallest actual predicted probability using the probit model is .00016. The regression prediction for this individual is a "probability" of voting for McGovern of −.41587. Similarly, the largest OLS "probability" is 1.62091, which has a corresponding probit predicted probability of .99999 for that case. Thus for these two individuals as well as others, the OLS prediction is nonsensical. We have plotted the predicted OLS regression line on Figure 3 over the range of actual observations. The differences in the two probabilistic predictions are quite clear, and very similar to Figure 2. OLS regression, of course, yields a strictly linear prediction, while probit leads to quite nonlinear predictions. At the two bounds of probability, the probit model curves or "flattens" to approach 0 and 1 only in the limit, while OLS exceeds the limits by large amounts. Further, within the nearly linear range of probit probabilities (e.g., between about .25 and .75), the linear increase is steeper than the comparable regression.

Our basic interest thus far has focused on "predicting" or "explaining" the dependent variable. Researchers are often concerned with the independent variables, e.g., in measuring their relative "importance" in the analysis. We might consider the probit MLE coefficient and the slope or "b" of OLS as one measure of "importance." The rank order of the size of the coefficients for the two techniques is quite similar. The only difference in the ordering is that the MLE for taxation is larger than that associated with the busing issue in the probit, while the order is reversed in the OLS estimation. However, there are greater differences in the relative sizes of the coefficients. For example, statistically significant but smaller coefficients are generally larger in comparison with the strongest independent variable (the liberal/conservative continuum) in probit than they are in the OLS case. As an illustration of this point, the liberal/conservative coefficient is 3.4 times the size of that of taxation as estimated by OLS, while it is only 2.5 times as large in the probit estimate. This sort of result is consistent with other work. In a Monte Carlo study, Zechman (1974) has observed that OLS generally underestimates all coefficients with a trichotomous dependent variable. However, he found that the underestimation was more severe the smaller the true (and in Monte Carlo studies, the known) b and/or standardized "beta weight" in comparison with other included variables. This finding did not hold for probit estimates. Rather, they appeared unbiased.[12]

In summary, we have seen that the probit model much more adequately describes the data as seen in the much greater R^2, and it avoids the prediction of nonsensical results such as "probabilities" that exceed the true ranges of probability. We expect the same sorts of results to hold as the number of ordinal categories increases. We would also expect that the problems of underestimation and the like through the erroneous use of OLS regression would decrease as the number of categories of the observed dependent variable increases. However, a new problem is raised as we move from dichotomous to n-chotomous variables. In particular, if the dependent variable is in fact ordinal, then the numerical assignment of values is arbitrary up to the order constraint. Thus, if Y is, say trichotomous, we could assign the numbers 1, 2, 3 to the three categories in order. However, equally appropriate would be the assignment of −100000, 999, 1000. The use of n-chotomous probit is insensitive to such shifts, but OLS regression assumes that the interval properties are meaningful and could lead to dramatically different estimates in the two cases.

Discriminant Analysis

To this point, we have considered OLS regression as an estimation technique when the dependent variable is measured intervally, and probit as an estimating procedure when the dependent variable is observed only ordinally. In both cases, the value of the dependent variable for any case is assumed to be a function of a weighted linear combination of independent variables and a

[12] Zechman's work is based upon a comparison of small sample properties of probit. Recall that the properties associated with any maximum likelihood estimation method are applicable only in "large" samples. Generating small samples (N = 50) meeting the conditions of the probit model with a trichotomous, ordinal dependent variable, he observed not only that probit estimates appear to be unbiased, but that they outperform OLS regression by a wide variety of measures. This sort of result provides some comfort when the researcher is faced with small samples and an ordinal dependent variable.

John Aldrich and Charles F. Cnudde

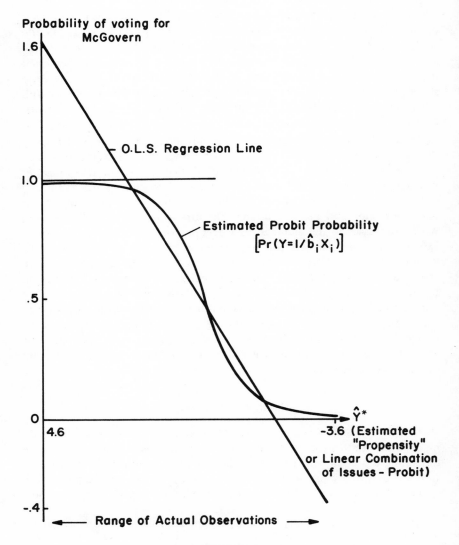

FIGURE 3
Comparison of OLS Regression and Probit Predicted
Probabilities of Voting for McGovern

function of a stochastic term that is random and normally distributed. Suppose, however, that the dependent variable is only categorical. That is, we can assume that the values of the dependent variable differentiate observations by classes which are mutually exclusive but do not necessarily form any order. For example, we can classify people into racial classes. This classification scheme does not allow for the formation of ordinal, and surely not interval scales of "race." The methodological question in this case may be put: "How do we predict the category of an observation as a function of its values on independent variables?" Quite clearly, neither probit nor OLS regression can serve as an estimating model.[13] Suppose, for example, that the dependent variable is trichotomous, with categories of x, y, z. If the variable is categorically measured, then the estimating technique should yield equivalent results if the arbitrary order is y, x, z, or x, z, y, or any other permutation. Neither OLS nor probit would meet this condition. The most similar technique to those we have considered for the nominal level variable is "discriminant analysis."

We can view discriminant analysis as a problem in classification.[14] How can we "best" classify observations to the nominal categories of the dependent variable on the basis of their values on a set of independent variables? Further, for the purposes of exposition, at least, we can present the technique in two distinct parts, the estimation of the parameters with respect to the independent variables, and (as a somewhat more distinct second step than previously) the treatment of the errors of classification.

Our first problem then concerns the relationship between the independent variables, the X's, and the dependent variable Y. Y is assumed to consist of, say, m classes or categories, one of which can be written as Y^i. Our prediction of the category of Y depends upon the values the observation takes on each independent variable. These values can be shown as a vector of observations $X = (X_1, X_2, \ldots, X_n)$ which is also equivalently shown as a point in a geometrical space of n dimensions. The basic idea behind discriminant analy-

---

[13] The one exception is the case of a dichotomous dependent variable which can be considered ordinal, and probit appropriately applied or categorical and discriminant analysis used. We have estimated the discriminant function (to be explained below) for the McGovern voting example. This function estimates a coefficient for each issue/ independent variable analogous to the probit and OLS regression estimates. Interestingly, the issue coefficients estimated by discriminant analysis are nearly identical to those obtained under the probit procedure. For example, the correlation between the two sets is .989.

[14] More extensive treatments of discriminant analysis are found in Anderson (1958) and Kort (1973).

sis then consists of dividing this n-dimensional space into m mutually exclusive and exhaustive regions, say $R_1, R_2, \ldots, R_m$, such that if an observation falls into region R_i it would be predicted as being a Y^i.

The treatment of the independent variables as defining an n-dimensional space does not differ from those techniques already discussed. What needs to be done is to consider the nature of the relationship between the "true" population classes and the independent variables. We assume, as discussed, that the space may be partitioned into separate and distinct regions—one for each category of the dependent variable. Moreover, we assume that within each population class observations are distributed normally across the independent variables, and with equal variances and covariances for each class, but allow for differing means. This normality assumption is stronger than that made earlier. Moreover, it represents a differing emphasis. In probit, for example, the normality of the stochastic term implies that, given a particular set of independent variable values and coefficients, remaining variation in Y (i.e., stochastic variance) will be normally distributed. In discriminant analysis, we must assume that the independent variables are normally distributed, given a particular value of Y. With this assumption it is possible to estimate the probability of each observation being in any one of the classes of Y. That is, we can define $P_i(x)$ as the (normality based) probability that an observation (with its particular values on the X's) would be a Y^i. Thus we could compare the probability that an observation is a Y^i versus a Y^j. In particular we would examine the $P_i(x)$ and $P_j(x)$, say by taking the ratio: $\frac{P_i(x)}{P_j(x)}$. In the dichotomous case, for example, if the ratio is greater than some constant (usually symbolized by K_{ij}), we would classify the observation as a Y^i; if it is less than K_{ij}, we would predict it as a Y^j. For this dichotomous case, this rule can be formalized as defining the regions of predicted Y classes as

$$\text{Region } R_i = \text{if } \frac{P_i(x)}{P_j(x)} > K_{ij} \tag{10}$$

$$\text{Region } R_j = \text{if } \frac{P_i(x)}{P_j(x)} < K_{ij} \tag{11}$$

We can define the "boundary" between region R_i and region R_j ("B_{ij}") as the set of points where the ratio exactly equals the constant K_{ij}. The probabilities, the $P_i(x)$'s, can be solved since we have assumed that they are all normally distributed and have the same variances and covariances. Then the only differences are in the means of the various classes of Y on the independent variables and the actual values of any given observation on the X variables.

If we let the mean values of Y^i on the X's be symbolized by $\overline{X}_i$ (i.e., the means of the observations of category Y^i on each independent variable), and the (assumed constant) variances and covariances summarized by the matrix S, the normality and other assumptions lead to the following rather long equations for solving for the two regions:

$$R_i = x'S^{-1} (\overline{x}_i - \overline{x}_j) - 1/2 (\overline{x}_i + \overline{x}_j)'S^{-1} (\overline{x}_i - \overline{x}_j) > \log K_{ij} \qquad (12)$$

$$R_j = x'S^{-1} (\overline{x}_i - \overline{x}_j) - 1/2 (\overline{x}_i + \overline{x}_j)'S^{-1} (\overline{x}_i - \overline{x}_j) < \log K_{ij} \qquad (13)$$

These equations are derived by substituting the definition of a normal distribution for the $P_i(x)$'s, taking logarithms (a permissible transformation), and algebraically manipulating the various terms. The first, leftmost, term in each equation [i.e., $x'S^{-1} (\overline{x}_i - \overline{x}_j)$] is the only term involving the individual observations, X. This term is called the *discriminant function,* and it is a *linear* function of the observations of the dependent variable. The rest of that term consists simply of differences in means of Y^i and Y^j weighted by the variances, S. The middle term is also based on weighted combinations of means. In effect, this can be considered as a measure derived from the distance between means for categories of Y. That is, it measures the distance or separation of the means of Y^i and Y^j on the independent variables. One way of conceptualizing the purpose of discriminant analysis is to define regions of classification which maximize the variation within the predicted classes as a proportion of the total variance. This middle term provides an indication of this "discriminability" of the independent variables as predictors of Y, and statistical tests can be performed on it. The final term in these equations is the constant K_{ij}, which depends on the criterion we employ with respect to error, which we will discuss shortly.

Extending the dichotomous case to a more general n-chotomous situation is straightforward. One simply has a set of ratios of probabilities to solve simultaneously, one ratio for each pair of classes. Thus in the trichotomous case (say Y^i, Y^j and Y^k) there would be three probability ratios and inequalities to solve. To define region R_i, we would have:

$$R_i = \text{Log} \frac{P_i(x)}{P_j(x)} > \text{Log } K_{ij} \text{ and Log } \frac{P_i(x)}{P_k(x)} > \text{Log } K_{ik} \qquad (14)$$

Again, the set of points where these inequalities (and the remaining ratio) are equal form the boundaries between regions B_{ij}, B_{ik} and B_{jk}.

The undiscussed constants, the K_{ij}'s, incorporate our criterion about errors in classification and are closely related to the success of the discriminant analysis. By changing the value(s) of the constant(s), the boundaries between regions are changed, but are only changed by defining a new set of lines *parallel* to the old.

An example may help to clarify many of the points we have been making. If there are two independent variables, the space to be divided into regions is a plane, and the boundary(ies) between regions will be lines through the plane. Changing values of the constants would change the boundaries by defining new lines that would be parallel to the original regional boundaries. For example, in Figures 4A and 4B, we have drawn a plane and regional boundary lines for a di- and trichotomous dependent variable, respectively. In Figures 5A and 5B we show the effects of changing the constant term(s); the boundaries have changed, but they are parallel to the original.

As we have pointed out, any observation on x can be represented as a point in the space. Given the definitions of the regions, an observation will be classified into a population class. For example, in Figure 4B, the point w would be predicted to be in Y^1. A set of such predictions leads to a table of predicted classes of the dependent variable versus the actual observations, the table which indicates the correct and incorrect predictions.

The discriminant function for which we have developed estimates is the "best" discriminant estimate, given the assumed normality and linearity

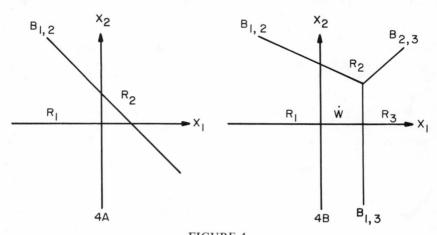

FIGURE 4
Examples of Discriminant Analysis of Di- and Trichotomous
Dependent Variables

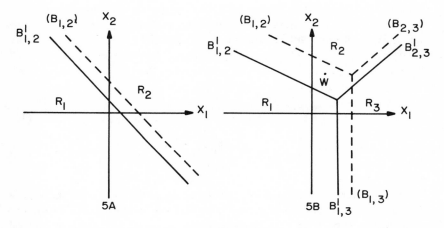

FIGURE 5
Two Examples of Discriminant Analysis with Varying Constants

constraints (i.e., the estimates of the population means and variances have a variety of desirable statistical properties). We can greatly alter the actual predictions of categories, however, by manipulating the constant terms. For example, in Figure 5B, we have altered the constant, and hence boundary lines between the regions, from those of Figure 4B. In this case, point w is now in region 2, not the initially estimated region 1, so we would estimate w as a Y^2 not a Y^1. Obviously, both the estimation of the $P_i(x)$'s and the K constants will be crucial.

A number of criteria have been proposed for the determination of these constant terms. The most obvious criterion is to let all K_{ij} be one. That is, if the ratio $\dfrac{P_i(x)}{P_j(x)}$ is greater than one, classify that observation in predicted class Y^i. If it is less than one, predict it as a Y^j. In other words, the criterion is simply to define the regions such that the probability of an observation being a Y^i is higher than any other class in Region R_i. Obviously, such a criterion has much intuitive appeal. However, if one approaches the problem of classification from a broader viewpoint, alternative criteria may be superior, since it can be shown that the posited rule "assumes" that there are equal probabilities of observing all categories. We are more often faced with the situation where there are very unequal probabilities of observing the various categories—race is an obvious example. Therefore we might want to incorporate additional information into the criterion. For example, we might "weight" the boundary-defining conditions by the actually observed proportion of Y^i's and Y^j's (presumably our "best estimate" of the true proportions). Thus our constant K_{ij}'s would simply be the ratios of observed sample frequencies of Y^j to Y^i. If we let P^{Yi} and P^{Yj} be the proportions of all observed Y's which are Y^i's and Y^j's, respectively, then we can define our two criteria of determining the K_{ij} constants as:

$$K_{ij} = 1 \text{ for all } i, j \quad (\text{i.e.,} \frac{P_i(x)}{P_j(x)} = 1 \text{ to define } B_{ij}) \tag{15}$$

$$K_{ij} = \frac{P^{Yj}}{P^{Yi}} \text{ for all } i,j \quad (\text{i.e.,} \frac{P_i(x)}{P_j(x)} = \frac{'P^{Yj}}{P^{Yi}} \text{ to define } B_{ij}) \tag{16}$$

As an example of the use of discriminant analysis, consider the choice among voting for Nixon, Humphrey, or Wallace in 1968. As a dependent variable, the 1968 vote is not measurable in terms of an ordinal or interval scale. Attempts to use party identification based concepts (e.g., the normal vote) which assume ordinality or more have floundered over the problem of what to do about Wallace voters.[15] One resolution is to employ discriminant analysis. As in our probit example, we will use the 7-point scales as a base to estimate the citizens' positions on the two issues of Vietnam and urban unrest.[16]

The estimations of the discriminant functions are presented in Table 2, these being the equations, as well, for the "boundary lines" to define the regions of the issue plane. We computed the constant coefficients by both assuming equal probability (i.e., $P^{Yi} = P^{Yj}$), so that K = 1 and log (K) = 0 in all pairs, and also using the proportionate vote division in the sample as an estimate of the true probabilities (in the 942 included respondents, 41.1% voted for Humphrey, 47.9% for Nixon, and 11.0% for Wallace). The two sets of regions are drawn in Figures 6 and 7, while the table of actual versus predicted vote categories is found in Table 3. Finally, we have reported a comparison table resulting from assuming that the coefficients for the two issues are equal. (The actually estimated ratios of the two coefficients for the three discriminant functions are found at the bottom of Table 2.)

First, let us consider the estimated relationships between the independent

<hr />

[15] See, for example, the dialogue between Boyd (1972a, 1972b) and Kessel (1972) on this point.

[16] While these two issues were very important in that election, so certainly were many others. However, 7-point scale format data were collected for only these two in 1968. It is also convenient to be able to visualize this two-dimensional example.

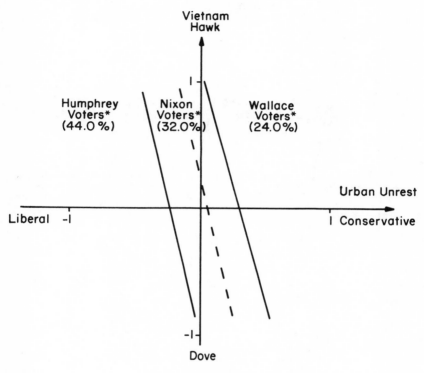

FIGURE 6
Discriminant Analysis of 1968 Voting, Based on Constants Equal to One

variables and the dependent variable, and then the error in classification. The Humphrey voters are estimated to be towards the liberal end of both issues, Wallace's region is to the right on both, and consequently Nixon voters are classified as those in between the other two. Notice, too, that the urban unrest issue is much more important than Vietnam in discriminating voters, its coefficients (the analogues to the regression b's and probit MLE coefficients) being 3.7 to 5.5 times as large as Vietnam's. Thus each candidate's region tends to cover almost the entire range of hawk to dove. Moreover, there is little difference between the discriminant functions defining the two regions, so that the Humphrey and Wallace regions in the range of actual observations do not touch. This sort of result is not typical of all applications of discriminant analysis. Indeed, the three categories of voting in 1968 appear

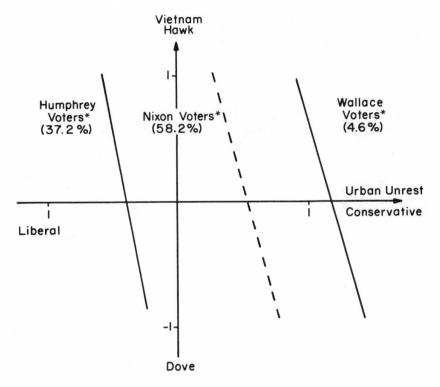

FIGURE 7
Discriminant Analysis of 1968 Voting, Based on Constants
Equal to Proportion of the Candidate Vote Actually Observed

to form an ordinal measure *with respect to the citizens' positions on these two issues.* Thus one possible use of discriminant analysis is to see if a measured dependent variable is approximately ordinally related to the independent variables of concern. This finding does *not* allow us to conclude that there is an ordinal measure of voting for the three candidates in 1968. Rather, we can only conclude on the basis of this evidence that the dependent variable is approximately ordinal over the independent variables examined. This has an equivalent interpretation: that the three discriminant functions are approaching the extreme possibility of being equal to each other, differing but by an additive constant.

The effects of changing our assumptions about the constant terms, K_{ij}, are quite clear. The Nixon region is much narrower when we assume that all K_{ij}'s are equal. Using the sample proportions as an estimate of the true probabilities increases the size of his region, so that the proportion of voters found in his region increases from 32.0% to 58.2%.

Let us turn to the question of error in classification. In the first case, where $\log(K) = 0$ for all comparisons, we obtain 55% correct classification, with the greatest successes being in classifying Humphrey and Wallace voters (about 67% and 71% correct, respectively), our greatest error being concentrated in predicting Nixon voters. When we incorporate the "prior probabilities," our correct classifications jump by more than 7% to 62% correct. The effect of changing the boundaries is to move about 26% of Humphrey and Wallace predicted voters to the region of predicted Nixon voting. Such redefinition of boundaries greatly increases the success of classifying Nixon voters (from 41% correct to over 72% correct). This was accomplished at minimal cost in classification of Humphrey voters (an 8% reduction in correct predictions), but at a greater loss in classification of Wallace voters (down to 28% correct). However, the Wallace voters are such a relatively small group that error there can be absorbed with relatively little cost.

A comparison of these results to a comparable probit or OLS regression analysis would be useful at this point. Unfortunately, just what would constitute a comparable analysis is far from clear. First, one might run three

TABLE 2

Discriminating Voters on Issues, 1968

Discriminant Functions	Log K = 0	Log K = Log $\dfrac{(P^{Yj})}{(P^{Yi})}$
$Z_{HN} = -.3484 -.2233$ Vietnam -1.2257 Urban Unrest	(= 0)	(= + .152)
$Z_{HW} = +.1379 -.6724$ Vietnam -2.8962 Urban Unrest	(= 0)	(= −1.318)
$Z_{NW} = +.4863 -.4492$ Vietnam -1.6705 Urban Unrest	(= 0)	(= −1.471)

Relative Weightings	Vietnam/Urban Unrest
Humphrey-Nixon	0.182
Humphrey-Wallace	0.232
Nixon-Wallace	0.269

TABLE 3

Error in Classifying Voters, 1968

Predicted Vote Log (K) = Log $\dfrac{(P^{Yj})}{(P^{Yi})}$

		Humphrey	Nixon	Wallace			
	Humphrey	24.4%	16.5	0.3	41.1%	(307)	
Actual Vote	Nixon	12.0	34.7	1.2	47.9	(358)	
	Wallace	0.8	7.1	3.1	11.0	(82)	62.16% Correct
		37.2%	58.2	4.6	100%	(747)	
		(278)	(435)	(34)			

Predicted Vote Log (K) = 0

		Humphrey	Nixon	Wallace		
	Humphrey	27.7%	10.3	3.1	41.1%	
Actual Vote	Nixon	15.3	19.5	13.1	47.9	
	Wallace	1.1	2.1	7.8	11.0	55.02% Correct
		44.0%	32.0	24.0	100%	(747)
		(329)	(239)	(179)		

Euclidean Equidistant (UU = Viet) Log (K) = Log $\dfrac{(P^{Yj})}{(P^{Yi})}$

		Humphrey	Nixon	Wallace		
	Humphrey	27.0%	11.8	2.3	41.1%	
Actual Vote	Nixon	14.6	24.6	8.7	47.9	
	Wallace	0.5	3.5	7.0	11.0	58.64% Correct
		42.2%	39.9	17.9	100%	(747)
		(315)	(298)	(134)		

paired comparisons (i.e., Humphrey and Nixon, Humphrey and Wallace, Nixon and Wallace), thus generating six equations instead of three. Next, we must decide what to do about the dependent variable. Looking at the Humphrey-Nixon pairing, for example, what are we to do with Wallace voters? Three possibilities come to mind. We might code a "Nixon vote" variable as a one if the respondent voted for Nixon and as a zero if he voted for Humphrey or for Wallace (and perhaps for abstention as well). Alternatively, we might simply remove Wallace voters from the analysis. Finally, we might attempt to infer what Wallace voters would have done in the absence of the Wallace candidacy on the basis of some other data (e.g., the SRC's 100-point "thermometer" evaluation of candidates). Clearly, our choice among these three possibilities (and any others that might come to mind) will greatly affect our results. The instability in such estimations is convincingly demonstrated in Table 4, which briefly summarizes probit results of these three approaches to estimating Nixon support. The MLE estimates differ considerably, in some instances being more than double those of others. As in the comparison between probit and OLS, there are some similarities (e.g., the relatively larger size of the coefficient for urban unrest), as well as some important differences (e.g., the

TABLE 4

Probit Predictions of Nixon Voting When Paired with Humphrey

	MLE	SE	MLE/SE
Wallace Voters Removed			
Urban Unrest	0.453	0.075	5.835
Vietnam	0.081	0.048	1.695
Constant	−0.114		
−2 × LLR	48.55		
(chi square, 2 degrees of freedom)		N = 860	
Wallace Voters Coded "0" (Not Vote for Nixon)			
Urban Unrest	0.235	0.070	3.367
Vietnam	0.031	0.045	0.689
Constant	−0.273		
−2 × LLR	15.14	N = 942	
Wallace Voters Vote "Preference" (Via 100° Thermometer)			
Urban Unrest	0.377	0.070	5.381
Vietnam	0.064	0.045	1.431
Constant	−0.159		
− 2 × LLR	41.296	N = 942	

Vietnam coefficient is never statistically significant at the .05 level). However, the instability of the estimates is the overriding consideration, especially when it is recalled that the Wallace voters amount to less than 10% of the sample. Similar comparisons of pairings involving Wallace are almost completely determined by our approach to the incorporation of the 40% or so of the sample who voted for the candidate not in the pair. Thus, a categorical dependent variable is wholly unsuited for OLS or probit estimation.

Conclusion

We hope we have been able to demonstrate the following points in this paper. First we tried to show that there are a variety of powerful techniques, all grounded on a solid base of statistical theory. Moreover, one or more of these techniques is suitable for whatever level of measurement is used for the dependent variable. All too often it appears that the alternatives are simply OLS regression and contingency table analysis. This implies that if one's data are measured on less than an interval scale, one has only the choice of using regression erroneously or using an appropriate but much weaker method of analysis. Alternative techniques exist. The particular examples we chose were selected for their similarities in terms of their purposes, their assumptions, and the powerful analysis they allow, while at the same time being applicable to each of the three basic measurement levels.

Second, we have argued that the "level of measurement" can be a crucial consideration, but one based upon the theory underlying the statistical procedure. As our example applications have demonstrated, employing a procedure assuming a different level of measurement can seriously affect the estimates and lead to incorrect inferences and hypothesis tests. Thus, our comparison application of OLS to an ordinal variable seriously underestimated the overall fit of the model to the data. Further, the individual coefficient estimates are known to be biased in general, and we have seen that the bias is not uniform, so that there were some changes in the order of size of coefficients and more dramatic changes in their relative magnitudes as compared to the probit estimates. There were great difficulties in attempting to specify the nominal level dependent variable example to make a comparison with probit. If our procedures are acceptable, the resultant estimates exemplify differences in hypothesis tests. The coefficient for the Vietnam issue was significant in all cases in the discriminant analysis, while it was never significantly different from zero (at the .05 level) in the probit estimates.

It is clear, then, that the levels of measurement problem is real. Yet it is but one important factor in choosing an appropriate statistical technique. Other aspects must also be considered. For example, there are other differences in assumptions of the techniques. Probit necessarily assumes that the stochastic term is normally distributed, an assumption which may not be necessary in all instances in using OLS regression. The discriminant procedure assumes that observations on the independent variables are normally distributed within each category of the dependent variable. This assumption is much stronger than any comparable assumption made in probit or OLS. Therefore, the plausibility of these and other assumptions must be weighed along with the level of measurement. Further, the degree to which assumptions are violated must be considered. Thus, the bias in OLS when applied to an ordinal variable will be less serious the greater the number of ordinal categories (*all else remaining equal*). Finally, it must be recognized that techniques have differing properties and differing degrees of development. Regression, in particular, has been extensively analyzed and formally developed. Only it is suitable, at this time at least, for estimation of more complex relationships and multiple equation models (e.g., simultaneous equations, causal modeling, etc.). In short, the choice of an appropriate statistical procedure is complex and contingent on many criteria. The level of measurement is only one criterion; yet it is important and may well have direct consequences for the analysis.

Third, we have argued that the political researcher must very carefully examine the assumptions underlying the statistical technique, and consider their correspondence to the theoretical assumptions one has made in deriving one's hypotheses. The failure to carefully trace out this correspondence can lead to incorrect conclusions equally as well as the application of a technique to an unsuitable level of measurement. A simple illustration of this point concerns the prediction of the division of congressional seats in off-year elections. We assumed that there was relative stability in partisan preference. If this assumption were wrong (e.g., if we extended our series back through elections during the era of Republican hegemony), the model would lead to quite different estimates.

All too often, research is based on faulty priorities. We are all familiar with examples of research which appears to be based on a new statistical technique and where the substantive problem was chosen simply to show off methodological sophistication. The undue emphasis on technique must be eschewed. Yet we cannot ignore this crucial element of research. The choice of a statistical method inappropriate for the substantive and theoretical concern leads just as surely to worthless research. Yet that choice can be grounded in the assumptions underlying the method and the decision about whether they are appropriate to the substantive problem, rather than the conventional "levels of measurement" debate.

Manuscript submitted February 5, 1975.
Final manuscript received March 7, 1975.

APPENDIX

The purpose of this Appendix is to present copies of actual computer output of the three techniques and indicate how to interpret it. It has been our experience that there can be some confusion in understanding such output the first few times a program is actually used, regardless of the comprehension of the basic statistical principles involved.

OLS regression programs are widespread, commonly used, and well documented. Most statistical packages (SPSS, OSIRIS, BMD, etc.) have an OLS program, and as well it has been our experience that many university computer facilities have their own regression packages. Therefore, they require little comment. Figure A-1 is a copy of the SPSS output which is summarized in Table 1 (in which OLS regression and probit are compared). Summary characteristics of the overall regression are printed first. Attention is usually focused on the R^2 and its root, the multiple correlation coefficient (or correlation between predicted and observed dependent variable values) as indications of the "goodness of fit." The standard error (of the estimate) and F statistic are most relevant for statistical tests of significance of the whole regression. The remaining summary statistics are useful for constructing "Analysis of Variance" (explained or "regression," unexplained or "residual," and total sum of squares and variances), such as the "ANOVA" tables found in Johnston (1972, p. 143). Following these summary calculations are statistics relevant to individual independent variables. The first column is the regression "b's" or slope coefficients (what we call "$\hat{\beta}$"'s in Table 1). The "Betas" of the second column are standardized betas, the standardization being a multiplication of the regression coefficients by the ratio of the standard deviation of the relevant independent variable to the standard deviation of the dependent variable. This standardization, therefore, puts all independent variables in comparable units (sometimes referred to as "dimensionless") to facilitate comparisons between independent variables (note that no comparable standardization exists for probit, since the standard deviation of Y is undefined). Next is the standard error of the estimated regression coefficient and the F statistic for each variable to test for significance of each coefficient (in other programs, a t value may be produced which is simply the square root of this F value). These F's all have one degree of freedom in the numerator and degrees of freedom equal to the difference between the sample size and the number of parameters being estimated in the denominator (or $1130 - 10 = 1120$ in this case). Many other statistics can be obtained from regression packages. Those available under SPSS are carefully explained in the SPSS Manual (Nie, Bent, and Hull, 1970) and various updates.

Figure A-2 is a copy of the output of the probit example (also found in Table 1). The program used is that developed by McKelvey and Zavoina (to the best of our knowledge, probit is not included in any of the statistical packages). The output is well documented and rather straightforward. The "Maximum Likelihood Estimate" column is the MLE coefficient for each independent variable and the constant, comparable to the regression b-coefficients or "β" (hence, the reference to them as "BETA(.)" on the leftmost column of the output). The standard error column is self-explanatory. The ratio of the two, in the third column of the output, is useful for tests of significance much like the individual F statistics of regression. Recall that, as in all maximum likelihood estimates, properties of the probit estimates are "asymptotic" (i.e., are applicable with large sample sizes only). The ratio MLE/SE is, in large samples, approximately a standardized normal random variable, or "Z score." Thus, this Z score can be used to test whether the coefficient is significantly different from zero, as in the case of the individual F values for OLS regression. The comparable statistic to the F of OLS regression for testing "overall significance" is -2 times the log of the likelihood ratio. This statistic is a comparison of the probability of observing this sample if the MLE estimates are correct (i.e., the estimated log of the likelihood function which is also printed) to the situation if all coefficients were zero (i.e., the null model). As stated in the output, this statistic is, in large samples, a chi-square statistic with degrees of freedom equal to the number of independent variables. Other summary indicators are found after a case-by-case residual analysis in the McKelvey-Zavoina program (and may not be found in other probit programs). These calculations are also self-explanatory and for the most part have direct analogues in OLS regression. It should be pointed out, however, that all statistics under the heading "Estimated Analysis of Variance" are just that—estimated. This is so since the Y variable is not measured intervally. The estimates are derived by arbitrarily setting the residual sum of squares so that there is an equivalent to one unit error for each case (i.e., this figure will always be equal to the sample size). Given this arbitrary setting, the other statistic estimates follow. Of course, of some interest is the percent of the bases correctly predicted, which is not estimated

FIGURE A-1
An OLS Output from SPSS

```
REGRESSION VERSIONS OF SUPPORT FUNCTION MODELS 1972                                   05/16/74        PAGE   13

FILE   CSF72     (CREATION DATE = 04/29/74)

* * * * * * * * * * * * * * * * * * * * * * *  M U L T I P L E   R E G R E S S I O N  * * * * * * * * * * * * *   VARIABLE LIST  1
                                                                                                                 REGRESSION LIST  1
DEPENDENT VARIABLE..     VAR001      ACTUAL VOTE   MCGOVERN

VARIABLE(S) ENTERED ON STEP NUMBER  1..     VAR003      FEDERAL JOBS IDEAL
                                            VAR004      TAXATION IDEAL
                                            VAR005      VIETNAM IDEAL
                                            VAR006      MARIJUANA IDEAL
                                            VAR007      BUSING IDEAL
                                            VAR008      WOMENS RIGHTS IDEAL
                                            VAR009      RIGHTS OF ACCUSED IDEAL
                                            VAR010      AID TO MINORITIES IDEAL
                                            VAR011      LIBERAL CONSERVATIVE IDEAL


MULTIPLE R           0.58886             ANALYSIS OF VARIANCE    DF      SUM OF SQUARES       MEAN SQUARE            F
R SQUARE             0.34675             REGRESSION               9.         78.31571           8.70175          66.05674
STANDARD ERROR       0.36295             RESIDUAL              1120.        147.53916           0.13173
```

------------------ VARIABLES IN THE EQUATION ------------------   ------------- VARIABLES NOT IN THE EQUATION -------------

VARIABLE	B	BETA	STD ERROR B	F		VARIABLE	BETA IN	PARTIAL	TOLERANCE	F
VAR003	-0.08727	-0.14247	0.01754	24.765					
VAR004	-0.04951	-0.09014	0.01454	11.600					
VAR005	-0.14549	-0.20062	0.02043	50.711					
VAR006	-0.01897	-0.03929	0.01346	1.984					
VAR007	-0.06748	-0.10265	0.01889	12.756					
VAR008	-0.00960	-0.02259	0.01074	0.800					
VAR009	-0.01093	-0.02000	0.01540	0.503					
VAR010	-0.02995	-0.05167	0.01671	3.127					
VAR011	0.16815	0.21013	0.02537	43.926					
(CONSTANT)	0.30271								

ALL VARIABLES ARE IN THE EQUATION

SUMMARY TABLE

VARIABLE		MULTIPLE R	R SQUARE	RSQ CHANGE	SIMPLE R	B	BETA
VAR003	FEDERAL JOBS IDEAL	0.39247	0.15403	0.15403	-0.39247	-0.08727	-0.14247
VAR004	TAXATION IDEAL	0.43024	0.18513	0.03110	-0.29474	-0.04951	-0.09014
VAR005	VIETNAM IDEAL	0.52882	0.27965	0.09452	-0.43885	-0.14549	-0.20062
VAR006	MARIJUANA IDEAL	0.54294	0.29479	0.01514	-0.29057	-0.01897	-0.03929
VAR007	BUSING IDEAL	0.55827	0.31166	0.01687	-0.37627	-0.06748	-0.10265
VAR008	WOMENS RIGHTS IDEAL	0.55950	0.31300	0.00134	-0.16528	-0.00960	-0.02259
VAR009	RIGHTS OF ACCUSED IDEAL	0.56271	0.31666	0.00366	-0.30653	-0.01093	-0.02000
VAR010	AID TO MINORITIES IDEAL	0.56669	0.32113	0.00449	-0.35190	-0.02995	-0.05167
VAR011	LIBERAL CONSERVATIVE IDEAL	0.58888	0.34675	0.02562	0.47582	0.16815	0.21013
(CONSTANT)						0.30271	

FIGURE A-2
An Example Probit Output

```
********************************************************************
N-CHOTOMOUS PROBIT ANALYSIS:  PROBIT MODEL ESTIMATIONS FOR EXTREMIST SUPPORT USING MCKELVEY PROBIT
                              MCGOVERN SUPPORT FUNCTION 1972 EXTREMIST SUPPORT TEST
********************************************************************

        THE ITERATION HAS CONVERGED ON THE 4TH ITERATION.  MAXIMUM LIKELIHOOD ESTIMATES FOLLOW

------------------ BETAS ------------------                                    ------------------ MUS ------------------

                              MAXIMUM                                                    MAXIMUM                STANDARD
              REPRESENTS      LIKELIHOOD    STANDARD                                     LIKELIHOOD             ERROR       MLE/SE
COEFFICIENT   EFFECT OF       ESTIMATE      ERROR      MLE/SE           COEFFICIENT      ESTIMATE

BETA( 0)      CONSTANT        -0.71277      0.06167    -11.558          MU( 1)           0.00000
BETA( 1)      VAR # 1         -0.37502      0.08251     -4.545
BETA( 2)      VAR # 2         -0.25658      0.06607     -3.884
BETA( 3)      VAR # 3         -0.59260      0.09178     -6.457
BETA( 4)      VAR # 4         -0.07534      0.05805     -1.298
BETA( 5)      VAR # 5         -0.20547      0.08320     -2.470
BETA( 6)      VAR # 6         -0.03796      0.04549     -0.834
BETA( 7)      VAR # 7         -0.04552      0.06668     -0.683
BETA( 8)      VAR # 8         -0.13613      0.07161     -1.901
BETA( 9)      VAR # 9         -0.65921      0.11529     -5.642

LOG OF THE LIKELIHOOD FUNCTION= -445.0191

-2.0 TIMES LOG LIKELIHOOD RATIO = 441.6399
(THIS IS CHI SQUARED WITH 9 DEGREES OF FREEDOM)

ESTIMATED ANALYSIS OF VARIANCE

EXPLAINED SUM OF SQUARES =      1273.54577
RESIDUAL SUM OF SQUARES =      1130.00000
TOTALSUM OF SQUARES =          2403.54577
ESTIMATED R SQUARED =             0.52986

OTHER SUMMARY STATISTICS

PERCENT PREDICTED CORRECTLY =       0.82655
RANK ORDER CORRELATION- PREDICTED VERSUS ACTUAL =       0.53474
```

in the same sense but is a straightforward computation. In the dichotomous case, the predicted value is simply the category (0 or 1) which has a higher probability for that case, given the estimated coefficients and probit transformations, and is found by solving equations such as (8) and (9) in the text or their analogues in the more general, n-chotomous case.

A program for performing discriminant analysis has recently been added to SPSS and may be found in other statistical packages (though not in OSIRIS, at least not version 3). Figure A-3 is an example of the SPSS output for log K = 0 as reported in Table 2. The core of the output is listed under the heading "Discriminant Functions" and is that which is reproduced in Table 2 (note that 1 = Humphrey voter, 2 = Nixon voter, 3 = Wallace voter, "RCSELF" indicates self-placement on the Vietnam scale and "UCSELF" on the urban unrest scale—the two issue scales being modified by the scaling technique as described in the body of this paper). Preceding the discriminant functions are a variety of statistics relating to the history of the computation. The program can operate analogously to "stepwise regression" (in which each significant variable is entered in order), the basic test being whether or not it adds a significant amount to the prediction as determined by F statistics. As can be seen, both variables do add a "significant" amount. Options are also available to generate the means and variance/covariance matrix, for solving equations such as (12) and (13), as well as a correlation matrix of independent variables. Even more recent updates indicate that it is now possible to generate the regions either by using the "equiprobability" assumption (i.e., log K = 0) or by weighting the probabilities in any specified manner [e.g., log K = log $\frac{(P^{Yj})}{(P^{Yi})}$], and to output tables and/or scatter plots of predictions.

All of these programs produce a wide variety of other statistics and other sorts of information. The portions of the output we have discussed are, we believe, the most important and most commonly used results. Explanations of other portions of the output can be found in the program write-ups.

REFERENCES

Aitchison, J., and Silvey, S. D. 1957. "The Generalization of Probit Analysis to the Case of Multiple Responses," *Biometrika,* June 1957, pp. 131–140.

Aldrich, J. 1975. *Voting in Two U.S. Presidential Elections: An Analysis Based on the Spatial Model of Electoral Competition.* Unpublished dissertation, University of Rochester.

FIGURE A-3
An Example Output of Discriminant Analysis

VOTING BEHAVIOR AND PREFERENCE BY SPATIAL LOCATION

RCSELF   10.2813   UCSELF   80.2396

U=STATISTIC   0.75288   DEGREES OF FREEDOM   2   2   744
APPROXIMATE F   56.64926   DEGREES OF FREEDOM   4   1486.00

F MATRIX = DEGREES OF FREEDOM   2   743

GROUP VARIABLE   VOTE

                        1.00   2.00

GROUP

     2.00   46.339417

     3.00   109.614517   39.957336

F LEVEL INSUFFICIENT FOR FURTHER COMPUTATION

********** DISCRIMINANT FUNCTIONS **********

GROUPS 1.00, 2.00,
VARIABLE COEFFICIENTS (LAMBDAS) CHOSEN COEFFICIENT (LAMBDA/MIN. LAMBDA)
CONSTANT -0.3484
RCSELF -0.2233 -1.0000
UCSELF -1.2257 -5.4900

GROUPS 1.00, 3.00,
VARIABLE COEFFICIENTS (LAMBDAS) CHOSEN COEFFICIENT (LAMBDA/MIN. LAMBDA)
CONSTANT 0.1379
RCSELF -0.6724 -1.0000
UCSELF -2.8962 -4.3069

GROUPS 2.00, 3.00,
VARIABLE COEFFICIENTS (LAMBDAS) CHOSEN COEFFICIENT (LAMBDA/MIN. LAMBDA)
CONSTANT 0.4863
RCSELF -0.4492 -1.0000
UCSELF -1.6705 -3.7189

SUMMARY TABLE

STEP NUMBER	VARIABLE ENTERED	VARIABLE REMOVED	F VALUE TO ENTER OR REMOVE	NUMBER OF VARIABLES INCLUDED	U-STATISTIC
1	UCSELF		108.7951	1	0.7737
2	RCSELF		10.2813	2	0.7529

Aldrich, J., and McKelvey, R. 1975. "A Method of Scaling with Application to the 1968 and 1972 Presidential Elections," *American Political Science Review* (forthcoming).

Anderson, T. W. 1958. *An Introduction to Multivariate Statistical Analysis.* New York: John Wiley and Sons.

Boyd, R. W. 1972a. "Popular Control of Public Policy: A Normal Vote Analysis of the 1968 Election," *American Political Science Review,* June 1972, pp. 429–449.

_____. 1972b. "Rejoinder," *American Political Science Review,* June 1972, pp. 468–470.

Cnudde, C. F. 1971. *Democracy in the American South.* Chicago, Illinois: Markham.

Converse, P. E. 1966. "The Concept of the Normal Vote," in Angus Campbell, Philip E. Converse, Warren E. Miller, and Donald E. Stokes, *Elections and the Political Order.* New York: Wiley and Sons.

Finney, D. J. 1971. *Probit Analysis.* New York: Cambridge University Press.

Johnston, J. 1972. *Econometric Methods,* 2nd ed. New York: McGraw-Hill.

Kessel, J. H. 1972. "Comment: The Issues in Issue Voting," *American Political Science Review,* June 1972, pp. 459–465.

Kort, F. 1973. "Regression Analysis and Discriminant Analysis: An Application of R. A. Fisher's Theorem to Data in Political Science," *American Political Science Review,* June 1973, pp. 555–559.

McKelvey, R., and Aldrich, J. 1974. "A Method of Scaling with Application to the 1968 Presidential Election," a paper presented at the Annual Meetings of the Public Choice Society, New Haven, Connecticut.

McKelvey, R., and Zavoina, W. 1969. "A Statistical Model for the Analysis of Legislative Voting Behavior," a paper presented at the Annual Meetings of the American Political Science Association, New York, New York.

Nie, N.; Bent, D.; and Hull, C. 1970. *S.P.S.S. Statistical Package for the Social Sciences.* New York: McGraw-Hill.

Page, B., and Brody, R. 1972. "Policy Voting and the Electoral Pr ocess: The Vietnam War Issue," *American Political Science Review,* September 1972, pp. 979–995.

Zechman, M. 1974. "A Comparison of Small Sample Properties of Probit and O.L.S. Estimators with a Limited Dependent Variable," unpublished paper, University of Rochester.

GERALD C. WRIGHT, JR.

Linear Models for Evaluating Conditional Relationships *

Relationships among the variables in political and sociological analyses are often conditional; the magnitudes of relationships frequently change among different types of people, and in different contexts. A common practice in studying such relationships has been to calculate and compare correlation coefficients, or other standardized measures of association, among subsets of observations defined by the conditioning variable. This method is criticized, and in its place we advocate a general linear model approach to assessing the extent of change in relationships among groups of observations. The approach consists of comparing a series of linear regression models with three criteria being offered for evaluating differences among the models. The analysis strategy is then illustrated in partial replications of two earlier studies.

This paper is an essay on comparing relationships among groups of observations. Its purpose is to present a multiple regression technique for systematically assessing the extent of change in relationships that takes place across populations, such as those defined by differences in time, geography, social class, or any of the characteristics by which units are commonly grouped. The general model covered below may be viewed alternatively as (1) a means of examining "conditional" relationships in a regression context, (2) a means for building more interpretable statistical interaction terms in multiple regression, or (3) a simple regression solution to the usually cumbersome statistical manipulations of analysis of covariance. We will proceed in four parts. The first briefly discusses the importance for theory building of comparing relationships under different conditions. Second, we will illustrate the problems of the common practice of using standardized measures of association in comparing relationships. The third section presents an approach to the problem as part of an integrated linear regression model strategy. And fourth, we demonstrate some of the uses and extensions of the approach through partial replications of Riley and Walker's (1969) critique of Dye's (1969b) analysis of income inequality in the American states and Lineberry and Fowler's (1967) study of reformism and public policy in American cities.

Reprinted from AMERICAN JOURNAL OF POLITICAL SCIENCE, Vol. XX, No. 2, May 1976, pp. 349-373, Gerald C. Wright, Jr., "Linear Models for Evaluating Conditional Relationships," by permission of the University of Texas Press.

Types of Comparisons

Let us begin by making clear a distinction suggested by Schoenberg (1972) between two types of comparisons. The first, and the most common in social science, are comparisons among observations classified by one variable (X) to see if they differ on another variable (Y). For example, we might ask if the average Y score is greater among those high on X than among those low on X. Or more simply we often ask, "is X related to Y?" Comparisons of this first kind are usually the major type of propositions that are initially deduced from a given theory. The comparison of interest does not usually change with the imposition of control variables. Generally attention continues to focus on differences in Y between high and low X's, but now controlling for the possible spurious influence of third variables, say Z and W.

We may not, and usually are not, in a position to state the circumstances or conditions under which the deduced YX relationship will hold. It may apply in times of peace but not time of war, among whites but not blacks, among communist systems but not among democracies, and so forth. When we address the conditions under which the YX relationship holds we imply comparisons, not of observations, but of relationships. In this second type of comparison we seek to determine if the YX relationship is constant in two or more defined circumstances or groups. If the relationship is constant in all the defined conditions, we may then conclude that the theory implying the relationship is equally applicable under all of those conditions. If, however, the relationship is substantially different from one circumstance to the next, then we have begun to "specify" the conditions under which the relationship holds. The first major reason for comparing relationships, therefore, is to determine the conditions or the scope of applicability of a given theory.

A second reason for comparing relationships is that such comparisons are sometimes directly implied by one's theory. The real significance of some theories is the specification that pairs of variables will be related differently in two or more contexts. Such statements are generally implied whenever one discusses the theoretical conditions under which some attitudes or circumstances will lead to particular behaviors or policies.

Two types of comparisons, then, might be implied by a theory: first, those comparing observations (levels of Y among high and low X's), and second, those comparing relationships (between Y and X according to levels of some third factor). A simple substantive example will further illustrate the distinction between these types of comparison and how they fit together as a matter of research strategy. Assume that one is primarily interested in the influence of social class on political participation. The first and obvious comparison is between members of different social classes in terms of their respective levels of participation. But one might also wish to examine the hypothesis that the importance of social class increases with economic development of the state. Then one would make the second type of comparison, examining differences in the relationship between class and participation between more and less developed states. Procedures for making the first comparison, between social class and participation, are well established (one can select from a wide variety of bivariate measures of association), but appropriate methods for making the second comparison, looking at differences in the class-participation relationship among states with differing levels of economic development, are not widely appreciated. The need for a systematic approach to comparisons of the second kind will be apparent after we consider the problems with the common practice of using standardized measures of association in comparing relationships among groups of observations.

Comparing Relationships Using
Standardized Measures of Association

The problem we are addressing here is comparing the relationships between variables across groups of observations. To illustrate, let us consider the two artificial data sets displayed in Table 1 where we have, for both data sets, scores on Y and X for two groups of observations, S and N. The two groups might represent sample survey respondents from the South and the North. Assume that we need to determine if the relationship between X and Y is the same in the two regions. The most common contemporary practice in handling this type of problem is to calculate and compare correlations between X and Y for the groups being examined. Doing so for the first data set yields a greater correlation ($r_{YX} = .780$) for group N than for group S ($r_{XY} = .529$). Similarly, for the second data set the correlation is greater among group N ($r_{XY} = .960$) than group S ($r_{XY} = .745$). The correlations seem to indicate for both data sets that the relationship between X and Y is greater in group N than in group S. Comparisons of this sort are seen quite frequently in published research reports where relationships are being compared among such grouping variables as social class, types of party identifiers, or regions.

Comparing correlations is an almost "natural" thing to do, since the correlation coefficient is undoubtedly the most popular measure of association in social science. Its use is widespread, seemingly restrained only by some occasional qualms that one may not have interval or ratio level data. Even these doubts are less and less frequent, as methodologists point out that the

TABLE 1

Listing of Example Data Sets

Data Set 1			Data Set 2		
Region	Y	X	Region	Y	X
S	1	1	S	1	1
S	5	1	S	7	1
S	2	2	S	4	2
S	6	2	S	10	2
S	4	4	S	7	3
S	8	4	S	13	3
N	3	3	S	10	4
N	7	3	S	16	4
N	5	5	N	4	3
N	9	5	N	6	3
N	6	6	N	6	5
N	10	6	N	8	5
N	7	7	N	8	7
N	11	7	N	10	7
N	8	8	N	10	9
N	12	8	N	12	9
N	9	9	N	12	11
N	13	9	N	14	11
N	10	10	N	14	13
N	14	10	N	16	13
N	11	11			
N	15	11			

assumption that one's data are interval is relatively cheap compared to the increased power the assumption affords us (Labovitz, 1967, 1970; Boyle, 1970; Cohen, 1965), although such violations of measurement level assumptions have not gone unchallenged (Mayer, 1970, 1971; Schweitzer and Schweitzer, 1971; Vargo, 1971). And the correlation coefficient has much to recommend it, offering several alternative interpretations allowing it to serve more than one purpose (McNemar, 1969, ch. 9), and is easily extended with the partial correlation coefficient to dramatically increase the analytic power of correlational analysis (Blalock, 1961).

Despite its widespread use, the correlation coefficient is not the most appropriate statistic for comparing relations across groups of observations. The intent of such comparisons of a relationship is usually to determine whether the causal law linking variables is constant among the populations being compared. By "causal law" here we mean simply the average respon-siveness of the dependent variable to differences or changes in the indepen-dent variable. The appropriate statistic for describing this aspect of the relationship between variables—assuming one is willing to make the usual assumptions for correlation analysis—is the unstandardized regression coeffi-cient, b_{YX}.[1] This argument is made most often in discussions of using standardized versus unstandardized regression coefficients (Blalock, 1967a, 1967b, 1968; Schoenberg, 1972; Tukey, 1954; Wright, 1960). Comparisons of correlation coefficients, r_{YX}, between the same pair of variables calculated separately for different groups of observations may be quite misleading, since the correlation coefficient is a function of both the causal law relating the variables and the ratio of the standard deviations of the independent and dependent variables (Blalock, 1968, p. 190).

$$r_{YX} = b_{YX} (S_X/S_Y)$$

The sensitivity of the correlation coefficient to changes in the standard deviations of the variables among comparison groups quite frequently is not realized in political and social research. Some of the possible consequences of the dependence of the standardized measures of association on differences in standard deviation ratios are illustrated in a closer look at our example data.

We have already found that the correlation between X and Y in the data sets is greater in group N than in group S. When the data from the first set are plotted, however, as in Figure 1, we can see that the causal law relating Y to X is exactly the same in both regions. The faulty inference drawn from the correlation coefficients is completely attributable to the proportionately greater standard deviation ratio among group N.

Group S: $r_{YX} = b_{YX} (S_X/S_Y) = 1.0 (1.366/2.582) = .529$
Group N: $r_{YX} = b_{YX} (S_X/S_Y) = 1.0 (2.579/3.304) = .780$

The correct comparison is obtained by the regression coefficients. Calculating the regression of Y on X for group S and then group N, we find the relationship is the same ($b_{YX} = 1.0$) in both groups.

Our second data set shows that reliance on the correlation coefficient can actually lead to inferences opposite of what is correct. These data are plotted

---

[1] The analysis strategy suggested below is completely applicable when dealing with categorical data. Using weighted least squares estimating techniques and Chi-square significance tests, Grizzel, Starmer, and Koch (1969) and Lehnen and Koch (1974) discuss linear models for categorical data that yield effect parameters analogous to the unstandardized regression coefficient.

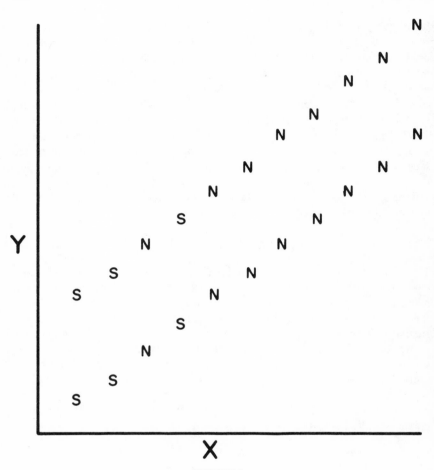

FIGURE 1

Example Showing Equal Strengths of Relationship and Unequal Standard Deviation
Ratios

in Figure 2, and here the responsiveness of Y to X is three times greater in
group S (b_{YX} = 3.0) than in group N (b_{YX} = 1.0). The standard deviation
ratio in group N, however, is proportionately even greater, so that comparing
correlation coefficients misleadingly suggests a stronger relationship in group
N than group S.

$$\text{Group S: } r_{YX} = b_{YX} (S_X/S_Y) = 3.0 (1.195/4.811) = .745$$
$$\text{Group N: } r_{YX} = b_{YX} (S_X/S_Y) = 1.0 (3.568/3.717) = .960$$

The point we wish to emphasize, which has been made by several others, is simply that standardized measures of association can be quite misleading when comparing relationships between or among groups of observations. Unstandardized regression coefficients, however, do provide the information required for determining the equivalence of the strength of relationships among groups.

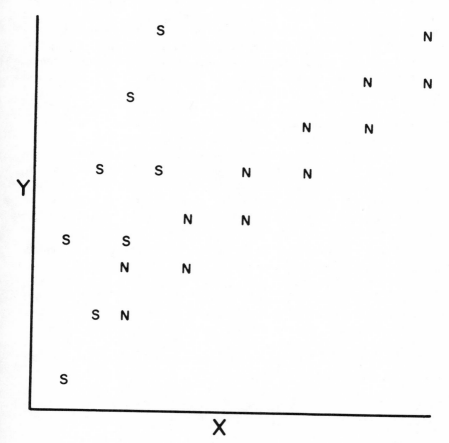

FIGURE 2

Example Showing Unequal Strengths of Relationship and Unequal Standard Deviation Ratios

Regression Models for Comparing Relationships

In the previous section we argued that unstandardized regression coefficients, rather than standardized measures such as the correlation coefficient, ought to be used to compare a relationship across samples. Our intention is now to present a strategy for making and evaluating such comparisons as one segment of a general data-analytic approach.

The strategy proposed here is derived from viewing multiple regression as an instance of the general linear model. A number of works have appeared in recent years which explain analysis of variance, multiple regression, and analysis of covariance as aspects of the general linear model (Bottenberg and Ward, 1963; Kelley, Beggs, and McNeil, 1969; Ward and Jennings, 1973). One widely appreciated relationship is between analysis of variance and "dummy variable" regression analysis (Suits, 1957; Jennings, 1967; Kerlinger and Pedhazur, 1973, pp. 102–115). The equivalence of these has been discussed by Cohen (1968) and Fennessey (1968) in terms readily comprehensible to most social scientists. Our interest in the present paper will therefore be restricted primarily to demonstrating a regression approach to what have been traditionally considered analysis of covariance problems. Analysis of covariance problems are simply a form of multiple regression with dummy variables, and the analysis of covariance test for the equality of slopes of the covariates among treatment groups is a case of statistical interaction in multiple regression (Blalock, 1972, pp. 498–502; Cohen, 1968, pp. 438–442; Finn, 1974, pp. 368–372; Searle, 1971, pp. 340–361).

The linear model approach to comparing relationships will be presented, using the example data from our second data set. The scoring used on these data for the following analysis is shown in Table 2. Although these data do not meet all the assumptions usually made for significance testing, they serve well our strictly illustrative purposes. Assume our primary interest is in the YX relationship and that we feel the need to test a categorical grouping variable, G, for both spuriousness and specification effects on that YX relationship. Begin by constructing a simple regression model expressing the overall YX relationship, completely ignoring the possible effects of G.

$$\text{Model I: } Y = a_0 + a_1 X + e$$

where

a_0 is the intercept;
a_1 is the slope of Y regressed on X;
e is the error term.

TABLE 2

Listing of Data for Models I, II, and III

		Model Variables			
Region	Y	X	$X^{(S)}$	$X^{(N)}$	$G^{(S)}$
S	1	1	1	0	1
S	7	1	1	0	1
S	4	2	2	0	1
S	10	2	2	0	1
S	7	3	3	0	1
S	13	3	3	0	1
S	10	4	4	0	1
S	16	4	4	0	1
N	4	3	0	3	0
N	6	3	0	3	0
N	6	5	0	5	0
N	8	5	0	5	0
N	8	7	0	7	0
N	10	7	0	7	0
N	10	9	0	9	0
N	12	9	0	9	0
N	12	11	0	11	0
N	14	11	0	11	0
N	14	13	0	13	0
N	16	13	0	13	0

If the unstandardized regression coefficient (a_1) is in the expected direction and significant, we would then generally conclude that the hypothesis relating Y and X is supported. Applied to the example data we see in Figure 3A a positive overall slope (a_1 = .71) with Model I explaining somewhat less than half the variance (R^2 = .458).

To test for spuriousness, and to determine the effects of the grouping variable, group membership, we construct Model II. Here group membership is a dichotomy scored as a dummy variable.

$$\text{Model II: } Y = b_0 + b_1 X + b_2 G^{(S)} + e$$

where

b_0 is the intercept;
b_1 is the slope of the independent variable X;
b_2 is the slope of group membership, $G^{(S)}$;
$G^{(S)}$ equals 1 if a case is in group S, and equals 0 otherwise.

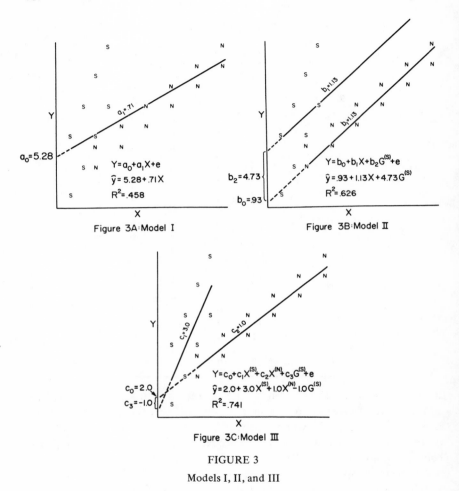

Figure 3A: Model I

Figure 3B: Model II

Figure 3C: Model III

FIGURE 3

Models I, II, and III

Model II is a linear additive regression model which may be conceptualized (see Figure 3B) as two parallel regression lines (the effect of X, b_1 = 1.13) separated by a "group effect" (b_2 = 4.73). Spuriousness would be indicated if the value of the regression coefficient for X from Model I (a_1) decreased to zero in Model II (i.e., if b_1 = 0). Since the coefficient for X is larger in Model II than in Model I, spuriousness due to the effects of group membership is ruled out. Moreover, we see that adding the group variable $G^{(S)}$ in Model II yields a substantial increase in the explained variance (R^2 = .626).

We are now in a position to test for the equality of slopes between groups S and N. This is done with Model III, which estimates separate slopes for each group within a single equation. The procedure for this is a simple extension of the usual dummy variable scoring (Cohen, 1968, pp. 427–429; Draper and Smith, 1966, pp. 134–142; Kerlinger and Pedhazur, 1973, Part 2).

$$\text{Model III: } Y = c_0 + c_1 X^{(S)} + c_2 X^{(N)} + c_3 G^{(S)} + e$$

where

c_0 is the intercept for the base category, group N;

c_1 is the slope of X for group S;

c_2 is the slope of X for group N;

c_3 is the difference between the intercept of group S and the intercept (c_0) of group N;

$X^{(S)}$ equals X for cases in group S and equals 0 otherwise;

$X^{(N)}$ equals X for cases in group N and equals 0 otherwise.[2]

Model III may be understood as two separate regressions within a single equation. It shows the coefficients of Y regressed on X among group N and the coefficients of Y regressed on X among group S. As two independent regressions, we get the following:

$$\text{Regression among group N: } Y_N = a_N + c_2 X^{(N)} + e$$
$$\text{Regression among group S: } Y_S = a_S + c_1 X^{(S)} + e$$

where

$a_N = c_0$ and $a_S = c_0 + c_3$

Although the same coefficients are obtained by both methods, there are

---

[2] Gujarati (1970) offers a slightly different, although mathematically equivalent means for constructing the variables in Model III. His procedures would suggest the equation

$$Y = d_0 + d_1 X + d_2 X^{(S)} + d_3 G^{(S)} + e$$

Here

d_0 is the intercept for the base group N;

d_1 is the slope for the base group N;

d_2 is the difference between the base group slope (d_1) and the slope for group S;

d_3 is the difference between the base group intercept (d_0) and the intercept for group S.

We follow the procedure here of retaining the unit vector in all the model equations (which means suppressing one category of each grouping variable) because the most widely used regression programs automatically supply it in generating solutions.

advantages in estimating a single equation for all cases, and these will be pointed out as we discuss the criteria for assessing the equality of slopes.

The first of these criteria is the actual subgroup regression coefficients; in the example data we see in Figure 3C that the slope for group S is much steeper (c_1 = 3.0) than for group N (c_2 = 1.0). This information can be obtained either through estimating an equation such as Model III, or alternatively through regressing Y on X separately for each group, as discussed immediately above. Information for the remaining two criteria, explained variance and statistical significance, is easily obtained only through estimating the coefficients in a single equation covering all cases.

The R^2 from Model III (not obtained from independent regression on the subgroups) permits a statement of the effects of allowing unequal slopes on our ability to explain the dependent variable. The difference in the R^2's of Models III and II indicates that by allowing the slopes to vary we can explain an additional twelve percent of the variance in Y (.741 − .626 = .115). The amount of increase in explanatory power necessary to be considered "important" depends upon one's purpose. If the primary goal is increasing overall predictive or explanatory power, then small increases in R^2's due to allowing slopes to vary may not be sufficient to warrant dealing with the more complex models. Particularly if one's theoretical interest is in the behavior of subgroups that are proportionately small compared to the entire sample increased, then explanatory power may be a relatively crude gauge. This is because very divergent slopes among numerically small groups may not add appreciably to overall explained variance. In these cases it may be advisable to rely primarily on differences in the magnitudes of the slopes (our first criterion) in conjunction with tests for the statistical significance of the differences among slopes.

Statistical significance is a third possible criterion that can be employed to determine the equality of slopes. However, it is important to be quite explicit about what is being tested. It is generally incorrect to calculate separate regressions (or correlations) for each subgroup and then test each of these coefficients for being *different from zero*. Our tests in comparing relationships should be differences between, or among, the slopes; we are usually interested in the test for whether subgroup slopes are significantly *different from each other*. This is a traditional question in analysis of covariance, although in its presentation concern is more generally with group differences than in equality of slopes of the continuous independent variable, or the "covariate" as it is usually called. Whether one's interest is in "treatment effects" while removing the effects of a "covariate" or in the relative responsiveness of the dependent variable to changes in the independent variable under different conditions, the mathematics are the same—we need to test for the equality of slopes among sets of observations. Such covariance tests are seldom seen in sociological or political science research, maybe because of a lack of familiarity, or perhaps due to a paucity of convenient computer programs.

By comparing models such as II and III, the difference between slopes can be tested quite readily from the information given as standard output from most regression programs. To illustrate with the example data, let us first test for the significance of the difference in slopes among groups S and N. To do this, we compare a "full" model which allows different slopes within each group (Model III) to a "restricted" model that has the restriction that the slopes of each group are equal (Model II). The criterion of significance is the F-test which can be calculated easily by comparing the explained variance of each model, corrected for differences in degree of freedom (Bottenberg and Ward, 1963, pp. 124–125; Kelley et al., 1969, pp. 63–68). The general form of the test is

$$F = \frac{(R^2_{full} - R^2_{restricted}) / df_1}{(1 - R^2_{full}) / df_2}$$

where

R^2_{full} is the proportion of variance explained by the "full" model;

$R^2_{restricted}$ is the proportion of variance explained by "restricted" model;

df_1 is the difference between the number of parameters estimated in the full model and the restricted model;

df_2 is the number of cases minus the number of parameters estimated in the full model.

Model III is the full model with four parameters (c_0, c_1, c_2, c_3), and Model II is the restricted model with three parameters (b_0, b_1, b_2). There are 20 observations in the example data, so the degrees of freedom for the test for the equality of slopes are one and 16 ($df_1 = 4 - 3 = 1$; $df_2 = 20 - 4 = 16$). Substituting these into the equation we obtain

$$F = \frac{(.741 - .626) / 1}{(1 - .741) / 16} = 8.74$$

which is significant at the .05 level.

This section has shown the construction of the regression equations for answering the question of the equality of relationships over different groups of observations. Hopefully we have made quite clear that linear regression techniques can be used to explore aspects of one's data well beyond simple or multiple additive regression models. Conceptualizing data analysis as different regression lines—parallel or not—among various groups allows, for many purposes, precise and readily interpretable statements about important relationships, as well as opening the way for models of greater explanatory power.

The question of the equality of relationships over populations may be addressed from a number of alternative perspectives. Where the third variable defines a set of conditions, the models function to test for whether a particular relationship is "contingent" or "conditional." The parallels in this regression context to the outcomes of Lazarsfeld's (1955, 1961; Rosenberg, 1968) "elaboration" of complex contingency tables, as suggested by Fennessey (1968, pp. 18–20), are fairly straightforward.

Our strategy for comparing relationships is also of direct relevance for the study of contextual effects; we find it increases considerably the power of the approach advocated by Davis, Spaeth, and Huson (1961). At a quite general level, the comparison of Models II and III is a simple test for statistical interaction between the grouping and continuous independent variables. The usual test for this is a multiplicative term for the interacting independent variables; however, while appearing statistically sound, this multiplicative procedure yields coefficients that are often difficult to interpret (Althauser, 1971; Cohen, 1968, pp. 437–441; Draper and Smith, 1966, pp. 222–227). The coefficients produced by Model III (and its extensions), in contrast, have the unambiguous interpretation of the slope of Y regressed on X in each category of G. Thus, the linear model approach for comparing relationships may be viewed from a number of statistically equivalent perspectives. Which perspective is chosen is likely to be a function of the literature in which the research is grounded and ease of interpretability.

Applications

In this section the approach discussed above will be applied in partial replications of two published studies. First, we will examine Dennis Riley and Jack Walker's critique of Thomas Dye's analysis of the determinants of income inequality in the 50 states. We believe the linear model approach advocated here gives an important insight into the Dye (1969a, 1969b) versus Riley and Walker (1969) controversy. Our second application is a replication of Lineberry and Fowler's (1967) study of reformism in American cities. Here we illustrate a generalization of Model III-type equations to situations with more than one continuous independent variable and more than two categories in the grouping variable. Relationships among subsets of observations were compared, using correlation coefficients in both of the original studies.

Gini Index Analysis. Dye's (1969a) analysis of state level determinants of degrees of inequality in the distribution of income within the states has been criticized by Riley and Walker (1969, p. 900, emphasis added) because "no effort was made to isolate regions within the country to find if *relationships change in different cultural or political settings.*" For evidence that Dye and others ought to consider relationships within regional groupings of states, Riley and Walker present correlations of a number of variables with the Gini Index measuring inequality of state income distributions. These are calculated for the eleven southern states of the Confederacy and compared to correlations based on the other nonsouthern states. Riley and Walker (1969, p. 900) find, in several cases, sizable differences in the correlations for the southern and nonsouthern states, and therefore label as "statistical artifacts" the correlations based on fifty states. Dye (1969b, p. 903) responds that he is more interested in generalizations that apply to all fifty states than in statements pertaining only to regional subsets of states. We intentionally avoid this aspect of their disagreement, restricting our comments to what we believe to be a better method for addressing the questions raised by Riley and Walker.

Two measures of state wealth will be related to the Gini Index using the South/non-South distinction as our grouping variable. The first measure of wealth, per capita income, was singled out initially by Riley and Walker in their comment on Dye's analysis. The other measure of wealth is median family income, and was included in Dye's original analysis but not in Riley and Walker's critique. Remembering that our primary purpose here is to illustrate a data analytic technique, we will try to keep the analysis simple by ignoring a whole host of other variables that were considered in the other studies.

The correlations for all fifty states of the Gini Index with per capita income is −.62, and with median family income it is −.76. By region, these correlations among the southern states are −.85 and −.88, while among the northern states the correlations are −.28 and −.47.[3] The relationships between the Gini Index and measures of wealth appear quite different in the South and non-South.

Changing to regression coefficients, and examining them through three increasingly complex models, yields quite different conclusions. The results

---

[3] Riley and Walker (1969, p. 900) report slightly different values for these correlations. The reason for the discrepancy is that their analysis is based on 48 rather than 50 states.

are shown in Table 3. First, looking at the per capita income variable, we see the bivariate regression of Model I yields a regression coefficient (a_1 = −.040) for all fifty states, with the model explaining a substantial amount of the variance in the Gini Index (Model I R^2 = .389). Adding the grouping variable, region, in Model II shows very sharp North versus South differences (b_2 = 37.47) and adds over 20 percent to the explanatory power of the model (Model II R^2 = .597). The impact of per capita income sharply decreases when region is included (from −.040 to −.018).

If the relationship between the Gini Index and per capita income is really substantially different within regions, then Model III, which permits different slopes within regions, should result in a still further increase in explanatory power. The increase is small, just over one percent (Model III R^2 = .615). The

TABLE 3

Models of Relationships between Gini Index
and Measures of Income and Region

Model	Equations*	R^2
Model I	$Y = a_0 + a_1 \, X \, E \, 3$	
Per Capita Income	$(520.7) + (-.040) \, X + e$	.389
Median Income	$(548.60) + (-.021) \, X + e$	.582
Model II	$Y = b_0 + b_1 \, X + b_2 \, G^{(S)}$	
Per Capita	$(467.0) + (-.018)X + (37.47) \, G^{(S)}$	.597
Median Family Income	$(502.06) + (-.013) \, X + (26.87) \, G^{(S)}$	.671
Model III	$Y = c_0 + c_1 \, X^{(S)} + c_2 \, X^{(N)} + c_3 \, G^{(S)}$	
Per Capita Income	$(459.35) + (-.050) \, X^{(S)} + (-.015) \, X^{(N)} + (97.60) \, G^{(S)}$	.615
Median Family Income	$(495.81) + (-.019) \, X^{(S)} + (-.012) \, X^{(N)} + (56.77) \, G^{(S)}$	.676

Tests for Significance of Difference between Models		
Model Contrasts	X = Per Capita Income	X = Median Family Income
I versus II df = 1,47	F = 24.31 (p<.01)	F = 12.72 (p<.01)
II versus III df = 1,46	F = 2.09 (p = NS)	F = 0.65 (p = NS)

*Y = Gini Index
X = Measure of Income; per capita income or median family income.
$X^{(S)}$ = Income among southern states; 0 otherwise.
$X^{(N)}$ = Income among northern states; 0 otherwise.
$G^{(S)}$ = 1 if a southern state; 0 otherwise.

absolute values of the regional slopes do reveal what appears to be a stronger relationship in the South ($c_1 = -.050$) than in the North ($c_2 = -.015$). The significance test contrasting Models II and III, shown in the bottom part of Table 3, suggests the difference between the slopes is not significant.[4]

Repeating the same analysis using median family income as the independent variable gives us a similar, but clearer, pattern. Almost 60 percent of the variance in the Gini Index is accounted for by just median family income (Model I R^2 = .582), and then adding the regional effect adds almost another nine percent to this (Model II R^2 = .671). Most importantly, however, we see that in Model III the relationship between the Gini Index and median family income is virtually the same within regions. This similarity is evidenced by (1) the similarity of regression coefficients of Model III ($c_1 = -.019$, $c_2 = -.012$), (2) the minimal increase in explained variance due to allowing the slopes to vary (Model II R^2 = .671 versus Model III R^2 = .676), and (3) the lack of significance in the contrast between Models II and III ($F = 0.65$).

It is not so obvious, therefore, that income and the Gini Index are related in fundamentally different ways in the South and non-South. While a discussion of measurement problems is beyond the scope of this paper, our findings of very minimal support using per capita income and no support using median family income do suggest that greater theoretical specification of the variables would be necessary to resolve that inconsistency. Our analysis does show, however, large regional differences in the Gini Index that are not accounted for by measures of state income, however measured. In this sense Riley and Walker appear quite correct in calling for greater effort at explaining these regional differences. That is, although the Gini Index/Income relationship is similar in the two regions, there does remain to be explained the greater inequality of income distributions of the southern states.

Reformism in American Cities. The analysis of the effects of reformism in American cities on revenue policies by Lineberry and Fowler presents an excellent example of the type of problem that requires comparisons of unstandardized regression coefficients. Lineberry and Fowler (1967, pp. 701–704) argue that cities with unreformed governmental structures (mayor-

---

[4] Presentation of significance tests seems to be the norm in comparative state politics studies, even though the states are not a sample but a population. The tests are presented here largely for illustrative purposes, although they are most interesting in light of the Riley and Walker (1969, pp. 902fn) procedure of choosing eleven states at random and recalculating their analysis. Our significance tests indicate that eleven states chosen at random could display slope differences of the magnitude observed for the income variables.

council form, partisan ballots, ward constituencies) differ in their policymaking processes from reformed cities (manager or commission form, nonpartisan ballots, at-large constituencies).

To give a partial reexamination of their analysis, as well as to illustrate our modelling strategy for more complex problems, consider their final hypothesis (1967, p. 713): "The higher the level of reformism in a city, the lower its responsiveness to socioeconomic cleavages in the population." Here reformism is hypothesized to inhibit the relationship between socioeconomic characteristics of cities and their public policies. The reformism variable is an additive index of form, constituency type, and kind of ballot. with four categories from least to most reformed (Lineberry and Fowler, 1967, p. 713). The dependent variables in their study are the ratio of total city revenue to total personal income (Taxes) and the ratio of total city expenditures to total personal income (Expenditures). The hypothesis implies that as one moves from least to most reformed cities the coefficients relating city socioeconomic characteristics to policy will increase. The socioeconomic characteristics examined will be the same four used by Lineberry and Fowler to test this hypothesis.[5]

A first test of the responsiveness hypothesis is to compare an additive model that allows reformism and SES effects to a model that allows different SES effects within each of the four reformism categories. These are simply extensions of Models II and III above, now with a grouping variable with four categories. To avoid confusion we will call them Model A and Model B respectively, and they may be expressed as follows:

$$\text{Model A: } Y = a_1 + \sum_{i=2}^{4} a_i R^{(i)} + bX + e$$

where

   Y is the dependent variable, Taxes or Expenditures;

   a_1 is the intercept;

[5] These variables are percent native-born or with mixed parentage (Ethnicity), percent of school-age children attending private schools (Private School Attendance), percent of dwelling units which are owner-occupied (Owner-Occupancy), and median years education of the adult population (Median Education). The sources of all data are the same as used by Lineberry and Fowler in the original study (*City County Data Book,* 1962; *Municipal Yearbook,* 1965). Following their procedure, we drew a random sample of 200 cities from those with 1960 populations over 50,000. With two of these having missing data, our study N is 198.

a_i are dummy variable regression coefficients for the ith reformism categories;

$R^{(i)}$ equals 1 if a city is in the ith reformism category, 0 otherwise;

b is the regression coefficient for the selected SES variable;

e is the error term.

$$\text{Model B: } Y = a_1 + \sum_{i=2}^{4} a_i R^{(i)} + \sum_{i=1}^{4} b_i X^{(i)} + e$$

where (as in Model A except)

b_i are the regression coefficients of the selected SES variable within the ith reformism category;

$X^{(i)}$ equals the value of the SES variable if the city is in the ith reformism category, equals 0 otherwise.

Support for the Lineberry and Fowler hypothesis would be indicated by (1) Model B explaining significantly more of the variance in Y than Model A, and (2) if the slopes in Model B monotonically decrease as reformism increases, i.e., $b_1 > b_2 > b_3 > b_4$. The analysis is repeated four times, once for each of the SES variables. The slopes of these variables within categories of reformism, as well as results of the significance tests for the differences between Models A and B, are presented in Table 4. Using correlation coefficients, Lineberry and Fowler reported (1967, p. 714) "some fairly consistent support for the hypothesis. Even when the decrease in the strengths of the correlations is irregular, there is a clear difference between cities which we have labeled 'most reformed' and 'least reformed.' " The data presented in our Table 4, using the more appropriate regression coefficients, do give some support to the hypothesis. Least reformed cities do appear more responsive to differences in Ethnicity and Private School Attendance for both policy measures, and to Owner Occupancy as well for Taxes. However, changes in these slopes are not monotonic, and in most cases allowing the slopes to vary does not add significantly to the explanatory power of the models.

We will take this analysis one step further while illustrating a means of including more than one continuous independent variable in the equation. The results in Table 4 are derived from Model B, which considered the SES variables one at a time without controlling the effects of the remaining SES variables. The simultaneous analysis of all four SES variables can be achieved by comparing a model with additive reformism effects and the effects of the four SES variables to a model allowing the slopes of all four SES variables to vary simultaneously within each category of the reformism variable. The

TABLE 4

Models of Simple Relationships between Policy Outputs
and Four Socioeconomic Characteristics, by Categories of Reformism

Dependent Variable	Reformism	Regression Coefficient from Model B (where X =)			
		Ethnicity	Private School Attendance	Owner Occupancy	Median Education
Taxes	Least (1)	.674	.488	−.801	−4.278
	(2)	.569	.690	−.294	−3.871
	(3)	.019	.017	−.314	−2.678
	Most (4)	.319	.238	−.586	−6.784
	Model A R^2	.268	.205	.310	.251
	Model B R^2	.306	.229	.332	.260
Signif. of the difference (df. = 3,190)		$F = 3.39$ ($p<.05$)	$F = 1.96$ ($p = NS$)	$F = 2.08$ ($p = NS$)	$F = 0.852$ ($p = NS$)
Expenditures	Least (1)	.782	.556	−1.193	−6.689
	(2)	.557	.740	−.196	−4.183
	(3)	−.093	−.204	−.472	−5.703
	Most (4)	−.119	−.271	−1.266	−18.833
	Model A R^2	.140	.128	.261	.249
	Model B R^2	.174	.153	.300	.302
Signif. of the difference (df. = 3,190)		$F = 2.64$ ($p = NS$)	$F = 1.84$ ($p = NS$)	$F = 3.51$ ($p<.05$)	$F = 4.82$ ($p<.01$)

former model (we will label it Model C) is a simple multiple regression
equation with a four-category dummy variable and four continuous variables:

$$\text{Model C: } Y = a_1 + \sum_{i=2}^{4} a_i R^{(i)} + \sum_{j=1}^{4} b_{.j} X^{(\cdot j)} + e$$

where (as above except)

b.$_j$ denotes the regression coefficient for the jth SES variable, constant
   across all reformism categories;

$X^{(\cdot j)}$ is the score of each city on the jth SES variable.

The full model, Model D, allows each slope of each SES variable to vary
within each category of reformism:

$$\text{Model D: } Y = a_1 + \sum_{i=2}^{4} a_i R^{(i)} + \sum_{i=1}^{4} \sum_{j=1}^{4} b_{ij} X^{(ij)} + e$$

where (as above except)

b_{ij} is the regression coefficient of the jth SES variable in the ith category of reformism;

$X^{(ij)}$ is the score of the jth SES variable if the city is in the ith category of reformism, 0 otherwise.

Notice that Model C is more parsimonious with eight parameters than Model D with twenty parameters. With Expenditures as the dependent variable, Model C explains 33.5 percent of the variance, while the full Model D accounts for 43.8 percent of the variance. This difference is significant at the .01 level. For the other dependent variable, Taxes, Models C and D account for 44.0 and 49.1 percent of the variance respectively, a difference that is statistically significant at the .05 level. The regression coefficients among categories of reformism from Model D are shown in Table 5.

Not even irregular support for the hypothesis is provided by the data in Table 5. None of the SES variables becomes systematically less strongly related to policy outputs as reformism increases. The one clear pattern emerging when all SES variables are considered simultaneously is that reformism intensifies the relationship between education and both Taxes and Expenditures. Most reformed cities appear to be most, rather than least, responsive to differences in education.

A very large number of alternative models can be formulated and compared within this general approach. For example, one might want to allow each of the SES variables' slopes to vary one at a time while imposing the same slope on the remaining SES variables. If so, then Model C above would be the reduced model, and the full model, assuming the first SES variable is the one whose slopes will vary within categories of reformism, might be expressed as:

$$\text{Model E: } Y = a_1 + \sum_{i=2}^{4} a_i R^{(i)} + \sum_{j=2}^{4} b_{\cdot j} X^{(\cdot j)} + \sum_{i=1}^{4} b_{i1} X^{(i1)} + e$$

where (as above except)

b_{i1} is the slope of the first SES variable in the ith category of reformism;

$X^{(i1)}$ equals the value of the first SES variable if the city is in the ith reformism category, equals 0 otherwise.

This Model E would have 12 parameters which we would compare to a reduced Model C with nine parameters. The difference in the R^2's between the two models would represent the additional explanatory power that would come with allowing the slopes of the one SES variable to change across

TABLE 5

Models of Simultaneous Relationships between
Policy Outputs and Four Socioeconomic Variables,
by Categories of Reformism

Dependent Variable	Reformism	Regression Coefficients from Model D			
		Ethnicity	Private School Attendance	Owner Occupancy	Median Education
Taxes					
	Least (1)	.555	−.036	−.695	.885
	(2)	.460	.195	−.117	−2.510
	(3)	.179	−.059	−.297	−2.134
	Most (4)	.477	−.174	−.410	−6.106
	Model C R^2 = .440 Model D R^2 = .491 difference: $F_{8,179}$ = 2.25(p<.05)				
Expenditures					
	Least (1)	.571	−.082	−1.061	.039
	(2)	.422	.262	.016	−3.270
	(3)	.270	−.338	−.373	−5.346
	Most (4)	.381	−.705	−.798	−16.263
	Model C R^2 = .335 Model D R^2 = .438 difference: $F_{8,179}$ = 4.07(p<.01)				

categories of reformism while controlling for the linear effects of the remaining SES variables.

Our primary purpose here, we would stress, is not to single out the Lineberry and Fowler analysis—their procedure of comparing correlations rather than regression coefficients remains a very common, although we believe inadvisable, practice. Our intention has been simply to first emphasize that standardized measures of association may be misleading when comparing relationships among groups of observations; second, we have attempted to present a better method for making such comparisons as part of a unified data analytic strategy in a multiple regression framework.

The flexibility and the precision in hypothesis testing permitted by the linear model approach is quite considerable. We believe that working with models such as these is a genuine heuristic aid in facilitating the researcher's effort to clearly state what he wishes to examine. Formulating hypotheses as alternative models sharpens our focus on the types of relationships that may be important. If nothing else, rather than automatically testing null hypotheses that all coefficients are equal to zero, this strategy encourages the investigator to explicate his theory sufficiently to determine the form of relationship among variables that the theory implies. Then, with the techniques for systematically evaluating the differences between formulated models, along with greater sensitivity to problems of measurement, this approach can contribute to a much greater explicitness and hence greater precision in our political research.

Manuscript submitted February 7, 1975.
Final manuscript received May 19, 1975.

REFERENCES

Althauser, Robert P. 1971. "Multi-collinearity and Non-additive Regression Models," in H. M. Blalock, Jr., ed., *Causal Models in the Social Sciences.* Chicago: Aldine, Atherton, pp. 453–472.

Blalock, Hubert M., Jr. 1961. *Causal Inferences in Nonexperimental Research,* Chapel Hill: University of North Carolina Press.

_____. 1967a. "Causal Inference, Closed Population, and Measures of Association," *American Political Science Review,* March 1967, pp. 130–136.

_____. 1967b. "Path Coefficients versus Regression Coefficients," *American Journal of Sociology,* May 1967, pp. 675–676.

_____. 1968. "Theory Building and Causal Inference," in H. M. Blalock, Jr., and A. B. Blalock, eds., *Methodology in Social Research.* New York: McGraw-Hill, pp. 155–198.

_____. 1972. *Social Statistics,* 2nd ed. New York: McGraw-Hill.

Bottenberg, Robert A. and Ward, Joe H. 1963. *Applied Multiple Linear Regression.* Springfield, Va.: U. S. Department of Commerce.

Boyle, Richard P. 1970. "Path Analysis and Ordinal Data," *American Journal of Sociology,* January 1970, pp. 461–480.

Cohen, Jacob. 1965. "Some Statistical Issues of Psychological Research," in B. B. Wolman, ed., *Handbook of Clinical Psychology.* New York: McGraw-Hill, pp. 95–121.

_____. 1968. "Multiple Regression as a General Data-Analytic System," *Psychological Bulletin,* December 1968, pp. 426–443.

County and City Data Book. 1962. Washington: Bureau of the Census.

Davis, James, A.; Spaeth, Joe L.; and Huson, Carolyn. 1961. "A Technique for Analyzing the Effects of Group Composition," *American Sociological Review,* April 1961, pp. 215–225.

Draper, Norman, and Smith, Harry. 1966. *Applied Regression Analysis.* New York: John Wiley and Sons.

Dye, Thomas R. 1969a. "Income Inequality and American State Politics," *American Political Science Review,* March 1969, pp. 157–162.

_____. 1969b. "Communications," *American Political Science Review,* September 1969, p. 903.

Fennessey, James. 1968. "The General Linear Model: A New Perspective on Some Familiar Topics," *American Journal of Sociology,* January 1968, pp. 1–27.

Finn, Jeremy D. 1974. *A General Model for Multivariate Analysis.* New York: Holt, Rinehart and Winston.

Grizzle, J. E.; Starmer, C. F.; and Koch, G. G. 1969. "Analysis of Categorical Data by Linear Models," *Biometrics,* September 1969, pp. 489–504.

Gujarati, Damodar. 1970. "Use of Dummy Variables in Testing for Equality Between Sets of Coefficients in Two Linear Regressions: A Generalization," *American Statistician,* December 1970, pp. 18–22.

Jennings, Earl. 1967. "Fixed Effects Analysis of Variance by Regression Analysis," *Multivariate Behavioral Research,* January 1967, pp. 95–108.

Kelley, Francis J.; Beggs, Donald L.; and McNeil, Keith A. 1969. *Research Design in the Behavioral Sciences: Multiple Regression Approach.* Carbondale and Edwardsville: Southern Illinois University Press.

Kerlinger, Fred N., and Pedhazur, Elazar J. 1973. *Multiple Regression in Behavioral Research,* New York: Holt, Rinehart and Winston.

Labovitz, Sanford. 1967. "Some Observations on Measurement and Statistics," *Social Forces,* December 1967, pp. 151–160.

_____. 1970. "The Assignment of Numbers to Rank Categories," *American Sociological Review,* June 1970, pp. 515–554.

Lazarsfeld, Paul F. 1955. "Interpretation of Statistical Relations as a Research Operation," in P. F. Lazarsfeld and M. Rosenberg, eds., *The Language of Social Research.* New York: The Free Press, pp. 115–125.

_____. 1961. "The Algebra of Dichotomous Systems," in H. Solomon, ed., *Studies in Item Analysis and Prediction.* Stanford: Stanford University Press, pp. 111–157.

Lehnen, Robert G., and Koch, Gary G. 1974. "A General Linear Approach to the Analysis of Nonmetric Data: Applications for Political Science," *American Journal of Political Science,* May 1974, pp. 283–313.

Lineberry, Robert L., and Fowler, Edmund P. 1967. "Reformism and Public Policies in American Cities," *American Political Science Review,* September 1967, pp. 701–716.

Mayer, Lawrence S. 1970. "Comment on 'Assignment of Numbers to Rank Order Categories,'" *American Sociological Review,* August 1970, pp. 916–917.

_____. 1971. "A Note on Treating Ordinal Data as Interval Data," *American Sociological Review,* June 1971, pp. 519–520.

McNemar, Quinn. 1969. *Psychological Statistics,* 4th ed. New York: John Wiley and Sons.

Municipal Yearbook. 1965. Chicago: International City Managers' Association.

Riley, Dennis D., and Walker, Jack L. 1969. "Communications," *American Political Science Review,* September 1969, pp. 900–903.

Rosenberg, Morris. 1968. *The Logic of Survey Analysis.* New York: Basic Books.

Searle, S. R. 1971. *Linear Models.* New York: John Wiley and Sons.

Schoenberg, Ronald. 1972. "Strategies for Meaningful Comparison," in Herbert L. Costner, ed., *Sociological Methodology 1972.* San Francisco: Jossey-Bass, pp. 1–35.

Schweitzer, S., and Schweitzer, D. G. 1971. "Comment on the Pearson r in Random Number and Precise Functional Scale Transformations," *American Sociological Review,* June 1971, pp. 518–519.

Suits, Daniel B. 1957. "Use of Dummy Variables in Regression Equations," *Journal of the American Statistical Association,* December 1957, pp. 548–551.

Tukey, John W. 1954. "Causation, Regression, and Path Analysis," in O. Kempthorn, et al., eds., *Statistics and Mathematics in Biology.* Ames: Iowa State College Press, pp. 35–66.

Vargo, L. G. 1971. "Comment on the Assignment of Numbers to Rank Order Categories," *American Sociological Review,* June 1971, pp. 517–518.

Ward, Joe H. Jr., and Jennings, Earl. 1973. *Introduction to Linear Models.* Englewood Cliffs: Prentice-Hall.

Wright, Sewell. 1960. "Path Coefficients and Regression Coefficients: Alternative or Complementary Concepts?" *Biometrics,* June 1960, pp. 189–202.

Scaling Techniques

HERBERT F. WEISBERG

Scaling Objectives and Procedures

A wide variety of scaling techniques are available for the analysis of the structure of a set of variables. These techniques generally analyze the similarities among a set of variables from a geometric perspective. Scaling techniques introduced in this chapter include Guttman scaling, unfolding analysis, cluster analysis, factor analysis, component analysis, and multidimensional scaling.

We shall use the term "dimensional analysis" to encompass a wide variety of data reduction techniques, the best known of which are Guttman scaling, cluster analysis, factor analysis, and multidimensional scaling. These techniques focus on the similarities (or the differences) among a set of variables, rather than tracing through causal processes as is the concern of the techniques described in the previous section of this book. Most statistical analysis deals with estimating the effects of independent variables on dependent variables, but that distinction between independent and dependent variables is not important in the dimensional realm. Instead, the scaling question is how similar (or different) is a set of variables. Scaling techniques analyze the structure of a set of variables when causation is not being considered,[1] and they do so on the basis of a geometric representation of the data.

The causal problem is so much more familiar than the scaling problem that it is worth pausing to give some examples of situations leading to dimensional analysis. Two basic situations can be distinguished. First, the researcher sometimes simply wishes to describe the dimensionality of a set of variables—a "dimensioning" concern. For example, the legislative researcher might want to determine whether a single liberal-conservative dimension underlies all roll call votes in a particular Congress, whether there are separate domestic and international dimensions, or whether there are actually several separate dimensions within the domestic and/or foreign realms. Similarly, the student of comparative politics might want to discover the dimensions underlying a party system in some nation.

Alternatively, the researcher sometimes wishes to derive unidimensional indices on which individuals can be scored—a use of scaling out of a concern

---

[1] Procedures developed by Jöreskog which combine causal and dimensional concerns will be described briefly at the end of this chapter.

with "positioning" individuals on scales with dimensional integrity.[2] For example, a survey researcher might want to combine several questions designed to measure political cynicism into a single scale so as to study the effect of that attitude on political participation, but a necessary first step would be to check whether all of the questions asked tap the same dimension of cynicism. Similarly, a researcher interested in the effects of social-economic status on political behavior might first want to see whether different indicators of the person's social-economic status are interchangeable or whether there are important differences among them. In these examples, the dimensionality is examined as a prelude to positioning the individuals studied on an underlying dimension, rather than out of a pure interest in the dimensionality *per se*.

These examples illustrate the variety of interests which motivate scaling, from data reduction and object classification to measurement improvement and assessing the commonality among a large number of measures. Dimensional analysis is often performed in an exploratory mode, seeing which dimensions are required to account statistically for a body of data. As such, it can be atheoretical, with the danger of accepting any result as meaningful even if it has no substantive significance. A case of this type of misuse of scaling would be collecting a few hundred indicators of the properties of different nations, seeking the dimensions underlying those indicators, and then giving interpretations of the dimensions that are obtained without external validation of the interpretations. Dimensional analysis is better when it is performed in a confirmatory mode, testing whether the data at hand conform to prior structural hypotheses. Unfortunately, the number of dimensional hypotheses we have at present is very limited, so exploratory analysis is more prevalent than confirmatory analysis.

Scaling makes direct use of a geometric metaphor, such as the concern in the above paragraphs as to whether a set of data can be explained in terms of a single dimension or require multiple explanatory dimensions. The meaning of this geometric metaphor is explored directly by Weisberg in the next chapter. In that chapter, Weisberg also presents some alternative interpretations of dimensionality and of unidimensionality that are inherent in different scaling techniques. Also, he provides further speculation on the philosophical underpinnings and implications of dimensional analysis.

Before proceeding to that chapter, it is useful to be familiar with some of the more basic scaling procedures, and these will be described in the remainder of this chapter. A wide variety of scaling techniques will be introduced in this

---

[2]The distinction between "dimensioning" and "positioning" was suggested by Donald Stokes (personal communication).

chapter, so the reader can have some familiarity with the concepts employed in the next two chapters and compare the techniques described in those chapters with other common dimensional procedures. Some of the purposes of scaling will also be explained in this chapter, both directly and by means of example, so the reader can better understand why these techniques are useful and what types of questions they are designed to answer.

Guttman Scaling: Unidimensionality as Cumulation

One of the most commonly used scaling techniques is Guttman scaling. To show the reasons that it is useful, we shall first describe a simple "nondimensional" procedure for data reduction.

Index Construction

The simplest way of combining several indicators into a single measure is to score each one and then add up the scores. By way of example, say that we are studying political participation, by which we mean not only voting but talking about politics, taking part in political campaigns, and joining political groups.[3] No single indicator would suffice here, since political participation involves a large number of acts, those just listed and many more. But if we want to study political participation as a whole rather than its separate facets, we must somehow combine those separate indicators. The "index construction" solution would be simply to count up how many activities a particular person performs. If only the four participatory acts listed above were included, then a total score of 4 would mean that the person participated in all four acts, 3 would indicate that the person performed three of those activities, and so on down to zero for the person who participated in none. Once respondents are thus scored on this index, the index could be correlated with other variables, so that one might study the relative effects of political cynicism and political interest on political participation.

A potential problem with this procedure is that some of the items in the index might measure different things from the other items. Perhaps one of the activities is really very different from the others and does not belong in the same index. Or perhaps political participation actually consists of distinctly different types of activities, with different types of people participating in the active "gladitorial" activities (taking part in campaigns and group membership) than

---

[3] The indicators employed here are those used by Matthews and Prothro (1966) in their study of political participation in the South.

in the more passive "spectator" activities (voting and political discussion).[4] If two of the indicators tapped one component and the other two tapped a different component, adding the four together in a single index would be like adding apples and oranges. Minimally, the index construction process has to be modified to check whether all the individual indicators indeed measure the same thing.

Beyond this, the index construction process equates the importance of the different constituent items, treating them as if they were of equal difficulty. People would receive a score of 1 on the above political participation index if they participated in only one of the four activities which have been listed, regardless of which activity that is—as if just taking part in a campaign is the same level of political participation as merely talking to somebody about that campaign. The simple index construction process is inadequate because it does not check whether the items are of unequal difficulty. But items can be of unequal difficulty while still measuring the same dimension, as in this example. This is the precise logic which leads to Guttman scaling.

Cumulative Scaling

Guttman scaling tests for a difficulty dimension underlying a set of data. If there is a difficulty dimension, then only certain data patterns should occur—ones which are "cumulative," such as those in the top five rows of Table 1. Only five patterns of political participation fit this scale: some people not participating at all, some performing only the easiest activity, some only the two easiest, some all but the hardest, and some all four. But cumulation implies that no person should "pass" a harder item while "failing" an easier item, so performing a "harder" activity (like taking part in a campaign) without performing the "easier" activities (like voting) constitutes "error" in the scale.

If all the items fit a cumulative pattern, we would have assurance that they constitute a single dimension. Actually, a perfect scale would be unlikely, as there is always some error (whether random error, measurement error, or violation of the unidimensional model). For example, a person whose only political activity is participating in a campaign (as in the last row of Table 1) would contribute error to the scale. A low amount of error would not invalidate a scale, but if the amount of error became high we would have to conclude that the items were not all unidimensional. If most of the error were found to be due to a single item, that item could be deleted from the scale. If, instead, the errors result because the different items measure, for example, two different dimensions,

---

[4]The distinction between "gladitorial" and "spectator" activities is due to Milbrath (1965).

TABLE 1

Hypothetical Guttman Scale of Political Participation

| | | Activity | | | | |
Person	Voting	Political Discussion	Group Membership	Campaigning	Score	Errors
1	Yes	Yes	Yes	Yes	4	0
2	Yes	Yes	Yes	No	3	0
3	Yes	Yes	No	No	2	0
4	Yes	No	No	No	1	0
5	No	No	No	No	0	0
6	No	No	No	Yes	0	1

Number of items = 4   Number of people = 6
Amount of missing data = 0
Number of valid responses = (number of items) (number of people) − (missing data)
$$= 4 \times 6 - 0 = 24$$
Total number of errors = 1
Guttman's coefficient of reproducibility = 1 − (number of errors)/(valid data)
$$= 1 - 1/24 = .96$$

then separate scales can be prepared and people scored separately on those two scales. In any case, it is important to have some statistic summarizing the quality of a scale.

Louis Guttman developed a "coefficient of reproducibility," which measures the proportion of responses which fit the scale, as illustrated in the calculations below Table 1. He recommended accepting as unidimensional only those scales with reproducibilities of at least .90 under his method of counting scale error. However, his measure has an upward bias; its minimum value is not .00 but depends on the proportion of people passing each item, so that in some cases the minimum reproducibility is actually quite high (.60 or .70 or even greater). To handle this problem, a "coefficient of scalability" has been developed. It normalizes the reproducibility coefficient by its minimum, given the item marginals. A scalability of at least .60 is usually required for a good scale. Actually, many other measures of scale quality have been proposed, and there is no single agreed-upon measure. But at least there is agreement on the need to measure fit to the cumulative model. Computer programs are available to assess the degree to which a set of variables fit a Guttman scale, in particular the GUTTMAN SCALE procedure in SPSS.

There are not good direct procedures for separating scales in a set of multidimensional data. A correlational approach is often employed for this purpose. The key to this approach is that if two items are perfectly cumulative, their cross-tabulation will contain a cell without any cases—since no one will pass the harder item while failing the easier one. Table 2 labels the cells in the fourfold table obtained by crosstabulating two dichotomous variables. If there is a perfect cumulative Guttman scale relationship between the two items, the c cell should equal zero. In terms of the measures of association described in earlier chapters, Yule's Q and some other "one-way measures of association" have the value of 1.0 in this case, which can be interpreted as perfect association. As a result, one way to locate Guttman scales among a large set of variables is to look for subsets of variables which all have very high Q values with one another. Automated procedures for such a search will be described later in this chapter.

To summarize, Guttman scaling is a technique for checking whether dichotomous data are unidimensional. It can be extended to multicategory data, mainly by first dichotomizing the variables. If the variables do not form an acceptable scale, an item with excessive error can be deleted. Or we can check whether the variables contain more than one subset of scalable variables, such as two separate dimensions. Guttman scaling employs a single theory of unidimensionality—the form of cumulation shown at the top of Table 1—but there are other forms of unidimensionality even for dichotomous data. The next chapter discusses some of those alternative models of unidimensionality, especially the proximity scale.

Unfolding Analysis: Unidimensional Preference Orders

The second procedure to be described in this chapter can be dealt with more quickly. It is Coombs's unfolding analysis, which is applicable to preference order data. If we have people order a set of alternatives from their first choice to

TABLE 2

Cross-Tabulation of Dichotomous Variables*

Easier Item	Harder Item		Total
	Yes	*No*	
Yes	a	b	$a + b$
No	c	d	$c + d$
Total	$a + c$	$b + d$	1.00

*Since the row item is the easier item, more people pass it than the column item. Thus, $a + b > a + c$, or $b > c$. If the items are perfectly cumulative, no one passes the harder item while failing the easier item, so $c = 0$. Yule's Q ($= \gamma$) $= (ad - bc)/(ad + bc)$, which, if $c = 0$, reduces to $(ad - 0)/(ad + 0) = ad/ad = 1.0$. Thus $Q = 1.0$ for cumulative variables.

their last, then the individual preference orders can be studied to obtain information about the underlying preference space.

Part of the idea of unfolding can be understood from the case of three alternatives. Say that there are three parties in a country and that public attitudes toward them are unidimensional. People at the left end of the polity would prefer the left party L the most, the center party C second, and the right party R least. People at the right end of the polity would like the right party R the most, center party C second, and the left party L least. Some people in the middle might be closest to C, then to L, then to R. Other people in the middle might be closest to C but then next closest to R and then L. This leads to four preference orderings occuring: LCR, CLR, CRL, and RCL (See Figure 1).

But, if the data are indeed unidimensional, no one would be closest to the left party L, second closest to the right party R, and furthest from the middle party C. And no one would be closest to the right party R, second closest to the left party L, and furthest from the middle party C. That is, two preference orders should not occur: the two with the middle party in third place, LRC and RLC. Thus, to scale a set of data, we would check how many parties are the last place choices of people. If everyone likes either L or R least, the data are unidimensional. (Or if they all like L or C least, then the data are unidimensional but the party ordering should be LRC instead of LCR; if they all like C or R least, then the data are unidimensional with the party ordering CLR.) But if L, C, and R all get substantial numbers of last place votes, then the data are not unidimensional.

This technique interprets preference orders as individuals picking up the underlying dimension at their most preferred ("ideal") point and then folding the dimension at that point to obtain their ordering of points (they prefer the alternatives nearer them regardless of direction—hence the folding idea). Since the analysis procedure seeks an underlying dimension which is consistent with the observed preference orders (the folded scales), it is termed "unfolding."

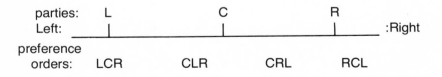

FIGURE 1

Preference Orders of a Party Dimension

For example, we could check whether Americans view partisanship as unidimensional by asking them to rate Democrats, Independents, and Republicans. If these groups were viewed as unidimensional with Independents in the middle, no partisan should like the other party more than Independents. In fact, most partisans like the opposite party more than Independents (see Table 3), so the preferences are not consistent with a Democrat-Independent-Republican ordering. They are actually more consistent with the ordering Republican-Democrat-Independent, but it is more appropriate to say that they are not unidimensional.

Unfolding analysis extends to more than three alternatives, though it rapidly becomes more complicated. With four alternatives, the occurrence of certain preference orders rather than others begins to give some information about the spacing of alternatives along a single dimension. We might find, for example, that the two left alternatives are closer to each other than are the two alternatives on the right. This is termed "ordered metric" information—information about the order of interpoint distances. Technically, this is a level of measurement between ordinal and interval, as it yields more than an ordering of the points but less than their precise locations on a dimension. The more alternatives being scaled, the more ordered metric information becomes available. With enough variables, the ordered metric information places severe limits on the possible

TABLE 3

Frequencies of Preference Orders Based on Thermometer Ratings of Democratic Party,
Republican Party, and Political Independents, January–February, 1980*

Order	Frequency
Compatible with Dem-Indep-Rep Dimension	
DIR	15%
IDR	14
IRD	10
RID	13
Total	52%
Not Compatible with Dem-Indep-Rep Dimension	
DRI	31%
RDI	17
Total	48%

*Preference orders are listed in first choice, second choice, third choice order. The total number of respondents with untied preference orders is 507. If each possible preference order of three alternatives were equally likely, two-thirds of the preference orders would be consistent with a single dimension. This table is taken from Table 1 (page 39), of Weisberg (1980) with the data based on the Center for Political Studies 1980 American national election survey.

locations of alternatives in the space, so that nonmetric unfolding of preference order data virtually pinpoints the variables in the space.

Unfolding analysis also extends to more than one dimension, but it is too complicated to calculate by hand. Fortunately, the nonmetric multidimensional scaling procedure mentioned later in this chapter and described in the last chapter can be used to unfold preference orders in one or more dimensions. But it basically just employs the principles mentioned already. If alternatives have fixed points in a space of limited dimensionality, then certain preferences orders should not occur. As a result, analyzing the pattern of preference orders can lead to information about the spatial structure. Moreover, the exact pattern of preference orders which occurs can place severe limits on the possible locations of alternatives in the space, so that nonmetric analysis of ordinal preference orders can yield spatial solutions nearly as precise as interval analysis provides.

Cluster Analysis: Separating Sets of Variables

Another important family of analysis techniques is designed to identify "clusters" of variables. A cluster of variables is a set of variables that are more similar to each other than to other variables. Sometimes a large set of variables can be decomposed into 2, 3, 4, 5, or 6 clusters, and it can be useful substantively to be able to talk about those clusters rather than the larger set of variables. A difficulty with cluster analysis is that there is no single well-defined procedure for clustering. Instead, the vague definition given here for clusters is compatible with a very large number of clustering approaches. As a result, there are literally hundreds of clustering routines that have been proposed over the years. Each has some advantages over the others, or at least its originator felt that it did. We cannot explain all clustering approaches in this short section, but the ideas behind cluster analysis can be introduced.

Simple Clustering

One clustering approach is to build up a cluster, starting with the most similar pair of variables—that with the highest correlation. Then the variable with the highest correlations with those first two variables is added to the cluster, followed by the variable with the highest correlation with those first three variables, and so on until none of the variables remaining to be clustered has high correlations with the variables already in the cluster. At that point, the first cluster is complete, and a second cluster is obtained by repeating the above process using only the unclustered variables. Further clusters can then be built according to the same procedure until all variables have been clustered or no remaining unclustered pair of variables has a high correlation.

This is a very simple clustering algorithm, but as stated so far, it is actually incomplete. Decisions have to be made about how high correlations have to be to put a variable in a cluster. The computer program for this type of clustering[5] permits the analyst to choose the limit after which variables are not added to a cluster and the limit after which new clusters are not formed. These are arbitrary decisions, but they can affect the clustering—different values would yield different sets of clusters.

Clustering Criterion

Additionally, the description in the above paragraphs did not define what it means to have "the highest correlations with variables already in a cluster." Does that mean the highest correlation with any variable in that cluster? If so, clusters are formed such that each variable has a high correlation with at least one variable in the cluster but not necessarily all of them. This possibility, called "single linkage," is useful in some clustering applications. For example, all that is necessary for the diffusion of a rumor through a communications network is for each person in a network to communicate with one other person in that network.

Alternatively, "the highest correlations with variables already in a cluster" could mean requiring high correlations with every variable in that cluster—or more precisely, that the new variable's minimum correlation with variables in the cluster is greater than the minimum correlation between the variables already in the cluster and any other unclustered variable. This condition leads to tight clusters, with a single low correlation being sufficient to prevent a variable from entering a cluster. The result, called "complete linkage," is a very common clustering criterion.

As a compromise between single and complete linkage, we could also use "average linkage," adding to a cluster the variable with the highest average correlation with the variables already in the cluster. This is a reasonable compromise, but it does operate at the interval level of measurement, while the other criteria use only ordinal properties of the correlations.

Hierarchical Clustering

Regardless of the linkage criteria chosen, the clustering approach described so far is limited in that it builds one cluster at a time. By contrast, another

---

[5]The computer program referred to here is the CLUSTER program in the OSIRIS computer package.

common clustering algorithm, Johnson's (1967) hierarchical clustering procedure,[6] can build several clusters at once. The pair of variables with the highest correlation starts the first cluster. Then, depending on which correlation is higher, either a second cluster is started with the pair of unclustered variables with the highest remaining correlation or a third item (having the highest correlations with the variables aleady in the cluster) is added to the first cluster.[7] At each following stage, a new cluster is formed, another item is added to one of the existing clusters, or existing clusters are merged, depending again on which correlation is higher.

This process can build several clusters at once, each from its nucleus out. The process continues until all items fit into a single cluster. For n variables, the procees gives a set of n clusters, a set of $n - 1$ clusters, a set of $n - 2$ clusters, . . . , a set of 3 clusters, a set of 2 clusters, and finally the 1-cluster solution. Since the clusters at any later stage are actually made up of combinations of those at earlier stages, this is termed a "hierarchical" procedure. Which stage gives the correct solution? The researcher is likely to look at auxiliary statistics to decide that, particularly at the proportion of high correlations that are within the clusters already formed at a stage rather than between variables in different clusters. The higher that statistic, the sharper the separation between the clusters. Generally, that statistic is high for a very large number of clusters, eventually falls as the number of clusters goes down, and then goes back up for a very small number of clusters. The best solutions seem to be those just before the statistic falls or just when it comes back up.

The types of clustering described so far are highly arbitrary. Although there is no formal mathematical justification for a particular clustering algorithm, clustering can give researchers a quick, if only partially adequate, view of their data's internal structure. As we have described it so far, clustering is actually nondimensional, but we have included cluster analysis in this chapter because it can be used for scaling purposes (see below) and because the next procedure to be described in this chapter can be considered a dimensional version of cluster analysis.

Coefficients for Clustering

The reader might have noticed that we have discussed clustering correlations in this section without indicating which correlation coefficients are to be used. The reason is that it depends—different correlations can be used for different

---

[6]This technique is available in the HICLUSTR program in the OSIRIS computer package.

[7]Any of the criteria mentioned above—single linkage, complete linkage, or average linkage—can be employed in judging the correlation of unclustered variables with those in the cluster.

purposes. With interval data, Pearson's r can certainly be used in clustering. The result would be to give sets of variables which vary together to a considerable degree. With noninterval data, two-way measures of association, like Kendall's τ *(tau)* would give similar results.

One interesting application of clustering is to cluster "agreement scores," measures of how often responses to two variables are identical. This application is most common when the focus is on clustering individuals, rather than variables, such as clustering legislators to see which legislators tend to vote together as blocs. The agreement score could simply count the number of times a pair of legislators vote together, and clustering could be applied to the matrix of agreement scores.

Another useful application is to cluster Yule's Q (or other measures of one-way association) as an approximation to Guttman scaling. It was mentioned in an earlier section that variables which are cumulative would have a high Q coefficient with one another. A set of variables with high Q's with one another would form a good quality Guttman scale. Cluster analysis thus can be used on Yule's Q to separate sets of variables which form Guttman scales from a larger set of multidimensional data. For example, Clausen and Cheney (1970) cluster a large number of legislative roll call votes to find what unidimensional Guttman scales exist in them.

Tree Analysis

Mathematical psychologists have recently developed an alternative to hierarchical clustering that represents similarity data as "additive trees" (Sattath and Tversky, 1977). An additive tree is a chart in which dissimilarity between objects is represented by the length of the path joining them. For example, Figure 2 shows an additive tree representation for the data of Table 4.

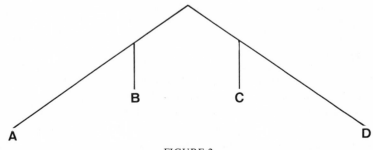

FIGURE 2
Additive Tree Representation of Table 4*

TABLE 4
Dissimilarities among Four Variables

	A	B	C	D
A	—	5.0	5.6	7.2
B		—	4.6	5.7
C			—	4.9
D				—

*Adapted from Table 1, Sattath and Tversky, p. 320.

There are two clusters: *A* and *B* on the left path in one cluster and *C* and *D* on the right path in the second. Additionally, the most similar (least dissimilar) variables are those closest together in the center—*B* and *C*—while the least similar (most dissimilar) are those at the opposite ends—*A* and *D*.

Additive tree analysis is related to multidimensional scaling as presented later in this chapter, except that the relations that count are those along the paths. The technique is most useful for classification purposes, when different paths along the tree can be different categories—subdividing the total set of variables into a few subsets, each of which is further subdivided. This procedure represents the data relations more completely than does conventional clustering.

Blockmodel Analysis

Another new clustering procedure is a "blockmodel" approach to analyzing relationships among individuals or other units. It decomposes a matrix of relations into blocks of individuals with similar relations to other blocks. Blocks need not be internally cohesive in this model; all that matters is that members of a block have similar relations with other blocks. The blockmodel procedure has been presented in a Workshop article by Panning (1982).

In a political example, Panning (1982) presents a blockmodel analysis of transfers among Senate committees to determine sets of committees with similar membership transfer relationships. He finds four sets of committees: six top committees (Foreign Relations, Appropriations, Agriculture, Finance, Judiciary, and Commerce), four at a second rung (Armed Services, Banking and Currency, Interior, and Labor and Public Welfare), three at a third rung (Public Works, Governmental Operations, and Rules and Administration), and two at the bottom (Post Office and District of Columbia). Membership transfers follow a general upward flow, except for equal flow back and forth from the second and fourth rung committees. The analysis does not differentiate within the four sets of committees, for all that matters is that there are similar relationships among the four sets. The analysis is hierarchical, moving individuals (or committees in this example) from set to set to try to maximize the fit between the actual data and the blockmodel. This technique seems to be particularly appropriate for "dominance" situations, as when seeking a hierarchy of importance—here of committees. And the blockmodel procedure can handle asymmetric relations, as when the number of moves from committee A to committee B does not equal the number from committee B to committee A.

It is too early to gauge the importance of the new blockmodel and additive tree approaches. However, it is clear that new and more applicable clustering procedures are being developed. The researcher interested in partitioning data into clusters can seek high-powered techniques that display many aspects of the data relations at once. The development of these techniques indicates a continued interest in mathematical psychology in finding appropriate geometric, cluster, and dimensional representations of complex data relations.

Factor Analysis: Dimensional Clustering

Factor analysis can be thought of as a dimensional clustering technique. Whereas the clustering procedures described so far view a variable as either in a cluster or not in it, factor analysis allows for the possibility that a variable is only partially in a cluster. The "factor loading" of a variable indicates the extent to which it partakes of the factor cluster—its correlation with the factor dimension.

Common Factor Model

The factor model interprets the standardized Z_{ij} score of a person i for variable j as a linear function of the person's position (F_{pi}) for each factor p and the extent to which the variable measures the factor (a_{jp}). In the one-factor case, for example, the person's score is

$$Z_{ij} = a_{j1}F_{1i} + e_{ij},$$

where the e is an error term. Different people have different values for the variable because of their different positions for the factor, the F_i. The reader might note that this is very similar to a regression equation, except that the "independent" variable (the F_i) is not observed and is just hypothesized to exist. In the more general multi-factor case, the model is that the person's score is

$$Z_{ij} = a_{j1}F_{1i} + a_{j2}F_{2i} + \cdots + a_{jm}F_{mi} + e_{ij}$$

where m is the number of factors. This is like a multiple regression equation, except that again the F terms are not observed.

The solution of the factor model requires some auxiliary assumptions. In particular, given that the factors are just hypothetical anyhow, we might as well assume that they are standardized and uncorrelated. Those further assumptions are sufficient to yield a decomposition of the correlation between two variables j and k which is known as the "fundamental factor theorem":

$$r_{jk} = a_{j1}a_{k1} + a_{j2}a_{k2} + \cdots + a_{jm}a_{km},$$

With one factor, this means that the correlation between two variables is just the product of their loadings on the underlying factor. With more factors, it means that the correlation is a linear sum of the product of their loadings on the respective factors. Factor analysis attempts to locate the variables in a dimensional space so as to satisfy this fundamental factor theorem.

In a geometric interpretation, factor analysis attempts to locate the variables on dimensions such that the correlation between a pair of variables (r_{jk}) equals the product of their distances from the origin ($d_j d_k$) times the cosine of the angle between them ($\cos \Theta_{jk}$). If the variables are perfectly correlated ($r = +1.0$), factor analysis would place them at the same point one unit from the origin, and they would be unidimensional. If the variables are independent ($r = .0$), factor analysis would locate them on orthogonal (right angle) dimensions.

For example, let us say that the correlations among five variables (labeled $A-E$) are as in Table 5. It is clear from the correlations that variables A and B have much in common, as do variables D and E, but those two sets are fairly distinct from each other. Furthermore, variable C is related to both sets. A geometric solution for these correlations is in Figure 3. The location of the variables on the dimensions are their "factor loadings." The loadings in this figure are given in Table 6.

The correlations can actually be "reproduced" from their loadings through use of the fundamental factor theorem. Variables A and B, for example, both

TABLE 5

Hypothetical Correlation Matrix Variable

	A	B	C	D	E
A	—				
B	.60	—			
C	.30	.50	—		
D	.00	.32	.50	—	
E	−.32	.00	.30	.60	—

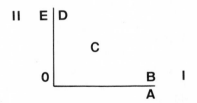

FIGURE 3
Common Factor Analysis of Table 5

have loadings of .8 for factor I and thus a product of .64. For factor II, A has a loading of − .2 and B has a loading of + .2, with a product of − .04. The sum of these products of loadings is then .64 + (− .04) = .60, the correlation given between variables A and B. Similarly, the other correlations can be reproduced exactly from the factor loadings.

In this example, it is possible to satisfy the correlation by locating the variables in a space of just two dimensions. Were that impossible, more than two dimensions would be used. As it is, two factors are required. Factor I is interpreted by examining what variables A and B have in common and factor II by examining what variables D and E have in common. Variable C is here related to both factors.

In a factor analysis, the use of Pearson's r correlations indicates that the variables are essentially standardized—means of zero and variances of one. If there were 5 variables, there would then be 5 units of variance being analyzed. Some of this variance is unique to each variable, but some is common variance. The type of factor analysis described in this section is termed the common

TABLE 6
Factor Loadings from Figure 3

| Variable | Factor | | Communality |
	I	II	
A	.8	− .2	.68
B	.8	.2	.68
C	.5	.5	.50
D	.2	.8	.68
E	− .2	.8	.68
Sum of Squares	1.61	1.61	3.22

factor model.[8] The amount of the variance of a variable which is accounted for by a factor is determined by squaring that variable's loading on the factor. Thus, variable A has a loading of .8 on factor I, so 64% of its variance is accounted for by that factor. Since its loading on factor II is $-.2$, 4% of its variance is accounted for by that factor. The sum of the squared values is known as the communality of the variable. Here the third column of the Table 6 shows that 68% of the variance of variable A is being accounted for by the factor analysis. This is less than 100% because variable A has some unique variance. In this case the variable with the least common variance is variable C.

How effective is the overall factor analysis? The sum of the communalities in the table is 3.22 units of variance. This is 100% of the common variance of the 5 variables, but it is not all of their total variance. Five standardized variables have 5 total units of variance, so that analysis accounts for 3.22/5.00 = 64.4% of the total variance. When the common factor model is employed, the common variance should be a reasonable proportion of the total variance. An analysis that accounted for 95% of the common variance would not be very meaningful if the common variance were only 10% of the total variance.

Another way of looking at the factor loading matrix is to examine the sum of squared loadings in each column. The first factor accounts for .64 of the variance in variables A and B, .25 for variable C, and .04 for variables D and E. When summed, this factor accounts for 1.61 units of variance. Similarly, factor II accounts for 1.61 units of variance. The column sum of squares (or "eigenvalue") shows the importance of the factor, and here the two factors are of equal importance.

An important question with factor analysis is how many factors to employ. The usual means of handling this decision is to perform a preliminary "component analysis" (to be described in the next section)—a factor analysis which analyzes the total variance of each variable. As many factors are extracted as there are variables being analyzed. If each variable contributes one unit of standardized variance, then a factor improves on the original variables only if it accounts for more than one unit of variance. This logic leads to "Kaiser's criterion"—the use of as many factors as have a sum of squared loadings (eigenvalues) greater than one. Once the number of factors is determined, then the common factor solution is obtained using that number of factors.[9]

---

[8]This corresponds to the PA2 type of factor analysis in SPSS.

[9]Common factor analysis is actually iterative. An estimate of the common variance of each variable is made (possibly by using the proportion of its variance that can be accounted for statistically by the other variables, as shown by the R^2 value with that variable as dependent and the rest as independent). The factor analysis is performed using that estimate as the correlation of the variable with itself. The variable's communality in that analysis—the proportion of its variance

We should note that the mathematics underlying factor analysis assumes use of Pearson's r as the measure of correlation. Since factor analysis makes interval level assumptions, there would be no gain in moving down to an ordinal level measure of association.

Factor Rotation

A complication is that the placement of the axes in the factor space is arbitrary. It is easiest to interpret the factors if they are rotated so that the variables tend to have high loadings on some factors and low on the rest. This amounts to seeking to place the axes through clusters of variables: "simple structure rotation." The solution given above is of this type and would correspond to the rotated solution in a factor analysis.

Actually, the factors need not be at right angles to each other. The solution shown above uses orthogonal axes (ones at right angles to each another) and corresponds to the commonly used "varimax solution." But the factors could be correlated, since there is no reason to expect that separate clusters of variables are completely independent of one another. Correlated factors require an examination of the "oblique axes." The best way to interpret correlated factors is to examine the oblique factor "pattern" which projects a point on the dimensions by drawing parallels to the other dimensions. This is illustrated in Figure 4, where variable X would be located on factor II but not factor I, since its projection is high only on factor II.[10]

Factor Analysis Problems

Factor analysis is often portrayed as a mindless data-crunching exercise. That is true in the sense that any statistical analysis routine is mindless—running a hundred cross-tabulations or regressions can be equally mindless. Factor analysis is probably most useful for testing an hypothesis about the

---

accounted for by the factors—is used as a new common variance estimate. The factor analysis is repeated until the communality estimates stabilize.

[10]If we had used the other system of projection, perpendicular projection of X onto the two axes, we would find that X has high values on both factors, which does not help us interpret the results. The perpendicular projection system is known as the factor "structure." It corresponds to the correlation between the variable and the factor, and it is employed in factor scoring applications.

In orthogonal space, the factor pattern and factor structure are identical, which is a good reason for using the simpler orthogonal solution unless there is a substantial correlation among the oblique factors. Often this means performing an oblique analysis, checking whether the factor correlations are high, and (if not) performing an orthogonal analysis.

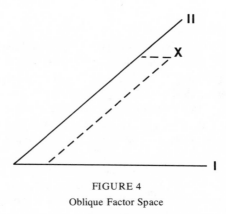

FIGURE 4
Oblique Factor Space

structure of a set of variables. This is termed the "confirmatory mode," in contrast to the "exploratory mode." A common application of the confirmatory mode is testing whether the common variance of a set of variables can be accounted for with a single underlying factor. However, we do not have many good structural dimensional hypotheses, so this theoretical mode of factor analysis is of limited usefulness.

Factor analysis is also often portrayed as plagued by indeterminacies, such as the choice of rotation. There are indeed indeterminacies, but the basic factor model is really the same basic general linear model which underlies regression analysis except that the "independent variables" are not observed but just hypothesized. Fortunately there are conventional ways of handling the indeterminacies that exist. These solutions may be arbitrary, but cluster analysis also involves a number of arbitrary decisions. The advantage of factor analysis over cluster analysis is that is allows variables to belong to the dimensional clusters to a partial degree. If we are willing to operate at the interval level of measurement, this method yields a more realistic portrayal of the data.

The final problem is one of interpretation of the solution. Factor analyses are often misinterpreted, as the users bend the interpretations to fit their desires. But that is not a problem with the technique so much as one with the researchers. No statistical technique can provide its own substantive interpretations. There are good ways to interpret the factors (generally by scoring the people on the factors and relating those scores to other variables as a means of testing different interpretations), but often we do not have enough data available to provide separate tests of the interpretations.

The discussion of factor analysis could go on endlessly. Instead, we shall stop here and turn more briefly to some related techniques.

Jöreskog Procedures

A special form of factor analysis should be mentioned that departs from the basic restrictions of this chapter. Jöreskog (1975) has developed a set of procedures for "exploratory factor analysis," "confirmatory factor analysis," "analysis of covariance structures," and "estimation of linear structural equation systems" that break down the conventional distinction between causal and scaling procedures. Basically, since the same general linear model is involved in regression and factor analysis, it can be generalized to handle the mixture of the two.

We shall give a single example to illustrate one Jöreskog procedure, but the reader should realize that the Jöreskog procedures are more general than this example. The Michigan elections studies include a large number of issue questions. It is reasonable to expect that these different issues questions tap a smaller number of underlying common dimensions, and factor analysis can be used to check for this possibility. In turn, these different dimensions can have different relationships to demographic variables, as can be determined by regression analysis using factor scores as dependent variables.

Knoke (1979) applied the Jöreskog procedure for the "estimation of linear structural equation systems with multiple indicators of unmeasured variables" (LISREL) to the 1972 Center for Political Studies national election survey. Specifically, he hypothesized a particular structure to the issue questions—making this a confirmatory rather than exploratory factor analysis—with some issues tapping only a social dimension (particularly attitudes toward marijuana and sex roles), some tapping only a racial dimension (specifically attitudes on minority rights), some both (attitudes toward rights of the accused), some only an economic dimension (attitudes on government action on inflation and on progressive taxation), and some both the racial and economic dimensions (busing, government guarantees of jobs, and government health insurance). The analysis confirmed that structure, finding a sizable (.62) correlation between social and racial factors, a moderate (.37) correlation between racial and economic, and none (.08) between social and economic.

Furthermore, the analysis found different causal patterns for the different factors. The social factor was most affected by age (younger people more liberal on social questions), education and occupation (people of higher socio-economic status more liberal). The racial factor was most affected by race (not surprising) and education (the more educated more liberal again) with some age effect (younger people more liberal). The economic factor was most affected by income (people of lower income more liberal), race (blacks more liberal), education (the less educated more liberal this time), and age (older people now the more liberal).

The success of this analysis rests on the ability of the analyst to make many assumptions, including which variables tap which dimensions as well as reliability estimates for some of the variables. Instead of allowing the analyst to explore a set of data without any prior expectations (as when a computer grinds out all possible crosstabulations of a set of variables), the researcher must be familiar with the data. The researcher must have an idea of what to look for in the data and where it is likely to be found. This is a good development, making it more difficult to capitalize on random features of the data and more necessary to develop good theories. The Knoke example nicely illustrates the interplay of theory and data analysis which is to be desired in any data analysis enterprise.

Component Analysis: Factoring Total Variance

There are actually several factor analysis "models." In addition to the "common factor model" described in the previous section, the "principal component model" is frequently employed.[11] It is particularly useful when trying to ascertain the extent to which a set of variables covary with one another. It differs from the common factor model in analyzing the total variance of the variable, not just its common variance.[12]

The principal component procedure seeks to locate a first component dimension in the space that accounts for a maximum proportion of the variance of the variables. If more than one component is required, the procedure locates the second to account for a maximum proportion of the variance not accounted for by the first component, subject to the constraint of orthogonal dimensions. This explanation holds for the *un*rotated component solution.

The first unrotated principal component thus serves as a general component, indicating the maximum proportion of the total variance which can be accounted for by a single component. If we wanted to construct a general index from the variables, we could use their loadings on the first component as their appropriate "weights." This would weight variables which tap the main underlying syndrome more heavily than those which do not.

If we wished to perform a component analysis on the example of Table 5 above, we would find the loadings in Figure 5 and Table 7. The principal component would correspond to the bisector of the two factors in the preceding figure, and there would be a second component. The first is the main compo-

---

[11]This corresponds to the PA1 type of factor analysis in SPSS.

[12]Operationally, this is achieved by analyzing the correlation matrix with values of 1.0 along the main diagonal (corresponding to correlations of unity between the varable and itself), whereas the common factor model puts the commonality estimates into the main diagonal in an iterative analysis.

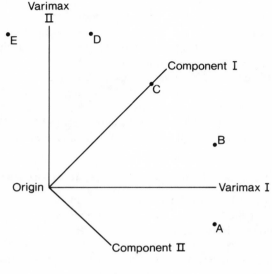

FIGURE 5

Component Analysis of Table 5

nent, since its sum of squares is larger (1.86 compared to 1.36), but the second is still to be retained, as its sum of squares (eigenvalue) is at least greater than 1.00.

This solution can be interpreted to mean that 1.86/5.00 or 37% of the total variance can be accounted for by a single component. All variables load on that component, though B, C, and D have the highest loadings. However, a second component exists, with A and E having higher loadings on it than the first component. That second component stresses the opposite character of A and E (and to a lesser extent B and D), with C not being related at all to the second component.

Model Choice

When is the component model used rather than the factor model? If the interest is in the extent to which a single component underlies a set of variables, the statistics underlying the component model make it highly appropriate. In more exploratory analyses of the structure of a set of variables, the common factor model is more likely to be used.

Incidentally, the mathematical difference in terms of the models is merely

TABLE 7

Factor Loading Matrix for Component Analysis (Figure 5)

| Variable | Factor | | Communality |
	I	II	
A	.42	−.71	.68
B	.71	−.42	.68
C	.71	.00	.50
D	.71	.42	.68
E	.42	.71	.68
Sum of Squares (eigenvalue)	1.86	1.36	

that there is no error term included for the component model, and there are as many components as variables. So, for n variables, the decomposition of Z_{ij} is
$$Z_{ij} = a_{j1}F_{1i} + \cdots + a_{jn}F_{ni}$$
Once again, the mathematics of the procedure is based on the use of Pearson's r correlations. Other coefficients are not usually employed.

Dichotomous Data

It should be noted also that the logic behind factor analysis fails for dichotomous data when Pearson's r is used (or its equivalent statistics with dichotomous data, Φ (phi) or Kendall's τ (tau) on a Guttman scale structure. With dichotomous data, Pearson's r would not equal 1.00 if the variables cumulate perfectly in a Guttman scale structure. As a result, factor analysis of Pearson's r's on dichotomous data can yield multiple factors when the data fit a single Guttman scale (Clausen, 1964) and indeed will obtain more factors the more variables there are on that scale (Weisberg, 1968).

An interesting application, however, emerges from the utility of one-way measures of association like Yule's Q for analyzing Guttman scale structures. Since high Q values would be obtained between cumulative variables and zero Q values between independent variables, the component analysis procedure is actually a fairly effective means of separating multiple Guttman scales in a set of data (MacRae, 1970; Weisberg, 1968) This usage is unconventional but seems to work fairly well.

Multidimensional Scaling: Nonmetric Similarity Analysis

A fairly new procedure for analyzing the dimensional structure of a set of data is nonmetric multidimensional scaling. It seeks a spatial solution of minimum dimensionality such that the more similar a pair of variables, the closer together they are in the space. While there are also some metric versions of multidimensional scaling, the nonmetric version is able to locate variables in a space quite well with merely ordinal interpretations of the similarity data. Since Rabinowitz explains the procedure in detail in the last chapter of this book, we shall not describe it further here.

How is multidimensional scaling used? It has been used on correlation coefficients (even Pearson's r, as in Weisberg and Rusk, 1970, and Rusk and Weisberg, 1972), but there are problems involved when there is a very small number of variables (Jones, 1974), and this procedure cannot be used to locate individuals in the same space as the variables (Rabinowitz, 1973). It can also be used on measures of similarity among the variables, or interindividual agreement scores. For example, the number of times members of a legislature vote together can be analyzed to obtain a spatial mapping of their relative locations (Hoadley, 1980). Rabinowitz (1976) has developed a particularly ingenious measure to be used in multidimensional scaling of thermometer data, where survey respondents rate political candidates from 100° (very warm feelings) to 0° (very cool feelings).

An interesting question is how multidimensional scaling and factor analysis differ. Both give multidimensional geometric interpretations of relationships among a set of variables, but factor analysis provides a metric translation of correlation coefficients into scalar products between variables in the space, whereas multidimensional scaling provides a nonmetric representation of similarity data as spatial distances. In the two chapters which follow, Weisberg and Rabinowitz give their evaluations of the differences between these important techniques. Minimally, it is clear that both techniques will remain frequently used analysis procedures for the foreseeable future.

Multidimensional Unfolding

A special application of multidimensional scaling programs is for the purpose of unfolding analysis. In this application, the procedure seeks to locate individuals and variables together in a space such that the higher a person ranks an alternative in his preference order, the closer the variable is placed to him in the space. This provides a practical means of performing the type of unfolding analysis described earlier in this chapter, even with multidimensional data.

Individual Differences Scaling

Finally, there is an important variant of multidimensional scaling logic which allows for the possibility of different individuals weighting the dimensions of a common space differently. For example, Converse's (1966) analysis of citizen preferences for French parties derives a two-dimensional structure—a left-right dimension and a cleric-anticleric dimension—but Converse goes on to show that different parties weight these dimensions differently: some parties stressing the left-right dimensions while giving little weight to the religious dimensions, others emphasizing the religious dimension while giving little weight to the left-right dimension, and still others giving fairly equal weights to the two dimensions. This same notion of individuals giving varying weights to common dimensions is embodied in Carroll and Chang's (1970) procedure for "individual differences scaling." Takane, Young, and de Leeuw (1977) have developed a particularly efficient procedure for such analysis, a procedure which can also be used for the basic multidimensional scaling analysis without the potential for local minimum problems.

Conclusions

No doubt the large number of procedures for dimensional analysis renders the area confusing. Often the nature of the available data serves to narrow down the choices. Yet it is important to consider a wide range of dimensional analysis procedures, rather than using a technique only because it has become conventional in a field without noticing that it has particular substantive implications that might not be fully warranted. There are a wide variety of alternative scaling models (see Coombs, 1964; Wolters, 1978). The chapter that follows picks up directly on this theme, illustrating some unconventional models which can be very appropriate substantively.

REFERENCES

Carroll, J. Douglas, and Chang, J. J. 1970. "Analysis of Individual Differences Multidimensional Scaling Via an N-way Generalization of 'Eckart-Young' Decomposition," *Psychometrika*, September 1970, pp. 283–319.

Clausen, Aage. 1964. "Policy Dimensions in Congressional Roll Calls: A Longitudinal Analysis." Ph.D. dissertation, University of Michigan.

Clausen, Aage R., and Cheney, Richard B. 1970. "A Comparative Analysis of Senate-House Voting on Economic and Welfare Policy: 1953–1964," *American Political Science Review*, March 1970, pp. 138–152.

Converse, Philip E. 1966. "The Problem of Party Distances in Models of Voting Change," in M. Kent Jennings and Harmon Zeigler, eds., *The*

Electoral Process. Englewood Cliffs, New Jersey: Prentice-Hall, pp. 175–207.

Coombs, Clyde H. 1964. *A Theory of Data.* New York: Wiley.

Hoadley, John. 1980. "The Emergence of Political Parties in Congress, 1789–1803," *American Political Science Review,* September 1980, pp. 757–779.

Johnson, S. C. 1967. "Hierarchical Clustering Schemes," *Psychometrika,* September 1967, pp. 241–254.

Jones, Bryan D. 1974. "Some Considerations in the Use of Nonmetric Multidimensional Scaling," *Political Methodology,* Fall 1974, pp. 1–30.

Jöreskog, Karl G. 1973. "A General Method for Estimating a Linear Structural Equation System," in Arthur S. Goldenberger and Otis D. Duncan, eds., *Structural Equation Models in the Social Sciences.* New York: Seminar Press, pp. 85–112.

Knoke, David. 1979. "Stratification and the Dimensions of American Political Orientations," *American Journal of Political Science,* November 1979, pp. 772–791.

MacRae, Duncan, Jr. 1970. *Issues and Parties in Legislative Voting.* New York: Harper and Row.

Matthews, Donald R., and Prothro, James W. 1966. *Negroes and the New Southern Politics.* New York: Harcourt.

Milbrath, Lester W. 1965. *Political Participation.* Chicago: Rand-McNally.

Panning, William H. 1982. "Blockmodels: From Relations to Configurations," *American Journal of Political Science,* August 1982, pp. 585–608.

Rabinowitz, George B. 1973. *Spatial Models of Electoral Choice: An Empirical Analysis.* Chapel Hill, North Carolina: Institute for Research in Social Science.

Rabinowitz, George B. 1976. "A Procedure for Ordering Pairs Consistent with the Multidimensional Unfolding Model," *Psychometrika,* September 1976, pp. 349–373.

Rusk, Jerrold G., and Weisberg, Herbert F. 1972. "Perceptions of Presidential Candidates," *Midwest Journal of Political Science,* August 1972, pp. 388–410.

Sattath, Shmuel, and Tversky, Amos. 1977. "Additive Similarity Trees," *Psychometrika,* September 1977, pp. 319–345.

Takane, Yoshio; Young, Forrest W.; and de Leeuw, Jan. 1977. "Nonmetric Individual Differences Multidimensional Scaling: An Alternating Least Squares Method with Optimal Scaling Features," *Psychometrika,* March 1977, pp. 7–67.

Weisberg, Herbert F. 1968. "Dimensional Analysis of Legislative Roll Calls." Ph.D. dissertation, University of Michigan.

Weisberg, Herbert F., and Rusk, Jerrold G. 1970. "Dimensions of Candidate Evaluation," *American Political Science Review*, December 1970, pp. 1167–85.

Weisberg, Herbert F. 1980. "A Multidimensional Conceptualization of Party Identification," *Political Behavior*, no. 1, 1980, pp. 33–60.

Wolters, Menno. 1978. "Models of Roll-Call Behavior," *Political Methodology*, no. 1, 1978, pp. 7–54.

HERBERT F. WEISBERG

Dimensionland:
An Excursion into Spaces*

Scaling analysis is based on a geometric metaphor. This workshop paper examines how our understanding of the metaphor affects our use of scaling. Instances which appear to be multidimensional are shown to be unidimensional under other scaling models. Conversely, some apparently unidimensional cases are found to be better described as multidimensional. Particular attention is given to the difference between multidimensional scaling and factor analysis. The philosophical implication of our dependence on the definition of unidimensionality is that scaling seeks only partial images of a real world that may be fundamentally unknowable.

Scaling analysis seeks the latent dimensions underlying a set of obtained observations. The variation across a set of variables is explained in terms of the different locations of these variables on hypothesized underlying dimensions. The dimensions are presumed to exist since their presence can make the variation across the variables explicable. Scaling techniques are used for two distinct purposes: description of data structure and measurement of individual behavior. The goal may be to describe the dimensionality of a set of variables—as in determining the dimensions underlying a party system. Or the intention may be to derive unidimensional indices on which individuals can be scored—as in constructing a scale of political efficacy which can be correlated with other attitudinal and behavioral measures.[1]

*This article benefits from Clyde Coombs's ideas on scaling models, from my collaboration with Richard Niemi and Jerrold Rusk on related projects, from the challenging comments of Lutz Erbring, Robert Friedrich, George Rabinowitz, and Stuart Thorson, from the suggestions by John Champlin and especially Sally Friedman for my leisure reading, and from the inspiration provided by a martyred square.

[1] The terms dimensional analysis and scaling will be used interchangeably in this paper, with factor analysis being included in this general rubric. The important general works on this subject include: Lee Anderson, Meredith Watts, and Allen Wilcox, *Legislative Roll-Call Analysis* (Evanston: Northwestern University Press, 1966); Clyde Coombs, *A Theory of Data* (New York: John Wiley and Sons, 1964); Harry Harman, *Modern Factor Analysis,* 2nd ed. (Chicago: University of Chicago Press, 1967); Duncan

Reprinted from AMERICAN JOURNAL OF POLITICAL SCIENCE, Vol. XVIII, No. 4, November 1974, pp. 743-776, Herbert F. Weisberg, Dimensionland: An Excursion into Spaces," by permission of the University of Texas Press.

But what is unidimensionality? The term is so familiar that we are easily lulled into fallacies in its usage. We assume it has a single meaning, so the dimensions produced by different scaling techniques are equivalent. Yet unless a formal proof is provided, there is no reason to believe that two scaling techniques have similar conceptions of what constitutes unidimensionality. Instead, unidimensionality may have different meanings which are appropriate in different substantive situations. As a result, a scaling technique may report that two dimensions underlie a set of data, even though the data might be considered unidimensional under some other conception of unidimensionality. Conversely, a unidimensional result may be obtained, although a two-dimensional representation would better satisfy the analyst's purposes. Thus a limited view of dimensions can restrict our success in determining dimensionality and in measuring individual positions.

A spatial analogy is intrinsic to scaling. A geometric model is used to represent certain of the relations among variables, with selected features of a geometric space being used to represent specific features of the observed data. Yet whenever we employ an analogy, our understanding of the phenomenon becomes limited by our understanding of the analogue. Spatial reasoning would not be helpful in communicating with a culture which does not employ geometric concepts. Similarly, the usefulness of dimensional analysis is limited by our own inabilities to comprehend fully the basics of geometry. Our restricted understanding of geometry limits our interpretation of the term "unidimensionality" and hinders our use of scaling.

How our limited understanding of the geometric analogue and how our limited use of the term unidimensionality restrict our ability to use scaling in studying political phenomena are but special cases of how our use of language can circumscribe our conception of the world.[2] The theme of how language limits and is limited by perceptions of the world is very general. "We learn language and learn the world *together*, ... they become elaborated and distorted together and in the same places."[3] Terms have meaning only to the

---

MacRae Jr., *Issues and Parties in Legislative Voting* (New York: Harper and Row, 1970); R. Rummel, *Applied Factor Analysis* (Evanston: Northwestern University Press, 1970); Herbert Weisberg, "Dimensional Analysis of Legislative Roll Calls," (unpublished Ph.D. dissertation, The University of Michigan, 1968). Measurement concerns are not of central importance here, but they are further discussed in Brian Ellis, *Basic Concepts of Measurement* (Cambridge: Cambridge University Press, 1966) and Warren Torgerson, *Theory and Methods of Scaling* (New York: John Wiley and Sons, 1964).

[2] See, for example, Hanna Pitkin's discussion of the themes discussed in this paragraph in *Wittgenstein and Justice* (Berkeley: University of California Press, 1972).

[3] Stanley Cavell, *Must We Mean What We Say?* (New York: Charles Scribner's Sons, 1968), p. 19.

extent to which our experiences supply meaning, so our experiential base inevitably restricts our language use. Conversely our understanding of phenomena is necessarily limited by our bounded store of concepts and terms. "The concepts we have settle for us the form of the experience we have of the world."[4] In the extreme, this may mean that "real" world phenomena seem to exist only insofar as we have developed terms with which to describe them. Thus we may be unable to recognize some phenomena as unidimensional until we recognize the full scope of the term.

When unidimensionality does not seem to suffice for a given set of data, we resort to more complicated multidimensional explanations. More generally stated, when events occur without a simple explanation, we devise complex causal mechanisms to justify their occurrence. However the apparent complexity may be due merely to the inadequacy of our concepts. Extension of our concepts may permit the ready comprehension of seemingly complex events. Simplicity always exists only with reference to a body of theory—events are never simple in themselves but only as part of a familiar framework. Yet Abraham Kaplan's "paradox of conceptualization" intrudes here: "the proper concepts are needed to formulate a good theory, but we need a good theory to arrive at the proper concepts."[5] Apparent multidimensionality may be due to an insufficiently general conception of unidimensionality, in which case much seemingly complex behavior would appear unidimensional if we revise our understanding of the term. Still our experience—with the geometry of the real world and with the common scaling approaches—makes it difficult for us to broaden sufficiently our conception of unidimensionality.

The role of spatial analogy in our comprehension of the real world is best made by reference to Edwin Abbott's classic tale of *Flatland.*[6] Flatland is a world of two dimensions whose inhabitants are triangles, squares, and the like. The women are lines, the men are shapes with angles; the greater the number of angles a person has, the higher is his class. The residents of this society cannot see outside of their plane, so all they can see are the line segments in their plane. They cannot conceptualize the existence of a third dimension since they are incapable of perceiving it. *Flatland* relates the saga of how A Square came to be the first citizen of his world to realize that a third dimension exists.

[4] Peter Winch, *The Idea of a Social Science and Its Relation to Philosophy,* ed. by R. F. Holland (New York: Humanities Press, 1965), p. 15.

[5] Abraham Kaplan, *The Conduct of Inquiry* (San Francisco: Chandler Publishing, 1964), p. 53.

[6] Edwin Abbott, *Flatland,* 6th ed. (New York: Dover Publications, 1952).

Events occur which defy understanding within Flatland's limited conception of space. For example, a sphere tries proving to the square that a third dimension exists by moving up off the Flatland plane. At first the sphere is a large circle (for all the square can see is the sphere's intersection with Flatland's plane), then a smaller circle as the sphere rises, then a dot, and finally the sphere disappears. Yet the square cannot comprehend this event since it is beyond accepted theories, and he puts it down as magic.

Another incident is the square's magical mystery tour to Lineland. Lineland is a world of one dimension whose inhabitants are line segments arrayed along the dimension. These line segments have length but no width, have fixed positions on the line, cannot move outside the line, and cannot understand how an outsider—the square—can "see" their order on the line. The square assumes his vision of Lineland is a bad dream, rather than realizing that careful examination of the difference between Lineland and Flatland would suggest the existence and nature of a three-dimensional world.

Finally the sphere bumps the square off the Flatland plane so the square can look down and see the structure of Flatland. He can see the insides of objects for the first time, since on the Flatland plane only object edges are visible. Suddenly he realizes that there is a third dimension and even a fourth (which the sphere regards as so inconceivable that he departs angrily when the square presses the point). Unfortunately for the square the other Flatland residents do not believe his new insight into the nature of the world, and the square suffers the imprisonment with which societies protect themselves from original thinkers.

Sphereland, a sequel to *Flatland,* is authored by the square's grandson—A Hexagon.[7] Flatland has come to realize that there are three dimensions, though the implications are poorly understood. It evokes the state of science in Europe immediately following Columbus's discovery of the New World but prior to complete revision of scientific theories to account for the new findings. *Sphereland* relates a series of mysterious events—mysterious until the hexagon develops the proper geometric understanding. For example, triangles are measured with new more accurate calibrating devices and it is found that their angles sum to more than 180°. This absurd event becomes explicable only when it is realized that Flatland's plane is actually curved.

These fables are intended to help readers understand the nature of spaces of more than three dimensions. We can comprehend such spaces only by analogy, and reading about Flatland and Lineland can sharpen our powers of

[7] Dionys Burger, *Sphereland* (New York: Thomas Crowell, 1965), tr. Cornelie Rheinboldt.

analogy.[8] But *Flatland* also serves to emphasize how our inability to compre-hend fully the basics of geometry limits our understanding of scaling. Like the square, we must be lifted out of our Flatland if we are to perceive the variety of dimensional forms. And we must extend our concepts to fit the complex world with a simple theory, rather than devising ad hoc explanations of why behavior does not always satisfy preconceived notions of unidimen-sionality.

The purpose of this paper is to explore the nature of unidimensionality. It rests on the assumption that most people are limited in their perceptions of dimensions and do not sufficiently question the use of the term. Six case studies will illustrate the variety of possible uses of the unidimensionality concept. In each instance what is multidimensional in one sense may be unidimensional in another, so our understanding of the world is directly affected by our interpretation of unidimensionality. What follows might thus be viewed as a series of mind-expanding games designed to explore the proper limits of the concept of unidimensionality.

Circleland: An Empty World without Ends

A circle is a two-dimensional geometric shape. What could be more obvious—or less true? A circle is only a straight line whose two ends have been joined together. If only the circumference of the circle is considered (and not its interior), then the circle is certainly unidimensional. Most scaling studies, however, unquestioningly treat circular solutions as two-dimensional rather than realizing that they are essentially unidimensional.

When we obtain two-dimensional solutions, we generally accept the fact that there are two dimensions and we go on to look at the ordering of points on them to help name the dimensions. Too often we do not even bother to plot the points in order to examine their shape. The argument is that some multidimensional solutions have shapes that *can* be interpreted as uni-dimensional. If, for example, the solution is exactly circular, then there is a distinct sense in which all that matters is the relative position of the points along their circle rather than their projections on artificial axes. Two dimen-sions would be required if some points were within the circle, but if all the

[8] For example, the residents of Lineland cannot see each other's interiors, while the square looking down on Lineland can see their middle points. The residents of Flatland cannot see each other's interiors, but when the square is lifted above Flatland he can see into their insides. The thought-provoking conclusion—which *Flatland* wisely leaves unstated—is that a four-dimensional creature could see our intestines!

FIGURE 1
Hoskin and Swanson's Multidimensional Scaling of the Colombian Party System*

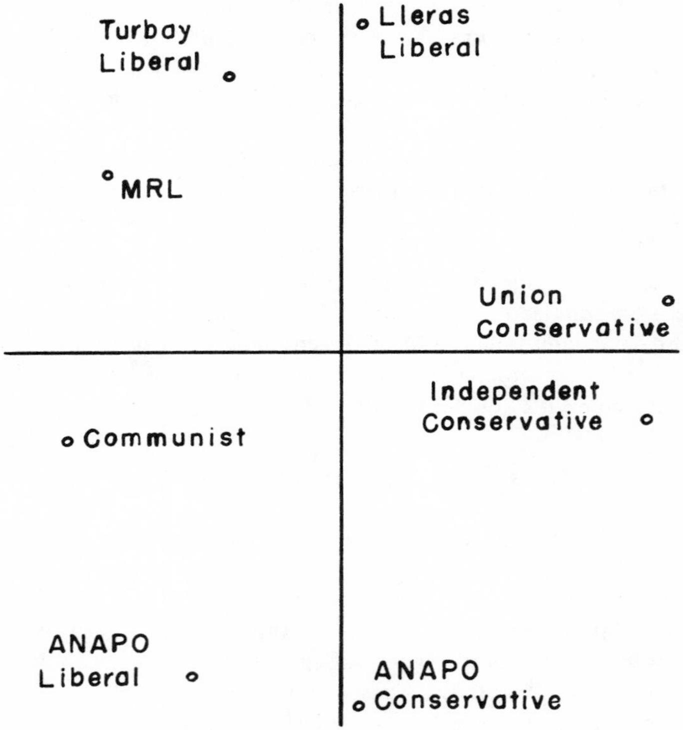

Turbay
Liberal   o

o Lleras
   Liberal

°MRL

Union   o
Conservative

Independent
Conservative   o

o Communist

ANAPO
Liberal   o

ANAPO
o Conservative

*From Gary Hoskin and Gerald Swanson, "Inter-Party Competition in Colombia," *American Journal of Political Science,* 17 (May 1973), 333.

points fall along the circle then each point can be described in terms of a single parameter—the angle formed by the line connecting it with the origin and the 0° line.[9]

Circular shapes may be expected for alliance structures and for vote coalitions where extremists of the left and right coalesce for particular purposes.[10] An example is provided by the Hoskin and Swanson study of the

[9] If this is viewed in terms of polar coordinates, the radius is constant since all points are along the circumference of the circle, and the single varying parameter is the angle. A circular representation may be employed when the radius values are virtually equal.

[10] See also the discussion of the similarity of theories of the radical right and left in Ole Holsti, "The Study of International Politics Makes Strange Bedfellows," *American Political Science Review,* 68 (March 1974), 217–242.

FIGURE 2
Circular Scale of Colombian Party System

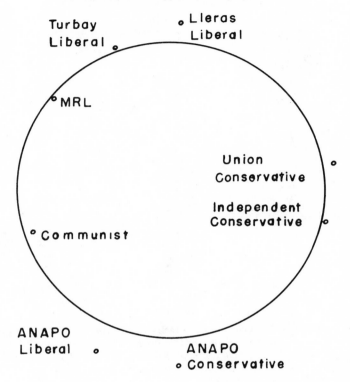

Colombian party system.[11] They asked leaders of Colombian political parties to rank order their preference for the several parties. Figure 1 reproduces their multidimensional scaling solution. They interpret this solution as involving a left-right dimension (the horizontal axis) and a government support-opposition dimension (the vertical dimension). However, note that there is a dependency between the dimensions such that no party is accorded a centrist position on both dimensions. Thus there is a sense in which this solution is essentially unidimensional, with party leaders ordering other parties by the distances from their own party along the circumference of the circle shown in Figure 2. The circle provides a very good fit to the solution.[12] Treating the

[11] Gary Hoskin and Gerald Swanson, "Inter-Party Competition in Colombia," *American Journal of Political Science,* 17 (May 1973), 316–350.

[12] A scaling algorithm could be developed to place parties closer together along the

FIGURE 3
Circular Scale of Swedish Party Voting in 1964 Riksdag*

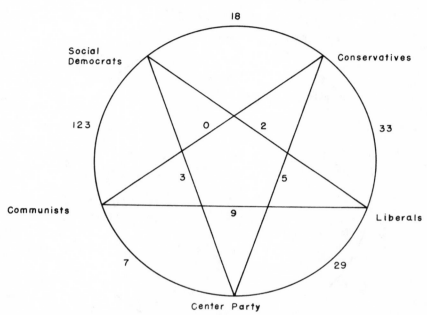

*The figures show the number of times each pair of parties voted together against the other three parties. The votes in the middle of the star between nonadjacent parties represent deviations from the circular scale. The data are from Nils Stjernquist and Bo Bjurulf, "Party Cohesion and Party Cooperation in the Swedish Parliament in 1964 and 1966," *Scandinavian Political Studies*, 5 (1970), Table 21, p. 151.

centrist Lleras Liberal and ANAPO Conservative parties as similar to one another on a left-right dimension would be to ignore their placement on opposite sides of the circle.

A circular pattern also fits voting coalitions in the Swedish Riksdag. Party cohesion is not perfect in the Riksdag, but it is so high that the parties can be considered the basic actors. The conventional unidimensional party order from left to right is: Communists, Social Democrats, Center party, Liberals, and Conservatives. However the best fitting dimensional pattern for their voting in 1964 is a circle with the Social Democrats moved between the

circle the more often they vote together, but this is more complex than it may appear, so adjacent parties have been equally spaced in Figure 2.

FIGURE 4
Hypothetical Curved Spatial Solution

Communists and Conservatives (see Figure 3).[13] Only on 19 of the 366 roll calls did nonadjacent parties in Figure 3 vote together, while 41 of the 366 roll calls would not fit if the Social Democrats and Communists were reversed. The ordering of the Social Democrats and Communists does not fit with the usual view of Swedish politics because the Social Democrats voted

[13] Data are from Nils Stjernquist and Bo Bjurulf, "Party Cohesion and Party Coopera-tion in the Swedish Parliament in 1964 and 1966," *Scandinavian Political Studies*, 5

more often with only the Conservatives than with only the Center party. And that is essentially a circular phenomenon—the parties of the left and the right sometimes vote together. The parties of the left and right are similar, at least in uniting against the center. A circular representation of this voting is appropriate to emphasize the closeness of the Social Democrats and Conservatives. Yet the data can be seen as unidimensional—but with the left and right extremes drawn together.[14]

When a computer program produces a circular solution, it is worth considering the unidimensional conceptualization of the circle. Even a curved solution should be examined as unidimensional. Figure 4 shows a hypothetical spatial solution. It is nothing more than a straight line that has been curved. Should this be interpreted as two-dimensional or unidimensional? Should the slight second dimension be given a substantive interpretation, or should we just examine the relations among the points themselves along the curved line? A solution of this shape should be considered suspect since the curvature might result from some distortion by the scaling technique rather than from the observed behavior. The points bear a unidimensional relationship to one another, and that essential unidimensionality should not be overlooked.[15]

The circular and curved cases directly raise the question of what is meant by a dimension. Perhaps the most basic definition would be to view a dimension as a one-parameter system where there are order relations on the parameter. Such a definition avoids the restriction of linearity. Yet it imposes

---

(1970), Table 21, p. 151. Similar results have been obtained for their 1966 data and from later data collected by Aage Clausen and Soren Holmquist.

[14] Another possible representation of the Swedish data would be as a unidimensional proximity scale, as described in the next section. A vote would fit that scale if only adjacent parties voted for it. But what if the three left parties and the right party vote for a bill while the remaining party votes against it? That would violate the proximity scale, since nonadjacent parties are voting together in support of a motion. A useful distinction here involves whether the agreement of nonadjacent parties is in opposition to proposals of the center (where the left and right vote together for opposite reasons) or in support of a common proposal to alter the status quo (as when the radical left and the conservative right unite to pass a bill providing for local control rather than the federal programs which the old left favors). The Swedish data are not available in a form to check whether the coalitions of left and right against the center are in opposition or in agreement to alter the status quo.

[15] Calculate the interpoint distances in Figure 4 using the Euclidean distance formula for two-dimensional space and then using the distances between the points along the curvature. Those two sets of distance figures will be monotone with one another. The unidimensional curvature representation loses no ordinal distance information that was present in a Euclidean two-space solution.

such few restrictions that it might allow a set of points to be considered unidimensional if they were in the shape of a numeral "2," "3," "5," "6," or even "8," where the one parameter would be how far from the beginning of drawing the numeral is each specific point. Are such cases "unidimensional?" How far is it *useful* to push our geometric conception of a dimension? For some purposes even these numerals might be regarded as unidimensional, though for most purposes an explanation of the shape would be required which would entail a two-dimensional view.

This discussion of circular dimensions is not intended to demonstrate that the Colombian or Swedish cases are circular. Substantive experts may or may not accept the circular representation. The purpose at present is to indicate that there is a reasonable model which is rarely used but which can be appropriate. It would be of interest to know whether the model fits these two polities, but it suffices to suggest the possible relevance. The shape cannot be tested unless the structure is first hypothesized as done there. Hopefully the hypothesis alone produces some insights which are substantively interesting.

Proximityland: A Conflictual World without Comparisons

Guttman scaling, one of the first scaling techniques, tests a cumulative view of the world: attitudes are unidimensional only if everyone willing to accept one statement is willing to accept all easier statements. An alternative view of a dimension is the proximity notion: attitudes are unidimensional if everyone is acceptant only of adjacent statements. For example, in the cumulative case, a legislator would be willing to support an appropriation value up to a certain amount; he might support any amount up to $3 billion while opposing any greater expenditure. In the proximity case the legislator might instead feel the program would be worthwhile only if it received reasonable funding (say $2–4 billion), but would oppose appropriations of less as worthless and would oppose appropriations of more as wasteful; only adjacent amounts within the reasonable range would be supported. The order imposed by adjacencies is as well defined as the order of cumulation.[16]

Alker has suggested that the proximity notion is appropriate for voter approval of political candidates.[17] Table 1 shows his hypothetical scale for

[16] The differences between the two models are presented in Herbert Weisberg, "Scaling Models for Legislative Roll-Call Analysis," *American Political Science Review,* 66 (December 1972), 1306–1315.

[17] Hayward Alker, Jr., "Statistics and Politics," in Seymour Martin Lipset, ed., *Politics and the Social Sciences* (New York: Oxford University Press, 1969), Table 2, p. 276.

TABLE 1

A Hypothetical Proximity Scale of 1964 Presidential Contenders*

State					Candidate					
	Fulbright	Kennedy	Rockefeller	Romney	Humphrey	Johnson	Jackson	Nixon	Reagan	Goldwater
Massachusetts	Yes	Yes	Yes	Yes	Yes	No	No	No	No	No
New York	No	Yes	Yes	Yes	Yes	Yes	No	No	No	No
Michigan	No	No	Yes	Yes	Yes	Yes	Yes	No	No	No
California	No	No	No	Yes	Yes	Yes	Yes	Yes	No	No
Arizona	No	No	No	No	Yes	Yes	Yes	Yes	Yes	No
Mississippi	No	No	No	No	No	Yes	Yes	Yes	Yes	Yes

*Source: Hayward Alker, Jr., "Statistics and Politics," in Seymour Martin Lipset, ed., *Politics and the Social Sciences* (New York: Oxford University Press, 1969), Table 2, p. 276.

1964 presidential contenders. Each voter (here residents of particular states) is asked to indicate the five candidates he or she likes most, and the perfect proximity scale means that all voters choose only adjacent candidates. If the left-right candidate order was not known, one would permute the candidates until each person chooses only adjacent candidates. The candidates are thereby ordered from left to right. The restriction to naming five candidates is not essential to the model; if the candidate space is unidimensional then the voters should like only adjacent candidates regardless of the number each names. The important point is that this is not a cumulative process: to be a liberal does not mean you must like all the candidates more conservative than you. A person can accept one candidate without accepting all more conservative (or liberal) candidates.

Multiparty coalitions can also be expected to follow proximity notions. Weisberg has shown that the cabinets of the French Fourth Republic form a proximity scale in that 17 of the 19 cabinets include only parties which are adjacent on a left-right dimension.[18] One of the two exceptions involves the absence of the MRP from the Mendes-France government, an unusual case in which Mendes took the exceptional step of negotiating with individuals rather than with the parties in forming his cabinet but the MRP party blocked his naming two MRP members to his cabinet.

When would proximity scales be found? The argument is that proximity scales will occur when two conditions are met simultaneously.[19] There must be some variance in individual preferences, so that not everyone most prefers a maximum (or a minimum) of the dimension. Additionally, the individuals must only indicate which alternatives they consider acceptable, rather than indicating which element of a pair comparison they prefer; for example the radical may prefer a moderate change to the status quo but still not consider the moderate change sufficiently useful to support it. Thus proximity scales may be expected where the *direction* of social change is at issue and where radicals oppose liberal reforms which ameliorate the situation without restructuring society. If either of these conditions is not met, Guttman scales (or their generalizations for nondichotomous and/or multidimensional data) will be more likely.

[18] Herbert Weisberg, "L'etude comparative des scrutins legislatifs," *Revue Francaise de Sociologie,* 12 (April–June 1971), 151–176. See also Robert Axelrod, *Conflict of Interest* (Chicago: Markham, 1970) and William Riker and Peter Ordeshook, *An Introduction to Positive Political Theory* (Englewood Cliffs, N.J.: Prentice-Hall, 1973), chapter 7.

[19] For a proof of these results see Weisberg, "L'etude comparative des scrutins legislatifs."

The considerable success of Guttman scaling cannot be lightly dismissed. The suggestion here is only that there exists a class of situations which can be treated as unidimensional even if Guttman scaling finds no cumulation. Yet those models are related. For a proximity scale, each person accepts adjacent alternatives, but that is also true of the circular and Guttman scales. The circular scale is the most general, the proximity next, and the Guttman scale is the most restrictive. For example, with dichotomous data there are 16 possible response patterns with four variables, of which 14 fit the circular model, 11 the proximity scale, and only 5 satisfy a Guttman scale. Thus we should always expect the circular and proximity scales to fit data better (or at least no worse) than the Guttman model. This means that the restrictive Guttman model would be employed unless the other models do a significantly superior job in fitting the data. Of course, the choice of model can be motivated by the nature of the underlying substantive process regardless of empirical fit, as in using a circular representation whenever the extremes unite in favor of a proposal that the center opposes.

Much depends on the purpose of the scaling endeavor. If one simply wishes to ascertain the nature of the substantive process, it is important to employ the widest possible definition of unidimensionality. There is no gain in describing a process as two-dimensional if it is unidimensional under a broader conception. Often, however, one scales to construct analytic measures, as when scaling legislative votes to obtain behavioral indices which can be correlated with constituency attitudes or characteristics. One then might want to obtain several measures of behavior even under a unidimensional process. For example, one might seek to measure extremeness as well as ideological position. Thus the choice of what is a unidimensional representation may depend on the purpose of the analysis.

Antiland: An Extremist World with Negative Peaks

Scaling models can have opposites, models which are their duals but with directions reversed. New scaling models arise when we consider these mirror image duals of the conventional models. This provides a series of negative models with distinctive substantive implications.

Scaling models for preference data assume that everyone has a point of *maximum* preference, known as an "ideal point." The person would rank order alternatives in terms of preferences, which means the person would like alternatives more the closer they are (or the closer the person thinks they are) to his or her ideal. The preference function is then single-peaked, as are the curves in Figure 5. For each person the greatest utility is being given by one

FIGURE 5
Single-Peaked Preference Functions

Utility

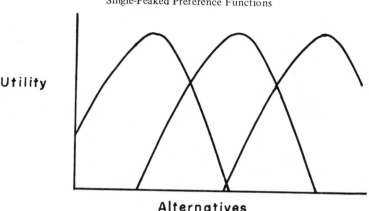

Alternatives

alternative and less utility is obtained as alternatives are further from the most preferred alternative. Single-peaked preferences constitute a common definition of unidimensionality.[20]

The mirror image concept is the anti-ideal. Each person has a point of minimum preference, an anti-ideal or a negative ideal point. The person intensely dislikes that alternative and dislikes other alternatives more the closer they are to that alternative. Unidimensional preference functions in this model are single-caved rather than single-peaked.[21]

This negative ideal model would apply to a situation where people are dissatisfied with moderate solutions and believe that sharp change is vital regardless of its direction. People dissatisfied with the conduct of a limited war may have a negative ideal at the status quo and have as their first choices either immediate withdrawal from the war or military victory (Figure 6).[22]

[20] Clyde Coombs, *A Theory of Data* (New York: John Wiley and Sons, 1964), chapters 5 and 9.

[21] The anti-ideal has been operationalized in Carroll and Chang's PREF-MAP computer program. See J. Douglas Carroll and Jah-Hie Chang, "Relating Preference Data to Multidimensional Scaling Solutions via a Generalization of Coombs' Unfolding Model," (Bell Telephone Laboratories, Murray Hill, N.J., 1967).

[22] A more realistic model for explaining preferences with regard to the Viet Nam war would be two-dimensional, with one direction dimension (ranging from withdrawal to victory) and one speed dimension (ranging from seeking an immediate solution to approval of gradual solutions). Many of the public favored a fast solution regardless of its direction, weighting the speed dimension much more heavily than the direction dimen-

FIGURE 6

Hypothetical Single-Caved Preference Functions on a Viet Nam War Involvement Scale

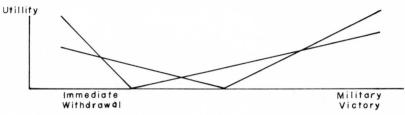

When the populace so despairs of moderate solutions that it demands change regardless of its direction, the negative ideal model is appropriate. The preference functions of Figure 6 would require multiple dimensions for scaling if normal scaling models were employed, but a single dimension would suffice for the negative ideal model. The fallacy would be in not using a unidimensional negative model when it is appropriate.

Coombs's unfolding analysis is the technique used for scaling preference orders under single-peakedness. If preferences are single-peaked, then no one would prefer both immediate withdrawal and military victory over intermediate solutions to a foreign war. To generalize, with unidimensional preferences the middle points on the dimension would never be selected as a person's last-place choice. Only the two end items of the dimension would be picked as last-place choices, as should be apparent from Figure 5. Inspection of Figure 6 suggests the corresponding conditions for the negative ideal model. If preferences are single-caved, no one would prefer both immediate withdrawal and military victory *less* than intermediate solutions. That is, with unidimensional preferences the middle points would never be selected as a person's first-place choice. Only the two end items of the dimension would be picked as first-place choices.[23] This is the reverse of the statement for

---

sion. Yet the negative ideal model does capture part of reality, since some citizens probably did have preference functions like those of Figure 6. To test the models one would have to ask people's preferences over a set of alternatives with time held constant, such as asking people if they prefer noninvolvement, limited involvement, or full involvement.

Figure 6 shows preferences over a limited set of alternatives in the sense that people's preferences might not continue to be more favorable as yet more extreme alternatives are raised. Even the hawks might give lower utility to the more extreme possibility of military victory through use of nuclear weapons. This suggests that the preference functions can only be considered over the range of realistic alternatives. The dimension may have to be bounded to apply the negative model.

[23] Consequently the negative model should be investigated whenever only two alternatives receive the bulk of first-place choices.

single-peaked preferences, and similar reversals occur throughout the conditions for unidimensionality under single-cavedness. As a result, to scale under the negative ideal model one need only apply conventional unfolding analysis to the reverse of each person's preference order. Negative models require no new scaling techniques; they require only stepping away from one's data to realize the data are the mirror image of conventional data.

We use scaling to describe and understand a complex political reality. Geometric models may be useful in this endeavor, but no single model should be expected to capture all of that reality. Multiple models may be appropriate, each describing part of reality. Each model draws attention to some aspect of the data: a circular model where extremists of the left and right behave similarly, a proximity model where extremists oppose desirable solutions that are too moderate, a negative model where people are dissatisfied with centrist solutions. Each model goes beyond conventional left-right notions without requiring us to posit the existence of multiple dimensions. Fairly complex attitudinal data can be ideologically unidimensional if our conception of unidimensionality is sufficiently general. Whether any particular example really fits these models is not important here, so long as these examples begin to suggest why such unconventional models require consideration.

Timeland: An Unseen World of Traces

The previous sections emphasized that sets of data which appear to be multidimensional can be unidimensional given the proper scaling model. The remaining sections switch to the opposite point: what seems unidimensional may sometimes be better understood as multidimensional.

One of the simplest interpretations of unidimensionality is a natural order. Objects can often be readily ordered but whether attitudes towards those objects are based on that ordering is an empirical question. Stimuli may be unidimensional with respect to some property, but preferences toward them need not be based on that dimension. For example, chocolates can be arrayed in terms of their sweetness, but preferences for chocolates may not be based on that natural order since many people prefer both sweet chocolate and bitter-sweet to the melange created by blending the two together. Natural orders may be irrelevant to preference behavior.

Time is one of the most important natural orders. Time is usually ignored in scaling, and we act as if all the observations were collected simultaneously even when that is untrue. But instead of viewing time as an unimportant complication, we can view time itself as the dimension. Time provides the backdrop against which objects develop. If time is viewed as a dimension, development over time can be scaled. Yet the argument above is that development need not be unidimensional, even if time is the relevant natural order.

Developmental processes can be described by a variety of models at different levels of complexity. The simplest notion is that development is a series of stages which follow in a predictable manner. Countries may pass through certain stages of economic development in an ever upward direction. The stage model breaks down for developmental processes in which acquisition of a new trait does not require deletion of all previous traits. Children may acquire new abilities in a specific order with complex skills not being acquired until prerequisite ones are in place, but acquisition of a new ability does not entail deletion of earlier traits.[24] A more complex model would permit ordered acquisition with deletion. A country moving up to a certain cultural level may retain most of its preceding cultural forms while deleting its most primitive cultural attributes. The deletion order may differ from the acquisition order, with an early trait lasting longer than some later acquired trait.[25]

Leik and Matthews have termed ordered acquisition with deletion a "developmental scale."[26] They suggest an example in terms of leisure time

[24] Snow has applied such a cumulative development model to political development in Latin America, with freedom of political organization for autonomous groups being the easiest trait to acquire and a modern bureaucracy the most difficult trait. See Peter Snow, "A Scalogram Analysis of Political Development," *American Behavioral Scientist*, 9 (March 1966), 33–36.

[25] A time model could actually be circular in the case of cyclical phenomena. For example, if one were to scale over time several indicators of interest in presidential politics (public interest as measured in surveys, newspaper column inches devoted to the campaign, and so on), interest would likely rise as the election approaches, peak at election day, fall sharply thereafter, and gradually increase as the next election approaches. If time were measured since the last presidential election, interest would fit a circular dimension. Such a cyclical development pattern would be violated if interest in presidential politics had a short-term surge around the congressional off-year elections.

Coombs and Smith present an even more general developmental model in which acquisition and deletion processes are independent. The traits are acquired in a fixed order and they are deleted in a fixed order, but the two processes are separate. Thus after acquiring traits A and B, some individuals may delete A to be left with trait B while others would acquire C to have traits A, B, and C. See Clyde Coombs and J. Keith Smith, "On the Detection of Structure in Attitudes and Developmental Processes," (Michigan Mathematical Psychology Program, 1972). The two-dimensional conjunctive scaling technique they suggest for this model is described in Clyde Coombs, *A Theory of Data*, chapter 12.

[26] Robert Leik and Merlyn Matthews, "A Scale for Developmental Processes," *American Sociological Review*, 33 (February 1968), 62–75.

TABLE 2

Hypothetical Scale of a Person's Leisure Time Activities

Activity	1–5	6–10	11–15	16–20	21–25	26–30	31–35	36–40	41–45	46–50	51–65	66–80
								Age				
Tricycle	Yes	No	No	No	No	No	No	No	No	No	No	No
Marbles	Yes	Yes	No	No	No	No	No	No	No	No	No	No
Bicycle	No	Yes	Yes	Yes	Yes	Yes	Yes	No	No	No	No	No
Bridge	No	No	No	No	Yes	Yes	Yes	Yes	Yes	Yes	Yes	Yes
Bowling	No	No	Yes	Yes	Yes	Yes	No	No	No	No	No	No
Squash	No	No	No	No	No	No	Yes	Yes	Yes	Yes	No	No
Knitting	No	No	No	No	No	No	No	Yes	No	No	No	No
Cribbage	No	No	No	No	No	No	No	No	No	No	No	Yes

TABLE 3

Developmental Scale of Votes at 1852 Democratic National Convention*

| Candidate | Ballot | | | | | | | | | | | |
	1	5	10	15	20	25	30	35	40	45	48	49
Cass	Yes	Yes	Yes	Yes	Yes	Yes	Yes	Yes	Yes	Yes	Yes	No
Douglas	No	Yes	Yes	Yes	Yes	Yes	Yes	Yes	Yes	Yes	Yes	No
Buchanan	Yes	Yes	Yes	Yes	Yes	Yes	Yes	Yes	No	No	No	No
Marcy	No	No	No	No	No	No	No	Yes	Yes	Yes	Yes	No
Pierce	No	No	No	No	No	No	No	No	Yes	Yes	Yes	Yes

*Yes indicates at least 29 of the 288 votes; No indicates 28 or less. Based on Richard Bain and Judith Parris, *Convention Decisions and Voting Records,* 2nd ed., (Washington, D.C.: The Brookings Institution, 1973), Appendix C.

activities. People adopt given leisure activities at certain times of their lives, continue them for a period, and eventually may drop them. Some activities may be continued throughout one's life, while others tend to be confined to a particular age period (youth, middle age, or old age). Table 2 shows a hypothetical person's developmental scale of leisure activities. The developmental scale algorithm begins with the order of time points known. Each trait is then checked to determine if it is possessed only during adjacent time points. The developmental pattern is violated if the trait is acquired, deleted, and then reacquired.[27]

Table 3 applies this logic to presidential nomination ballots at the 1852 Democratic national convention.[28] The candidates gained and lost strength along a time dimension. Cass and Douglas were strong throughout the balloting, Buchanan faded early, Marcy started late but lost, and another late starter won—Franklin Pierce won the nomination virtually unanimously on the 49th ballot even though he was still under 10% of the votes on the 35th ballot. Never did a candidate fall out of competition and then return, the pattern which would violate a developmental model.[29]

[27] The developmental scale is a proximity scale (or a Guttman scale if deletion does not occur) in which the order of alternatives is known in advance to be the time order. Thus the developmental scale is very restrictive since the order of alternatives is fixed rather than being chosen to maximize fit with the data.

[28] Data are from Richard Bain and Judith Parris, *Convention Decisions and Voting Records,* 2nd ed., (Washington, D.C.: The Brookings Institution, 1973), Appendix C.

[29] The use of a 10% cutoff is an arbitrary device to permit the developmental scale to be displayed in the proximity scale mode. An alternative procedure would be to plot for each candidate the number of votes obtained (on the ordinate) against the ballot number

Yet this unidimensional result is not a necessary outcome. A vivid contrast is presented by the 1924 Democratic nomination. John W. Davis began with only 31 of the 1098 votes, peaked at 129.5 on the 23rd and 24th ballots, fell to a low of 40.5 votes on the 58th ballot, and then went back over the 10% mark on the 95th ballot and won the nomination on the 103rd. Development need not follow a linear pattern. Indeed the most interesting cases to study might well be those like the 1924 nomination where development was not unidimensional.

In scaling developmental processes, our interest is in whether there is an orderliness to the development. We may not find regularized stages of development; indeed we may find that development goes back and forth without advancement. We assume that time is the dimension against which development occurs, but the developmental scaling fails if that assumption is in error.[30]

Natural orders, such as time, can sometimes form the basis for dimensions. Temporal evolution of attitudes can occur, such as in the argument that people become more conservative as they age.[31] Yet preferences and behavior may not always be based on a preconceived natural order, and even development need not be monotone with time. The existence of a natural order does not suffice to guarantee that a unidimensional perspective is appropriate.

Cumulativeland: A Unidimensional World without Single-peakedness

To what extent do different scaling models employ compatible notions of unidimensionality? Niemi and Weisberg have shown that two of the most

---

(on the abscissa). A developmental model would suggest single-peaked shapes for these plots, as in Figure 5, whereas deviation from developmental patterns would yield multipeaked curves. The actual vote totals for the 1852 convention data are much more bumpy than suggested by Table 3. For example, Cass started with 116 votes, slipped to 33 by the 30th ballot, but then went all the way up to 131 votes on the 35th ballot.

[30] Time processes can also be generalized by defining the abstract characteristics of time sets as in Thomas Windeknecht, *General Dynamic Processes* (New York: Academic Press, 1971), pp. 13–16. Monetary values would qualify as a time set in that they are nonnegative real numbers with addition of zero not changing their values, so similar procedures could be used to test whether preferences toward spending various amounts of money on government programs are consistent with the money dimension.

[31] See the discussion of time-related attitude change in M. Kent Jennings and Richard Niemi, "Continuity and Change in Political Orientations," paper delivered at 1973 American Political Science Association meetings, New Orleans.

common meanings are in conflict—and by implication that different techniques may yield very different types of dimensions.[32]

The first meaning they consider is single-peakedness. In attitude theory a prime interpretation of unidimensionality involves everyone having single-peaked preferences over a common dimension as in Figure 5. Single-peakedness plays an important role in formal theory. Black, for example, shows that the paradox of voting cannot occur if all individuals have single-peaked preferences.[33] Thus social choice is rational in a unidimensional culture. Clyde Coombs developed "unfolding analysis" to test preference order data for single-peakedness.[34] However preference orders are often not available, so we would like to be able to test other types of data for single-peakedness.

A second meaning of unidimensionality is that of cumulation. Cumulation occurs if people accept a proposal only if they accept all weaker proposals. Guttman scaling ascertains the fit with unidimensional cumulation. Guttman scales are spoken of as unidimensional, and Guttman scaling is thus a procedure for testing unidimensionality of dichotomous data. Indeed it may be the most common test for unidimensionality in attitude research.

The question is whether these two meanings of unidimensionality are equivalent. If single-peakedness connotes unidimensionality and if a Guttman scale is unidimensional, can we use Guttman scaling to test for single-peakedness? Niemi and Weisberg provide a counter-example to demonstrate that such an identity is fallacious. Figure 7 shows their example. The acceptances fit a cumulative Guttman scale perfectly, assuming that each person will accept items only if they provide the indicated minimum of utility. However not all preferences are single-peaked. The three preference functions have been devised so that single-peakedness will not hold for all individuals regardless of any reordering of the alternatives along the horizontal axis. Thus Guttman scales do not guarantee single-peakedness.[35]

[32] Richard Niemi and Herbert Weisberg, "Single-Peakedness and Guttman Scales: Concept and Measurement," *Public Choice,* forthcoming.

[33] Duncan Black, *The Theory of Committees and Elections* (Cambridge: Cambridge University Press, 1958).

[34] Clyde Coombs, *A Theory of Data,* chapter 5.

[35] A complete proof also requires demonstration that Guttman scales do not imply single-peakedness when individual responses are based on choosing which of a pair of alternatives the person prefers more. The proof is as simple as that given here, but the reader is referred to Niemi and Weisberg, "Single-Peakedness and Guttman Scales" for the counter-example. They also push the argument further to demonstrate that a person's Guttman scale score is not indicative of the person's ideal preference point on the dimension. Note that it has only been shown that Guttman scalability does not imply single-peakedness; under appropriate conditions, single-peakedness may still imply Guttman scalability.

FIGURE 7
Preference Functions over a Single Dimension*

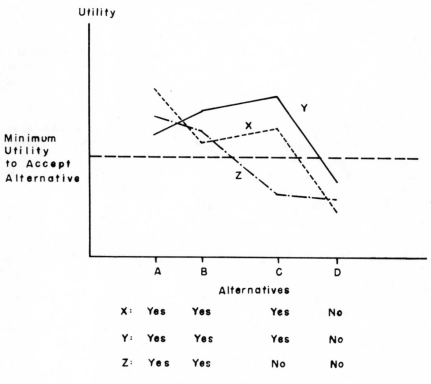

X: | Yes | Yes | Yes | No

X: Yes Yes Yes No

Y: Yes Yes Yes No

Z: Yes Yes No No

Response Patterns

*Taken from Richard Niemi and Herbert Weisberg, "Single-Peakedness and Guttman Scales: Concept and Measurement," *Public Choice,* forthcoming.

It would be folly to interpret this case as showing that some other scaling technique (such as factor analysis or multidimensional scaling) should be used in preference to Guttman scaling. The problem is in the type of data available: single-peakedness can be tested only with preference order data, however difficult they are to obtain.[36] Only unfolding analysis treats "single-peakedness"; other scaling techniques just test whether the data conform to a single-parameter ("unidimensional") model.

[36] The difficulty found in Figure 7 might not occur if the data were multicategory rather than dichotomous, but only complete preference order data suffices to guarantee the detection of multipeaked preferences.

Factorland: A Mechanized World of Extra Dimensions

Some scaling techniques are usually considered in a complex multi-dimensional context. To understand them it is necessary to determine what they treat as unidimensional, so that the choice between alternative procedures can be based on which notion of a dimension is most appropriate. Nonmetric multidimensional scaling and factor analysis are two of the most important multidimensional techniques, but their understandings of unidimensionality are quite disparate.

Nonmetric multidimensional scaling, as developed by Shepard and Kruskal, seeks to obtain a spatial representation of data such that the more similar are a pair of stimuli (such as, the higher is their correlation), the closer together are their points in the space.[37] That is, the interpoint distances are monotone with the corresponding data values. A single dimension is found if objects can be uniquely ordered with the most different at opposite ends and with smaller distances representing smaller differences. The dimension orders the objects along a continuum according to how different they are from one another. More than one dimension is obtained if the distance relations between points cannot be satisfactorily accommodated with a single dimension.

The principal component factor analysis model instead represents correlations by the cosines of the angles between vectors.[38] For example, a correlation of zero would be displayed by $90°$ separation between the lines connecting the variables' points with the origin. A single dimension is found if variables covary perfectly, which is to say if the variables are identical to one another except for linear transformations. The dimension shows the extent to which the variables are saturated with the same common element. Variables at opposite ends of a dimension are opposites of one another.[39] Table 4 summarizes some of the differences in the two scaling models.

[37] See J. Kruskal, "Multidimensional Scaling by Optimizing Goodness of Fit to a Nonmetric Hypothesis," *Psychometrika,* 29 (March 1964), 1–27. The essential concepts are similar to those of smallest space analysis as developed by Guttman and Lingoes; see Louis Guttman, "A General Nonmetric Technique for Finding the Smallest Coordinate Space for a Configuration of Points," *Psychometrika,* 33 (December 1968), 173–192.

[38] The component model of factor analysis is considered throughout this section rather than the common factor model which represents correlations by scalar products (cosines multiplied by the product of the lengths of the two vectors). For a more general discussion of the differences between multidimensional scaling and factor analysis, see George B. Rabinowitz, "An Introduction to Nonmetric Multidimensional Scaling," *American Journal of Political Science,* forthcoming.

[39] Multiple dimensions would be obtained only if the variables can be partitioned into fairly separate clusters. Trivial factors based on error in the data would be excluded by Kaiser's criterion of using only factors which explain at least one unit of variance.

TABLE 4

Differences between Multidimensional Scaling and Factor Analysis

	Multidimensional Scaling	Factor Analysis
Spatial representation:	distances	cosines of angles
Unidimensionality:	unique ordering with interpoint distances monotone with data values	perfect covariation
Opposite ends of dimension:	most different stimuli	variables that are opposites
Located at same point:	no differences between the stimuli	perfect covariation of the variables
Type of dimension:	difference continuum	saturation factor

These are two different spatial representations which are appropriate in distinct situations. If the data consist of distance measures, then multidimensional scaling is clearly required. The cosine formulation of factor analysis might be essential in other instances, as in dealing with numeric attribute data. However there are some cases, such as the analysis of correlation coefficients, in which either display is possible. In some situations the two techniques will yield different results, so there must be a choice made between the two representations. Specifically the question to be addressed is how the techniques differ in the analysis of correlation statistics. There has been little systematic study of this topic, though a preliminary set of conjectures can be advanced.

A preliminary difference is that factor analysis can yield more dimensions than multidimensional scaling.[40] This is partly due to the fact that multi-

[40] Factor analysis also can yield more dimensions than Guttman scaling; see Aage Clausen, *Policy Dimensions in Congressional Roll Calls* (Unpublished Ph.D. dissertation, The University of Michigan, 1964). This is due to the choice of correlation coefficient for the factor analysis; see Herbert Weisberg, *Dimensional Analysis of Legislative Roll*

FIGURE 8

Multidimensional Scaling of Independent Sets of Variables

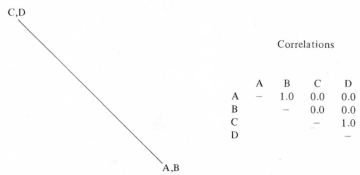

Correlations

	A	B	C	D
A	–	1.0	0.0	0.0
B		–	0.0	0.0
C			–	1.0
D				–

dimensional scaling only takes account of the ordinal features of the data while factor analysis considers their interval values. The simplest example is that distances between three objects can always be represented in one dimension using a nonmetric solution,[41] but two dimensions may be required for a metric fit.[42] Also, factor analysis can involve an extra dimension because it employs an origin to permit angle calculations, while the interpoint distances considered in multidimensional scaling do not depend on the placement of an origin. Thus Figure 8 shows that multidimensional scaling requires only a single dimension to portray the distinction between two sets of points without an origin, while factor analysis of the same data (Figure 9) requires two dimensions since the independence of the two sets of points can only be shown with respect to an origin.[43] One more dimension may be

---

Calls, chapter 5. The differences described in the text may similarly be due to analysis of the wrong type of correlation coefficient with one of the techniques, but the conclusions still show some important relationships between the techniques.

[41] Let the points with the greatest distance be at opposite ends of the dimension. Place the third point closer to the point with which it has the least distance. Necessarily then the middle distance is between the third point and the other point.

[42] For example, if A and B are two units apart, A and C are three units apart, and B and C are four units apart, then two dimensions are required for a metric fit. A nonmetric solution would simply place B and C at opposite ends of a single dimension with A positioned on that dimension closer to B than to C.

[43] In these and later figures, at least two variables are always located at the same point with perfect correlations among them. Multidimensional scaling can obtain trivial solutions when there are small numbers of variables with many equal correlations, so the perfect correlations are used here to force meaningful multidimensional scaling solutions.

FIGURE 9

Factor Analysis of Independent Sets of Variables

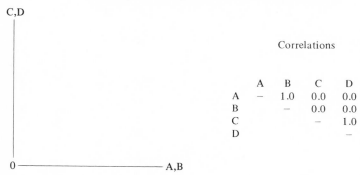

Correlations

	A	B	C	D
A	–	1.0	0.0	0.0
B		–	0.0	0.0
C			–	1.0
D				–

necessary for factor analysis since one more point—the origin—is to be scaled.

The extra dimension produced by factor analysis is essential when locating individuals in the space. If individuals were assigned factor scores on the basis of Figure 9, each individual would obtain two scores which would be independent of one another. Figure 8 is based on the same data, but there is no way of scoring individuals in multidimensional scaling to yield the same information. When individuals are to be located in the space, factor scores are more appropriate than multidimensional scaling of correlations.

But when does factor analysis yield one more dimension than multidimensional scaling, and what is the meaning of that dimension? Three cases must be distinguished. The conditions defining the cases will not be specified in precise terms here, but the differences in the relationship between factor analysis and multidimensional scaling will be emphasized.

The first case is when all variables have the same direction so that virtually all correlations are positive. Say there are perfect correlations among variables A–D and among variables E–F but only .50 correlations between the two sets. The multidimensional scaling solution for these correlations is unidimensional with the two clusters of points at opposite ends of the dimension. The factor solution of Figure 10 instead employs two dimensions. [44] The clusters are separated most on the second axis, and that axis best captures the multidimensional scaling solution. Since the variables have the same direction, they all have positive loadings on the first factor component.

---

[44] Figures 10 and 11 give unrotated principal axes. Oblique rotated solutions would place one axis through the A–D cluster and another through the E–F cluster, with the angle between the axes being the angle whose cosine is the between-set correlation.

FIGURE 10

Unrotated Factor Analysis of Positively Correlated Sets of Variables

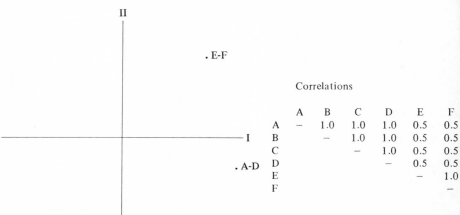

	A	B	C	D	E	F
A	−	1.0	1.0	1.0	0.5	0.5
B		−	1.0	1.0	0.5	0.5
C			−	1.0	0.5	0.5
D				−	0.5	0.5
E					−	1.0
F						−

All variables have high loadings on the most important principal axis, which is a general component that emphasizes what the variables share in common. Rather than order the variables in terms of how different they are from one another, the first component shows the extent to which each item is saturated with the common factor.

The second case is when one set of variables has the opposite direction of another set of variables, so that the between-set correlations are essentially negative. Again let there be perfect correlations among variables A–D and among variables E–F, but let the between-set correlations be −.50. The multidimensional scaling solution remains as above, but the factor analysis principal components are now those of Figure 11. The clusters are separated most on the first principal component. The opposite directions of items is captured by the first principal axis, and that is the main difference between items which would dominante a multidimensional scaling space. The second factor component is of substantially less importance.

The final case is when there are more than two sets of variables with zero or negative correlations between the various sets. Figure 12 gives an example in which there are sets of negatively correlated variables which are independent of other sets of negatively correlated variables. The two techniques yield identical solutions for this case. As many dimensions are required to capture

FIGURE 11

Unrotated Factor Analysis of Negatively Correlated Sets of Variables

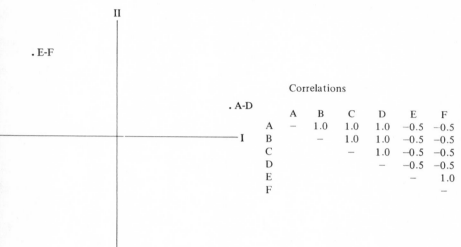

	A	B	C	D	E	F
A	–	1.0	1.0	1.0	−0.5	−0.5
B		–	1.0	1.0	−0.5	−0.5
C			–	1.0	−0.5	−0.5
D				–	−0.5	−0.5
E					–	1.0
F						–

the differences between the variables in multidimensional scaling as are necessary to give angular representations to the correlations in factor analysis. This is the case where the two techniques report the same dimensionality.

Altogether, the first factor analysis principal axis gives two types of information. It shows the item directions and, ignoring signs, it shows how saturated the variables are with a common factor. The items are not ordered in terms of their differences from one another but in terms of how much they partake of the central core. This latter piece of information is actually a part of classical statistics. When we distinguish between independent and dependent variables, we use regression to determine how much of the variance of the dependent variable can be accounted for by the independent variables. When the distinction between independent and dependent variables is inappropriate (as in analyzing the structure of a party system), factor analysis is used to determine how much of the variance of the total set of items can be accounted for by a single hypothetical construct—the first principal component—and to what extent each variable measures that common element. Thus the component model of factor analysis provides a classical solution to a statistical question, while multidimensional scaling has no analogue to this information.

How will multidimensional scaling results differ from factor analysis?

FIGURE 12

Multidimensional Scaling and Factor Analysis of Independent Bipolar Structure

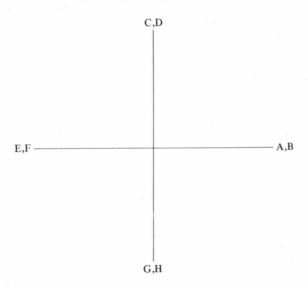

Correlations

	A	B	C	D	E	F	G	H
A	–	1.0	0.0	0.0	−1.0	−1.0	0.0	0.0
B		–	0.0	0.0	−1.0	−1.0	0.0	0.0
C			–	1.0	0.0	0.0	−1.0	−1.0
D				–	0.0	0.0	−1.0	−1.0
E					–	1.0	0.0	0.0
F						–	0.0	0.0
G							–	1.0
H								–

Comparison of Figures 10–12 suggests a complex answer. When the items have the same direction, the multidimensional scaling solution will correspond to the factor space deleting the first general component. When the items have different directions, the first principal components of the two techniques will be similar. Indeed when there are sets of items with opposite directions which are independent of other such sets, the two solutions will be similar for all dimensions. Other differences between the two techniques seem to have little impact on the solutions.[45] This statement should be regarded as a conjecture based on a set of simple data structures. These results would not hold exactly in the analysis of real data since the two techniques handle error differently, but tests of the conjecture on real data are very encouraging.

This conjecture has been tested on correlations between attitudes toward presidential contenders in the 1972 American national election survey of the University of Michigan's Center for Political Studies.[46] Feelings toward Republican and Democratic leaders were negatively correlated, and both techniques focused most attention on that distinction. Consequently there was a .998 correlation between the first principal axes obtained by multidimensional scaling and factor analysis.[47] To test the conjecture further, scores given to some candidates were reversed so that a 100° thermometer score would always mean a liberal response.[48] That is, variables with negative loadings on the first factor of the original analysis were reversed so all items would have the same direction. The analyses were performed a second time on the revised data. The correlation between the first principal axes fell to $-.004$; only half of the variation on the first factor could be accounted for by linear prediction from the three multidimensional scaling dimensions. Yet the second factor had a .996 correlation with the first multidimensional scaling

[45] Factor analysis represents data by scalar products between vectors while multidimensional scaling employs interpoint distances. Yet even this difference will not cause sharp discrepancies in solutions, except that the scalar product representation necessitates an origin. For example, the scalar product between points j and k can be written in terms of the distance d_{jk} between the points and the distances, d_j and d_k, of each point from the origin: $-.5 \, (d_{jk}^2 - d_j^2 - d_k^2)$ which equals $c - .5d_{jk}^2$ if all variables are a constant squared distance c from the origin. According to that result, the scalar products would be monotone with the squared interpoint distances which are obviously monotone with the unsquared interpoint distances. Consequently nonmetric analysis of scalar products and interpoint distances will differ only as items are unequal distances from the origin.

[46] The data are the candidate feeling thermometers from the preelection survey. They were made available by the Inter-University Consortium for Political Research. Neither the original investigators nor the Consortium bear any responsibility for the analysis or interpretations presented here.

[47] The correlation reported here is the correlation between each variable's loading (projection) on the first factor component with its loading on the first multidimensional scaling dimension. Note also that the multidimensional scaling solution employed here is a principal axis rotation around the centroid of the points. That rotation possesses statistical meaning since it can be shown to account for a maximum proportion of the variance of the points with each successive orthogonal dimension.

[48] The reversing of candidate thermometers is intended only to illustrate the difference between the two analysis techniques, and not as a substantively useful procedure.

dimension, and the third factor had a .870 correlation with the second multidimensional scaling dimension. When all items have the same directions, the first factor component is unrelated to the multidimensional scaling space while the later factors correspond closely to the multidimensional scaling solution. Thus both parts of this test confirm the conjecture developed above.

Factor analysis can produce extra dimensions which serve particular purposes: indicating the extent to which variables share a common core, providing the item directions, and giving a space for scoring individuals. But what is more fundamental is that factor analysis and multidimensional scaling involve different types of dimensions. In some instances they provide identical information, but when they do not the factor analysis of correlation matrices provides more information and can be used for multidimensional scaling purposes. Multidimensional scaling seems appropriate only when it yields the same dimensionality as factor analysis or when a distance model is required.[49]   Overall, these two multidimensional procedures differ in their interpretations of unidimensionality, so considerable care is essential in the choice between them.

Dimensionland: An Analogue World of Games

The existence of different forms of unidimensionality and nonequivalent types of dimensions permits no simple conclusions as to the true nature of unidimensionality. This should not be interpreted as questioning the scientific utility of scaling, but rather should emphasize the importance of considering a wide variety of alternative scaling models. Geometric models are employed to facilitate understanding the nature of political reality, so limiting the breadth of geometric models is unnecessarily restrictive. This perspective implies avoiding resort to multidimensional explanations when the data are unidimensional according to some other applicable meaning of unidimensionality, while still adopting multidimensional measurements when models permitting unidimensional fit are inappropriate. This is basically a plea for

[49] If the items have meaningfully different directions which should not be corrected (as when scaling attitudes toward presidential contenders), the multidimensional scaling solution is quite proper. When the items have artificially opposite directions which are not intended to be the focus of the analysis (as when scaling legislative roll call votes—which occasionally have yes as a liberal response and other times no as a liberal response—with an interest in finding the underlying dimensional structure without regard to item direction), the multidimensional scaling solution is useless unless the items are properly directed in advance and even then the analysis in the text suggests that factor analysis would be more useful.

flexible use of scaling models, but it has some intriguing philosophical implications that merit explicit attention.

First, different scaling models permit representation of different aspects of reality, so a complete portrayal of political reality may require the use of several scaling models and multiple images. This contradicts the simplistic notion that objective scientific methods can yield unique solutions. As Abraham Kaplan argues, "Truth may be one, but if so, this proposition holds at best only for literal statements; there is no limit to the metaphors by which we can effectively convey what we know. . . . If the model is not conceived as picturing reality, we can make good use of several models, even if they are not compatible with one another."[50] Science thus becomes the search for a multiplicity of partial images. This does not signify a shortcoming of scaling methodology, but just illustrates the role of models in science. Metaphors—geometric as well as other types—are used in scientific inquiry, but all of the real world behavior can never be captured in a single metaphor. Multiple models are useful, and it is worth being reminded that no single representation is ever identical to the world one seeks to describe.

Second, our limited set of familiar and usable scaling models must inevitably restrict our ability to describe the political world. Our store of models determines our potential for understanding political reality. This underlines the dependence of scientific conclusions on proper concept development. Science describes the world, but only within the context that science prescribes. Reality cannot be distinguished from the manner in which we study it. This view is similar to the Sapir-Whorf hypothesis of linguistic determinism operating on culture. Linguistic relativity states that "all observers are not led by the same physical evidence to the same picture of the universe, unless their linguistic backgrounds are similar."[51] The consequence is that "human beings do not live in the objective world alone, . . . but are very much at the mercy of the particular language which has become the medium of expression for their society."[52] Substitute the term "scientific concepts" for "linguistic backgrounds" and "language" in these statements and one has the result that the set of concepts available to science at any point of time must inevitably limit the conclusions that science can make. Furthermore, differences in scientific concepts yield different views of the real world.

[50] Abraham Kaplan, *The Conduct of Inquiry*, p. 287.

[51] Benjamin Whorf, as quoted in John B. Carroll, ed., *Language, Thought, and Reality: Selected Writings of Benjamin L. Whorf* (Cambridge, Mass.: MIT Press, 1956), p. v.

[52] Edward Sapir, *Selected Writings in Language, Culture, and Personality*, edited by David Mandelbaum (Berkeley: University of California Press, 1964), p. 162.

Finally, the very existence of a knowable reality may well be questioned. The inhabitants of Abbott's Flatland live in a two-dimensional world, and the discovery of more dimensions has minimal effect on their existence. Similarly, our existence is necessarily confined to a three-dimensional world, so the possibility of extra dimensions cannot be verified even if analogy permits understanding the nature of larger spaces. Ultimately, "objective reality" may be fundamentally unknowable, always a captive of our finite frames of reference. The consideration of scaling models is then just a case study in the limits of scientific methodology.

We may find it useful to adopt a spatial analogy in describing a political world, but the representation cannot convey all of that political world. We may be intrinsically limited to partial representations, confined by our conceptual bases, and seeking to describe a reality that can never be fully known. Partial images of an unknowable reality—a challenging agenda for a flight into Dimensionland.

Manuscript submitted January 10, 1974.
Final manuscript received June 26, 1974.

GEORGE B. RABINOWITZ

An Introduction to Nonmetric
Multidimensional Scaling*

Nonmetric multidimensional scaling methods are useful for spatially representing the interrelationships among a set of data objects. In this, they are similar to factor analytic methods. The assumptions and procedures associated with these methods are, however, somewhat different from those associated with factor analysis, and are more appropriate to certain political data. In this paper the logic underlying nonmetric multidimensional scaling methods is described, and some guides for using these procedures are offered.

Nonmetric multidimensional scaling techniques are among the set of procedures available to investigators interested in spatial representation of political objects. These techniques are useful in illuminating the structure hidden in a complex data matrix, and form an important addition to the factor analytic methods which have been widely used in the discipline. They have achieved considerable popularity in recent years, primarily for three reasons. First, they often yield solutions in a sufficiently low dimensionality to permit a visual examination of the structure. This is an invaluable interpretative aid. Second, they permit the investigation of many matrices which cannot be congenially analyzed using factor analysis. Third, they make only ordinal assumptions about the data, which is often advantageous given the "weak" nature of most social science data. This paper is a general introduction to nonmetric multidimensional scaling.[1]

*I wish to thank Stuart Rabinowitz, Herbert Weisberg, the members of the Comparative Politics Discussion Group at the University of North Carolina, and three unknown reviewers for the valuable suggestions they have made.
[1] The strategy used in these procedures is quite flexible and can be applied to a wide variety of problems. These include the direct analysis of preference data (data in which individuals indicate which of a set of objects they prefer) and nonmetric factor analysis. However, the wide familiarity and availability of metric factor analytic procedures and technical problems which arise in the direct analysis of preference data have limited the application of this approach in these areas. In this piece we will limit our focus to more conventional nonmetric multidimensional scaling.

Reprinted from AMERICAN JOURNAL OF POLITICAL SCIENCE, Vol. XIX, No. 2, May 1975, pp. 343-390, George B. Rabinowitz, "An Introduction to Nonmetric Multidimensional Scaling," by permission of the University of Texas Press.

An Intuitive Example

Let us launch the discussion by way of a particular example. Suppose that we were interested in an individual's perception of five political candidates: McGovern, Humphrey, Nixon, Percy, and Wallace. We might ask the individual a variety of questions. For example, we might ask how much he likes each candidate, or what the good and bad points of each candidate are. One task would be particularly rewarding for the information it produces: Ask the individual to order pairs of candidates according to the degree of similarity that he perceives among them. If the individual organizes politics (and politicians) along a liberal-conservative continuum, we would expect him to perceive candidates of like ideology to be relatively similar; if he organizes politics on the basis of party affiliations, we would expect him to perceive candidates of the same party to be relatively similar; if he has an incoherent or idiosyncratic view, we would expect no recognizable pattern to emerge. Let us suppose, then, that we asked him to rank pairs of these candidates on the basis of their similarity, and he ordered them as follows:

Most similar: 1. Humphrey - McGovern
               2. McGovern - Percy
               3. Nixon - Wallace
               4. Nixon - Percy
               5. Humphrey - Percy
               6. Humphrey - Nixon
               7. Humphrey - Wallace
               8. McGovern - Nixon
               9. Percy - Wallace
Least similar: 10. McGovern - Wallace

This ranking, while of interest, does not adequately convey a sense of the manner in which the individual's perceptions of these political figures are organized. If the ranking were used to locate points representing the candidates in a visualizable space, the underlying structure of his perceptions might be revealed more clearly.

In a technical sense, locating objects in a representational space involves assigning to each object a series of numbers, one number for each of the dimensions in the space. The numbers position the object points on the dimensions. If one dimension is involved, one number is assigned to each object. If the space is two-dimensional, two numbers are associated with each object. The first number positions the point on the first axis; the second number positions the point on the second axis. If three dimensions are involved, three numbers are assigned to each object, and so on.

In order to assign these numbers in a rational way, it is necessary to associate a mathematically meaningful property with the observed data. For example, think of creating an ordinal scale of objects on the basis of their physical weight. The real number properties of *greater, equal,* and *less than* can be associated respectively with an object weighing more than, the same as, or less than another object. On this basis, given any finite number of objects and a simple balance, it would be possible to assign a number to each object such that whenever one object is heavier than another and tips the balance in its direction, a higher number is assigned to it.

What mathematically meaningful property might be associated with our pairwise ranking of candidates? It does seem that *the more similar a pair of candidates are perceived as being, the closer the points representing these candidates should be when they are located in the space.* With this as a criterion we can approach the problem of scaling these points.[2]

Can these points scale in one dimension? The most dissimilar pair is McGovern and Wallace; hence on a single dimension these will have to lie at opposite ends of the scale. Humphrey-McGovern are the most similar pair; hence they must lie next to each other on the scale. This situation is depicted in Figure 1. Now consider the location of the Percy point. Percy is more similar to McGovern than to Humphrey; hence his point should be closer to McGovern's than to Humphrey's. This creates a problem. We have already decided that Wallace and McGovern must lie at opposite ends of the scale; hence Percy cannot be located at P_1 or any point to the left of McGovern. We also decided that Humphrey must be immediately next to McGovern; hence Percy cannot be located at P_2 or any point between McGovern and Humphrey. If we were to try to locate Percy at the Humphrey point or anywhere

FIGURE 1
Illustration of the Impossibility of a Unidimensional Representation of the Data

[2] This assumption appears quite reasonable; however, it is by no means the only, or necessarily the "correct," assumption to apply to these observations. Its usefulness depends on the degree to which the individual's psychic perception of proximity corresponds to physical proximity. Nevertheless, unless strong reasons dictate the assumption is *not* valid, it is an excellent choice.

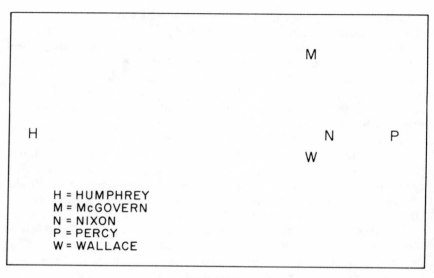

FIGURE 2
A Random Configuration of the Five Points

to· the right of Humphrey (i.e., at P_3), the Percy point would be closer to Humphrey than to McGovern, which reverses the similarity order. With the McGovern, Humphrey, and Wallace points positioned at acceptable locations, there is no adequate place for the Percy point; thus no perfect representation of these similarities is possible on a single dimension.

Can we scale the points in two dimensions? Clearly, this is more complicated. Let us start with a rather arbitrary decision. We will initiate the process by randomly locating five points in the space, one point for each candidate.[3] In Figure 2 the randomly generated configuration of points is displayed. Obviously, this configuration does not even approach satisfying the scaling criterion. The Humphrey and McGovern points which should be closest are quite far apart and generally the points are scrambled incoherently.

How might we proceed? A naive, but reasonable approach would be to move the points in the space so that the distances between them are more

_____

[3] The process of placing the points can be likened to a dart-thrower tossing five labeled darts, each aimed at the same bull's-eye. The location of each dart would depend only on the chance fluctuation of the throw. Similarly, the location of the five points is entirely arbitrary and depends only on chance factors.

consistent with the similarities. However, it is not entirely clear how the points should be moved. For example, if we moved the Humphrey and McGovern points very close together, it might bring McGovern too close to Nixon and Wallace, it might take McGovern too far from Percy, or somehow violate the relation of Humphrey to the other candidates. Ideally, when moving each point, we would take into consideration all of its interrelations. One reasonable tactic would be to generate a set of target values, one for each pair, which could be used to guide the moves.

Let us draw a graph. Each point on the graph will represent a pair of candidates. Location on the Y axis will be determined by the rank order similarity of the pair, and position on the X axis by the interpoint distance in the scaling space. It is important to distinguish between the *scaling space* and the *graph*. The *scaling space* appears in Figure 2; it is the space in which the candidate points are represented. It contains five points, one for each candidate, and is two-dimensional, but could be of one, three, four, or any finite

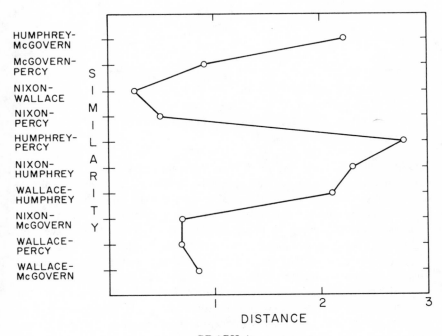

GRAPH A
Plot of Distance Against Similarity–Random Configuration

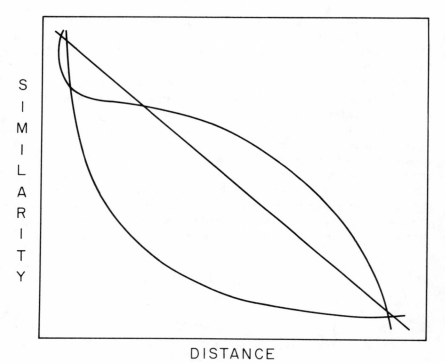

S
I
M
I
L
A
R
I
T
Y

DISTANCE

GRAPH B
Plot of Three Monotonic Lines

dimensionality. It is the end product of the scaling procedure. The *graph* has ten points, one for each pair of candidates, is *always* two-dimensional (y = similarity, x = distance), and is useful in creating the target distances. The graph associated with the scaling space in Figure 2 appears in Graph A.

What would this graph look like had our scaling effort been successful? Our scaling objective is to locate the points so that the distance between pairs of points increases as pairs are perceived to be less similar. Had we successfully located the candidate points, when we connected the ten points on the graph the resulting line would have moved down and to the right, indicative of increasing distance as we moved from the most to the least similar pair.

Lines which move consistently in one direction are called monotonic lines. In Graph B three lines appear. Notice, all three lines are monotonic—they continually move to the right, indicative of increasing distance as one moves down from the most to the least similar pair. However, the three lines are quite different: one line is almost straight, another a smooth hyperbolic curve, and the third slightly S-shaped. That each of the lines satisfies the scaling criterion illustrates the nonmetric nature of the scaling goal. If the procedure were metric, there would be an exact relationship between the similarity measure and the interpoint distances. For example, if we insisted that our interpoint distances be a linear function of the similarities, then only straight lines would be acceptable. Algebraically, insisting on a linear function requires that for every unit change in the similarity measure there be a fixed change in interpoint distance. Any such assumption presupposes that the units of the similarity measure are meaningful. Since in this case we started with only the rank order of pairwise similarity, making this assumption would be inappropriate. In general, by allowing for *any monotonic relation* we allow greater flexibility in our attempts to locate points in the scaling space and make only ordinal assumptions about the measure of interpair similarity.

Now let us look back at the graph associated with Figure 2. Quite clearly, the line in Graph A is not moving uniformly down and to the right. In Graph C this line reappears along with another line. The second line is constructed to be as similar to the first line as possible (in a least squares sense) with the restriction that it never move down and to the left. Using the more technical vocabulary, the distance values on the second line are restricted to be *monotonically* decreasing with (as a function of) perceived similarity. There-fore, as one moves from more to less similar pairs, the distance associated with each successive pair on the graph never decreases. This second line will always move either straight down or down and to the right. (In the literature, the graph in which both the actual and monotonic distances appear is called a Shepard Diagram.)

Our object in the scaling process is to have distances between pairs decrease monotonically as pairs are perceived to be more similar. Our object in constructing targets is to generate a set of values which can guide us when we move the points in the scaling space. Notice that when the first line is zigzagging, not at all satisfying the original scaling criterion, the second line runs straight down and seems to be a "smoothed out" version of the first line which is consistent with the scaling criterion. Clearly, it would be a consider-able improvement of the configuration which appears in Figure 2, if the actual interpoint distances were more like the values associated with the second of these two lines. Hence, these second values will make excellent targets, and we shall use them for that purpose. (In the literature, target values are called *disparities*. They are also sometimes identified as d-hats, $\hat{d}$, or d-stars, d*.)

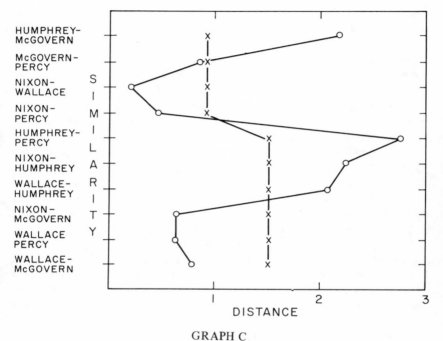

GRAPH C

Plot of Distance Against Similarity for Actual Distances (O's) and
Target Values (X's)—Random Configuration

The numerical values of the distances and targets appear in Table 1. The strategy for calculating the targets is to set them equal to the actual distances except when violations of the monotonicity requirement occur. When violations do occur, targets are calculated by averaging as few actual distances as possible to resolve the violation. Note that when a series of target values are the same, they are simply the average of the actual distances over the series of pairs. Hence, a pair whose actual distance is satisfactory will tend to have a target value equal to the actual distance; a pair whose actual distance is smaller than that of pairs which are perceived to be more similar will tend to have a target value larger than its actual distance; and a pair whose actual distance is larger than that of pairs which are perceived to be less similar will tend to have a target value smaller than its actual distance. A detailed example showing how these target values are calculated appears in Appendix A.[4]

_____

[4] This least squares method is not the only way we could calculate targets; it is,

The strategy for moving the points is exceedingly straightforward. If two points are farther apart than they should be—that is, if the actual distance for the pair is greater than the target value—the points will be moved closer together; if the points are closer together than they should be, they will be moved farther apart. The relative amount of movement will be determined by the difference between the actual and target distances. The greater the difference, the more the two points will be moved. Points will always be moved directly toward or directly away from each other—that is, they will be moved along the line linking the two points.

Generally, when the points are moved the new actual distances will *not* equal the target values. It would be possible to pick any *single* distance, such as the Humphrey-McGovern distance, and make that actual distance equal to its target; it is ordinarily not possible to make *every* distance correspond. The targets provide a *guide* for moving the points. Our goal in moving the points is only to improve the configuration. Once we have succeeded in improving the solution by making the actual distances more like these targets, we can then calculate new targets and repeat the entire procedure in the hope of further improving the configuration. Eventually, we should obtain a solution in

TABLE 1

Actual Distances and Target Values Corresponding
with the Initial Configuration Which Appears
in Figure 2

Pair	Actual Distance	Target Value
Humphrey - McGovern	2.218	0.961
McGovern - Percy	0.909	0.961
Nixon - Wallace	0.239	0.961
Nixon - Percy	0.479	0.961
Humphrey - Percy	2.766	1.554
Nixon - Humphrey	2.288	1.554
Wallace - Humphrey	2.130	1.554
Nixon - McGovern	0.662	1.554
Wallace - Percy	0.666	1.554
Wallace - McGovern	0.815	1.554

however, a particularly reasonable approach. Any method we use would have to share two features with it: first, the target values must be based on the actual distances; second, the target values must be a monotonic function of the original rank order of pairs. Another common method is the rank image method. An example using this method appears in Appendix B.

which the actual distances are a monotonic function of similarity, if such a solution is possible.

Let us now go down the list of Table 1, moving pairs of points. The first pair, Humphrey-McGovern, should be moved toward each other and moved quite a lot since the difference between the actual and target distances is considerable. The next pair, McGovern-Percy, should be moved slightly apart, since the target distance is a little larger than the actual distance. This is the second move for the McGovern point, and in general, each point will be

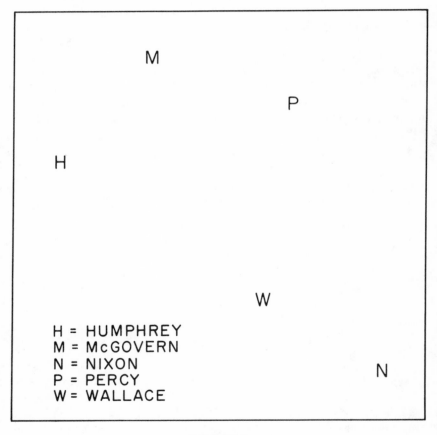

FIGURE 3
The Configuration of Five Points after the First Set of Moves

TABLE 2

Actual Distances and Target Values Corresponding
with Configuration after the First Iteration Which
Appears in Figure 3

Pair	Actual Distance	Target Value
Humphrey - McGovern	0.856	0.856
McGovern - Percy	0.864	0.860
Nixon - Wallace	0.856	0.860
Nixon - Percy	1.739	1.588
Humphrey - Percy	1.437	1.588
Nixon - Humphrey	2.366	1.822
Wallace - Humphrey	1.511	1.822
Nixon - McGovern	2.381	1.822
Wallace - Percy	1.218	1.822
Wallace - McGovern	1.634	1.822

moved several times in the course of any particular sequence. After making
the ten moves indicated on the list, we would have a new configuration of
points. Such a configuration appears in Figure 3. Clearly, this is a considerable improvement over the configuration which appeared in Figure 2.
However, it is still far from perfect. For example, Nixon and Percy are farther
apart than Percy and Wallace, while they should be closer together. Once
more, we can move the points and try to further improve the configuration.

The distances and target values associated with the pairs of points as they
are located in Figure 3 appear in Table 2 and are plotted in Graph D. The new
target values are again calculated to be as similar to the new distances as
possible while still satisfying the monotonicity requirement. Notice that the
new target values are much closer to the new distances than were the previous
targets to the previous distances. If the solution were "perfect," the target
values would be identical to the distances.

We can now proceed to move the points, making one modification in our
strategy this time. While we again will move the points in relation to the
difference between the actual and target distances, we will in general move
the points less, since we are interested in changing the configuration less
radically. (In the nonmetric multidimensional scaling literature, the amount a
configuration is changed from iteration to iteration is called the *step-size*.)
The configuration of points recovered after this second move is displayed in
Figure 4. The configuration is better than the previous one, but still not
perfect. Clearly, we could continue to repeat the process indefinitely in the

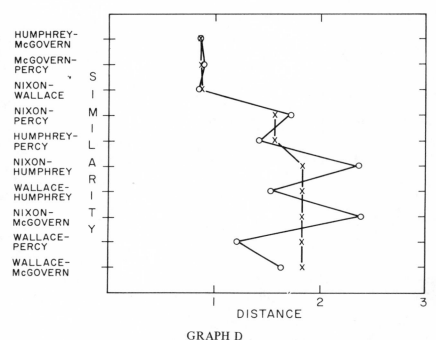

GRAPH D

Plot of Distance Against Similarity for Actual Distances (O's) and
Target Values (X's)–Configuration after First Set of Moves

hope of improving the configuration each time. We would stop when the actual distances and target values are in exact correspondence, indicating that the solution is perfect, or should that never occur, when we succumb to general fatigue. The configuration recovered after three additional iterations appears in Figure 5, and in Table 3 are the interpoint distances and target values associated with Figures 4 and 5. The final configuration displayed in Figure 5 is perfect; the distances consistently increase from the most similar Humphrey-McGovern pair to the least similar Wallace-McGovern pair.

The two-dimensional solution in Figure 5 gives us an image of the way in which the individual perceived these five candidates. It seems that both party identification and left-right ideology might have influenced his perceptions. We will postpone further discussion of the configuration until a later section when we will consider both the general interpretation problem and the interpretation of this configuration in more detail.

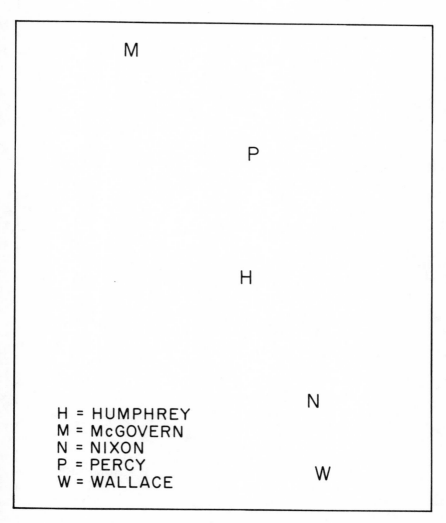

FIGURE 4
The Configuration of Five Points after the Second Set of Moves

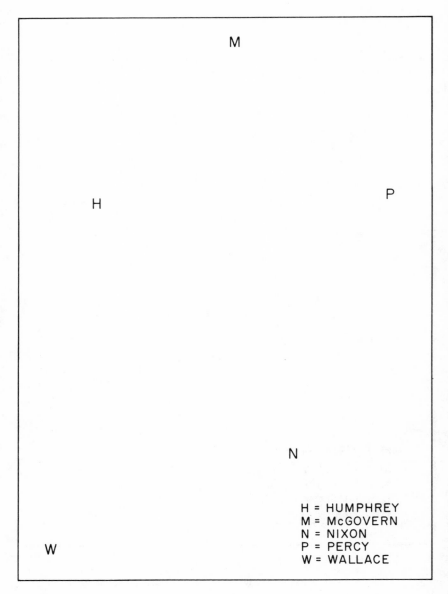

FIGURE 5
The Final Configuration of Five Points Obtained after the Fifth Set of Moves

TABLE 3

Actual Distances and Target Values Corresponding to
the Configurations Displayed in Figures 4 and 5

Pair	Figure 4		Figure 5	
	Actual	Target	Actual	Target
Humphrey-McGovern	1.501	.954	.937	.937
McGovern-Percy	.914	.954	.973	.973
Nixon-Wallace	.447	.954	1.141	1.141
Nixon-Percy	1.503	1.021	1.257	1.257
Humphrey-Percy	.742	1.021	1.283	1.283
Nixon-Humphrey	.818	1.021	1.408	1.408
Wallace-Humphrey	1.243	1.243	1.568	1.568
Nixon-McGovern	2.318	2.133	1.876	1.876
Wallace-Percy	1.948	2.133	2.195	2.195
Wallace-McGovern	2.741	2.741	2.421	2.421

The Analytic Procedure

While the procedure we used to locate the points seemed successful in this five-candidate example, it had two very critical drawbacks. First, there was no measure available to indicate the adequacy of the solution. Second, unless we achieved a perfect solution, there was no way of knowing when we could stop the procedure. Both of these would constitute serious problems in more complex and realistic situations. The motivation for performing nonmetric multidimensional scaling procedures is to help elucidate the structure in a complex data matrix. Even when such matrices are quite structured, idiosyncratic features are almost invariably present and mitigate against perfect solutions. Realistically, our goal is not to find a perfect configuration, but rather the best one possible. It is therefore essential to confront the problems of (a) defining a measure which reflects the adequacy of any particular solution and (b) delineating a method for determining when the iterative procedure should be terminated.

The strategy used to move the points involved two basic steps. First, given the set of similarities and the interpoint distances in the scaling space, the target values were calculated. Second, the points were moved in order to make the actual distances more like the target values. The object of the scaling process is to have the actual distances a monotonic function of the original similarities. The target values were created to be as similar to the distances as possible, with the restriction that they be a monotonic function of the original similarities. A natural measure of how close the solution is to satisfying the monotonicity goal would be the average (or mean) squared difference·between the actual distance and the target values. The smaller the average difference, the better the solution would be. Formula A represents the mean squared difference.

Formula A

$$\sum_{i=1}^{\text{\# of pairs}} \frac{[(\text{Actual distance pair i}) - (\text{Target value pair i})]^2}{\text{\# of pairs}}$$

It should be apparent that the formula is sensible. If the actual distances were a monotonic function of the similarities, then the actual distances and target values for each pair would be identical, and all the differences would be zero. As the actual distances depart from the monotonicity goal, the actual distances and target values will diverge and the differences will increase. Since the differences are squared, their signs will not influence the measure.

There is, however, a major problem with this measure; it is quite sensitive to the scale factor used to calculate distances. No basic unit of measurement is present when one performs nonmetric multidimensional scaling. All that is critical is the relative distance between points. Were we, for example, to double every interpoint distance, the solution would be neither better nor worse than before. However, as a result of doubling, our measure would change dramatically. The actual distances are doubled; hence the targets would double. Since both target values and actual distances are doubled, their differences would double. Based on squared differences, the measure would quadruple.

Formula B

$$\frac{\sum_{i=1}^{\text{\# of pairs}} \frac{[(\text{Actual distance pair i}) - (\text{Target value pair i})]^2}{\text{\# of pairs}}}{\sum_{i=1}^{\text{\# of pairs}} \frac{[(\text{Actual distance pair i}) - (\text{Mean actual distance over all pairs})]^2}{\text{\# of pairs}}}$$

This problem can be alleviated by adding an appropriate denominator to the measure. Formula B modifies Formula A by dividing it by the variance of the interpoint distances. Should the scale factor be changed, both the numerator and denominator would be affected equally, and hence the effects would cancel out, leaving the measure unchanged.

The revised measure can be interpreted as the proportion of the total variance in interpoint distances *inconsistent* with the monotonicity constraint. It is similar to the ratio of unexplained to total variance central to regression and analysis of variance. This measure will vary between 0 and 1. For perfect solutions it will be zero; as solutions depart from the monotonicity constraint, its value will increase to a maximum of one.

In keeping with statistical tradition, we might make one more change in the measure. Generally, one does not work directly with variances or squared correlations, but rather with their square roots, standard deviations and simple correlations. Hence, we shall define a final measure which is the square root of the previous one. This measure appears in Formula C and is rewritten in Formula C'. In Formula C' the "# of pairs" term which appears in the numerator and denominator simply cancels out and is removed.

Formula C

$$\left[\frac{\displaystyle\sum_{i=1}^{\text{\# of pairs}} \frac{[(\text{Actual distance pair i}) - (\text{Target value pair i})]^2}{\text{\# of pairs}}}{\displaystyle\sum_{i=1}^{\text{\# of pairs}} \frac{[(\text{Actual distance pair i}) - (\text{Mean actual distance over all pairs})]^2}{\text{\# of pairs}}} \right]^{\frac{1}{2}}$$

Formula C'

$$\left[\frac{\displaystyle\sum_{i=1}^{\text{\# of pairs}} [(\text{Actual distance pair i}) - (\text{Target value pair i})]^2}{\displaystyle\sum_{i=1}^{\text{\# of pairs}} [(\text{Actual distance pair i}) - (\text{Mean actual distance over all pairs})]^2} \right]^{\frac{1}{2}}$$

The final measure will also vary from 0 for perfect solutions to a maximum of 1.

In the nonmetric multidimensional scaling literature this measure is called *Stress 2*. The term "Stress" follows from the fact that the measure increases as the solution gets worse, the "2" from the fact that it was the second of two Stress formulas developed.[5]

Given a measure of the badness of fit of a particular solution, the problem of determining when to terminate the iterative procedure can be easily handled. Generally, we would expect that each successive solution would be closer to satisfying the monotonicity requirement than the solution which preceded it. Hence, if the Stress does not improve over several iterations, the procedure can be reasonably terminated.

We now have enough information to delineate a complete procedure.

1. Initially, locate the points, one for each of the objects to be scaled, in a space of fixed dimensionality.

2. On the basis of the interpoint distances and the similarities, construct a set of target values.

3. Calculate the Stress of the solution.

4. If the solution is perfect or if the basic procedure has been repeated several times (undergone several iterations) and the Stress has not improved, stop the entire procedure. Otherwise, go on to step 5.

5. Move the points in order to make the actual distances more similar to the target values, with the magnitude of the move adjusted to reflect the desired amount of change.

6. Repeat the process starting at step 2.

---

[5] The original Stress formula, *Stress 1*, differs only in the denominator. In Stress 1 the variance of distances term is replaced by the mean square distance. The formula for Stress 1 is:

$$\left[\frac{\sum\limits_{i=1}^{\# \text{ of pairs}} [(\text{Actual distance pair i}) - (\text{Target value pair i})]^2}{\sum\limits_{i=1}^{\# \text{ of pairs}} (\text{Actual distance pair i})^2} \right]^{\frac{1}{2}}$$

Stress 1, like Stress 2, is sensitive to the difference between the actual distances and target values and insensitive to the scale factor. The Stress 1 denominator will always be greater than or equal to that for Stress 2. Hence, Stress values will be lower using Stress 1 than Stress 2. While Stress 2 has a more intuitive interpretation and provides certain technical advantages over Stress 1, both measures perform well as measures of badness of fit. In the text, when we refer to the Stress of a solution we will mean the Stress calculated according to any satisfactory measure of badness of fit, such as Stress 2 or Stress 1.

The procedure seems quite reasonable. However, its development has not been very rigorous. It would be useful to approach the task of scaling the points in a more analytic fashion. Underlying much of the procedure is the notion that the lower the Stress, the better the solution. Analytically, we could define the problem as one of finding the configuration of points for which the Stress value is minimized.

In minimizing such complex functions mathematicians use what are called *negative gradient* or *steepest descent* techniques. These methods work as follows:

1. One determines how much the measure will improve for a very small change in each of the independent variables. (The independent variables in the Stress formula are the locations of the points on the axes. Each coordinate location is something that we can manipulate. Hence, if we have 5 points to locate in 2 dimensions, we have 5 × 2 = 10 independent variables). Technically, the amount the function improves with a very small change of an independent variable is called the *partial derivative* of the function with respect to that variable.

2. One then changes the values of each independent variable in proportion to the relative amount of improvement; variables are changed more if the improvement (partial derivative) calculated was large. One then repeats the procedure iteratively until a change in any of the independent variables will cause no (or negligible) improvement. This occurs when all the partial derivatives are zero or close to zero.[6]

Analytically, we can solve the problem of minimizing Stress by calculating the partial derivatives and using them to relocate the points. When one goes through the analytic solution, it is remarkably like the intuitive procedure we developed earlier. That is, it turns out that points are always moved directly toward or away from each other with the relative amount of movement determined by the difference between the actual and target distances. However, placing the problem in an analytic context is still useful. First, we know

[6] If we list these partial derivatives in order, starting with that associated with the first point on the first dimension and continuing to the last point on the last dimension, the resulting set of ordered partial derivatives is called the *gradient*. The gradient is a vector whose direction summarizes the direction in which the points are moved. The size of the gradient is the square root of the sum of the squared partial derivatives, and hence offers some information about the rate of change for a very small movement of the points. It is easier to technically discuss some aspects of the procedure in terms of the gradient; hence this vector is regularly referenced in the literature.

that our intuitive solution did not miss an alternative approach which would have been easier and more accurate. Second, when we moved the points in the intuitive procedure we worked pair by pair. In the intuitive procedure each point was moved several times in the course of a single iteration; these moves may have been in the same or in quite different directions. The partial derivatives for each point on each axis represent the sum of all the pairwise moves. Hence, using the partial derivatives is slightly more efficient.

Third, our only stopping criterion occurred when the Stress failed to improve after several iterations. Now when the partial derivatives are all zero, we know all our moves cancel out and we have reached some kind of optimum solution. Fourth, we never had a satisfactory way to decide how much to change a configuration on any given iteration. It happens that if we change our solution just enough so that our last move gives us no information about our next move, we are changing our configuration just the right amount. While this is a little technical, it nevertheless is useful to know that once we have broached the problem analytically we have a better notion of how radically we should change the configuration from iteration to iteration.

Comparison with Factor Analysis

The procedure is well defined and can be programmed to run on a computer. Once programmed, it can easily be applied to problems of substantive interest. Since factor analysis has been the most widely used multidimensional scaling procedure, an obvious question is "how do these methods compare?"[7]

Obviously, they differ in terms of the level of measurement they presume; factor analysis assuming interval level data, nonmetric multidimensional scaling, ordinal level data. However, this distinction is somewhat artificial. It is feasible to construct a nonmetric factor analysis procedure or a metric multidimensional scaling technique. There is a more fundamental difference between the two methods.

Most critically, the basic models underlying the methods are different. Factor analysis is based on a *scalar product* model; nonmetric multidimensional scaling is based on a *distance* model. While this is a rather technical sounding distinction, it is of some significance. In Figure 6 two points, X and

---

[7] A full discussion of factor analysis is beyond the intended scope of this paper. In this section the most critical difference between factor analysis and multidimensional scaling is emphasized. Because the discussion is brief, it is necessarily somewhat more technical than those sections which precede and follow it.

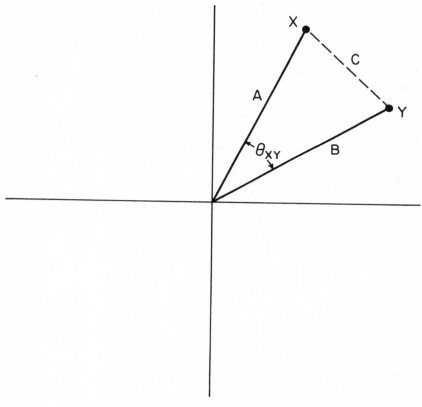

FIGURE 6
Basic Scalar Products with Points Equidistant from Origin

Y, appear. The length of the line labeled C is the distance between the two points. The length of the line labeled A is the distance of point X from the origin. In keeping with standard notation, we will denote this distance $|X|$. In general, the distance of a point from the origin will be denoted by the symbol representing the point surrounded by two vertical lines. The length of the line labeled B is the distance of the Y point from the origin or $|Y|$. The angle made by the intersection of these two lines we will denote as θ_{XY}. The scalar product between X and Y is equal to the length of X from the origin times the length of Y from the origin times the cosine of the angle between them; that is, $|X| \, |Y| \cos \theta_{XY}$.

How is this scalar product related to the interpoint distance? When the points are all equidistant from the origin, the distance and the scalar product will depend only on the angular separation. As the angle becomes larger, the distance will increase and the scalar product will decrease. Under this condition there is an inverse monotonic relation between distances and scalar products. The larger the distance, the smaller the scalar product and vice versa.

In instances where the distances of the points from the origin are not equal, this relationship breaks down. In Figure 7 we see three points, X, Y, and Z. Here $|X| = |Y|$, but $|Z|$ is quite a bit larger than $|X|$ and $|Y|$. The largest

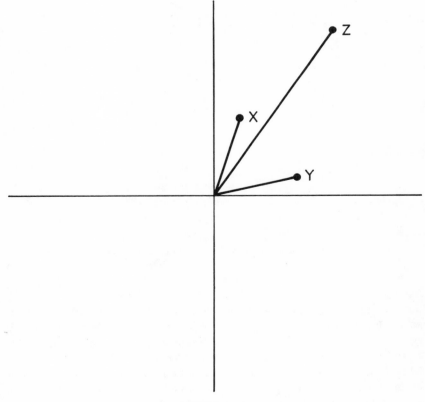

FIGURE 7
Illustration Where Scalar Products Are Not Monotonically Related to
Interpoint Distance

scalar product will be between X and Z, since |Z| is large, and the angle between X and Z is small. The next largest scalar product will be between Y and Z; |Y| |Z| = |X| |Z|, but the angle between Y and Z is greater than that between X and Z. The smallest of the scalar products will be between X and Y, since |X| and |Y| are both small and the angle between them is the largest of all. Now look at the distances; it is obvious from inspection that the XY distance is the smallest, the XZ distance next, and the YZ distance the largest. Here, there is no monotonic relation between distance and scalar product; the pair with the smallest scalar product has the smallest distance, the pair with the largest scalar product has the middle distance, and the pair with the middle scalar product has the largest distance. In general then, when all points are equidistant from the origin, the scalar product is monotonically related to the distance; when points are not equidistant from the origin, the scalar product is not monotonically related to the distance.

The basic difference between factor analysis and nonmetric multidimensional scaling should now be clearer. Factor analytic procedures treat input data as scalar products; a "perfect" configuration following a factor analysis is one in which the interpoint *scalar products* match the values in the input data matrix. In contrast, a "perfect" configuration following a nonmetric multidimensional scaling analysis is one in which the *interpoint distances* match the input data values.

Both covariance matrices and Pearson product-moment correlation matrices are scalar product matrices. However, Pearson product-moment correlations are scalar products between standardized variables, hence between variables of identical length. Either factor analysis, which is directly a scalar product model, or nonmetric multidimensional scaling, which requires data to be a monotonic function of distance, can legitimately be used to analyze product-moment correlation matrices, The standard nonparametric measures of association are conceptually similar to standardized scalar products; hence they lend themselves to either nonmetric multidimensional scaling analysis or (nonmetric) factor analysis.

How similar will the results be using these methods? Since the models underlying the two methods differ, we would in general expect them to produce somewhat different results. The principal component variant of factor analysis keeps all variables of constant length and should produce results more similar to those obtained using nonmetric multidimensional scaling. Since nonmetric multidimensional scaling procedures are nonmetric, which implies less restrictive criteria of fit, they usually achieve solutions in the same or lower dimensionalities than metric factor analysis or principal component analysis.

In many instances we collect similarities data which are not scalar product measures, but are measures the analyst wishes to treat as a monotonic function of distance. For example, a measure of internation hostility or internation trade, sociometric choice, individual perceptions of interobject similarities (such as in the five-candidate example), and the line-of-sight measure of pairwise similarity are all proximity rather than scalar product measures.[8] In these instances the nonmetric multidimensional scaling model is correct to apply, and the factor analytic model is not.

Which method should be chosen to analyze a particular set of data? As a general rule, factor analytic procedures should be used when one is creating standard indices, such as an efficacy or civil rights index, or if one is interested in testing the dimensionality or viability of items for forming potential indices. This type of scaling is metric and is usually consistent with the linear model underlying classic factor analysis. Nonmetric multidimensional scaling methods are most useful in analyzing proximity structures such as party or candidate spaces, internation relations, and legislative voting patterns. Nevertheless, it is the measure of similarity which determines which method to apply, and an analyst should give careful thought to the substantive implication of the particular similarity measure he applies. If the measure is a proximity measure, a nonmetric multidimensional scaling method should be used. If the measure is an unstandardized scalar product measure, a factor analytic method should be used. If the measure is a standardized scalar product, it is often useful to apply both methods.[9]

Guidelines for Use

A researcher interested in using a nonmetric multidimensional scaling program should be familiar with some basic guidelines. We will now discuss those issues which an investigator confronts when he applies this methodology to research problems.

Data

Data input into a nonmetric multidimensional scaling program is usually a matrix of values reflecting the similarity or dissimilarity among pairs of

[8] The line-of-sight measure of pairwise similarity is discussed in Rabinowitz (1973, Chapter 2). It is designed to measure the relative similarity between pairs of objects (such as political parties) from individual ratings of those objects, under the assumption that the individuals have common perception but different evaluations of the objects.

[9] A full treatment of proximity measures is beyond the scope of this paper. See MacRae (1970), Weisberg (1968), Morrison (1972), and Rabinowitz (1973) for discussion of some of the standard measures of association and their utility for spatial analyses.

TABLE 4

Matrix of Perceived Intercandidate Similarity

	McGovern	Humphrey	Nixon	Percy	Wallace
McGovern	——				
Humphrey	1	——			
Nixon	8	6	——		
Percy	2	5	4	——	
Wallace	10	7	3	9	——

objects. In our five-candidate example we had arranged our ten candidate pairs in a list proceeding from most to least similar. We could have supplied the same information in a conventional matrix form. Such a matrix appears in Table 4. An entry in this matrix is the rank order similarity of a candidate pair. Hence, a 1 is assigned to the Humphrey-McGovern pair, a 2 to the McGovern-Percy pair, and so on through the list. When this matrix is input to a nonmetric multidimensional scaling program the numerical values will be used only to sort the pairs from most to least similar, and a list identical to the one we used in the five-candidate problem will be formed by the program. Correlation matrices contain essentially similar information. Each entry in a correlation matrix is a number reflecting the similarity between two objects, and these numbers can be used to rank the object pairs from most to least similar.

If one is working with a correlation matrix, it is necessary to be sure that items are coded consistently. For example, if we are analyzing a set of roll calls with Yea coded 1 and Nay, 3, and if on some of these votes Yea is liberal and on others Yea is conservative, all the items should be recoded so that a liberal vote receives consistently one score and a conservative vote another. Artificial negative (or positive) correlations due to question wording or coding must be avoided, since this will lead to artificially large (or small) distances between object points.

Interpretation of Results

The usual objective in performing a nonmetric multidimensional scaling analysis is to uncover the structure present in a complex data matrix. To do this an analyst must deal with three basic questions:

1. What is the correct dimensionality for the spatial representation of the data matrix?

2. How satisfactory a solution has been achieved? That is, what does any particular Stress value tell us about the solution?

3. How can the spatial configuration recovered be substantively interpreted?

Determining dimensionality. Every nonmetric multidimensional scaling solution takes place in a space of *fixed* dimensionality. The analyst first chooses the number of dimensions in which he wishes to work and then obtains a solution in that dimensionality. For example, in the five-candidate problem, we first tried a one-dimensional solution, decided a perfect one-dimensional solution was impossible, and then went on to try a separate two-dimensional solution.

The primary guide in selecting the number of dimensions in which to perform the analysis is the substantive knowledge the user brings to the problem. Invariably the analyst has an a priori notion concerning the number

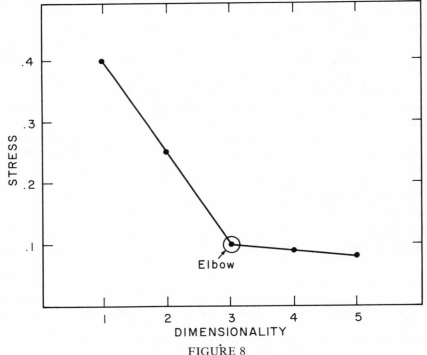

FIGURE 8

Illustrative Plot of Stress against Dimensionality with a Clear Elbow at
Three Dimensions

of dimensions underlying his data matrix. If very strong substantive reasons indicate that only a specific dimensionality is appropriate, the analyst can obtain solutions in only that dimensionality. More usual is the case where the analyst feels the solution should be within a certain range of dimensions, but is not sure which dimensionality is correct. The normal procedure in this case is to obtain a solution in each of the relevant dimensionalities and to use these results to select the correct one.

Figure 8 contains a plot of Stress against dimensionality for some hypothetical set of solutions. The Stress values for the one- to five-dimensional solutions are respectively .4, .25, .1, .09, .08. Notice that Stress decreases markedly as one goes from one to two and two to three dimensions, but then seems to level off, decreasing only slightly as we add dimensions after that. We know Stress will always decrease as we add dimensions, since as we add dimensions we are increasing the number of coordinates which we will estimate and hence increasing the number of manipulable independent variables.[10] In this example, it seems that the first three dimensions are each capturing a significant part of the structure present in the original data matrix, while the fourth and fifth dimensions seem to be capturing idiosyncratic features, or perhaps only random error. Notice the elbow in the curve at the third dimensional point. This elbow occurred because of the drop in the rate of change in Stress after the third dimension was added. The appearance of an elbow in the Stress against dimensionality curve provides a good indication of the correct dimensionality. In this example the dimensionality is three.

Unfortunately, in many empirical instances there is not a clearly discernible elbow. In these instances an analyst must draw on his substantive expertise to select the dimensionality he will report. When there is neither a clear substantive nor a clear empirical basis for selecting a specific dimensionality, then it is often useful to report the solution in several different dimensionalities.

Interpretation of Stress. The following guidelines are useful in relating Stress to the quality of solution.

Quality of Solution	Stress 2	Stress 1
Perfect	0.00–0.05	0.000–0.025
Excellent	0.05–0.10	0.025–0.050
Good	0.10–0.20	0.050–0.100
Fair	0.20–0.40	0.100–0.200
Poor	0.40–1.00	0.200–1.000

[10] Occasionally, Stress will be higher for a higher than for a lower dimensional

While valuable, these guidelines must be applied cautiously. Stress, ideally, would be insensitive to the number of points used in the analysis. However, as the number of points increases, Stress tends to increase. In addition, one-dimensional solutions tend to be disproportionally prone to high Stress. If one is analyzing data with a large number of objects ($N > 30$) or if one is working in one dimension, it is reasonable to extend these ranges slightly. On the other hand, if the number of points analyzed is small ($N < 10$) or if when we form the ratio of the number of points to the number of dimensions, this ratio is small (ratio < 4), the resulting Stress might be lower than the quality of solution warrants. Nevertheless, in most situations the guidelines are satisfactory.

Interpreting a Configuration: Traditional Method. When interpreting a spatial representation of data, our first instinct should be to delineate the basic cluster pattern present in the configuration. One of the great advantages of nonmetric multidimensional scaling is its tendency to produce solutions in a limited number of dimensions, thus giving us a visualizable picture of the major interrelationships among the objects in our data matrix. By getting this overview, we are much less likely to fall into those misinterpretations which arise when we are forced to work dimension by dimension, without a sense of how the entire space fits together.

In Figure 9 the final configuration of the five candidate points is redrawn with the representational axes included and some of the major groupings demarked. We can identify two broad patterns. The regular Democrats, Humphrey and McGovern, are drawn together to the upper left side of the space; the two regular Republicans, Percy and Nixon, to the middle right. Similarly, the more liberal group of McGovern, Percy, and Humphrey are located toward the top of the space, while the more conservative group of Nixon and Wallace lies toward the bottom. The clustering pattern is weak, since the distances within clusters are quite large; nevertheless, it does seem that party and idealogy effects are represented in the space.

If we want to move from this general description to an analysis of the structure in dimensional terms, we move to mathematically tenuous grounds. The problem is familiar to anyone who has studied factor analysis. In a

---

solution. *This result only occurs artificially,* either because the procedure was terminated prematurely, or because a false or local minimum was obtained. (In a later section the problem of local minima will be discussed.)

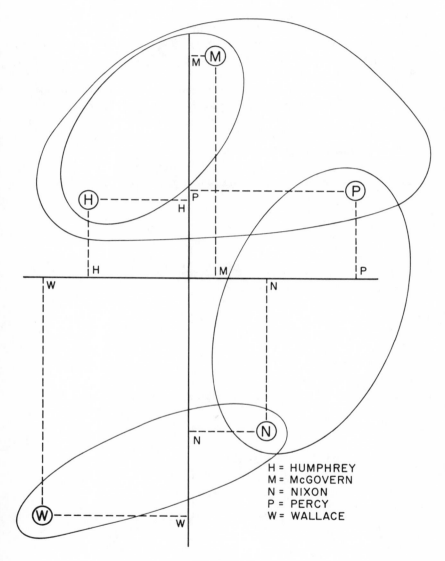

FIGURE 9
The Final Configuration of Five Points Redrawn with the Representational
Axes Included and the Major Groupings Demarked

Euclidean space, the particular axes we use as a basis on which to locate our points are entirely arbitrary. If, for example, we had rotated our axes and represented our points as in Figure 10, the solution would have identical Stress and be mathematically equivalent to our initial one. Notice, however, that the X and Y coordinates for the two solutions are quite different. When analysts interpret spatial configurations dimensionally, they do so in terms of the location of the points on specific axes. This makes the selection of the axes very critical, and puts the analyst in the somewhat awkward position of interpreting a configuration in terms of specific dimensions which are mathematically irrelevant to the solution obtained.

Factor analysts cope with this problem by defining specific *simple structure* criteria for selecting axes. The idea underlying simple structure is to have

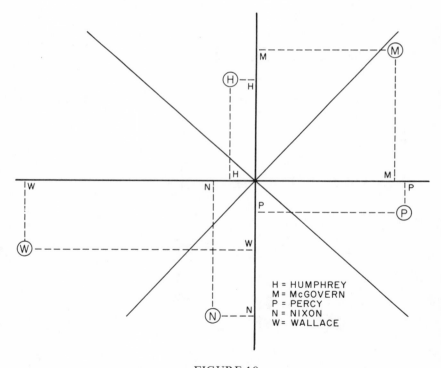

FIGURE 10
The Final Configuration Redrawn after a Rotation
(Previous representational axes are also shown.)

axes run through clusters of points. Axes are then interpreted in terms of the clusters they pass through. When clusters are well defined, this tends to encourage interpretations similar to those one would make when visually overviewing the structure. If no strong clustering pattern is present, then these rotational methods are less useful. In addition, if we are interested in interpreting dimensions as underlying factors or causes and clusters are formed because of the interrelation of several different factors, these methods produce misleading results.

The standard rotational methods used in factor analysis are divided into two types: orthogonal, in which the axes are kept at right angles and hence are independent; and oblique, in which the axes are allowed to correlate. The most common orthogonal rotation is the varimax rotation. The most common oblique rotations are the direct and indirect oblimin rotations. In general, the orthogonal rotations are most useful as a vehicle for overviewing structure, since the nonassociation between axes makes comparisons between objects easier. The oblique rotations are better suited to delineating dimensions, since "real world" attributes of legitimate substantive interest are likely to be interrelated.

It is appropriate to apply these standard rotational procedures when performing a nonmetric multidimensional scaling analysis as well. However, there is a caveat: in a nonmetric multidimensional scaling solution the origin is arbitrary. That is, the origin can be changed without altering the Stress or any essential attribute of the structure. Since rotations are around a fixed point, this could be a problem. Fortunately, the centroid of the configuration, the point in the middle of the space, is a natural origin for these solutions and is a very reasonable point about which to perform rotations. The standard nonmetric multidimensional scaling programs all locate the origin at the centroid.

It is important, of course, *not to* interpret the origin and distance from the origin as one would in a factor analysis. Factor analysis is a scalar product model; hence the origin is fixed and distance from the origin is an important piece of information. When performing a nonmetric multidimensional scaling analysis, even after a "standard rotation" interpretation of axes must rest on the *relative,* not the absolute, location of points on the dimensions. In addition, because of the nonmetric nature of the algorithm, the structure of the space will be insensitive to any factors which are common to the entire set of items. For example, in a factor analysis, the first principal component will often have high loadings for all the items when the items in the matrix tend to be positively correlated. In a nonmetric factor analysis or a nonmetric multidimensional scaling analysis this first component will not appear, because it does not discriminate between items.[11] *Nonmetric multidimensional scaling solutions emphasize those dimensions which lead to discrimination between items.*

Interpreting a Configuration: External Criteria. In both nonmetric multidimensional scaling and factor analysis, there are other and perhaps better ways to approach the problems of dimensional interpretation. These involve using external criteria to help select dimensions. If an investigator is seriously interested in explicating the structure among his data objects, he is likely to have an a priori sense of what the underlying dimensions are. If the research design can be controlled, it should be possible to include in the analysis both the means to test dimensional hypotheses and the means to locate axes in the space.

When we asked the individual to rank the candidate pairs according to how similar he perceived them to be, we noted that if the individual organized politics (and politicians) along a liberal-conservative continuum, he would perceive candidates of like ideology to be relatively similar; if he organized politics on the basis of party affiliation he would perceive candidates of the same party to be alike; if he had an incoherent view of politics he would display no discernible pattern in his pairwise perceptions. The two underlying dimensions which we identified as most likely to shape his political orientations were party and ideology. Let us suppose that when we asked him for his perceptions of pairwise similarities, we also asked him to locate the five candidates on two independent continua, one party, the other liberal-conservative. This produced two dimensions independent of (external to) the space created on the basis of the similarity judgments, which are displayed in Figure 11.

How might we use this external information to clarify our understanding of the similarity space? If the individual had used either party or ideology exclusively as a guide in his perceptions of candidate similarity, then the configuration recovered on the basis of the similarity judgments should have been unidimensional and should have corresponded to one or the other of the two external dimensions. If the individual had used both party and ideology, we would expect the similarity space to be two-dimensional and reflect both a party and an ideology component. The space is two-dimensional and seems to be influenced by party and ideology, but it is unclear to what extent each component influences the spatial structure and how an axis representing each component can be located in the space.

---

[11] A nonmetric factor analysis differs from a metric factor analysis in that the scalar products need only preserve the same rank order as the input data values rather than duplicate the actual values.

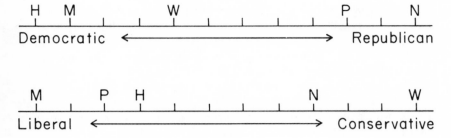

FIGURE 11

Individual's Perception of the Five Candidates on a Democratic-Republican
and a Liberal-Conservative Dimension

Inserting a new axis in the space is geometrically equivalent to drawing a
line through the space running through the origin. If we are interested in
seeing whether or not the spatial structure can reflect a specific external
dimension, like the party or ideology dimension, it would be reasonable to
determine the single axis in the space on which the projections are most like
those of the externally determined dimension. If the projections on the
internally drawn axis are quite similar to those on the external axis, we would
have evidence which supports the hypothesis that the external dimension is
one of the underlying causes of the structure; if the projections on the best
fitting internal dimension and the external dimension are quite different, the
hypothesis could be rejected. This raises two closely related questions: First,
"How can we determine the internal axis which most closely corresponds to
the external axis?" Second, "How can we measure the degree of fit between
the projections on the internal and external axes?"[12]

The basic numerical information we have at the end of a nonmetric
multidimensional scaling procedure is numbers which locate the object points
on each of the (arbitrary) representational axes. Associated with each axis are
as many numbers as there are points in the space. Conceptually, we can think
of the axes as standard analytic variables. Suppose we performed an unstandardized multiple regression using as the independent variables the representational axes and using as the dependent variable the externally determined
axis. We would obtain the linear combination of the representational axes
which most closely corresponds with the external axis. That is, for each

[12]To clarify any ambiguities in the text, we mean by an "external axis" an axis
defined completely independent of the recovered configuration, and by an "internal
axis" an axis actually drawn through the space.

representational axis we will have a weight which reflects how important that axis is in predicting position on the external dimension. If we orient a new axis in the space such that it corresponds with each representational axis in proportion to the magnitude of the regression coefficient (weight), we will have the single internal axis which is most like (in a least squares sense) the external axis. The degree of fit can be measured by the Pearson product-moment correlation between the internal and external axes. This bivariate correlation is identical to the multiple correlation between the representational axes and the external dimension.

The regression equation to determine the orientation of the party axis would be

$$b_1 \, axis_1 + b_2 \, axis_2 + constant + error = external \; party \; dimension,$$

where the b values are unstandardized regression coefficients, the constant and error terms are those associated with an ordinary least squares regression, and $axis_1$ and $axis_2$ are variables representing the location of the points on the representational axes. On each variable ($axis_1$, $axis_2$, and the external party dimension) there are as many observations as points in the space, in this case five. While the particular representational axes used will influence the b values and the constant term, the eventual orientation of the axis representing party will be entirely independent of them. Similarly, the multiple correlation coefficient will not be influenced by the particular representational axes used.

To determine the orientation of the axis, we calculate its slope by taking the ratio of the b coefficients. For example, if $b_2/b_1 = 3$, the axis should be drawn so that for each one-unit change on the first representational axis there is a three-unit change on the second representational axis. When we actually perform the regression with these data our results are:

$$10.8 \; axis_1 - 5.7 \; axis_2 + .002 + error = external \; party, \; and$$

$$1.2 \; axis_1 + 6.5 \; axis_2 + .200 + error = external \; ideology.$$

The b_2/b_1 ratio used to orient the party axis internal to the space is $-5.7/10.8 = -0.528$; the b_2/b_1 ratio used to orient the internal ideological axis is $6.5/1.2 = 5.417$. Both of these axes are drawn in Figure 12.[13] The

---

[13] A simple procedure which can be used to construct an axis once the b coefficients have been determined is to mark the point with coordinate (b_1, b_2) and then draw the line determined by that point and the origin. This line is the appropriate internal axis.

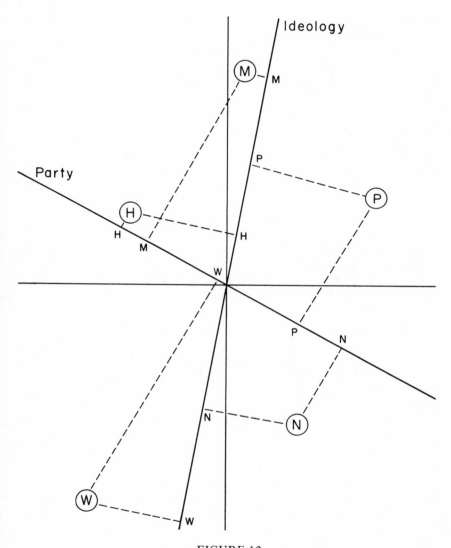

FIGURE 12
The Final Configuration of Five Points with Representational and Party
Identification and Ideology Axes Inserted

correlation between the projection of points on the internal party axis and external party dimension is .996, and that between the internal ideological axis and the external ideological dimension is .995. The close correspondence is apparent if one compares the projection of points on the internal axes in Figure 12 with the external dimensions in Figure 11.

The results support the hypothesis that party and ideology were critical in determining the observed spatial structure. Of course, the small N of five candidates warrants considerable caution. In general, the use of external dimensions to reveal the underlying basis for a spatial structure is a potent addition to the rotation methods. By using external dimensions, the analyst determines axes with real substantive interpretability and obtains a measure of fit between the hypothesized determinants of the structure and the spatial structure which has been observed.

Problems with the Method

As with most analytic procedures, these methods present problems to which an investigator should be sensitive before applying them in his research. Problems arise from two sources, one the nonmetric nature of the procedures, the other the iterative strategy used in arriving at a best fit solution.

Problems Associated with the Nonmetric Assumptions

These techniques make only ordinal assumptions and return metric results. The jump in level of measurement occurs because of the metric constraints present in this type of data. One need work only a few examples by hand to realize that for most similarity matrices only a single representation is possible. However, when the number of dimensions becomes large relative to the number of variables, the constraint essential to these procedures starts to evaporate. One can then obtain solutions with low Stress that do not represent the data well. Hence, *the procedure should not be applied (or should be applied very cautiously) to data when the ratio of objects to dimensions is small (ratio < 4).* Similarly, *analysis with less than ten, and certainly with less than eight points should be avoided.* (We have violated both these caveats with our five-candidate problem in order to present an example with greater intelligibility.)

There is another caveat which arises from the nonmetric nature of the procedure. Let us again violate the constraint restrictions and suppose that we have six points whose correct location is displayed in Figure 13. Notice that the five points, excluding f, are located in two distinct clusters: the A,B,C cluster and the D,E cluster. The similarity order obtained using just the ten

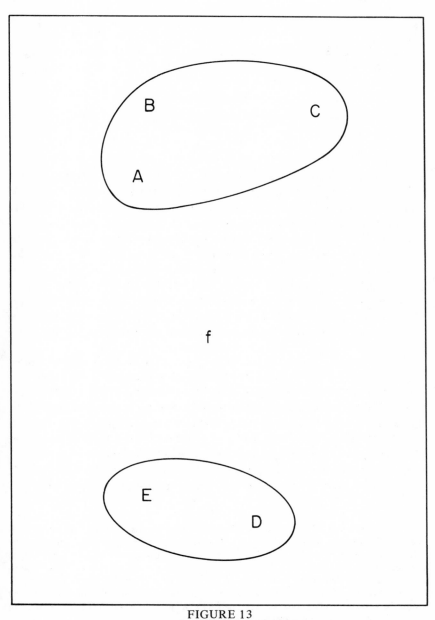

FIGURE 13
Illustration of a Potentially Degenerate Configuration
(Excluding f, all within-cluster distances are less than between-cluster distances.)

FIGURE 14

A Degenerate Solution Incorrectly Locating All Within-Cluster Points at the
Same Position

pairs formed from these five points is AB, DE, BC, AC, AE, AD, BE, CD, CE,
BD. This ordering can be broken into two distinct halves—the within-cluster
pairs AB, DE, BC, and AC, followed by the between-cluster pairs AE, AD,
BE, CD, CE, BD. When this condition arises a nonmetric procedure cannot be
appropriately applied, for a "perfect" solution can always be obtained by
locating each point in a cluster at exactly the same point in the solution
space. For example, using just the five points, the obviously incorrect unidimensional solution in Figure 14 will be "perfect." The AB, DE, BC, and AC
pairs will all have an actual distance of 0.0 and the AE, AD, BE, CD, CE, and
BD pairs will all have an actual distance of 1.0. These distances satisfy the
monotonicity requirement so targets will equal distances and the Stress will
be zero.

This condition usually arises when an analyst is using a very limited
number of points. For example, the presence of the ƒ point in this case would
be enough to prevent the solution from degenerating.[14] Nevertheless, it is
important, particularly if the data are expected to be severely clustered, to be
on the lookout for this type of degeneracy. It is easy to detect; Stress will be
very low, even in one dimension, and points will be located in *very tight*
distinct clusters. The occurrence of this degeneracy informs the analyst that
his data are quite clustered, but gives him no insight into their finer structure.
The problem can be circumvented only by performing a metric analysis.

---

[14] The rank order of pair similarity with f included is: AB, DE, BC, Ef, Af, AC, Df,
Bf, Cf, AE, AD, BE, CD, CE, BD. If A, B, and C were located at the same position, the
AC distance would be zero. This implies that the Af distance must be zero, since Af
precedes AC in the similarity order. This in turn implies the f point would also have to
be located at the same position as A, B, and C. However, the Ef pair precedes the Af pair
in the similarity order; hence, the Ef distance would also have to be zero. Clearly, Stress
would become very high were E positioned with A, B, and C; hence a different solution
would be sought and the degeneracy would not occur.

Problems Associated with the Numerical Method (the Iterative Strategy)

In Figure 15 a curve is drawn. Notice that it has two low points, one at A and one at B. Point A is called a global minimum, since it is associated with the lowest point on the curve. Point B is called a local minimum, since it is associated with the lowest point on the curve in its immediate vicinity. If we

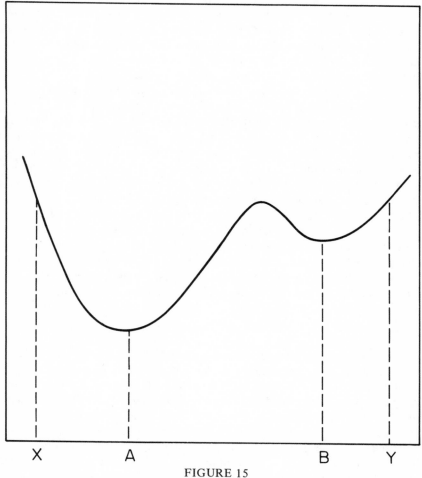

FIGURE 15
Illustration of a Local Minimum at B and a Global Minimum at A

start at point X and move to a minimum, we will wind up at A, the global minimum. If we start at point Y and move to a minimum, we will wind up at B, the local minimum. Notice that if we had a procedure oriented to obtaining a minimum from a fixed starting point, we would not know that B was a local and,not a global minimum. In analogous fashion, the procedure we use to minimize Stress is not sensitive to whether the minimum found is local or global. In either case, Stress would decline fairly consistently from iteration to iteration until the minimum was achieved.

If one does have a local minimum, it is usually easy to detect, in that Stress is high and *the solution does not make sense empirically*. Often, this is not a real problem since only one minimum exists, which must therefore be a global one. However, to help insure the analyst that the solution he reports is indeed the global minimum, several strategies are available.

The particular starting configuration we use is an important determinant of the likelihood of a local minima solution. We started our five-candidate problem by randomly (arbitrarily) locating five points in the space. If we had started with a more reasonable configuration, for example, one based on a metric analysis of the same data matrix, we would have been much closer to the eventual best solution. In general, a rational (as opposed to a random) start is an excellent way to reduce the risk of hitting a local minimum. Another good strategy is simply to perform the analysis several times using *different random* starting configurations, and then choosing the one solution with the lowest Stress. Either of these approaches is effective in nullifying potential local minima problems. The "safest" of all strategies is to run one solution with a rational start and several with random starts to check on the result. Most of the nonmetric multidimensional scaling programs allow for either a series of random starts, some type of rational start, or both.

Programs Available

There are several programs available to perform nonmetric multidimensional scaling. The three which have been most widely used are MDSCAL (new version KYST), TORSCA (new version POLYCON), and SSAI (this program is regularly updated). *The programs produce quite similar results and may be used interchangeably.* The main distinctions between the programs are technical, and involve the way in which target values and the measure of fit (Stress) are calculated and how one obtains the initial configuration to start the analysis. The basic algorithm in each of these programs is essentially identical to the one described in this paper.

Summary

We have completed a general introduction to nonmetric multidimensional scaling. Let us now summarize the major points.

Assumption

When points representing objects are located spatially, if, according to the measure used, one pair of objects is more similar than another pair, the points in the more similar pair should be located closer in the space.

Procedure

Points representing the objects are located in a space of fixed dimensionality and are then moved iteratively until a minimum Stress configuration is obtained. Stress is a measure of badness to fit; it ranges from 0.0 for a perfect solution to 1.0 for the worst possible configuration.

Guidelines for Use

1. Input data is a matrix which reflects the similarity or dissimilarity between pairs of objects.
2. The researcher specifies the dimensionalities in which he wishes to obtain solutions. The eventual decisions on dimensionality are based on substantive expertise and the plot of Stress against dimensionality.
3. The adequacy of a solution is determined using the following guidelines, realizing that the guidelines are not perfect and are sensitive to the number of points used in the analysis.

Quality of Solution	Stress 2	Stress 1
Perfect	0.00–0.05	0.000–0.025
Excellent	0.05–0.10	0.025–0.050
Good	0.10–0.20	0.050–0.100
Fair	0.20–0.40	0.100–0.200
Poor	0.40–1.00	0.200–1.000

4. The solution should be interpreted initially by describing the overall clustering pattern. If a dimensional interpretation is desired, either the standard rotational methods or the use of external criteria is appropriate.

Caveats

1. Be very circumspect about solutions where the ratio of the number of points to the number of dimensions is less than four.
2. Do not work with less than eight and preferably not less than ten points.
3. If Stress is very low and points are located in tight distinct clusters, the solution is probably degenerate. Check the original matrix to see if all the within-cluster pairs are more similar than any between-cluster pairs.
4. Beware of potential local minima problems.

Annotated Bibliography

General

There is an extensive nonmetric multidimensional scaling literature. The articles which develop the theory underlying the three major nonmetric multidimensional scaling programs are: Shepard (1962a, 1962b), Kruskal (1964a, 1964b), Guttman (1968), and Young (1968); of these, the Kruskal (1964a) piece is the most readable for a nontechnical audience. The algorithm used in nonmetric multidimensional scaling is quite flexible and can be applied to a wide variety of problems. A sense of the variety of potential uses is provided in Young (1972) and Lingoes (1972). The most common alternate use is in the direct analysis of preference data; procedures appropriate to this application are discussed in Green and Carmone (1970), Gleason (1969), and Rabinowitz (1973). An overview of current scaling procedures not restricted to nonmetric multidimensional methods appears in Shepard (1972). Many of the programs Shepard discusses are considered in more detail in Green and Rao (1972).

MacRae and Schwarz (1968) and Weisberg (1968) compare nonmetric multidimensional scaling and factor analysis in the analysis of legislative roll calls. Weisberg (1974) compares principal component analysis and nonmetric multidimensional scaling more generally. Weisberg and Rusk (1970), Rusk and Weisberg (1972), Mauser (1972), and Rabinowitz (1973) provide applications of nonmetric multidimensional scaling techniques. They all analyze the dimensions underlying candidate evaluations. Taken together, the Weisberg and Rusk, Mauser, and Rabinowitz pieces illustrate the scope of data to which the method can be legitimately applied and the importance of the similarity measure in determining the eventual spatial configuration.

Sources

The nonmetric multidimensional scaling programs referred to in the paper are available from the sources listed below.

MDSCAL and KYST

>   Computer Program Librarian
>   Bell Laboratories
>   Murray Hill, New Jersey 07974

TORSCA and POLYCON

>   Professor Forrest Young
>   Psychology Department
>   University of North Carolina
>   Chapel Hill, North Carolina 27514

SSAI

>   Professor J. C. Lingoes
>   1000A N. University Building
>   The University of Michigan
>   Ann Arbor, Michigan 48104

For a comparison of the effectiveness of TORSCA, SSAI, and MDSCAL, see Spence (1972) and Lingoes and Roskum (1973).

Metric Constraint and Interpreting Stress

The degree of spatial constraint present in an ordinal data matrix is examined in Shepard (1966).

Detailed investigations of the relation between Stress and the adequacy of solution appear in Young (1970) and Sherman (1972). Spence and Ogilvie

(1973) present tables which delineate realistic upper bounds for Stress values given a fixed number of points and a fixed dimensionality.

Factor Analysis and Metric Multidimensional Scaling

There are many texts dealing with factor analysis. An excellent general text is Harman (1967). A less technical and quite readable text is Rummel (1970).

A method for performing metric multidimensional scaling appears in Torgerson (1958, pp. 247–297).

Interpreting Structure

For a good discussion of the use of unidimensional scales in interpreting spatial structure, see Cliff and Young (1966). A very useful, but fairly difficult article which deals with some alternate approaches to interpreting a nonmetric multidimensional scaling solution is Degerman (1972).

Appendix A

Calculation of Target Values Using the Least Squares Criteria

Let us suppose that the actual interpoint distances were those displayed in the second column of Table 5. Let us calculate the target distances associated with these actual distances. The calculations are displayed in the next five columns of Table 5.

We start by simply listing the actual distances until we have a violation of the monotonicity requirement. The first four pairs all have their distances in the correct order. Hence, initially these target distances are the same as the actual distances. The fifth distance, however, is smaller than the fourth distance; this violates the monotonicity requirement. To try to rectify this violation we will simply average the fourth and fifth distances. The fourth distance is 7.0; the fifth distance is 2.0; their average is $(7.0 + 2.0)/2 = 9.0/2 = 4.5$. However, this still does not solve the problem; our new target of 4.5 for the fourth pair is less than the target of 6.0 for the third pair. To keep the targets monotonic we must also include the third pair in the average. The new average is $(6.0 + 4.5 + 4.5)/3 = 15.0/3 = 5.0$. The target values for the first five pairs are now monotonic (2.0, 4.0, 5.0, 5.0, 5.0), so we can proceed to the sixth pair. Again we will set the target distance equal to the actual distance unless there is a violation in the monotonicity requirement. The

TABLE 5

Illustration of Target Value Calculation Using Least Squares Method

Pair	Actual Distance	Calculation of Targets					Final Target	Actual Distance
1	2.0	2.0	2.0	2.0	2.0	2.0	2.0	2.0
2	4.0	4.0	4.0	4.0	4.0	4.0	4.0	4.0
3	6.0	6.0	6.0	5.0	5.0	5.0	5.0	6.0
4	7.0	7.0	4.5	5.0	5.0	5.0	5.0	7.0
5	2.0	2.0	4.5	5.0	5.0	5.0	5.0	2.0
6	7.0				7.0	7.0	7.0	7.0
7	8.0				8.0	8.0	8.0	8.0
8	9.0				9.0	9.0	9.0	9.0
9	10.0				10.0	9.5	9.5	10.0
10	9.0				9.0	9.5	9.5	9.0

sixth, seventh, eighth, and ninth distances have actual distances consistent with the monotonicity requirement, so their targets are set equal to their actual distance. The tenth pair has an actual distance of 9.0, which is less than the target distance of 10.0 associated with the ninth pair. These two must be averaged to form the targets for the ninth and tenth pairs. Their average is $(10.0 + 9.0)/2 = 19.0/2 = 9.5$. This creates no new violations of the monotonicity requirement; hence our ten targets are now calculated.

The full set of targets appears in the next-to-last column of Table 5. The actual distances reappear in the last column. Notice that the target distances do seem to serve their purpose. The pair most clearly out of order is the fifth pair, where the actual distance is too small. Here the target distance is considerably greater than the actual distance. Were the two pairs immediately preceding it in the order closer together, the fit would also improve, and for them the target distances are less than the actual distances. For the first, second, sixth, seventh, and eighth pairs the target and actual distances are the same, and these pairs do seem to have reasonable interpoint distances. The ninth and tenth pairs are slightly out of order, and here the ninth target is slightly smaller and the tenth slightly larger than their respective actual distances.

Appendix B

To calculate the targets using the rank image method, one simply sorts the actual distances and uses the smallest distance as the target for the most

TABLE 6

Illustration of Target Value
Calculations Using Rank
Image Method

Pair	Actual Distance	Target Distance
1	2.0	2.0
2	4.0	2.0
3	6.0	4.0
4	7.0	6.0
5	2.0	7.0
6	7.0	7.0
7	8.0	8.0
8	9.0	9.0
9	10.0	9.0
10	9.0	10.0

similar pair, the next smaller distance as the target for the next most similar pair, and so on. The actual and target distances appear in Table 6 below. Notice, the targets are simply the actual distances, now sorted to run from the most to least similar.

Manuscript submitted February 7, 1974.
Final manuscript received December 19, 1974.

REFERENCES

Cliff, Norman, and Young, Forrest W. 1968. "On the Relation Between Unidimensional Judgments and Multidimensional Scaling," *Organizational Behavior and Human Performance,* August 1968, pp. 269–285.

Degerman, Richard L. 1972. "The Geometric Representation of Some Simple Structures," in R. Shepard, A. K. Romney, and S. B. Nerlove, eds., *Multidimensional Scaling, Volume I, Theory.* New York: Seminar Press, pp. 193–211.

Gleason, Terry. 1969. *Multidimensional Scaling of Sociometric Data.* Ann Arbor: Institute for Social Research.

Green, Paul E., and Carmone, Frank J. 1970. *Multidimensional Scaling and Related Techniques in Marketing Analysis.* Boston: Allyn and Bacon.

Green, Paul E., and Rao, Vithala R. 1972. *Applied Multidimensional Scaling.* New York: Holt, Rinehart, and Winston.

Guttman, Louis. 1968. "A General Technique for Finding the Smallest Coordinate Space for a Configuration of Points," *Psychometrika,* December 1968, pp. 469–506.

Harman, Harry H. 1967. *Modern Factor Analysis.* Chicago: University of Chicago Press.

Kruskal, Joseph. 1964a. "Multidimensional Scaling by Optimizing Goodness of Fit to a Nonmetric Hypothesis," *Psychometrika,* March 1964, pp. 1–27.

_____. 1964b. "Multidimensional Scaling: A Numerical Method," *Psychometrika,* June 1964, pp. 115–129.

Lingoes, James C. 1972. "A General Survey of the Guttman-Lingoes Nonmetric Program Series," in R. Shepard, A. K. Romney, and S. B. Nerlove, eds., *Multidimensional Scaling, Volume I, Theory.* New York: Seminar Press, pp. 52–68.

Lingoes, James C., and Roskam, Edward E. 1973. "A Mathematical and Empirical Analysis of Two Multidimensional Scaling Algorithms," *Psychometrika,* December 1973, Monograph Supplement, pp. 1–93.

MacRae, Duncan, Jr. 1970. *Issues and Parties in Legislative Voting.* New York: Harper and Row.

MacRae, Duncan, Jr., and Schwarz, Susan B. 1968. "Identifying Congressional Issues by Multidimensional Models," *Midwest Journal of Political Science,* May 1968, pp. 181–201.

Mauser, Gary A. 1972. "A Structural Approach to Predicting Patterns of Electoral Substitution," in R. Shepard, A. K. Romney, and S. B. Nerlove, eds., *Multidimensional Scaling, Volume II, Applications.* New York: Seminar Press, pp. 245–287.

Morrison, Richard. 1972. "A Statistical Model of Legislative Roll Call Analysis," *Journal of Mathematical Sociology,* July 1972, pp. 235–248.

Rabinowitz, George B. 1973. *Spatial Models of Electoral Choice: An Empirical Analysis.* Chapel Hill: Institute for Research in Social Science.

Rummel, Rudolph J. 1970. *Applied Factor Analysis.* Evanston: Northwestern University Press.

Rusk, Jerrold G., and Weisberg, Herbert F. 1972. "Perceptions of Presidential Candidates: A Midterm Report," *Midwest Journal of Political Science,* August 1972, pp. 388–410.

Shepard, Roger N. 1962a. "The Analysis of Proximities: Multidimensional Scaling with an Unknown Distance Function, I," *Psychometrika,* June 1962, pp. 125–140.

_____. 1962b. "The Analysis of Proximities: Multidimensional Scaling with an

Unknown Distance Function, II," *Psychometrika*, September 1962, pp. 219–246.

_____. 1966. "Metric Structures in Ordinal Data," *Journal of Mathematical Psychology*, July 1966, pp. 284–315.

_____. 1972. "Introduction to Volume I," in R. N. Shepard, A. K. Romney, and S. B. Nerlove, eds., *Multidimensional Scaling, Volume I, Theory*. New York: Seminar Press, pp. 1–22.

Sherman, Charles R. 1972. "Nonmetric Multidimensional Scaling: A Monte Carlo Study of the Basic Parameters," *Psychometrika*, September 1972, pp. 323–355.

Spence, Ian. 1972. "A Monte Carlo Evaluation of Three Nonmetric Multidimensional Scaling Algorithms," *Psychometrika*, December 1972, pp. 461–486.

Spence, Ian, and Ogilvie, John C. 1973. "A Table of Expected Stress Values for Random Rankings in Nonmetric Multidimensional Scaling," *Multivariate Behavioral Research*, October 1973, pp. 511–517.

Torgerson, Warren S. 1958. *Theory and Methods of Scaling*. New York: John Wiley and Sons.

Weisberg, Herbert F. 1968. *Dimensional Analysis of Legislative Roll Calls*. Unpublished doctoral dissertation, University of Michigan.

_____. 1974. "Dimensionland: An Excursion into Spaces," *American Journal of Political Science*, November 1974, pp. 743–776.

Weisberg, Herbert F., and Rusk, Jerrold G. 1970. "Dimensions of Candidate Evaluations," *American Political Science Review*, December 1970, pp. 1167–1185.

Young, Forrest W. 1968. "TORSCA—A FORTRAN IV Program for Nonmetric Multidimensional Scaling," *Behavioral Science*, July 1968, pp. 343–344.

_____. 1970. "Nonmetric Multidimensional Scaling: Recovery of Metric Information," *Psychometrika*, December 1970, pp. 455–473.

_____. 1972. "A Model for Polynomial Conjoint Analysis Algorithms," in R. Shepard, A. K. Romney, and S. B. Nerlove, eds., *Multidimensional Scaling, Volume I, Theory*. New York: Seminar Press, pp. 69–104.

Contributors

John Aldrich is associate professor at the University of Minnesota; his Ph.D. is from the University of Rochester.

Herbert B. Asher, one of the co-editors of this volume, is professor at the Ohio State University. He has served as co-editor of the *American Journal of Political Science*. His Ph.D. is from the University of Michigan.

Terence Ball is associate professor at the University of Minnesota. He holds a Ph.D. from the University of California at Berkeley.

Jere Bruner is associate professor at Oberlin College; he received his Ph.D. from Yale University.

William Buchanan is professor and department chairman in political science at Washington and Lee University. He taught at the University of Tennessee in 1962–1965, and he has a Ph.D. from Princeton University.

Charles F. Cnudde is professor and department chairman in political science at the University of Texas at Austin. He received his Ph.D. at the University of North Carolina at Chapel Hill.

Morris Fiorina is professor at Harvard University. He received his Ph.D. from the University of Rochester.

Charles O. Jones is a professor at the University of Virginia. His Ph.D. is from the University of Wisconsin, and he has served as managing editor of the *American Political Science Review*.

Charles Plott is professor at the California Institute of Technology. He holds a Ph.D. in economics from the University of Virginia.

George B. Rabinowitz received his Ph.D. from the University of Michigan. He is associate professor at the University of North Carolina at Chapel Hill.

Herbert F. Weisberg, one of the co-editors of this volume, is professor at the Ohio State University. He has served as co-editor of the *American Journal of Political Science*. His Ph.D. is from the University of Michigan.

Gerald C. Wright, Jr., is associate professor at the Indiana University. He holds a Ph.D. from the University of North Carolina at Chapel Hill.

About the Book and Editors

In this book twelve eminent political scientists discuss research methods in the social sciences. Part I addresses theory building, including formal theory and the philosophy of science. Part II focuses on data analysis, including measures of association, regression models, and scaling techniques.

The editors discuss important conceptual and methodological problems that social scientists encounter in their research activities. Some chapters introduce advanced methods, such as nonmetric multidimensional scaling and probit and discriminant analysis, while other chapters address more familiar procedures, including measures of association and regression analysis. Attention is also paid to the use of formal models in empirical research and to Kuhn's idea of paradigms and paradigm shifts.

The focus throughout is on central concerns of social science research. Data analysts and teachers need not have extensive training in mathematics to understand and apply the methods described.

Contributors: John Aldrich, Herbert Asher, Terence Ball, Jere Bruner, William Buchanan, Charles F. Cnudde, Morris Fiorina, Charles O. Jones, Charles Plott, George B. Rabinowitz, Herbert Weisberg, and Gerald C. Wright, Jr.

Herbert B. Asher, John H. Kessel, and Herbert F. Weisberg are professors of political science at the Ohio State University. W. Phillips Shively is professor of political science at the University of Minnesota.

Index

Theory-Building and Data Analysis in the Social Sciences was set into type on the Mergenthaler VIP in ten point Times Roman with two point spacing between the lines. This book was designed by Muriel Underwood, set into type by Computer Composition, Inc., Nashville, Tennessee, printed offset by McNaughton-Gunn, Inc., Ann Arbor, Michigan, and bound by John H. Dekker & Sons, Grand Rapid, Michigan. The paper on which the book is printed is designed for an effective life of at least three hundred years.

THE UNIVERSITY OF TENNESSEE PRESS / KNOXVILLE